Strait Talk

STRAIT TALK

United States–Taiwan Relations

and the Crisis with China

NANCY BERNKOPF TUCKER

HARVARD UNIVERSITY PRESS
Cambridge, Massachusetts
London, England

First Harvard University Press paperback edition, 2011

Library of Congress Cataloging-in-Publication Data
Tucker, Nancy Bernkopf.
Strait talk : United States-Taiwan relations and the crisis with China /
Nancy Bernkopf Tucker.
p.   cm.
Includes bibliographical references and index.
ISBN 978-0-674-03187-6 (cloth : alk. paper)
ISBN 978-0-674-06052-4 (pbk.)
1. United States—Foreign relations—Taiwan.
2. Taiwan—Foreign relations—United States.
3. United States—Foreign relations—China.
4. China—Foreign relations—United States.
5. Taiwan—Foreign relations—China.
6. China—Foreign relations—Taiwan.   I. Title.

E183.8.T3T829 2009
327.7305124'9—dc22   2009031361

For Josie,
who didn't stay long enough
(1950–2008)

Contents

THE END OF THE COLD WAR

SEARCH FOR A NEW WORLD ORDER

WAR AGAINST TERRORISM

Illustrations

Acknowledgments

SEVERAL PEOPLE and organizations provided exceptional support during the years that this book grew and changed. Josie Woll offered constant encouragement, needed prodding, and an occasional shove when I wanted to do just a little more research or became sidetracked with other interests and responsibilities. Ultimately, she came to the rescue, editing the manuscript and imposing discipline, economy, and an end date. She did this and more in spite of personal trials—heroically and selflessly. Throughout the decades of our friendship she shared her strength and wisdom. For these reasons and more I have dedicated this book to her.

I also benefited from the challenging questions and criticism of two generous and meticulous readers—James Mann, author and onetime journalist, and Richard Bush, former director of the American Institute in Taiwan, who subsequently has served as director of the Center for Northeast Asian Policy Studies at the Brookings Institution. They weighed my words and helped shape my ideas. I wish I had listened sooner and more often to their advice. Bonnie Glaser read portions of the text and sharpened my insights on many issues. I profited from the assistance of two talented researchers and translators who helped me work with Chinese language materials, Natalie Liu in Washington and Hsu Hsing-yi in Taiwan.

I am deeply grateful to the Smith Richardson Foundation and especially its Senior Vice President, Marin Strmecki, and Allan Song, its Senior Program Officer for International Security and Foreign Policy, for their patience and generosity. They waited a long time for this book, cheerfully accepting an interim solution in 2005, an edited volume called *Dangerous Strait*. The Rockefeller Foundation Bellagio Center gave me an inspirational month in paradise to begin the project, and the Institute for Advanced Studies helped bring it to an end, allowing me the time and space to draft the manuscript. Dean Robert Gallucci of Georgetown University granted time off and financial assistance, which Assistant Dean Peter Dunkley facilitated.

The National Security Archive in Washington, under the dedicated leadership of Thomas Blanton, deserves special praise for the extraordinary work it has done in making historical records accessible. I have been particularly well served by William Burr, who has repeatedly helped me find important documents. Charles Stuart Kennedy, the director and engine behind the Association for Diplomatic Studies and Training Oral History Project, assisted me in mining his valuable interviews, even permitting me to help him with some. Archivists at several presidential libraries rendered much-appreciated assistance in navigating the files they curate and the difficult declassification process, especially Regina Greenwell at the Lyndon Johnson Library. Authorization to see the otherwise unavailable diplomatic records of the Republic of China, although limited, was secured by Tien Hung-mao, a veteran scholar who at the time served as Taiwan's foreign minister. David Lee Ta-wei, also a scholar-diplomat, recently Taiwan's representative in the United States, assisted as well.

Our shared interest in U.S.–Taiwan relations, and their good nature, led more than one hundred participants in these events to agree to be interviewed for this book. I could not have written it without them. They made me see the crucial connections, the peculiar reasoning, the bureaucratic struggles, and the key turning points that documents do not capture. Not everyone who helped was free to accept open recognition, so the list that appears at the back of the book cannot be complete. I am grateful to them all.

Kathleen McDermott, editor for History and Social Sciences at Harvard University Press, insisted on a leaner, tighter manuscript, which made this a better book. A somewhat different version of Chapter 2 appeared in the *Journal of American History* in June 2005 with the expert assistance of editors there.

Finally and impossibly, I want to thank Warren I. Cohen, who unfailingly assisted me, giving excellent advice and sacrificing many things he would rather have done. His partnership in everything is indispensable.

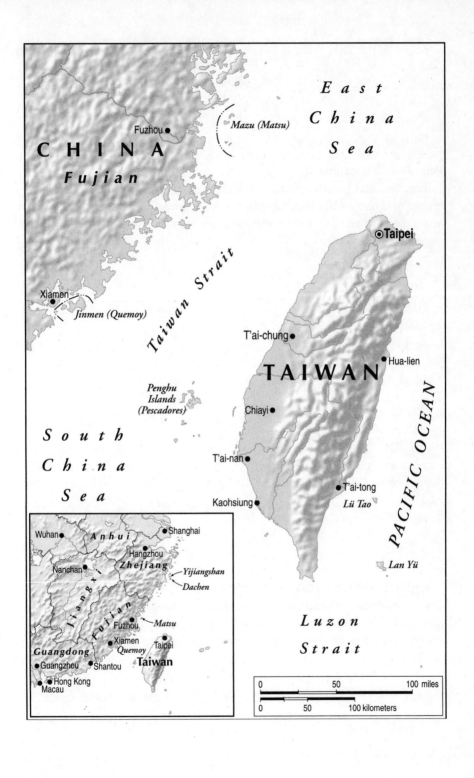

East
China
Sea

CHINA
Fujian

Fuzhou ●

Mazu (Matsu)

Xiamen ●
Jinmen (Quemoy)

Taiwan Strait

Taipei

T'ai-chung ●

Hua-lien ●

TAIWAN

Penghu
Islands
(Pescadores)

Chiayi ●

South
China
Sea

T'ai-nan ●

PACIFIC OCEAN

Kaohsiung ●

T'ai-tong ●

Lü Tao

Lan Yü

Wuhan ●
Anhui
Shanghai ●

Hangzhou ●
Zhejiang

Nanchan ●

Jiangxi

Yijiangshan
Dachen

Fujian

Fuzhou ●
Matsu

Guangdong

Xiamen ●
Quemoy

Taipei ●

Taiwan

Guangzhou ●
Shantou ●

Hong Kong ●
Macau ●

Luzon
Strait

| 0 | 50 | 100 miles |

| 0 | 50 | 100 kilometers |

Introduction:
Landscape and Memory

> The great majority of mankind is satisfied with appearances as
> though they were realities.
>
> MACHIAVELLI

TODAY CONFRONTATION in the Taiwan Strait represents the single most dangerous challenge for the United States in the world. Although the war on terror preoccupies Americans, a Taiwan Strait clash is the only conflict in which the US could confront a nuclear power with a huge military establishment. It would be an immensely destructive war with repercussions not just for the adversaries, but also for the region and the world. Should hostilities begin—whether through miscalculation, misunderstanding, accident, or intention—the United States might wish to stay out, but it would have difficulty remaining disengaged. The security of the United States, Taiwan, and China is tightly intertwined. Their politics, ideals, and interests are broadly divergent. The result is suspicion and mistrust.

In the spring of 2008, elections in Taiwan abruptly diminished the near-term likelihood of war, although they did not eliminate underlying disputes or change the enormity of potential conflict. The election of Ma Ying-jeou and a strong Kuomintang-led government created space for compromise, bringing to power a coalition that emphasized cross-Strait economic integration and accepted unification as a distant possibility. Relief in Washington and Beijing was immediate and overwhelming.

But relief could be premature if new attitudes—flexibility, generosity, equity, and, especially, trust—do not follow. Signals are mixed. Washington and Beijing missed the chance to reach out before Ma's inauguration: Beijing rejected a Taiwan-observer seat at the May 2008 World Health Assembly, and Washington rebuffed Ma's desire to visit the United States. These decisions reflected uncertainty about Ma's intentions and the domestic politics with which he contends. Subsequently, both the US and China embraced Ma, but real progress requires a breadth and depth of cooperation and trust not characteristic of past interaction.

Mistrust plays a crucial part in complicating and weakening relations between the US and Taiwan as both try to cope with China. Analysts and diplomats focus on building confidence across the Taiwan Strait between Beijing and Taipei, to remedy instability and reduce threats. They seek to diminish suspicion between Beijing and Washington to facilitate cooperation and ease friction. But the mistrust that characterizes Washington's relations with Taipei remains largely unacknowledged because it is awkward and embarrassing. Doubts in Washington and Taipei about each other's trustworthiness and reliability have poisoned their history and endanger their future. So even as Americans welcome Ma's election, trust remains an issue. Some in Washington have too much confidence in his ability to solve problems, while others fear that intentionally or inadvertently he will sell Taiwan out.

The chance that war could erupt over Taiwan, long a disturbing undercurrent in US–China relations, burst into the consciousness of average Americans in March 1996, when President Bill Clinton reacted to Chinese missiles plunging into waters just off Taiwan's coast by dispatching two aircraft-carrier battle groups to the scene. Before that, government officials, members of Congress, and the media had not been paying much attention to Taiwan. There had been a brief flurry of excitement when Taiwan's President Lee Teng-hui visited in 1995, and before that sparks of admiration for Taiwan's growing democracy. China got more notice, but usually in the context of trade deficits and human rights controversies. The tragic events of Tiananmen Square defined the parameters of interest.

Flying missiles and sailing ships signaled that the US believed Taiwan to be endangered and sought to prevent escalation. No military alliance demanded that Washington fight alongside Taipei. Indeed, Washington enjoyed official relations with the People's Republic of China (PRC), having shifted recognition from Taipei to Beijing on January 1, 1979. Thereafter, for the US, the PRC constituted the sole legal government of China, a so-called one-China policy, and in the subsequent Taiwan Relations Act, Washington pledged nothing more than arms sales and maintenance of a capacity to resist force and coercion by China. Whether US assistance will come again, and under what circumstances, remains a central question in US–Taiwan relations.

War, actual or potential, has always been at the core of the relationship between the United States and Taiwan. Chiang Kai-shek and his Nationalist Chinese followers fled defeat in the Chinese civil war in 1948–49 to seek refuge in Taiwan, surviving only because the US interceded. American money and military assistance poured in—as they had during the Japanese invasion of the mainland in World War II—preventing a collapse and thwarting an attack and takeover of the last piece of "Free China."

Washington sent warships repeatedly to support Taiwan. The 1996 operation in many ways harked back to confrontations in 1954 and 1958, when Americans sailed to the Taiwan Strait to reassure the Nationalist Chinese and preempt further action. Beijing's use of force to score political points regarding Taiwan's status and behavior turned stalemate into confrontation in the 1990s, as it had in the 1950s. And as it had in the 1950s, the US delighted Taipei and shocked Beijing in its willingness to deploy substantial military capabilities despite strains in US–Taiwan relations: in the 1950s over garrisoning of, and guarantees to, several offshore islands; in the 1990s over Lee Teng-hui's manipulation of the US political system. Furthermore, although in 1996—as in the 1950s—the incident jeopardized US security, Washington chose strengthening the island's defenses over cutting military aid and abandoning Taiwan. In the 1950s Washington signed a treaty and based sophisticated weapons on the island. Half a century later the US sold Taiwan advanced weaponry and expanded assistance for strategic planning and training.

But neither Taipei nor Washington embraced the relationship fully. US strategic, political, economic, and financial support and Taiwan's posture as Free China never eradicated deep and barely hidden reservoirs of mistrust. On both sides differences in priorities and perspectives through generations of leaders and their advisers have raised questions about the wisdom and durability of the alignment.

Demands to disengage have arisen in the US because Taiwan is distant, unknown, and dangerous. During and after World War II, dismay over the ineffectiveness and corruption of the Nationalist Chinese government soured the White House and State Department on Chiang Kai-shek. President Harry Truman, having concluded that Chiang's associates had embezzled millions of aid dollars, balked at providing more. Chiang, in turn, interpreted pressure for reform as barely concealed coercion to oust him. He demanded US aid to reconquer the mainland. Truman and his secretary of state believed diplomatic relations with Chiang's Chinese communist adversaries, who governed the vast majority of the Chinese, might be a necessary and wise solution.

But other developments precluded renouncing Taiwan. Denying Taiwan to monolithic communism in the wake of North Korea's attack on the

South suddenly appeared vital. The island emerged as a strategic outpost in the cold war, and Chiang—however authoritarian—became a symbol of freedom in contrast to Mao Zedong's communist tyranny. Taiwan soon became a base for intelligence and sabotage operations, particularly aerial reconnaissance, signal monitoring, and coastal raids. In time, as Taiwan experienced an economic boom, it became a significant American trade partner. Ultimately, Taiwan developed into a democracy.

Despite shared interests, the enormous disparities in power, culture, size, and development rendered cooperation between the US and Taiwan difficult. The United States balanced global responsibilities. Americans who paid attention to foreign policy were oriented toward Europe, and they devoted appreciably less attention to problems in Asia. Few knew much about China, and fewer still about Taiwan, even at times of crisis.

In Taiwan, a majority also focused on domestic challenges.[1] They sought to create a viable society and economy; never more than 20 percent were committed to recovering the mainland. Images of the US captured its actions as liberator from Japan, provider of generous aid, and advocate of democratic values, but also as a conspirator in, and facilitator of, Kuomintang (KMT) repression. Among neither the majority nor the minority did much sympathy exist for Washington's insistence that Taiwan join the cold war struggle against Moscow.

With such different priorities, leaders often appeared inattentive, irresponsible, and untrustworthy to each other. Even before Richard Nixon conceived of a new framework for dealing with China and Taiwan in the 1960s, Washington and Taipei doubted each other's reliability. Whether it came to resolving the Vietnam War or thwarting China's development of an atomic arsenal, their impulses and plans diverged sharply. Officials had trouble just communicating because they used identical words to describe different ideas.

The US, most famously, established a security alliance with Taiwan that it never intended as a war-fighting pact. The value of the alliance lay in dual deterrence—of Taipei as well as Beijing. Washington wanted not merely to boost Taipei's morale, but also to tie Chiang's hands. President Dwight D. Eisenhower and his secretary of state, John Foster Dulles, cultivated a policy of strategic ambiguity to keep friend and foe, Taipei and Beijing, guessing about the circumstances under which the US might intercede in a military conflict in the Strait. From the 1950s forward each successive administration adopted a version of strategic ambiguity.[2]

Mistrust in conditions of great uncertainty invited Taiwan to struggle for influence over its destiny in the United States. The Republic of China

(Taiwan) became known as a lobbying juggernaut second only to Israel in its ability to manipulate Washington. Despite its status as a dependent, Taiwan eschewed passive acceptance of whatever the US chose to give. Rather, it made demands and followed policies independent of, and sometimes directly contrary to, American interests.[3]

Time and circumstance altered the lobby and the pattern of its success. As the old China lobby fought less to return to the mainland and more to strengthen Taiwan, its vaunted—if exaggerated—coherence and power declined. First, new constituencies and sources of money (Taiwanese Americans as well as Chinese Americans) promoted different, diverse, and, sometimes, more militant political causes. Second, by the mid-1960s the intimidating political environment of McCarthyism that had empowered the early lobby had disappeared. With the election of Richard Nixon, lobby membership dropped significantly as supporters, prematurely, declared victory. Third, an opposing China lobby materialized that promoted ties to Beijing, a lobby that included and cooperated with portions of the American business community. But Taiwan not only encountered rivalry in lobbying, it found Americans mesmerized by the drama of normalizing relations with China, of fighting the cold war with Beijing's help, and of witnessing China's economic transformation.

Taiwan utilized propaganda, espionage, and bribery to reach the chronically inattentive American public, the recurrently new and ignorant members of Congress, and the largely preoccupied executive branch. In those early years it magnified distrust by plotting to steal missiles and develop nuclear warheads. It committed human rights abuses on American soil to monitor and curb political opponents and independence activists. And, because it did not believe it could rely on the US government, it acquired intelligence from those willing to spy and leak.

Taiwan's leaders, however, could not find a formula that would end America's romance with China. These traditional men had difficulty overcoming cultural restraints and setting aside partisan and personal ambition to counter or work with the US. Portraits of them as titans of lobbying and masters of the US political system, although imaginary, generated anxiety about and mistrust of Taipei. Successive administrations, therefore, shrouded US initiatives in secrecy, going well beyond the standard efforts of diplomats to protect their policies. The effect on Taiwan, unsurprisingly, was to persuade the leaders and the public that they could not trust the US.

Mistrust accelerated with the democratization of Taiwan. As political reform took hold, Taiwan politics became more turbulent and unpredictable. New leaders had fewer ties to the US, and a raucous legislature forced bargaining on issues such as arms sales, where approval had always been automatic.

Democracy has also opened up the question of Taiwan's future. Although the majority advocates the status quo, shunning independence and unification, the public has become more culturally and politically "Taiwanized." But whatever their goal, this aroused citizenry insists on the right to decide its future. Americans, as a result, have had to tread carefully between their one-China policy and demands for self-determination. Ironically, Woodrow Wilson introduced the vocabulary of self-determination to the Chinese during World War I, having borrowed the expression from Lenin. Wilson, however, was no revolutionary, distrusting third-world peoples and their unpredictable governments. Chinese everywhere felt betrayed when Wilson did not support them.[4] Similarly, today the limits to US cooperation with Taiwan's democracy surprise and disturb many who listened for decades to Washington's promotion of democratic principles. Some simply refuse to believe that Washington's commitment is conditional, persuaded that whatever Taiwan does, the US will be there.

THE purpose of this book is to examine unsparingly that history of mistrust, the damage it has caused to US–Taiwan relations, and the jeopardy in which it has put both sides. Ignorance, indifference, carelessness, and secrecy have allowed politicians and diplomats to pretend that the relationship works, although in many ways it has become increasingly dysfunctional. Responsibility for these developments rests with everyone discussed in these pages, since continuing and varied actions have contributed to the existing predicament. All distrust cannot be eliminated, of course, but mutual confidence could grow if it were based on greater transparency and mutual respect.

This volume also expands a meager literature on how the US and Taiwan interact. For every study of US–Taiwan relations, dozens have been written examining US relations with China. This may appear reasonable, given China's greater size and growing power, but for the foreseeable future Taiwan holds a critical key to peace in Asia. Being uninformed is dangerous.

This book, accordingly, seeks to explore and explain US–Taiwan relations. It has been undertaken in the firm belief that knowledge can overcome mistrust, diminish misunderstanding, and avoid miscalculation. It focuses on the actions and thinking of policy makers and the diplomats who implement those policies. It drills down into the political and strategic concerns that have forced cooperation and compelled confrontation.

Since Richard Nixon entered the presidency in 1969, determined to repair Washington's sundered ties to China, Taiwan has had to function with many fewer than normal diplomatic ties. Making interaction work under these highly unusual and deeply fraught conditions distinguishes US–Taiwan relations from most international exchanges. Yet the absence of formal diplomatic relations has not led to Taiwan's collapse, and so the successes as well as the failures in these years are worth studying.

No effort has been made to look at the relationship comprehensively. Although trade and investment are critical to sustaining US contact with Taiwan, this study does not deal with economic affairs. It does not detail concerns about society, culture, or human rights except as they have an effect on the central themes. Furthermore, Congress and interest groups are largely absent. It is not that these issues and actors are unimportant; they are critical and have captured my attention elsewhere. Most of them, however, have functioned relatively smoothly as part of the informal relationship. It is in the security and political arenas that the critical challenges undermining trust and mutual confidence exist. It is on these questions, therefore, that this book attempts to broaden and enrich understanding.

This volume also seeks to place US–Taiwan relations in context. For Washington, Taiwan has always been a relatively minor concern compared to its other worldwide commitments. Taiwan, however, has few friends and none willing to provide continuing, if circumscribed, political and military support. Generations of US officials have noted this disparity and, although some lamented it, most have believed it provided useful leverage. The China factor does not totally define the relationship, and yet few things remain untouched by it. Each entertains different expectations regarding China and the benefits or threats of dealing with it. For decades Washington and Taipei have seen China differently, calculating actions on the basis of disparate needs and not always mindful of the implications for each other of their China policies. The growth in Chinese power, wealth, and influence means that they continue to do so at increasing peril.

The final reason for writing this book has been to demonstrate that history matters. Current relations and future problems can be fully understood only through a historical framework. Policy makers often believe themselves too busy to consult the past regarding the needs of the future. They draw on analogies unpredictably and inaccurately. They assume that some policies are foreordained and others shapeless, open to thorough reformulation.[5] All too often Americans have been ahistorical in seeking to influence Taiwan's path. Taipei and Beijing have stepped in and interpreted the past competitively. When memory is absent, those who wish to create their own reality have free rein. Given the jeopardy in which this puts the United States, this book seeks to help decision makers avoid adding to the mistrust they have inherited.

Mistrust has been just one feature of US–Taiwan relations, but it has been the most central, damaging, and persistent. Understanding and eliminating mistrust should be a critical priority. That goal informs this book. Anything less could easily lead to catastrophe.

IN THE CONTEXT OF
THE COLD WAR

DURING THE years from 1945 to 1969, the United States defined the world in terms of a cold war contest with the Soviet Union and its allies. Washington considered its most crucial arena to be Europe, where US allies recovered slowly from the Second World War, watched their colonial empires disappear, and lurched among domestic political alternatives that sometimes left them precariously vulnerable to communism. Americans met these threats by expanding national influence overseas, creating a new global empire. If the Soviets did not always pose the economic, social, and political challenges that US leaders saw, imagined, or pretended to face, much of the world nonetheless succumbed to bipolar thinking and organization.

In the ensuing confrontation, Americans measured China against the Soviet Union—better or worse, a puppet or rogue state. Moscow stood at the heart of the cold war, with its atomic bomb, its European Iron Curtain, and its emplacement of missiles in Cuba. But the fanatical Chinese sometimes seemed more frightening to Americans—whether in the administration, in the Congress, or among the public—when, for example, they fought Americans on the Korean peninsula, prolonged the Vietnam war, or fulminated against the US and its leaders. Accordingly, "Free China" became an ally despite its policies and politics.

The imperatives of the cold war also accelerated the rebalancing of American political institutions. An imperial presidency suited the demands of bipolarity and advancing technology: crises became constant, nuclear war seemed imminent, information expanded vastly but grew harder to amass and control, and decisiveness commanded a premium. Congress, animated by anticommunist passions, could, in the person of a Senator Joseph McCarthy, crusade against alleged communists in the government and disrupt executive decision making. But more often, Congress sought to shape policy through appropriations and oversight, conceding final authority to the executive.

Congress had the greatest say when propelled by public opinion and united behind policies that presidents already favored. When disunited, or unsure, Congress had far less significance. President Dwight Eisenhower operated quite independently, toppling governments in Iran (1953) and Guatemala (1954) while also arrogating potential war-making powers through the Formosa (1955) and Middle East (1957) resolutions. John F. Kennedy barely informed Congress during the Cuban Missile Crisis (1962), and Lyndon Johnson bent members to his will over Vietnam with the Tonkin Gulf Resolution (1964).

On China and Taiwan, where few knew much, influence remained uneven, episodic, and diffuse. A vociferous minority—the Walter Judds and William Knowlands—motivated by missionary zeal, ideology, markets, and battlefield enmity, pressed an activist agenda and sometimes compelled presidents to modify policy. But the siren call of parochial constituent interests and the hostility of many executive branch officials more often eliminated Congress from important China-related decision making. Public opinion at times provided a more effective constraint, given the power of retributive voting. But, ultimately, high-level officials and foreign affairs specialists determined the direction of US relations with Beijing and Taipei.

CHAPTER ONE

The Origins of Strategic Ambiguity

WHEN RICHARD NIXON took the oath of office as the thirty-seventh president of the United States, Taiwan's leaders celebrated the triumph of a cold warrior and friend of the Republic of China (ROC) who would, they assumed, vigorously guard the cause of Free China. There had been signs during the preceding years that Nixon might be rethinking some of his anti-PRC views, but in January 1969 no one expected the changes soon to be wrought in Sino-American relations. On the contrary, in the US, Taiwan, and China, most observers of Nixon's victory saw it in the context of his anticommunist political career.

The environment also resonated with assumptions about US–Taiwan relations. Most Americans who paid attention to Asia judged the US to be, overall, Taiwan's benefactor and protector. They ignored periodic flare-ups over policy choices and believed good intentions and generosity excused cultural missteps. Neither side acknowledged mutual distrust. Yet, in the two decades between Chiang Kai-shek's arrival in Taiwan and Nixon's arrival in the White House, the US–Taiwan relationship was by no means an uncomplicated marriage of congruent needs and interests. Both dominance and dependency could be, and sometimes were, troublesome and exhausting.

Washington played on a far larger stage than did Taipei, and the differences in outlook and priorities produced recurrent tension. The US subordinated most of its foreign policy to fighting the Soviet Union and its minions in the communist bloc. Thus, American presidents sought allies everywhere, among the industrialized powers and the less developed states. In America's broad vision, Taiwan could be useful if it restrained and embarrassed Beijing, whereas China could be helpful so long as it drained Soviet resources and distracted Moscow from the larger cold war contest.

The Nationalist Chinese in Taiwan agreed that communism constituted a menace, especially communism in its Chinese guise. Chiang Kai-shek (CKS) and others among the Kuomintang (KMT) leadership who sought Washington's assistance cared about the wider struggle only when it impinged on their prospects for survival and recovery of the mainland. When Americans briefly looked to the Chinese communists to help fight Japan during World War II, the KMT also dispensed with ideology to flirt with Moscow.[1]

Political outlooks similarly diverged. The democratic government of the US found its association with the repressive and dictatorial KMT authorities necessary and convenient—but awkward, given American principles of political liberalism, free enterprise, and sociocultural diversity. The KMT, although almost totally dependent on the US, ignored American proselytizing. Its leaders devoted their energies to exploiting Washington's support to build a strong economy and a viable military, while pretending to care about a shared struggle for freedom and democracy.

Washington sporadically considered severing its links to the KMT, yet—given the options—it always relented. The Kuomintang, in turn, tolerated the indignities of dependency, becoming increasingly adept at manipulating its great power patron.

The most notorious misunderstanding concerned the battle against Japan in the 1940s. Washington believed Chiang put his civil war struggle first, hoarding supplies and troops even as he impeded the efforts of communist Chinese soldiers to confront Japanese armies. Chiang contended that he wanted to attack, but Washington and London limited his resources and dictated how, when, and where to fight. Unsurprisingly, distrust and resentment followed.[2]

In the same way, anxious to find a solution to the Chinese civil war so that Japan's surrender would not spark renewed fighting, Harry Truman and Secretary of State Dean Acheson sent General George Marshall to mediate in 1945. But Chiang considered Marshall's effort at neutrality to be disloyal, and he proved more resistant to negotiation than the communists. The US gave up, ultimately supporting the KMT in renewed warfare. Both Chinese sides had by then concluded that the US couldn't be trusted.

By 1949 Truman and Acheson felt little but contempt for Chiang Kai-shek and seriously considered abandoning the Kuomintang. Truman had become convinced the KMT government was inept and shortsighted as well as corrupt. Acheson, never a patient man, thought Washington should no longer squander funds and advice on someone incapable of using either effectively. During 1948 and 1949, as Chiang lost the mainland, the administration divided over the issue of Taiwan's strategic importance, arguing about its location along sensitive sea-lanes and the inherent dangers in Soviet control.[3] But in NSC 48/2, signed December 30, 1949, it finally ruled out a military defense of Taiwan just weeks after Beijing had begun to plan for a cross-Strait war in 1950–51.[4] Expecting that Taiwan would fall, the administration directed American diplomatic missions worldwide to explain to host governments that the island possessed no strategic significance and that Washington had no responsibility for it.[5] Truman and Acheson followed this with public announcements that the US would not again intervene in the Chinese civil war, signaling that they saw Taiwan as expendable.[6]

The Republic of China's sojourn in the wilderness proved brief. With the outbreak of war in Korea on June 25, fear of a monolithic communist conspiracy based in, and directed from, Moscow, which sought domination of East Asia, overwhelmed all other considerations. Washington's immediate military response led to a major war almost certainly unanticipated by both Beijing and Moscow. The confrontation and its ideological impact disrupted US–China relations for almost thirty years.

Even after war began, the alignment between Washington and Taipei remained open to adjustment. Truman ordered the US Seventh Fleet to the Taiwan Strait in June 1950 to prevent the Korean conflict from engulfing the region. Fearing a KMT assault on the mainland as much as he worried about the Chinese communists seizing Taiwan, Truman declared that all operations against the mainland must stop. He intended to withdraw the US Navy as soon as these dangers had passed. Although he declared the disposition of Taiwan to be undecided and poured military and economic assistance into the island, Truman had no plans to create two Chinas or to secure independence for Taiwan.

Eisenhower, Dulles, and Contradictions over Taiwan

Truman's successor, Dwight Eisenhower, wanted to use the Nationalist presence across the Strait to threaten China and accelerate a settlement in Korea. The US became Taiwan's primary source of assistance, which allowed Chiang to stabilize KMT rule and refurbish the armed forces. Chiang then began to press for a mutual defense treaty, only to discover that supposedly sympathetic leaders in Washington did not want to give it to him.

China emerged as the key to Chiang's treaty much as Mao Zedong's support for North Korea's attack in June 1950 had been the answer to regime survival. In September 1954 Mao shelled Jinmen, an island off China's coast still under Nationalist control. He did not hope to seize it, lacking the capability. He did intend to deter a defense treaty, create friction between Washington and Taipei, and force the international community to pay attention to the Taiwan issue. Secretary of State John Foster Dulles, however, concluded that the crisis left him no other choice but, grudgingly, to sign the treaty.[7]

Although now in a formal alliance with Taipei, Americans did not embrace the KMT government uncritically.[8] The mutual defense treaty provided the KMT urgently needed support, but it also gave Washington the ability to circumscribe, if not prevent, Nationalist Chinese risk taking. Chiang, for instance, desperately wanted to safeguard not only Taiwan and the Penghu Islands but also Jinmen and Mazu. The State Department refused. Rather than offer an explicit pledge, Washington would say only that, in extremis, coverage might extend to "such other territories as may be determined by mutual agreement."[9] At Eisenhower's behest, Congress bolstered the assurance with the Formosa Resolution in 1955, authorizing the president to assist the Nationalists in defending Taiwan, Penghu, and unspecified "related positions."

The confrontation with China dragged into March, and the Eisenhower team began to talk, privately and publicly, about using atomic weapons to end it.[10] How influential these threats were in Beijing's decision to renounce its misadventure remains uncertain. Washington's atomic diplomacy may have been more important in fortifying Taipei. Zhou Enlai went to the April 1955 Bandung Conference seeking support from the "third world," but he recognized that the Strait crisis wasn't winning Beijing friends. He softened China's position, and diplomatic talks with the US followed, along with the end of the confrontation.

It is clear that the 1954–55 Taiwan Strait crisis had three fundamental, long-term effects on US–Taiwan–China interaction. Washington's attempted nuclear intimidation of Beijing led Mao to develop China's atomic capability, raising the stakes of confrontation.[11] Second, Washington's difficulties controlling its ally and deterring its adversary produced the enduring, if sometimes reviled, policy of strategic ambiguity. Eisenhower and Dulles judged that it was hazardous to tell Beijing exactly which territories Washington would defend because the People's Liberation Army (PLA) would seize the rest. At the same time, they refused to clarify the extent of their assistance lest Chiang Kai-shek become overconfident and produce a new crisis. Strategic ambiguity also allowed Eisenhower to defend himself against an intrusive Congress. Third, Taipei concluded that its approach to relations with Washington was working. As had happened on the mainland in the 1940s, Washington might be angered and it might not grant the KMT unlimited support, but, lacking alternatives, it would ultimately stand by the Republic of China. It would do so even when KMT behavior jeopardized American interests and security.

So, largely unchastened by the Strait crisis, Chiang repeatedly reached for more than America was prepared to bestow. He urged Washington to help him establish an Asian defense association to parallel the North Atlantic Treaty Organization. He suggested to a series of American presidents that ROC soldiers could help fight in Vietnam as he had earlier, unsuccessfully, offered to assist in Korea, eager for the prestige of marching alongside Americans.[12] More important, he tried to persuade US officials to see attacks against Communist China as necessary extensions of their existing battle plans. Bringing down Mao was vital to sustaining peace in Asia.

Washington, however, dismissed Nationalist forces as inadequate, fit for nothing more than reconnaissance or commando raids, and likely to be a burden rather than an asset in serious fighting.[13] Still, neutralizing Taiwan would not serve US strategic interests and was specifically disavowed in 1953. Indeed, the mere existence of ROC forces tied down PLA units, and since the entire cost of annual economic and military assistance to Taiwan equaled no more than the price of equipping and feeding a single US division at home, it seemed a bargain.[14]

As for Chiang's motives, US leaders became ever more convinced that the Generalissimo cared little about containment of the Soviet bloc, but rather wanted to embroil the US in a war with China to facilitate the KMT's return to the mainland. After the 1954–55 crisis, far from removing his troops from islands within range of Chinese artillery, he had tripled their numbers.[15] In the summer of 1956 Chiang initiated a secret "Plan K" for joint navy, marine, and army landings in Fujian and Guangdong provinces. Scaled back from proposals to attack Shanghai or the Shandong peninsula, nearer Beijing, this venture, Chiang argued to Washington, would recoup losses in Vietnam and Korea. Washington refused assistance, contributing fatefully to Taipei's decision to stage a riot in 1957 that destroyed the US Embassy in Taiwan.[16]

The US did not jettison the Kuomintang and Taiwan in spite of this friction. Dulles's ire always passed, and the continuing propaganda allure of a Free China kept critical American diplomats at bay. Indeed, Dulles and Eisenhower both remained chary of the China lobby, especially in Congress. Neither man could doubt that for them to lose Taiwan, as their predecessors had "lost China," would be politically costly.

Washington also feared that its credibility as a friend and ally would be undermined by abandonment of Taipei. In particular, to bolster policies of "brinkmanship" and "massive retaliation," Dulles and others believed there could be no doubts about US resolve to act in a crisis. Nor could Washington allow the PRC to rupture the US defensive perimeter, thereby exposing sea-lanes vital for trade and military traffic or leaving Asian friends suddenly vulnerable.

Instability might also result from Taipei's secret contacts with Beijing that began in 1955, following the offshore islands crisis. The CIA concluded that "Peking shifted to . . . sowing suspicion between Washington and Taipei," an apparently clever tactic since both Taipei and Washington worried about betrayal. In fact, Chiang Ching-kuo (CCK), the Generalissimo's son, reported the initial contacts to Washington only when they leaked to the press, and the CIA worried about whether and why some exchanges might be hidden from Washington even though CCK generally sought to reassure the US. Tsao Chu-jen, a shady Hong Kong journalist with ties to Zhou Enlai and CCK, on whose staff he may have served, proved especially persistent. None of these communications, however, yielded identifiable changes.[17]

In 1958 the US, having been unable to persuade CKS to reduce his exposure on the offshore islands, responded to renewed PRC shelling by sending warships again. Washington installed eight-inch howitzers on Jinmen capable of hitting China with atomic shells and provided the first Sidewinder air-to-air missiles to be used in combat.[18] Mao—who sought to drive Chiang from the islands, test US determination, energize domestic reform, and challenge domination of the international order by Washington and Moscow—admitted to having been shocked by the US response. "I simply did not calculate . . . that the world would become so disturbed and turbulent," he later observed.[19] He renounced his hopes of capturing Jinmen and Mazu, realizing that increasing the geographic distance between the mainland and Taiwan would contribute to the creation of two Chinas.[20] Beijing also paid a price with the Soviet Union: Moscow, about to send a prototype atomic device to China, concluded that the Chinese were too irresponsible and refused to ship the bomb.[21]

Having backed CKS forcefully, Dulles nonetheless distrusted him and told the press on September 30, 1958, that it would be foolhardy to sustain large deployments on the precarious offshore islands if a cease-fire could be negotiated. Dulles compelled CKS to agree to a communiqué declaring that Taiwan would rely on political means to recover the mainland.

Dulles was respectful of the potency of the China lobby, which had hounded his predecessor; his public utterances always remained of the fire and brimstone sort, and even privately he welcomed opportunities to curtail Chinese Communist Party (CCP) power and influence.[22] But he sympathized with the Chinese communists who were being asked to tolerate "an active base for attempting to foment civil strife."[23] As a step toward realizing the two-Chinas policy he preferred, he repeatedly raised the idea of seating both Chinas in the United Nations (UN) rather than maintaining the pretense that Taipei still represented all of China.[24] In 1956 he contemplated a plan to substitute India for China as a permanent member of the UN Security Council, which would allow the administration safely to acquiesce in the representation of both Chinas in the General Assembly. Further, ignoring pressure from Taipei and Congress, he refused to promise to use the veto against Beijing's admission, although he conceded that he might have to do so.[25]

Eisenhower declined to take political risks to deal openly with the experiment in China, but he considered diplomatic relations and trade with Beijing inevitable. Thus, he and Dulles threatened China but never allowed CKS to attack it, rebuffed his request for nuclear warheads and missiles, engaged in diplomatic talks with Beijing, and explored the possibility of dual representation in the UN, as well as opposing Taipei's use of its veto to keep Mongolia out.[26] At no point did Eisenhower or Dulles wish to abandon the KMT, but, contrary to common wisdom, they wanted a more realistic relationship with both Chinas.

As would be the case often in the US–Taiwan relationship, Americans thought to be sympathizers disappointed Taipei once in office. Dulles never served as an advocate for Taiwan. Instead, he appeared willing to come to terms with Beijing if Chinese leaders would break with Moscow. Lobbyists and businessmen who staunchly supported Chiang Kai-shek misled Taipei into believing Washington would be friendlier. So too did the enormous economic assistance Washington lavished on Taiwan, which helped launch an extraordinary economic boom. Taiwan's leaders had trouble looking beyond their own agenda and understanding where it converged with or diverged from US national interests.

Kennedy's Unexpected Taiwan Policy

Surprisingly, things improved with the election of John F. Kennedy, despite Taipei's opposition to a Kennedy victory. Kennedy had voted against the 1955 Formosa Resolution, had spoken of a potential relationship with Beijing, and during the presidential campaign had dismissed the offshore islands as "unnecessary to our security" as well as indefensible.[27] As Kennedy settled into office, Taiwan conducted military exercises to prepare for unilateral action against China, should it have to engage alone.[28]

To Chiang Kai-shek's immense relief, however, Kennedy went further than Eisenhower in thwarting Beijing's international aspirations and assuring the ROC's status. Kennedy secretly guaranteed that he would cast a veto at the UN to keep Beijing out, which Eisenhower and Dulles had refused to do.[29] Chiang prompted Kennedy's guarantee by threatening to veto Mongolia's UN admission because it remained part of China rather than being an independent state. Mongolia's entry had been administratively linked to that of French-speaking Mauritania, so blocking Mongolia meant alienating eleven Francophone African governments.[30] In retaliation they might reverse policy and vote to oust Taiwan and seat China. Kennedy feared CKS would then attack China, precipitating a disaster in US domestic politics as well as in the Strait. Kennedy preemptively decided to make a pledge on the veto.[31]

Ray Cline, the CIA station chief in Taipei, facilitated this secret promise, bypassing both the US ambassador and the ROC Foreign Ministry.[32] National Security Adviser McGeorge Bundy told Kennedy that Cline was "the ablest officer in any service on the island, and . . . the one who has the closest confidence of the Generalissimo and his son." He had become the younger man's drinking buddy and sometime traveling companion.[33] Bundy, who had briefly served at the CIA with Cline, urged the president to listen to the station cheif's insights into the KMT's thinking and his warnings that its leaders felt ignored and mistreated by the State Department.[34]

Meanwhile, Kennedy's State Department sought to deal with the Chinese representation issue through a "successor states formula." This argued that two Chinas existed as offshoots of the Republic of China, established in 1912, and both ought to be seated in the UN.[35] The veto pledge undercut this strategy, but Kennedy didn't care, aware that Republicans in Congress opposed any initiative encompassing two Chinas.[36] Instead, the administration called the China seat an "important question" and demanded a two-thirds vote in the General Assembly rather than a simple majority. Kennedy considered this tactic awkwardly transparent but—believing questions of China recognition and representation were political dynamite—unavoidable.[37]

Secretary of State Dean Rusk, whom historians and diplomats have blamed for thwarting China initiatives under Kennedy, told his son that he was, in fact, "leaning toward a two-China policy in 1961." He maintained that he broached the subject with Kennedy early on, only to be rebuffed.

Whether he pursued the issue as circumstances changed, or more characteristically kept silent in view of Kennedy's strong opinions, is unclear.[38] Certainly Rusk had disliked and distrusted Chiang Kai-shek since the Truman administration, and he found it hard to credit talk about reform in Taiwan.[39] Chiang's inflexibility on the UN issue stirred up old enmities, undermining Rusk's customary self-control. Believing Taipei's veto on Mongolia to be "political suicide," he told Assistant Secretary of State Walter McConaughy, a KMT sympathizer, to make clear that the administration would see to it that the American people lost all compassion for Chiang Kai-shek.[40]

Ultimately, Mongolia entered the UN, Chiang did not cast a veto, and word of Kennedy's pledge did not leak. US–Taiwan relations showed the strains of intense diplomatic maneuvering, tensions not assuaged by Chiang's persistent demands that he be allowed to attack China. In the spring of 1961 his military chief sought to fire nuclear-tipped artillery shells from Jinmen; the US refusal to supply the shells shut this plan down.[41]

Chiang's determination to attack the mainland to trigger a revolution continued to draw strength from the agricultural and industrial disarray in China. Reports of a massive famine following Mao's catastrophic Great Leap Forward—which may have killed as many as 30 million between 1958 and 1962—were widely disseminated by Chiang's Asian People's Anti-Communist League.[42] Kennedy recognized that flatly rejecting Chiang's ambitions would be politically perilous at home, could provoke a desperate lunge at China, and might undermine morale on the island, destabilizing Chiang's regime and undermining US credibility. He also found it personally unacceptable to write off the struggle against communism in China. But he did not trust Chiang. He knew Chiang believed that "once the Nationalist troops had established a bridgehead anywhere on the mainland, the Americans would surely provide all necessary aid."[43] Even short of forcing a Sino-American war by diverting resources to a military buildup, Chiang would jeopardize economic stability on the island.[44]

In June 1962 US intelligence discovered that major troop movements had begun on the mainland opposite Taiwan, a response to preparations for military operations on the island. A debate ensued among US officials whether Chinese forces would be restricted to a defensive mission or might attack the offshore islands.[45] Roger Hilsman, director of the Bureau of Intelligence and Research, convinced the administration to ready forces but be ambiguous about using them, because any firm decision would quickly leak.[46]

On the diplomatic track, Washington took several actions. Ambassadorial talks between the US and the PRC had been launched in May 1954 to deal with citizen detainee issues. They quickly became mired in irresolvable Taiwan Strait problems, but they continued sporadically to keep a dialogue going. Thus, in 1962 US Ambassador John Cabot could use them to tell his counterpart, Wang Bingnan, that Kennedy sought no war and would not support an attack on China.[47]

Beijing had assumed that the appointment of Alan Kirk, an admiral, as Kennedy's new ambassador to the ROC meant Washington intended to ready ROC forces for amphibious warfare. Kirk, however, demanded CKS not give Beijing excuses to strike or opportunities to portray the US and ROC as aggressors. CKS rapidly came to see Kirk as unfriendly and complained that the US was protecting the enemy by binding Taiwan "hand and foot." He also objected to the US initiative at Warsaw and emphasized the Hong Kong talks with China more as his trust in Washington diminished.[48]

Kennedy simultaneously tried to use the Soviet Union to pressure China, regarding Moscow's communists as more reasonable and underestimating the Sino-Soviet split. Soviet Ambassador Anatoly Dobrynin might not have been eager to help with Beijing but was aghast that Kennedy would contemplate "help[ing] defend the off-shore islands."[49]

Perhaps it was to rein in Chiang as well as to propitiate him that Kennedy considered visiting Taipei in 1963. American plots to replace him had long since been abandoned, and Kennedy turned instead to flattery and coaxing to get cooperation with American priorities.[50] Further, a presidential visit would promote deterrence of the PRC and highlight Taiwan's economic success as a model for other Asian states. Initially the plan involved an October 1963 trip to Japan and Korea, allowing time in Indonesia, Malaya, or the Philippines, with a one-day stop on Taiwan. When CKS heard of the possibility, he immediately extended an enthusiastic invitation. Scheduling soon slipped to 1964, and Kennedy died before serious planning could begin.[51] But even without the symbolism of Kennedy arriving in Taiwan, the mere mention of a visit gratified Chiang. By 1963 it was clear that Kennedy shared many of the Generalissimo's concerns, among them the development of a PRC nuclear weapon and Chinese expansionist · appetites.[52]

Ironically, sympathetic historians would later portray Kennedy as a prescient thinker on China, a man who would have radically changed US–China relations, recognizing the PRC and rectifying a misguided attachment to the ROC. Those seeking to explain his lack of meaningful progress between 1961 and 1963 blamed it on Dwight Eisenhower: allegedly, Ike had warned Kennedy that if the young man tried to change China policy, he would emerge from retirement to fight it.[53] This story, however, is difficult to reconcile with Eisenhower's views about the inevitability of diplomatic relations with China and its UN admission. Nevertheless, reference to this Eisenhower threat became such a common feature of the thinking about China that after Kennedy's death the Johnson administration continued to be restrained by it.[54]

The immediacy of a Strait crisis had in any case lessened by the autumn of 1963. Reports from the US Embassy in Taiwan noted that preparations for an attack against China had diminished substantially. Chiang Ching-kuo, on a visit to Washington, assured Ray Cline that there would be no invasion unless a revolution seemed imminent. But, in return for caution, Taipei wanted more support for covert operations. Above all, CCK asserted, the US and ROC must not allow the communists to relax and consolidate their power.

Although US officials had stopped thinking of CCK exclusively as the sinister head of ROC intelligence, Washington remained skeptical of the motives of both Chiangs. Ching-kuo tried to heighten interest in an incursion with reports that Taipei had identified missile and atomic facilities and would be willing to cooperate with Washington in removing them. Bundy, however, guardedly reminded CCK that rather than toppling the PRC, an American-supported invasion would probably bring Beijing and Moscow back together.[55] As for direct attacks on nuclear weapons factories, Kennedy, although fixated on the dangers of a Chinese bomb, told Chiang he doubted that they could penetrate Communist defenses and believed that they lacked adequate intelligence.[56]

Chiang's Ambitions and Lyndon Johnson's Interests

Kennedy's attitude and that of his successor, Lyndon Johnson, reflected the difference in responsibilities and interests of Washington and Taipei. For Johnson as for Kennedy, Ike, and Truman, priorities looked very different from the two capitals. This became apparent shortly after Johnson assumed the presidency and France decided to establish diplomatic relations with the PRC.

Neither Chiang nor Johnson welcomed the French move. Johnson stressed that the US had appealed at the highest levels to deter Paris. But when Chiang planned an immediate rupture, Washington urged him to be patient. If the French maintained relations with Taiwan, an embarrassed Mao Zedong might be forced to reject France, or if France succeeded in having relations with both Beijing and Taipei, this could be generalized into a broader worldwide movement. Chiang, however, refused even to see the US ambassador, unwilling to condone the concept of two Chinas.[57] To the Generalissimo these disastrous events were the fault of the Americans, who had blocked his recover-the-mainland campaign. When on January 21 an armored division attempted a coup to overthrow Chiang, he also blamed this on Washington.[58] In the end France broke relations, ending the dispute but leaving behind enmity in Taipei and Washington about the inability of each to understand the priorities of the other.

Smoother cooperation existed in the crucial area of joint intelligence gathering, begun when the KMT still ruled on the mainland. The Pentagon, CIA, and National Security Agency focused on signals intelligence, providing equipment and training for Chinese Nationalist aerial reconnaissance and telecommunications monitoring. According to the Ministry of National Defense in Taipei, electronic sources yielded plentiful data on PLA deployments (air, land, and sea), PRC military analysis, and modernization efforts, because China depended heavily on easily monitored radio transmission. The ROC could also listen to domestic and international communications, supplying hundreds of native linguists who understood nuances impenetrable to all but the very best nonnative speakers. Aerial photography produced additional information on military maneuvers, war-related manufacturing, and the development of industry and agriculture. Planes gathered airborne debris to study Chinese nuclear testing. Aircraft, often piloted by airmen from Taiwan, carried out surveillance just twenty miles from China's coast. In 1964 the CIA installed over-the-horizon radars that provided the opportunity to track PRC missile launches.[59]

Washington and Taipei regularly shared the fruits of their labors but suspected each other of holding back information. The PRC aggravated distrust by generating misleading intelligence, penetrating spy networks, and infiltrating collection facilities. Human intelligence gathering caused the most problems, particularly in the early years, when the US and Taiwan often bought secrets, which contributed to the corruption and duplicity of informants.

As Beijing's capacity to shoot down surveillance aircraft improved in the late 1950s, Taiwan lobbied for more agile and advanced aircraft. Sophisticated technology raised security concerns, however: if planes crashed or were shot down in China, Soviet as well as Chinese communist authorities would acquire valuable secrets. Nevertheless, in July 1960, with Eisenhower's approval, Lockheed Aircraft sold two high-altitude U-2 spy planes to Taiwan.[60] At almost the same moment Moscow succeeded in downing Francis Gary Powers and his U-2, thus ending reconnaissance flights in Eu-

"But you can't quit now. Think of your obligation to those generations of crackpots yet unborn."

rope. Ray Cline did not believe that China had equally effective missiles and insisted Taiwan should continue collecting valuable intelligence. By the time China downed the first U-2 in 1962, the missions were too important to stop. Indeed, the U-2 not only photographed China's missile bases, but also established how drastically the departure of Soviet technicians had slowed China's nuclear program and subsequently revealed China's progress toward building its own bomb.[61]

The October 1964 Chinese nuclear detonation had long been expected and dreaded. Kennedy, Johnson, and others projected a shift in the balance of power and influence in the Asian region. CKS agreed, seeing a psychological effect "that could not be overestimated." In an emotional meeting with Cline, who had been dispatched for hand-holding, Chiang emphasized Taiwan's vulnerability. US promises to retaliate meant little to Taiwan's people who would already be dead.[62] What Chiang wanted, he would later write to Johnson, was the "wherewithal to destroy the ChiCom nuclear installations."[63] Chiang discounted deterrence; he was worried that Washington would be constrained by "world opinion [which] would consider that Peking has a perfect right to bomb a part of its own territory." Two years later Chiang's anxieties remained obvious enough that Rusk wrote to Johnson, "I did not draw him out on what conclusions he drew from his fears because I rather thought that he would immediately recommend a first strike against mainland Chinese nuclear installations."[64]

Chiang's proposals in 1965 and 1967 to seize five southern Chinese provinces seemed similarly unrealistic and irresponsible. Although he insisted it could be done without US troops or nuclear weapons, Americans did not believe it could be done at all, seeing the parallel with their own failure in the Cuban Bay of Pigs invasion—but on a spectacularly bigger scale.[65] After visiting Taipei, Chairman of the Joint Chiefs of Staff Earle G. Wheeler recommended Washington be brutally frank about not invading China because a posture of "interested but uncommitted onlookers" would not work.[66] Jim Thomson of the National Security Council (NSC) staff described the situation as "rather eerie: the GRC [government of the Republic of China] knows that we don't believe . . . [the return to the mainland story]; and we know that they know we don't believe it; and we suspect that some of them don't believe it; but no one says it. The result is that our every relationship is affected by the unmentionable dead cat on the floor."[67]

During 1966, with Congress holding hearings on US relations with China and "containment without isolation," Chiang Kai-shek decided that the tide of American policy had turned against Taiwan. Cline found him and his son dispirited. Arthur Hummel, deputy chief of mission at the embassy in Taipei, wrote that the Nationalists and the Americans "have sharply divergent views of the world." The Taiwan government operated on the premise "that there is a war on already and has been for many years"; Washington "is committed to exploration of steps toward peace." Both sides were careful to avoid a breakdown in their dialogue about cooperation, but the US increasingly found that the Nationalist government was "not being candid with us on a number of its operations."[68]

As the US and the Republic of China stood on the brink of policy realignment, Taiwan miraculously won a reprieve because of a sharp deterioration of domestic conditions inside China after the outbreak of the Great Proletarian Cultural Revolution. Johnson, in a speech on July 12, 1966, observed that China's people should not continue to be isolated from the world. His advisers ever more strongly encouraged a two-Chinas approach, arguing that much could be gained in international opinion to offset criticism of the Vietnam War by embarking on a new, more rational position on China.[69] But Mao's efforts to recreate his revolution, accelerate economic growth, and purge his rivals led to such mayhem that the world community reconsidered embracing the People's Republic. Much of the pressure to rectify representation in the UN evaporated, lessening mistrust between Washington and Taipei. CCP irrationality seemed to confirm ROC judgments of the mainland system, restoring an identity of interests with the US. And once vote tallies in the UN ceased to run in Beijing's direction, Taipei slackened demands that the US pledge to wield its veto or leave the UN if the PRC was admitted.

Lyndon Johnson, in any case, remained preoccupied with waging war in Vietnam. For him the most interesting fact about Taiwan may well have been Chiang Kai-shek's willingness to send troops to help fight. The president had become increasingly desperate, involving Washington's friends to alleviate domestic pressure on his administration. To Johnson's chagrin, his advisers insisted that accepting Taipei's troops would be too provocative. Johnson had to be satisfied with covert special forces operations.[70]

GIVEN that the relationship between Taipei and Washington remained so difficult, repeatedly disrupted by crises that put the US in harm's way or made Taipei fear abandonment, it is extraordinary that the partnership lasted as long as it did. But Taiwan literally had no place else to go. No other nation in the anticommunist alliance would have done as much for Taiwan as the US. In fact, European allies periodically lectured Washington that its passion for Chiang Kai-shek was ill starred and ill fated.

Although it flirted with Moscow, Taiwan's only real alternative was reconciliation with Beijing. It appears reasonably certain that, had the US pushed harder to unseat the Kuomintang, its leaders would have considered compromise across ideological lines more seriously. The Communist Chinese from early on offered KMT leaders entrée into high-level positions on the mainland. There would probably have been wealth if not power associated with capitulation. But it would have been surrender without guarantees.

The United States similarly had few choices. Discarding Taiwan entailed political penalties, but the uses of Taiwan remained limited. Support for a Free China as a symbol served Washington's needs at home and abroad, demonstrating its loyalty and reliability by championing Taiwan's survival, recovery, and growth.

Militarily, even after the US trained and supplied Taiwan's forces, the ROC comprised no more than a strategic reserve. Rusk refused the Defense Department's suggestion that Chiang's troops could be deployed in Southeast Asia. The secretary argued that fielding Nationalist forces ensured escalation because it would (1) induce the PRC to intervene if it wasn't already involved, (2) weaken Taiwan's defenses, thus tempting Beijing to attack the island, or (3) suggest that the real motive was to topple CCP control in China. Moreover, Rusk doubted the worth of Taiwan's fighting men.[71]

For Americans, Taiwan's location was valuable but not crucial. Basing forces in Taiwan might contribute to a defense of Japan, South Korea, or Southeast Asia, but less provocative alternatives existed. Raids on China from Taiwan that interrupted trade and slowed modernization would be more productive and desirable in theory than in reality. Taiwan offered only one actual strategic advantage: a staging area for intelligence operations, particularly electronic eavesdropping, however unreliable the information collected.

Nonetheless, the symbiotic relationship continued right up to the eve of Richard Nixon's inauguration.[72] One of the central lessons learned in the years following World War II was that anger, contempt, and mistrust did not necessarily undo a relationship. Despite disappointments and betrayals, between 1949 and 1969 Taipei and Washington found each other useful in their shared opposition to communism in China.

DÉTENTE

During Richard Nixon's tenure, the Soviet Union's challenge escalated as Moscow achieved parity with the United States in nuclear weaponry and international involvement. Washington entered into arms control agreements with Moscow—the 1972 Strategic Arms Limitation Treaty and Anti-Ballistic Missile Treaty—and made trade concessions that were contingent on Soviet good behavior. The policy of détente sought to integrate the Soviet Union into the world community and anchor its activities in accepted norms—to make it a stakeholder in the international system. Détente, however, failed, a victim of Moscow's desire to preserve a free hand among developing nations and strong opposition in the US.

Richard Nixon and Henry Kissinger wanted to bring American foreign policy into alignment with resources diminished by the Vietnam War through a far-reaching reconceptualization of America's role in the world. Abjuring regional responsibilities, they deputized select nations, such as Iran and Japan, to handle local discontent. It did not always work. Arab-Israeli clashes produced war in 1973 and locked Kissinger into "shuttle diplomacy." Where ideational or economic threats forced attention, as in Chile in 1973, Nixon and Kissinger did not hesitate to conspire to overthrow the government.

In their broad repositioning of US policies, China loomed large. Washington wanted to use Beijing as leverage against Moscow and Vietnam. China needed Washington to deter Soviet threats along its northern border. Moscow, dismayed by Sino-American reconciliation, feared Washington would establish military ties with Beijing. Its dread of the "yellow peril" led to consideration of destroying Chinese nuclear weapons facilities, a suggestion Kissinger quickly revealed to China (1973–74).

Nixon energetically pursued his personal political agenda, determined to be the man who "opened" China. He overlooked the tumultuous events of China's Cultural Revolution (1966–76) and the stark human rights abuses of Chinese leaders. He ignored promises to keep Japan and Taiwan forewarned of policy changes deeply affecting their security. Instead, Nixon and Kissinger engaged in prolonged secret diplomacy, excluding almost all allies abroad and virtually everyone at home: the public, the Congress, and the government's China specialists. They scored a notable triumph, although Congress and the public were far more open to change than imagined then and since. Initiating relations with China did not, however, outweigh Nixon's misuse of power in the Watergate imbroglio. To Beijing's surprise, Congress and the public forced Nixon's resignation in 1974. Nixon's departure, however, complicated progress toward diplomatic relations.

CHAPTER TWO

Taiwan Expendable?

THERE WERE two stories of Sino-American relations in the 1960s and 1970s, the oft-told tale of normalization with the People's Republic of China and the less well-noted saga of friction with, and final abandonment of, the Republic of China. These chronicles of triumph and tragedy progressed simultaneously, with nearly identical casts of characters on the American side and with the pivot of action for both the crucial decision to alter Washington's official commitments in East Asia. For the United States this could be seen as a coming-of-age story: the Americans finally facing reality, accepting the PRC's existence after decades of denial, triggering choruses of relief worldwide. In fact, because the change in policy was so radical, a myth came to surround it, originated and cultivated by Richard Nixon and Henry Kissinger; it told of a bolt-from-the-blue initiative undertaken at great political risk but carried out with consummate skill by the only individuals who could have realized it. One day the US was wedded to its ROC ally, and the next it had opened relations with China.[1]

As is true of myths in general, this one encompassed elements of truth and fiction, papering over sins and weighing heavily on future efforts to understand not just the development of US relations with China, but especially the trajectory of US relations with Taiwan. The legend of Nixon and Kissinger's outwitting the American China lobby, slaying the Taiwan dragon, and storming the Gate of Heavenly Peace to engage Mao Zedong and Zhou Enlai obscures a variety of issues. Reexamination of the opening to China clarifies the dynamics of foreign policy making at a watershed in the cold war. Once Kissinger went to Beijing and reached an understanding with his Chinese hosts, after all, the US had more communists on its side than did the Soviet Union.

Analysts generally agree that Nixon and Kissinger acted in the national interest when they launched normalization.[2] The central argument of this new look at the China "opening," however, is that the means to this laudable end were deeply flawed, that they fundamentally undermined US credibility and sowed the seeds of continuing distrust in US–Taiwan and US–China relations. Nixon and Kissinger wanted so intensely to realize their goal that they surrendered more than was necessary to achieve it, and the price was paid, not in the near term by the Nixon White House, but over the long term by the people of Taiwan and by US diplomacy writ large. Indeed, their promises were bigger, their compromises more thoroughgoing, and their concessions more fundamental than they believed the American people would readily accept. Thus, they relied on secrecy and "China fever" to mask the collateral damage. Subsequently, they ensured that for decades the historical record would remain inadequate and inaccurate. What biographers, commentators, and historians wrote under such circumstances continued to mislead, subject as they were to the complex interplay of misunderstanding, misperception, and falsehood.

To Nixon and Kissinger the overarching geopolitical significance of a relationship with China justified eliminating all intervening obstacles. Thus, the effort to replace an established relationship with the ROC in favor of an exciting new tie with a more exotic mainland China progressed in secret, involving a minimum of staff to provide analysis.[3] The pace was grueling, and the focus relentlessly on Beijing. Although Nixon understood that to placate domestic political constituencies he had to create an appearance of concern about Taiwan, neither he nor Kissinger worried about the survival of the government under Chiang Kai-shek or thought seriously about the will of the people on the island. Indeed, the record that can be assembled today shows that Nixon and Kissinger rarely reflected on Taiwan at all.[4]

The place of Taiwan in the calculus of the American China initiative illustrates the problem of relating to US client states, given the dynamic ways democracy may intervene in foreign policy making. If Taiwan appeared expendable to those in the White House who were defining policy, others in the government, the Congress, and the public did not agree. This disagreement set up a struggle on the right and left of US politics, and it ought to have mobilized the reputedly indomitable China lobby, with its potent American and Taiwan branches, to keep the Nixon administration from damaging Taiwan's interests. But derailing the rush to Beijing proved a mighty challenge even for a force conventionally rated second only to the pro-Israel lobby for its effectiveness in Washington.[5]

Developments in the US during the 1960s troubled Taiwan, yet they did not spur officials to attempt serious preemptive actions. Taipei did little more than complain about US fickleness, and it failed to rally supporters, to reinvigorate the movement against the People's Republic, or to restore interest in the fate of what cold warriors called Free China. Indeed, Nixon's presidency worsened the situation: at first Taipei misperceived him as a friend and then found the secrecy imposed by the White House virtually impenetrable. Both factors provided excellent excuses for inaction, relieving the mission in Washington and the government in Taipei of responsibility for preventing something they presumably could not have known about. Delay also became a central element of strategy, as Taipei hoped some event would disrupt Sino-American reconciliation. But, although the historical record shows awareness of changing trends among Taiwan policy makers, those who could have shaken Taiwan out of its lethargy—having perhaps become too accustomed to dependence—fecklessly ignored signs and remained largely inert. Taiwan could not have deterred the US from a goal that its leaders had come to see as a key security interest. On the other hand, it failed even to attempt a coherent strategy.

Finally, notwithstanding normalization mythology, history did not begin with Kissinger's secret trip to Beijing. Earlier events had created an environment that permitted bolder action and lessened the potential for political retribution. The oft-repeated claim that only Nixon could have gone to China exaggerates the courage required for his change in policy and obscures the near certainty that, building on preceding trends, others would have made the journey if Kissinger and Nixon had not.[6] In fact, the records of White House conversations reveal alarm that someone else, most likely a member of Congress, would get to Beijing first. Nixon therefore insisted that the Chinese not allow other political figures to upstage him. Even in such small ways the urgency felt in the Nixon White House ensured that Taiwan would pay the price.

Historical Precursors

Although the US–Taiwan relationship remained a formal alliance in 1969, interest in the new China had been growing among policy makers and the general public. Nixon and Kissinger would later take credit not simply for instigating a revolutionary breakthrough in American foreign policy but also for overcoming the resistance of the diplomatic corps, the Congress, and public opinion. Beneath the surface of animosity toward Beijing and encouragement of Taipei, however, a movement had gradually gathered force in the corridors of power, in the minds of key actors, and among the citizenry that pointed to the need to rationalize America's China policy.

The shift grew out of a more complex coincidence of factors than the machinations of two individuals on a crusade. For instance, even at the height of the cold war, when the PRC stood indicted as a puppet of Moscow, Washington and Beijing conducted a continuing, if erratic, diplomatic dialogue. These ambassadorial talks, convened in Geneva and Warsaw, solved few problems but brought China into direct contact with the US more often than with most other states with which it enjoyed formal relations.[7]

As indicated in chapter 1, Eisenhower supported the KMT but lamented that "so many members of Congress want to crucify anyone who argues in favor of permitting any kind of trade between the free nations and Communist China." This stifled incentives for people to rise up against communist oppressors and eliminated "a means of weakening the bonds between Soviet Russia and Communist China."[8] Neither he nor his secretary of state educated the opposition, however, deferring to right-wing Republican pressures and giving higher priority to improving relations with Moscow.[9]

Over the following decade, changes in public attitudes and small alterations in official policies demonstrated a slow but rising awareness that "Red China" would not collapse. Instead, it grew more powerful and influential in the world community, especially among newly emerging postcolonial states. In 1959, when the Senate Foreign Relations Committee had commissioned a study on options for China policy, the resulting Conlon Report, written by the political scientist Robert Scalapino, called not just for relations with Beijing, but also, to Taipei's anger and chagrin, for rerecognizing the Republic of China as the Republic of Taiwan.[10]

During the early 1960s, although John F. Kennedy allowed evidence of Chinese fanaticism to dominate his administration's view of the PRC, travel restrictions eased and the State Department reorganized to begin independent analysis of China.[11] Roger Hilsman, Kennedy's assistant secretary of state, told the Commonwealth Club of San Francisco, shortly after JFK's death, that the US ought to encourage development of a more pragmatic China while continuing to protect Taiwan, but in the context of a "two-Chinas" world. Just before his assassination Kennedy had declared that the US was "not wedded to a policy of hostility to Red China." Jim

Thomson of the NSC staff, who had participated in drafting Hilsman's text, pressed Lyndon Johnson to abandon a US strategy of encircling and preaching to China.[12]

As most important American officials stopped deluding themselves into believing that the communist government on the mainland would disappear, Taiwan's international standing and the possibility of independence became more frequent topics for discussion. US military units on Taiwan might deter the PRC, prevent private deals with Beijing, and reduce the need for expensive military assistance; but critics feared the permanent commitment to Taipei and the certainty of charges that the US was occupying Taiwan. Taiwanization—the emergence of a new generation that culturally and politically identified with the island more than the mainland—seemed another likely, although distant, way to preserve separation.[13]

By the mid-1960s polling surveys suggested considerable support for a two-Chinas approach on representation in the UN, for increased contacts with the PRC, and even for eventual rapprochement. Hearings held in 1966 by the Senate Foreign Relations Committee may have been the most important milestone, introducing the concept of "containment without isolation," which sought greater inclusion of China in the world community.[14]

Taiwan's Response to Shifting US Policy

Taipei, perpetually wary of the smallest suggestion of an American softening toward Beijing, nevertheless contented itself with a framework for Taipei-Washington interaction that did not adjust to trends in the US. The KMT leaders on Taiwan through the 1950s and early 1960s absorbed themselves in domestic political reorganization and economic restructuring, which American advisers had ardently encouraged and their own experience showed to be essential. Though less active, Chiang Kai-shek remained the deciding voice on government policies. Purges of corrupt and incompetent officials and suppression of factionalism meant not greater democracy but stronger control by the Chiangs—father and son. Taiwan nonetheless prospered: its programs of land reform, infrastructure development, and industrialization were more farsighted and better implemented than those on the mainland, all assisted by American funding—US nonmilitary aid averaged $100 million a year from 1950 to 1965.[15]

But innovation did not extend to foreign and security policy. The views of Chiang Kai-shek and his inner core of advisers remained fixed on civil war frustrations. Officials responsible for external affairs focused their attention on old battles: international recognition for Taipei and the isolation and destruction of Beijing. They increasingly feared that the US, unreliable in the past, might abandon them or compel them to adopt dangerously conciliatory policies. Chiang, however, believed that the US had no alternative to backing him.[16]

During the 1950s and into the early 1960s, the efforts of the China lobby appeared so successful that there seemed no need for a change in strategy or tactics. This amorphous and informal coalition of US officials, members of Congress, businessmen, publishers, journalists, scholars, church officials, and missionaries, as well as representatives from Taiwan, kept aid flowing, the PRC out of the UN, and diplomatic relations in place. There was friction, of course, but despite Washington's anger at an unruly client state, its support continued, a support bolstered by anticommunism, domestic partisanship, and the cold war.[17]

By the mid-1960s, however, the picture had begun to look more uncertain to Taipei. On the one hand, Taiwan's growing involvement in Vietnam, both as host to twenty thousand American supply personnel and as a base for tactical nuclear weapons, produced a new strategic tie to Washington.[18] On the other hand, US flirtation with Beijing—modifying its travel ban, for instance—eroded Chiang Kai-shek's confidence in the US. When the PRC tested a nuclear device in 1964, Chiang insisted that the US mount immediate strikes on Chinese reactors and was deeply disturbed when the embassy rebuffed his entreaties. Chiang, his son, and others at the top of the ROC government concluded that Taiwan had to defend itself and launched a covert nuclear program.[19] Moreover, as American intelligence agencies reduced their funding of surveillance and sabotage against the People's Republic, CIA agents noted a new level of hostility among their Taiwan interlocutors. Services from the two states "began to watch each other as much as they cooperated."[20]

The Johnson administration sought to allay Taipei's apprehensions with expedited delivery of aircraft, continued cooperation in gathering intelligence from signals and surveillance flights by U-2 planes, briefings on the ambassadorial talks, and invitations to visit Washington.[21] Perhaps more comforting to the Taipei government, however, was the inability of the Johnson administration to turn its minor initiatives into a new beginning for US–China relations. Officials on Taiwan could see a reassuring constancy in disputes between Washington and Beijing over many issues, including the fiction that Taipei governed all China.

Nixon and the New Direction in China Policy

Taipei would have been more anxious had its leaders realized how far the thinking of the next American president, Richard Nixon, had evolved on the need to deal with Beijing. Taiwan's leaders put their faith in the Nixon who had built his political career as an anti–Red China cold warrior. They knew, although few others did, that his 1950 Senate campaign had benefited from the help of Allied Syndicates, a public relations firm with a large ROC account dedicated to blocking Beijing's admission to the UN and protecting sizable KMT assets in the US. Nixon had advocated using Chiang's troops to fight the Korean War, and a decade later, in his campaign against Kennedy, he pledged to veto any attempt to replace Taipei with Beijing in the UN. Nixon claimed friends among the KMT elite, and in an interview years later he declared, "I didn't need to be lobbied on [the Republic of] China. It would be like carrying coals to Newcastle."[22]

Nixon's sympathies for the ROC had, however, been diminished by his expanding foreign policy experience and changes in the importance of Taipei and Beijing. As vice president, he had listened to Chiang Kai-shek talk of his expected return to the mainland, knowing that the dream would not come to pass. In the 1960s, out of office but planning his rehabilitation, Nixon traveled extensively to build his image as an international states-man. He would later write of his dismay to find that "to our Asian friends and allies it looked as if . . . political expediency, public apathy . . . and partisan politics [were] undermining America's will to fight against com-munism in Asia." Chiang insisted that only invasions of North Vietnam and China would resolve the Vietnam conflict and the Red China threat because the only way to defeat communists was with "bullets." Nixon later remarked, "Chiang was a friend and unquestionably one of the giants of the twentieth century. I wondered whether he might be right, but my pragmatic analysis told me he was wrong."[23]

In 1965, during a trip to Asia, evidence of Nixon's reorientation became known to a scattering of individuals. In Taipei Nixon told the American diplomat Arthur W. Hummel Jr. that the Nationalists would never go back to the mainland and that Washington would have to improve relations with the PRC. Nixon and Hummel both knew that the future presidential candidate's room at the Grand Hotel was bugged and that his reflections would be reported to Chiang.[24] Thus, from quite early on, unless a critical intelligence failure occurred, knowledge of Nixon's apostasy existed at the highest level of Taiwan's leadership. Nixon went on to tell Roger Sullivan, in the American embassy in Singapore, the rough outlines of his later path to normalization with Beijing. On a subsequent trip he argued to an unenthusiastic Chester Bowles, then serving as US ambassador to India, that "good relationships with China were more important than good relations with the Soviet Union."[25]

These private indicators of Nixon's changing views became public in his 1967 *Foreign Affairs* article asserting the need to end China's "angry isolation." On one level a campaign document, the piece suggested Nixon's subsequent choices, yet many supporters of the ROC missed its clear operational message. Marvin Liebman, impresario of conservative causes and head of the Committee of One Million against the Admission of Communist China to the United Nations, remarked on that fact to a longtime proponent of the ROC, congressman Walter Judd (R-Minn.) just days after Nixon's election. "Prophetically," wrote the committee's chronicler, Stanley D. Bachrack, Liebman cautioned that they "might be too confident about Nixon's dedication to existing China policy."[26]

China issues had had far less influence on Henry Kissinger before Nixon brought him to the White House as national security adviser. Kissinger had written about a possible future Sino-Soviet rift in 1961, evidently unaware that the crucial split had already occurred. As the foreign policy adviser to the presidential candidate Nelson Rockefeller in 1968, Kissinger dealt with China questions, but he exhibited little curiosity and minimal expertise. Early on, Kissinger's biographers Marvin and Bernard Kalb observed, "Kissinger was a mere passenger on the Administration's China train. The President was clearly its sole engineer."[27]

Kissinger apparently became interested in China only when he realized how seriously the president took efforts to improve relations with China and how much strategic leverage against the Soviet Union a US relationship with China could offer. He believed that the US could play the USSR and the PRC each against the other and enjoy better relations with each than either had with the other. Having given Beijing a starring role in a strategic contest of such immense import, Kissinger dismissed Taiwan as inconsequential, little more than a domestic political pawn. Throughout his negotiations with the Chinese, Kissinger would consistently minimize the significance of Taiwan as an issue for Beijing and as an impediment to progress.

To implement the early phases of his China policy, Nixon used the State Department, but he told its China specialists nothing about his broader intentions, allegedly believing they were wedded to a pro-Taipei perspective that would interfere with rapprochement. In fact, opinion throughout the government was mixed, but the first initiatives taken by the White House were based on State Department proposals, including the idea of exchanging high-level emissaries. Nixon and Kissinger, nevertheless, preferred to divert State Department and CIA analysts with task forces and studies. One CIA veteran, James Lilley, recalled that "as we bickered over the finer points [of policy, we] . . . were taken by surprise when news of Kissinger's July trip to Peking was made public even though we represented some of the most informed and experienced China hands in the U.S. government."[28]

Some secrecy surrounding the opening to Beijing was necessary to avert attack by proponents of the Republic of China. Nixon, who had reveled in pillorying the Democrats for their softness on communism, understood better than most how easily efforts to alter China policy could disintegrate into a vicious political brawl.[29] Although he knew that the China lobby had declined in importance, he believed Taipei could muster a powerful coalition to stop a new venture if it became public prematurely. In fact, by the time of Nixon's election, the Committee of One Million was in disarray, its chief money raiser having moved to London. In April 1970 the *New York Times* proclaimed the China lobby's virtual demise. Soon after, the ROC embassy had difficulty arranging a welcome breakfast for the heir apparent, Chiang Ching-kuo.[30]

Nixon, however, insisted that Kissinger keep in contact with China lobby leaders and meet with the ROC ambassador to assure them that only modest steps were being taken to better relations with China. He even appeared to seek approval for reaching out to China, as when he instructed Kissinger to consult Senator Karl Mundt (R-S.D.), a Chiang Kai-shek stalwart, "and see whether he would be willing to have another move in that direction."[31] Nixon worried about being condemned for betrayal of old friends. He would not do "what the Kennedy administration did to [Ngo Dinh] Diem either physically or philosophically. . . . [It] has Diem's blood on its hands."[32] But once he had a scheduled visit to Beijing, the president expected to stun the liberals who normally belittled him and carry all but the diehards in his own party when he stood for reelection.

As it turned out, secrecy did not just deprive policy makers of advice and information as the China opening proceeded. Concealment also hampered smooth relations with Taiwan. Nixon and Kissinger were acutely aware of the need to distract, if not satisfy, domestic supporters of the ROC as well as Taipei without making commitments that would hamper agreement with Beijing. As time passed, American officials withheld growing amounts and wider varieties of information to deprive Taipei of a clear sense that a US opening to China was gaining momentum and to prevent confrontation or sabotage.[33] "Even the fact that we had sat down to talk with the Chinese Communists [at Warsaw] was bad news from Chiang Kai-shek's viewpoint," recalled Ralph Clough, a foreign service officer deeply involved in the process. "We kept Chiang Kai-shek generally informed, but, of course, he wasn't confident that we were telling him everything."[34] Indeed, the Nixon administration failed to brief Taiwan's representatives before the Warsaw sessions, as had been routine, and provided unsatisfactory summaries afterward. Walter McConaughy, the US ambassador to the ROC, repeatedly importuned his superiors to clarify their intentions to Chiang; otherwise, Beijing might be able to offer its version to create a rift between Washington and Taipei.[35] The US consul general in Hong Kong, David Dean, could see that the PRC had already begun to use the talks "to worry Taipei and particularly cast doubt in . . . [Taiwan officials'] minds about the steadfastness and reliability of its U.S. ally."[36]

An early indicator of the difficulties ahead arose when Chiang Ching-kuo visited Washington. Nixon and Kissinger worried about Beijing's reaction, but the younger Chiang's future leadership role as successor to his aging father called for broad exposure to US officials and institutions. Furthermore, trust between Taipei and Washington was being eroded not just by inklings of changing China policy, but also by declining US support for South Vietnam. Nguyen Van Thieu, an old friend of Chiang Kai-shek's, had stopped in Taipei en route home from his unsettling summit with Nixon in June 1969. Alerted that the Americans would be withdrawing troops from Vietnam, CKS unhappily asked Thieu, "Why did you let them do it?"[37] He sent his son to Washington primed for a discussion of seven key issues in US–Taiwan relations. His chief adviser on American affairs, Frederick Ch'ien Fu, laid them out: (1) US compromise with China on ROC interests; (2) US preservation of the ROC's Security Council and General Assembly seats at the UN; (3) US protection of the offshore islands; (4) US defense of Taiwan against nuclear attack; (5) US termination of support for independence activists; (6) US acquiescence in an assault on the mainland in the event of civil war there or Sino-Soviet conflict; and (7) US maintenance of a military balance across the Strait. The Foreign Ministry urged Washington to sign an upbeat communiqué incorporating at least some of those points to demonstrate US commitment to Taiwan.[38]

When, after several postponements, CCK arrived in spring 1970, the administration greeted him with a ceremonial welcome ordinarily reserved for heads of state. The young Chiang stayed at Blair House, enjoyed a black-tie dinner, and met with top officials—with Nixon for a surprisingly generous seventy-five minutes. The president sought to be comforting about plans for improving relations with China, pledging, "I will never sell you down the river." Kissinger, also attempting encouragement, emphasized that the US believed in standing by its friends and would never yield to any communists on any issue.[39]

His discussions in Washington neither mollified nor persuaded Chiang. Indeed, the trip convinced him that relations with the US would soon change decisively; Washington would continue to protect the island, but Nixon would normalize with Beijing, undermining the one-China policy that had sustained Taipei since Japan's surrender, thus fatally challenging Taipei's status as the legitimate capital of China and thereby drastically weakening the KMT's hold on power.[40]

Taiwan did enjoy the continued backing of high-level but essentially powerless members of the administration, a group aptly symbolized by Vice President Spiro Agnew. Nixon repeatedly dispatched his vice president to Taiwan, but he never informed Agnew about plans for a China opening and kept him on a tight leash in Taipei. Agnew was directed to say that cuts in military assistance had been unfortunate but unalterable and that the US did not support a return to the mainland. He could neither endorse the ROC as the only legitimate government of China nor accept that it had "the exclusive right to the *only* seat for China" in the UN. He should support the US–ROC Mutual Defense Treaty of 1954 but emphasize that Taiwan must not impede relations with Beijing.[41]

Preparing carefully for talks with the vice president, Chiang's advisers could not know that Nixon saw Agnew's visits as a sop. Their agenda ran the gamut from military cooperation and creation of an Asia-Pacific security system to defense of Taiwan's UN seats. If officials in Taipei had reservations about the Agnew channel, they kept them private.[42] And Agnew spoke up for them, telling the press that reduced support for Taipei was "bothering the hell out of me." Of course, Agnew's views had no influence on the president, who was enraged when reporters wrote of Agnew's opposition to normalization. Dismissing the vice president as incompetent, Nixon called him his "insurance policy against assassination." Agnew's sympathies and expendability, then, made him a good emissary for soothing Taipei's anxieties.[43]

Meanwhile, evidence of changing US priorities mounted. On April 6, 1970, the public phase of rapprochement began with the invitation a Chinese Ping-Pong team extended to its American counterpart to play in China. The US government accepted, and on April 14 news of Americans being greeted in China by Zhou Enlai reached Taipei and media outlets around the world. Less dramatic but also important was a statement by the State Department spokesman C. W. Bray early in the month that China and Taiwan ought to negotiate the status of Taiwan directly, since it remained undetermined. Bray's remarks roiled the waters in both Taipei and

Beijing. The PRC protest was shrill and received wide attention, but the ROC, whose survival depended on nuances and definitions, was far more dismayed.[44] Foreign Minister Chow Shu-kai reminded McConaughy that the Cairo and Potsdam declarations had affirmed that Japan should return Taiwan to the Republic of China and that both the peace treaty with Japan and the 1954 Mutual Defense Treaty had explicitly recognized Taiwan as a part of ROC territory. Nixon at the American Society of Newspaper Editors on April 16, 1971, "confided" to his audience that he had advised his daughters to travel to China as soon as they could and that he himself hoped to do so, a statement that shocked Chiang Kai-shek. To the president's special envoy, Ambassador Robert Murphy, he asserted "the various overtures Washington has made to placate Peiping [Beijing] have reached a maximal limit, beyond which any further steps would bring disasters."[45]

Taipei leaders understood more clearly than their American counterparts that Beijing wanted rapprochement not just to protect against the Soviet threat, to secure admission to the UN, or to trade with the US, but to recover Taiwan. In the 1950s the PRC had adopted the position that no breakthrough on any issue could be considered until agreement had been reached on the Taiwan problem. The US had insisted that progress required a Chinese renunciation of the use of force. If Sino-American relations now appeared on the brink of change, that could mean only that either the Americans were blind to Beijing's manipulation or Washington stood ready to capitulate.

Rapprochement and Taiwan's Future

The White House did in fact decide that Washington could accommodate Beijing's long-sought preconditions in order to facilitate talks, as Ambassador Walter J. Stoessel was instructed when he prepared to meet with Lei Yang, the Chinese ambassador to Poland on January 20, 1970. During the Warsaw encounter, where Lei emphasized Taiwan to the exclusion of almost everything else, Stoessel asserted that the American military presence on the island constituted no threat to China. But, acknowledging that Beijing wanted more than vague reassurances, he explicitly pledged, "We will also not support and in fact will oppose any offensive military action from Taiwan against the mainland . . . and it is our hope that as peace and stability in Asia grow, we can reduce these facilities on Taiwan that we now have." He also made clear that Washington was prepared to accept a negotiated resolution between Beijing and Taipei.[46]

What made 1971 the first truly viable occasion for rapprochement was the strategic impetus provided by Soviet aggression. Under the Brezhnev Doctrine of 1968, Moscow claimed the right to violate sovereignty to "protect socialism," thereby placing China's security at risk. Nixon and Kissinger shared Chinese eagerness to stop Moscow's expansion. But as eager as Mao and Zhou might have been for a US counterweight to Moscow's threats, they were not willing to make any fundamental sacrifices that would impede the recovery of Taiwan. Nixon later recalled that among the first messages transmitted through Bucharest as the US and China reached out to each other was the Chinese assertion that "there is only one outstanding issue between us—the U.S. occupation of Taiwan."[47]

In July 1971, when Kissinger finally stepped off the aircraft onto Chinese soil, protection of Taiwan's interests did not rank near the top of a US agenda that focused on anti-Soviet maneuvering and efforts to end the Vietnam War. Kissinger and his entourage were astonished simply to be in Beijing, and the significance of their arrival overwhelmed them, as it would the American people when the trip became public. In his memoir *The White House Years*, Kissinger maintained that during his foray to Beijing, he barely discussed Taiwan and never jeopardized its interests. But declassified transcripts of the first meeting between Kissinger and Zhou Enlai demonstrate that this contention is simply not true. Zhou immediately challenged Kissinger to address China's core interests: acknowledgment that Taiwan was part of China and withdrawal of military forces and facilities from the island in a limited time. Zhou harked back to the history of US–China interaction over Taiwan, reminding Kissinger that in 1949 "the U.S. stated . . . that it had no territorial ambitions regarding Taiwan" and would not "interfere in China's internal affairs." After "the Korean war broke out . . . you surrounded Taiwan and declared the status of Taiwan was still unsettled. Even up to the present day . . . this is your position. That is the crux."[48]

On that very first day, in his opening statement to Zhou, Kissinger gave Beijing more than it could have expected. Cautioning the Chinese to be discreet because Nixon had authorized him to make offers before vetting them inside his government or with Congress, Kissinger withheld only formal recognition. He agreed to remove US troops from Taiwan: two-thirds with the end of the Vietnam War and the other third progressively as relations improved. He did not demand that Beijing renounce force, and he asserted that the military issue would not be "a principal obstacle between us." He ruled out pursuing a policy of two Chinas or of one China, one Taiwan. He pledged that no one in the US government would give any support to the Taiwan independence movement and promised to enforce the policy himself. The US would also refrain from running covert CIA or other intelligence operations out of Taiwan.[49]

On the second day, Zhou reiterated, in tough terms, his insistence on his Taiwan agenda to make certain the Americans understood his priorities. Zhou observed "the Taiwan question is a very small matter to you. As you said, it was created by President Truman, and what use is Taiwan to you at the present moment?" But Zhou wanted to impress on the Americans that for Beijing "Taiwan is not an isolated issue." Without settlement on Taiwan, he insisted, there would be no reconciliation. Washington had yielded ground on Taiwan and must go further, abandoning the position that its status remained in any way undetermined. To Zhou's delight Kissinger gave up more. Kissinger added that the US would not give Chiang Kai-shek assistance for an assault against the mainland, which rendered such a venture impossible. The US would also favor China's entry into the UN even as it tried to keep a seat for Taiwan. To Zhou's objections, Kissinger responded that this was a necessary, but hardly permanent, expedient. Finally, Kissinger reassured Zhou that "we will strongly oppose any Japanese military presence on Taiwan."[50]

Given the difficult and lengthy exchange on Taiwan, Kissinger's subsequent comment that he found the Chinese "relaxed" on the Taiwan question seems disingenuous. Yet Kissinger may have spoken with conviction because, himself dismissive of Taiwan, he never grasped its importance to Beijing. Domestic American politics and the anticommunist struggle had given the KMT influence on the US government, but the island never appeared to possess great intrinsic value. In 1950 the US military had been willing to see it fall to the Chinese communists rather than expend men and materiel to save it. Although Douglas MacArthur had called it an unsinkable aircraft carrier, Washington had no desire for a base of military operations against the mainland. Kissinger, whose interest in Asia was purely strategic, could comfortably imagine, even more readily than Nixon, bartering away Taiwan's interests to reconfigure the cold war.[51]

Nixon had ideological baggage, personal experience, and political instincts that made his position on China and Taiwan more complex. As a young congressman he had worried about Chiang Kai-shek because the Generalissimo fought in the front lines against communism. He knew Chiang personally, had visited Taiwan, had worked alongside the stalwarts of the China lobby in Congress, and had benefited from right-wing, pro-Taiwan money. But for Nixon as president, the demands of the cold war and electioneering had become more intense. Whereas standing behind Taiwan might ensure backing from his customary supporters, it would not win the adulation his ego and his campaign required. Nixon instructed Kissinger, "Having in mind the fact that . . . [the Chinese] have to be tough on Taiwan, . . . we've got to be tough on Taiwan in order to end up where we're going to have to end up." Still, a slightly chagrined Nixon urged, "I wouldn't be so forthcoming . . . until necessary."[52] The ROC could not be ignored but must not stand in the way of his expected foreign policy triumph.

Second, Kissinger's view that the Taiwan situation did not constitute an urgent priority for the People's Republic may best be understood in the context of the first remarks that he delivered in Beijing. Kissinger consistently believed that his advisers and academic China experts exaggerated the emphasis China placed on the future of Taiwan. He considered it inconsequential to his Chinese interlocutors compared to the opportunity to gain US support against the Soviets. Beijing, purposefully or not, proved to be misleading on this point. China quite naturally emphasized a common anti-Soviet agenda. Washington, moreover, had conceded so much on Taiwan, had met China's preconditions so fully, that the PRC leadership believed it could wait before trying to extract more. Thus, Beijing yielded ground on timing, accepting the idea that US troop withdrawals would come not instantly but in stages linked to increased peace and stability in the region. Similarly, although the Mutual Defense Treaty remained illegitimate in the eyes of Mao and the Politburo, and they made an agreement to withdraw US troops a prerequisite to Nixon's visit, they also accepted a termination of the treaty undertaken over the twelve-month period prescribed in the treaty.[53] These Chinese compromises, however, did not equal those by Nixon and Kissinger, which left China's leaders much to savor after Kissinger's July visit.

Warnings from Chinese leaders that American Taiwan policy could jeopardize cooperation never stopped, but perhaps because they were muted, they failed adequately to trouble the hopeful American practitioners of rapprochement. Kissinger, even after his trip to Beijing, told a former foreign service officer, John S. Service, that the Chinese were not serious about Taiwan; they were just using it as a bargaining chip.[54] Nixon assured French President Georges Pompidou at a December 1971 meeting in the Azores that the Chinese "do not view the talks as producing immediate results in Taiwan . . . [but] regard these talks as the beginning of a long process."[55] In fact, Beijing reasonably expected that Kissinger's visit would rapidly lead to diplomatic relations. After that the Chinese and many others, including many on the island, thought Taiwan—isolated and vulnerable—would quickly collapse.

Did Kissinger believe that Taiwan would survive rapprochement as either a separate state with which the US enjoyed diplomatic relations or as a political entity clinging to some form of autonomy? Although the PRC would lack the military capabilities to attack and occupy the island at least for some time to come, Zhou asserted to Kissinger without hesitation that "the US must recognize that the PRC is the sole legitimate government in China and that Taiwan Province is an inalienable part of Chinese territory which must be restored to the motherland." Kissinger replied, "As a student of history, one's prediction would have to be that the political evolution is likely to be in the direction which Prime Minister Chou En-lai indicated to me." Kissinger continued by assuring Zhou, "We will not stand in the way of basic evolution."[56]

Chinese leaders, then, came away from their July 1971 meetings with Henry Kissinger encouraged to assume that their most cherished goal had been accomplished. The Americans would not stand in the way; Taiwan would be theirs. The fact that this did not happen—that Beijing subsequently felt misled—engendered a sense of betrayal that simmered below the surface of rapprochement. It did not have a significant effect so long as no radical departures in Taiwan's politics, cross-Strait interaction, and US–Taiwan relations occurred. Once the balance began to shift in all those areas, however, the course set by Richard Nixon and Henry Kissinger came back to haunt the corridors of power and decision making.

Taiwan and the Diplomacy of the
Opening to China

Taipei learned of the Kissinger mission just thirty minutes before Nixon announced to the world that he had initiated the opening to China and would himself be traveling to Beijing in 1972. By contrast, Anatoly Dobrynin, the Soviet ambassador, heard directly from Kissinger almost twelve hours before Nixon's television broadcast. CCK immediately assembled his advisers and, although he had met privately with Kissinger in Washington just a year earlier, grilled Frederick Ch'ien on the man's character and strategic thinking.[57] Chiang, suddenly confronted with the long-expected and much-dreaded event, had to decide on his government's immediate and long-term reactions.

For Taiwan's leaders the disadvantages of dependence had never been more conspicuous and the grounds for despair never clearer. Even as the White House reached out to the Soviets with what Dobrynin called goodwill gestures, Secretary Rogers offered James Shen, the ROC ambassador, neither adequate information nor constructive compensation for previous and prospective slights.[58] Even Walter McConaughy, the US ambassador in Taiwan, did not learn of the Kissinger mission until an hour before its public announcement; the timing undercut if not contradicted Nixon's statement to him that, regardless of the attempt to better relations with China, the US was "trying to continue our close primary relations with" the ROC.[59] Nixon, however, had concluded that the opening to China was inevitable "and it better take place when they've got a friend here rather than when they've got an enemy here." Kissinger responded, "It is a tragedy that it has to happen to Chiang at the end of his life. But we have to be cold about it." And Taiwan's friend in the White House responded, "Yeah, we have to do what's best for us."[60]

The US government at first did little to reassure Taipei. American officials assumed that Taipei would be shaken by the event and the president's announcement. They were not surprised when the National Assembly denounced Nixon for betraying Taiwan and both the government-controlled and the independent press castigated the US for its treachery.[61] To Ambassador Shen, Nixon and Kissinger emphasized that Taipei must "do nothing to rock the boat"; Shen took the statement as a warning not to "spoil the American plans."[62] Over time Washington grew more concerned about Taiwan's reaction. In August, Richard Helms, director of the CIA, sent Kissinger the transcript of a conversation between two ROC air force officers in which they discussed using a flight by a U-2 plane to provoke the PRC into canceling the Nixon trip. Helms admitted that such an incident seemed unlikely, particularly since it would mean Taiwan's loss of a critical intelligence link to the US, but he was worried enough to caution Kissinger.[63] Zhou Enlai similarly warned that Chiang could not control rogue elements who would "deliberately . . . create trouble for him, and for you. That's why we maintain defenses along our coast."[64]

Although no militant demonstrations erupted, Nixon decided to solicit a staunch supporter of Taiwan to try to mollify the ROC government. California's Governor Ronald Reagan agreed, with some misgivings, to go to Taiwan for the ROC's National Day observances on October 10 as part of a wider trip to Asia.[65] Nixon was sending not a close confidant but a man whom, like Agnew, he found "'strange,'" someone who "'isn't pleasant to be around.'" According to the American diplomat Roger Sullivan, "Taiwan didn't want to be briefed, didn't ask to be briefed. So it was a symbolic kind of gesture so they wouldn't feel they were being abandoned. Maybe a gesture to protect Richard Nixon from his own people in the US."[66] Reagan's status secured a meeting with Chiang Kai-shek, but Chiang reportedly sat "like a stone, looking straight ahead silently" as the emissary tried to explain why Nixon had chosen to send Kissinger to Beijing.[67] Of course, for Taiwan the crisis had not passed: as Reagan spoke, a struggle at the UN for the China seat raged. Indeed, the governor would barely be out of Taipei when a new disaster struck.

The United Nations

In October 1971 two events significantly undermined Taiwan's international status and prospects for survival. Washington and Beijing were aware of the approaching vote on the United Nations China seat when they agreed on a date for Kissinger's second visit to China. The documents reveal that Beijing proposed October and that Kissinger refused to change the timing when the coincidence surfaced. He later explained that his Chinese plans needed to be fixed before the ROC's expulsion from the UN or announcement of a Soviet-American summit could derail them.[68] Indeed, Nixon feared that domestic backlash from Taiwan's ouster would undermine the China initiative. The two men therefore preferred to lie to the secretary of state and pretend that they had asked the Chinese to reschedule, rather than actually to do so.[69] Ultimately, Nixon would instruct Kissinger to delay his return to avoid a triumphal homecoming on the day of the vote, but that gesture in no way lessened the US contribution to the Taiwan debacle.

As early as March 1970, Rogers had written to Nixon urging that efforts to improve relations with Beijing not interfere with the UN membership question. But the president required no reminder of the Chinese representation issue that had plagued Eisenhower and each president thereafter. Mounting pressures for PRC admission, interrupted by years of Cultural Revolution violence, had resumed and required a new US policy. By autumn 1970 the US itself no longer advocated unconditional exclusion of Beijing, having shifted to a posture of keeping Taiwan in rather than the mainland out. American diplomats feared that UN members viewed Taiwan as a "sinking ship," assuming its removal to be unavoidable. The president reminded Kissinger that he wanted "a position in which we can keep our commitments to Taiwan" but not be embarrassed by them.[70]

American policy makers faced a complicated and ultimately unmanageable combination of obligations. Seeking a reasonable and pragmatic solution, US diplomats leaned toward a dual-representation formula that would place both the PRC and ROC in the UN. But any dual-representation initiative (and National Security Study Memorandum 107 examined six variations) faced enormous obstacles, most formidably the reality that neither China considered any version acceptable. Moreover, the UN membership would probably see US sponsorship of such an arrangement as a cynical manipulation of the system: Americans had previously promoted it partly because Chiang Kai-shek could be compelled to accept it, whereas Beijing's rejection would shift the burden for exclusion onto the communist Chinese.[71]

In 1971 Nixon and Kissinger, convinced that Beijing would never tolerate dual representation and would be angered by Washington's advocacy, concluded that they should withhold White House support.[72] Nixon personally may also have found the policy unpersuasive. He remarked to Ambassador McConaughy that keeping the ROC in the Security Council is "why the whole two China thing is so really rather ridiculous."[73] But officials at the State Department and the National Security Council believed that if the US worked vigorously, a majority for dual representation could be mustered, along with a provision awarding the Security Council seat to Beijing while leaving a place for Taipei in the General Assembly. That would be better than being held responsible for Taipei's ouster.[74]

Taiwan, appalled that Washington might acquiesce in, or even cosponsor, a dual-representation resolution, declared that it could not stay in the UN if Beijing occupied the Security Council seat. Chiang Kai-shek instructed his foreign minister to emphasize that the ROC presence in the General Assembly and Security Council remained "inseparable and indivisible." Having been a founding member of the organization, the ROC could not relinquish the Security Council seat without undermining its legal rationale for existence.[75] Chow Shu-kai had long implied that "whether a bandwagon mood in favor of PRC admission develops depends in large measure upon the US attitude." Assistant Secretary Green attempted to convince ROC officials that their hold on the UN would be weakened by their refusal to explore options. If Taipei quit the UN, not only would it be isolated, but its intransigence might psychologically release the US from promises to protect Taiwan.[76]

Much of the diplomacy on the issue had to be conducted by Taiwan's ambassador in Washington, James Shen, who did not strike Americans as a first-rate diplomat or "a source of new initiatives."[77] Unforgivably, he had publicly criticized the administration; predictably, his démarches and entreaties made little headway. In July he sought to prick Rogers's conscience, reminding him of Nixon's pledge not to allow the PRC to take China's UN Security Council seat: "This will be looked on as a test case of your repeated assurance that you will not do anything at [the] expense of an old friend."[78] By August 1971, as the UN clock ticked, Shen could reach Kissinger only by inviting him to dinner "to see if [an ROC] . . . cook couldn't equal or excel the level of the Chinese cooks in Peking."[79]

Washington understood that the final decisions on Taiwan's stance belonged to Chiang Kai-shek and that he would not be easy to persuade. Chiang, Deputy Assistant Secretary for East Asia Arthur Hummel later remarked, "was a very old fashioned, authoritarian figure. Not very well educated. Not understanding . . . how we work, what Congress does, what can be done, and what can't be done. He was very narrow minded" and, diplomats feared, would doom their efforts through stubbornness and illusion.[80] Chiang dismissed compromise with the "bandits" in Beijing because "there is no room for patriots and traitors to live together [*hanzi buliangli*]"; he expected the US to live up to promises to use its veto in the UN. Not only John F. Kennedy and Lyndon B. Johnson but also Nixon in his 1960 campaign had made such promises.[81] To a Nixon emissary he remarked caustically, "Should the ROC one day leave the UN, the world would know that she has been forced out not by the Communists, but by the US."[82]

To others in Taipei, the thought of Beijing enjoying UN privileges while Taiwan watched from the outside seemed worse. In the legislature and the press, they argued that Taiwan should "fight the bandits from within."[83] Taiwan representatives at the UN and in Washington repeatedly confided to American officials that they agreed with the US position, but were dismissed at home as "unduly pessimistic." After Kissinger's astonishing secret trip to China became public, however, frightened Taipei officials capitulated, abandoning months of resistance. Accordingly, in August 1971 Rogers asked Taiwan to speak out in favor of dual representation, throwing the Foreign Ministry into disarray. Taiwan did instruct all ROC ambassadors to ask their host governments to vote for the resolution even though Taipei would not, but Frederick Ch'ien, CCK's adviser, conceded that some ambassadors refused to follow ministry guidance. Even Ambassador Shen, having watched the process from his perch in Washington, recalled in his bitter memoir that "when asked by governments friendly to us how we would wish them to vote, we did not know what to say. . . . As a result, many of our friends were in a quandary. In the end this proved to be our undoing because they did not know what we really wanted them to do."[84]

Having acquiesced to the possibility of a dual-representation vote, Taipei still had to decide on its reaction to the result. The foreign minister told McConaughy in the greatest secrecy that there had been quite a fight among the highest officials during a full-day meeting in the capital on September 9. Hard-liners passionately advocated a principled, if doomed, response regardless of the consequences. Internationalists, however, appeared to triumph, convincing Chiang Kai-shek to make the "painful" decision not to threaten to walk out. Washington could not expect Chiang to go further than that. As Rogers averred to the president, "Taipei has come a very long way toward developing a more pragmatic foreign policy— much farther than many would have predicted."[85]

As it turned out, arduous lobbying and clever maneuvering failed to preserve an ROC seat in the United Nations. Coexisting China delegations in the UN may have been unattainable from the start. Kissinger dismissed the effort as an "essentially doomed rearguard action" mounted because it was "the only piece of the action on China under State Department control."[86] The administration, in any case, declared it would neither threaten to use its Security Council veto nor withhold financial support to keep the PRC out.[87]

But Kissinger's October trip to Beijing swept aside any hope for dual representation, signaling that Washington considered normalization its highest priority. Rogers ineffectually opposed the visit, perhaps partly out of pique at being left behind again, but also because of the delicate UN situation. Although he reassured Taipei that the trip would not influence the vote, Rogers argued in Washington that changing the date of the mission made more sense than carrying out an advance trip four months before the president would actually go to China. "It almost looks as if we were suckers," he warned, "to do it right at the time that we've got the most important issue between us coming to a vote." Kissinger in retrospect insisted that "the problem was not any one trip but the basic trend." Anticipating a loss, Kissinger simply preferred not to go as a "defeated man," and he shared the president's concern that "there may be some pressure," exerted by the Congress and the public, "to reconsider if we should go to China" at all.[88]

George H. W. Bush and the other exhausted members of the US delegation at the UN struggled vigorously, if forlornly, through the grueling days and weeks before the vote. Asserting the principles of universality, reality, and practicality, Bush made the case that Taipei, exerting effective control over a population of some 14 million, should not be cavalierly ejected from an international forum dedicated to peace, particularly since membership would have no bearing on the final resolution of the Taiwan-China dispute. Harry Thayer, the mission deputy, felt "there was no question that Bush was convinced that this was the right thing to do. He was indefatigable in lobbying for this policy. . . . He had a marvelous touch in dealing with the human beings behind the title, invited them out to his home town . . . to seats at a baseball game. . . . So when he said we, the US, will do this . . . people believed him."[89] Bush, perhaps naively, expected to be able to win in the UN. "I know for a fact that the president wants to see the policy implemented," he told the *Washington Post*.[90] But Bush, a relative novice in foreign affairs, did not enjoy the full confidence of his superiors. Rogers dismissed him as a "lightweight" and Kissinger told Nixon that Bush was "too soft and not sophisticated enough" to represent the US in the Beijing negotiations with Zhou Enlai—a judgment with which Nixon agreed.[91] Bush waged a ferocious campaign on what he believed to be Nixon's orders, not knowing that just days before the final vote Kissinger doctored a Rogers speech, dropping references to UN universality and to the fact that the population of Taiwan exceeded the populations of two-thirds of member states.[92]

As a man with aspirations to higher office, Bush barely complained about being undermined by the White House and abandoned by allies. Years later, he recalled the "bitterness" and "disgust" he felt at the countries that reneged on pledges to vote alongside the US and the delegates who, dancing in the aisles, celebrated Taiwan's expulsion and their success in weakening Washington's influence within the international organization. For many, he believed, "Taiwan wasn't really the issue. Kicking Uncle Sam was." Taiwan's representatives, angry and humiliated, walked out before the final ballot had been cast. Bush strode from his seat to catch Taiwan's UN ambassador and momentarily "put an arm on his shoulder." But Bush felt it was not just foreign governments that had let down Taipei and the US mission to the UN. Although he agreed with the Nixon administration's China initiative, he nevertheless saw Kissinger as the instrument of Taiwan's shameful ouster. "What was hard . . . to understand was Henry's telling me he was 'disappointed' by the final outcome of the Taiwan vote. . . . Given the fact that we were saying one thing in New York and doing another in Washington, that outcome was inevitable."[93]

Nixon seemingly had more difficulty accepting the idea of a UN defeat than did Kissinger. Until the end, he believed there might be a chance to keep Taiwan's seat and hoped to rally countries that owed the US support, such as Israel, Venezuela, Turkey, and Greece. The president, who sought to use normalization with China in a vast geopolitical maneuver against the Soviet Union, wanted to maintain leverage against Beijing as well by keeping Taipei in the General Assembly. But he also worked hard at rationalizing his willingness to allow Taiwan to be superseded at the UN, which he dismissed as a "damn debating society." "What good does it do?" he asked McConaughy rhetorically in June. "Very little. . . . No, my feelings about the UN, I must say, that . . . none of our vital interests have ever been submitted to the UN and will never be while I'm here. . . . I think [Taiwan] . . . ought not to give much [of] a damn what happens at the UN. I don't think it hurts them one bit."[94] Besides, whatever the potential cost for Taiwan, Nixon told Kissinger, "there's nothing in it for us to start slobbering over the [ROC] Chinese and have . . . [the UN] slap us in the face."[95]

Kissinger made a brief attempt in Beijing to persuade Zhou not to push ahead with the UN campaign. He pointed out that some 62 percent of Americans opposed Taiwan's ouster and suggested that a clash on this issue could disrupt rapprochement. But when Zhou did not respond, Kissinger let the matter drop, assuring the Chinese that the administration had no intention of backing away from promises made in July, whether UN entry was pressed and whether Beijing declared that it would settle the Taiwan question by peaceful means. Kissinger did finally take a tough stand against abandoning Taiwan, telling Zhou that such behavior by Washington would hardly be a good basis for a new bond with China.[96] Zhou remembered Kissinger's paean to loyalty some months later when, in discussing Vietnam and Taiwan, he observed cynically, "That is still your old saying—you don't want to cast aside old friends. But you have already cast aside many old friends."[97]

In the end, Nixon and Kissinger benefited from the misguided actions of Taiwan's leaders. During the months of maneuvering over the UN, Chiang Kai-shek and his associates forced Washington to wheedle, to plead, and to threaten in order to mount something resembling a unified position. But so long as Taipei insisted that Taiwan was part of China, it doomed any argument that the 14 million residents—who determined their own affairs on territory they ruled—ought to be entitled to representation under the UN's universality principle. When Taipei claimed to be the capital of all of China, it undermined confidence in the government's grasp of reality. Finally, so long as Taipei demanded that countries choose between Taiwan and China, it blocked efforts to keep both parties in the UN.[98] At no point, in October 1971 or the weeks and months before, did CKS permit a vigorous initiative to capture the imaginations of Taiwan's flagging supporters. Admittedly, even a creative proposal would probably not have withstood the Nixon-Kissinger July shock, but Taiwan's passivity in the face of almost-certain defeat suggested poor choices and ineffective leadership.

RICHARD NIXON and Henry Kissinger had been successful in redirecting US foreign policy. They had unquestionably been right to press ahead to normalize relations with the People's Republic, a policy too long in coming and clearly in the national interest. A case can even be made that some secrecy helped facilitate the effort, although they carried it to an extreme that threatened the enterprise, and, to undermine competition, they imposed an urgency that engendered needless complications.

Less defensibly, they willingly betrayed an ally, conceding Taiwan's interests before negotiations began. Nixon and Kissinger forfeited not simply the right of Taiwan's people to self-determination, but potentially their ability to avoid communist rule. Having realized their policy, they then capped it by facilitating the loss of Taiwan's international representation. Although William Rogers argued against this unnecessary act, Nixon and Kissinger ignored him, and Taipei condemned him as either disingenuous or uninformed. Few in Washington, however, were deeply troubled by what had happened. Taiwan's strategic location and the autocratic nature of its rulers excused a lot, even if the balance between ideals and realism crucial to Americans' definition of themselves had tilted very far in one direction.

CHAPTER THREE

Survival

IN THE wake of the July Nixon-Kissinger shock and the October UN debacle, the US–Taiwan relationship fell into disarray. Over the next seven years Taiwan and the US remained tied to the formalities of a decaying alliance while Washington negotiated terms for full normalization and neutralized domestic political opposition. To avoid raising false hopes about a change in direction, US officials afforded little more than grudging compliance with commitments. Trade with and arms sales to Taiwan continued, but for American officials the key priority was to protect rapprochement.

In Taipei illusion and disillusion paralyzed policy makers. Before Nixon's February 1972 trip, Taipei's ambassador to Washington had tried, and failed, to secure a congressional resolution affirming treaty obligations. After the trip, torn between the desire for retribution and the need for help, officials hoped for a miracle and seemed unsure of what else to do. Although the China-Taiwan lobby continued to be talked about in reverential terms, it could not stall the steady progress toward US–China diplomatic relations.

Thus, during the 1970s, although the US relationship with Taiwan looked almost unchanged, the rules of engagement—for solving problems, for seeking help, for registering complaints, and for providing security—were all unclear. This caused a myriad of problems. Within the US government normalization suddenly took precedence, but residual loyalties to Taiwan, hostility toward the PRC, and simple inertia intruded on policy formulation and execution. Tension was often greatest between agencies in Washington, which saw benefits of the opening to China most clearly, and officers in the field, who sympathized more with Taiwan's plight.

After July 1971 Taiwan's options narrowed. Responsiveness by the Nixon administration to inquiries and requests deteriorated. Cuts in financial assistance for military programs paralleled withdrawal of troops and equipment. Fewer American officials traveled to Taiwan, and access to the government in Washington declined, circumstances that expanded opportunities for misunderstanding and mistrust. When Gerald Ford took the helm, conditions improved modestly, but Taipei found no way to translate the new administration's political constraints into gains.

Regrouping

In late 1971, as the boisterous celebration of UN delegates faded, questions arose at home and abroad regarding future relations with the international organization. At the most extreme, Senator Barry Goldwater (R-Ariz.) demanded the US cut funding, renounce membership, and oust UN headquarters from New York.[1] The US backlash, however, proved to be temporary and limited.

Conservatives and China lobby stalwarts in the US who might have responded to a vigorous rallying cry remained disorganized. Even though the pundit William F. Buckley Jr. broke with the president, questioning Nixon's conservative credentials, many were loath to attack Nixon and swallowed their discontent. Ronald Reagan, for instance, had supported the China opening only to see Taiwan expelled from the UN, and he chafed at the stain on his credibility. Kissinger sought to reassure him, promising there would be consequences "for every country that voted against us that didn't have an overpowering reason." Kissinger counseled patience, explaining, "We feel we have to do it in our own devious way," and Reagan went along because he put the anti-Soviet thrust of administration policy ahead of Taiwan's interests. Walter Judd, a former congressman and China lobby leader, secretly pledged support for the president, confidentially telling Kissinger that reports of his opposition would actually "strengthen . . . [the national security adviser's] hand" in negotiations with the Chinese.[2]

For Taiwan the consequences were serious. Chiang Kai-shek initially wanted to proclaim that, having violated its charter, the UN no longer was worthy of ROC participation. The hope of retaining membership in vital international organizations connected to the UN, such as the International

Monetary Fund and World Bank, however, constrained him. Taipei did not yet realize that Washington would not expend political capital to help; in fact, it secretly notified its embassies in Europe and Asia that there would be no major effort to preserve places for the ROC in these institutions.[3]

Diplomats from Taiwan, meanwhile, renewed their lobbying for assistance from Washington. The ROC Embassy was very small in the early 1970s; its political section consisted of no more than five people, all of whom were novices at congressional liaison work, previously the province of Madame Chiang Kai-shek. CCK, determined to control as well as energize the operation, asked S. K. Hu, an air force general and head of the embassy's procurement mission, to become special assistant to the ambassador and reorganize legislative liaison operations. He recruited a group of young, American-educated officials to broaden ties with members and their key staff aides. By 1972 Hu had created a dedicated congressional section, one of the few embassies to have one, and had begun to broaden contacts on the Hill beyond traditional ties to conservative Republicans.[4]

Although Taiwan welcomed all support, weapons sales, more crucial psychologically than for defense, took precedence.[5] American analysts did not expect a Chinese attack on Taiwan, believing China would not endanger the American opening and could not muster the requisite forces. Given the mysterious death of Lin Biao, the defense minister and Mao's heir apparent, a military campaign seemed especially unlikely. The rejection of Taiwan by the international community made infiltration and sabotage of the newly vulnerable island more plausible. Taipei officials and angry demonstrators considered rendering greater assistance the least Washington could do as compensation for permitting the UN ouster.[6]

As plans progressed for Nixon's trip to China, Taiwan staged commando raids on China's Fujian coast on December 10, 1971, and January 10 and January 22, 1972. US officials concluded Taipei hoped to cause friction between Washington and Beijing, possibly disrupting Nixon's visit, but they did little to allay Taipei's anxiety.[7] Nevertheless, CCK assured Ambassador Walter McConaughy that he would not allow his government to provoke an incident during Nixon's stay on the mainland.[8]

Taiwan Remains China's Focus in Negotiations

During the October trip that may have tipped the UN vote on Taiwan's expulsion, Kissinger's purpose had been to craft the agenda and draft the communiqué for Nixon's February 1972 summit in China. Taiwan com-

China's Membership in the United Nations: A New Seating Plan?

manded primary attention, and the Chinese pressed forcefully for language that would make their position clear. Zhou Enlai insisted that the US drop the word "equitable" in expressing support for "an equitable and peaceful resolution of the relationship of Taiwan and the mainland" lest it be interpreted as a call for self-determination through a plebiscite. Kissinger agreed. Although he could not guarantee Nixon's concurrence, he felt "quite sure the President will go along."[9] Chinese negotiators also designated Taiwan a province of China, to which neither Kissinger nor his American team objected, a position they would find unsustainable. At the time, the fact that Taiwan was not a democracy may have made this stance more palatable. More important, neither Nixon nor Kissinger wanted to see the emergence of an independent Taiwan that would demand US protection and stymie their anti-Soviet priorities. But Kissinger also faced Zhou's implacable will and his threats that reconciliation could founder on the Taiwan issue. Zhou insisted that China had been flexible, removing time limits for US military withdrawal and requiring only, but absolutely, that Washington commit to a final result. To Kissinger's alarm he urged, "Please report to your President our view, and the situation that only such a formulation is acceptable."[10]

When Alexander Haig traveled to China in January to refine trip preparations, he alerted Zhou to efforts in the US to disrupt Nixon's trip and prevent rapprochement; he urged greater flexibility on the Taiwan issue. But Haig did not propose a change in China's actual requirements on independence and troop withdrawal; rather, he called for alteration of language to produce "a formulation that is somewhat less truthful and somewhat less precise than the language which Dr. Kissinger carried away with him during his last visit."[11] Zhou rebuffed Haig, increasingly attuned to Nixon's domestic political imperatives and sure the president would come.

Thus, upon Nixon's arrival in China in 1972, the parameters had already been set for agreements on Taiwan, as had the practice of saying different things in public and in private. When he opened his substantive dialogue with Zhou on February 22, Nixon immediately raised Taiwan and reiterated understandings reached by Kissinger, hoping to set the issue aside and discuss matters that interested him more. "Principle one," he began, "there is one China, and Taiwan is a part of China." He went on to disavow support for Taiwan independence movements, Japanese involvement, references to Taiwan's status as undetermined, and military action against the PRC. Nixon emphasized his fears that domestic groups would manipulate the Taiwan question to block his China initiative. Language had to be found to disguise concessions so that a joint communiqué between the US and the PRC that set out areas of agreement at the end of the president's visit "would not stir up the animals," thereby motivating them to hurl charges that "the American President went to Peking and sold Taiwan down the river." Under such circumstances, he might be "forced . . . to make a strong basically pro-Taiwan statement," which would obstruct implementation of commitments on both sides. "The problem here," Nixon told Zhou, "is not what we are going to do, the problem is what we are going to say about it."[12]

Zhou did not prolong discussion of Taiwan, but his remarks regarding "peaceful liberation" were pointed rather than patient. If Taiwan refused to entertain the prospect of reunification, then China would have to take other actions once US troops had been removed. Nixon presumably had signaled his understanding of these realities, Zhou observed, when, in November 1969, he ended the US Navy's Taiwan Strait patrols. Furthermore, Zhou added, "It would be good if the liberation of Taiwan could be realized in your next term of office," since China's leaders were old. "I should say very frankly that when Dr. Kissinger said that it would take ten years, that would be too long. . . . I can't wait ten years."[13] Zhou's determination to resolve the Taiwan impasse had not diminished. His message was not forbearance; he sought to draw lines.[14]

Zhou, therefore, persisted in seeking a clear statement of US intentions regarding removal of US forces from Taiwan despite Nixon's preference for vague phrasing. Nixon was willing to say to the premier that he planned to withdraw US troops from Taiwan in his second term, by

1976 for example, but he did not want to make a written or oral pledge. He could then tell Congress and the press that no deal had been struck. Kissinger and his negotiating team ultimately found compromise language that linked force reduction to growing peace in the region and final withdrawal to a full settlement. But ironically, at this crucial moment in the China initiative, the president's insistence on secrecy and ambiguity raised fewer problems with the Chinese than with his own diplomatic corps.

Discussions of what would become the Shanghai Communiqué had proceeded for months without direct participation by the Department of State. By exposing Marshall Green, assistant secretary for East Asia, and Secretary of State William Rogers to the full text for the first time only after the CCP Politburo had approved it, Nixon created a crisis of sorts. Kissinger characterized the vehement objections of Rogers and Green as "bickering" and dismissed them as "trivial," commenting elsewhere that "hell hath no fury like a bureaucrat scorned." But Nixon concluded he could not afford to ignore their input and return home with a divided delegation.[15]

Green saw danger in the references to both Taiwan's status and Taiwan's security. The definition of one China and who adhered to it, the most troubling long-term question in the China-Taiwan stalemate, immediately caught Green's attention. The proposition asserted, "All Chinese on either side of the Taiwan Strait maintain there is but one China and that Taiwan is a part of China." Kissinger had been able to undo his October error in accepting the designation "province" by substituting the word "part." Green, however, pointed out that saying "all Chinese" did not accurately represent reality, since only a minority of those living on Taiwan thought of themselves as Chinese. Alternatively, if "all Chinese" meant those socially, culturally, and ethnically Chinese, then virtually everyone on the island fell into the category, but this majority did not agree that they belonged to China.

The communiqué text also threatened Taiwan's security by conspicuously omitting the US-ROC Mutual Defense Treaty from a list of defense pacts in Asia. Green saw a dangerous parallel with the notorious Acheson speech of 1950 that had placed Korea outside the US defense perimeter in Asia. Five months later, administration critics had assailed the secretary of state for inviting North Korea to attack the South. Green believed memories of this event would "unravel the whole document."[16]

Kissinger had some success despite his fury at having to reopen the talks. When the Chinese refused to permit reference to the Mutual Defense Treaty between the US and Taiwan, he convinced them to eliminate all mention of treaties from the communiqué. Instead, he engineered a press query in Shanghai that allowed him to speak of the Taiwan treaty as one of several "continuing commitments" in Asia. He did not do as well salvaging self-determination. His irate Chinese interlocutor berated him for implying that any reputable person on Taiwan might not identify himself as Chinese or consider Taiwan part of China. Kissinger capitulated.[17]

The resulting Shanghai Communiqué did not tell the people of the United States, Taiwan, or China that Nixon had privately accepted Beijing's key demand. Rather, in this first agreement between the US and the PRC on the normalization of their relations, Americans said that the US "acknowledges" and "does not challenge" the idea "that all Chinese on either side of the Taiwan Strait maintain that there is but one China and that Taiwan is a part of China," a view shared at the time by authorities in both Beijing and Taipei.[18] Indeed, in 1972 their dispute centered not on independence for Taiwan, but on which government rightfully ruled all of China. So Washington outwardly assumed a neutral posture, emphasizing that resolution of the Taipei-Beijing conflict must be peaceful, but not asserting what the outcome should be.

Beijing sought to use rapprochement to destabilize Taiwan and imply that Washington had shifted its affections to the mainland despite continuation of the Mutual Defense Treaty. Mao instructed the CCP that "Simultaneously with the improvement in the Sino–U.S. relations," a clear benefit of his decision to deal with Nixon would be "a gradual alienation in the relations between the United States and the Chiang gang. . . . [Now] . . . the Chiang gang is no longer able to get tough."[19]

The obvious gains for Beijing tempered Taipei's relief at retaining diplomatic relations. Nixon had conferred legitimacy on Mao's bandit regime. He had embarrassed himself and his country by virtually kowtowing to China. Years of promises that Washington would never negotiate about Taiwan's interests without ROC officials in the room were dramatically broken. The leadership had been seriously undermined, the more so since Chiang learned of the trip from men he deemed low-level emissaries, a mere assistant secretary of state and a member of the NSC staff. Further, the disregard of the Taiwanese on the island angered and energized the independence movement.[20] Taipei officials who compared the Chinese and English versions of the Shanghai Communiqué, moreover, asserted that Beijing had fooled the Americans by weakening wording that opposed the PRC use of force.

CKS refused to meet with Green and John Holdridge, but his son calmly and confidently received them, recalling repeated American pledges that both diplomatic and defense commitments would remain intact. They emphasized that no deadlines had been agreed on and no specific plans made to advance normalization. Indeed, CCK later contended that they said the US would work toward "better," not formal relations with Beijing.[21] Ambassador McConaughy, a staunch supporter of the ROC, no doubt contriubted to CCK's confidence since, according to the deputy chief of mission, "he could not conceive that his country would de-recognize an old ally," and Green either would not, or could not, be explicit enough to convince him.[22]

Nixon and Kissinger extended similar assurances to Ambassador James Shen in Washington. During strained sessions in March, Shen protested that the communiqué had used the word *Taiwan,* not the official designation, ROC, and did not explicitly cite the US–ROC defense treaty. Kissinger acknowledged and downplayed both lapses, emphasizing continuing US–Taiwan diplomatic and military ties and their importance, when, within five years, Mao died. This would open opportunities as internal turmoil and possible Sino-Soviet conflict materialized, requiring a collaborative Washington-Taipei policy. Nixon denied that he had made secret deals and warned against arousing American isolationism with repeated demands for support. The president insisted to the guarded ambassador that Beijing had not been "hard" on Taiwan, neither urgently demanding a solution nor threatening to use force.[23]

The president and his national security adviser automatically assumed that entrenched interests would oppose the opening to China, and they decided to bypass them during the heady days of secret diplomacy. In many cases this wariness proved justified. But problems often reflected not so much individual loyalties or resistance to change as legalities, practicalities, and procedures. Indeed, many diplomats viewed Taiwan's governing authorities with a jaundiced eye, recalling that in the 1940s and 1950s the China lobby, with support from the ROC, had tried to drag the US into war with Mao and had helped fuel anticommunist purges at the State Department. The careers of men like John S. Service and John Carter Vincent had been shattered and the China service handicapped for years thereafter.[24]

The ROC had been treated as a nation and an ally, even if American officials were sometimes privately patronizing or contemptuous. Washington could not alter the public face of policy precipitously. In January 1973 President Nixon met with the ROC's Vice President Yen Chia-kan, who had traveled to the US to attend Harry Truman's funeral. Nixon reassured him of defense commitments and diplomatic relations. Yen came with his own message. He told the president that Taiwan would do everything it could to coordinate policies with the US on Vietnam and most likely on everything else, since it needed US support.[25]

Taiwan tried to follow Washington's lead on all policy issues and to give the US assistance whenever an opportunity arose, consciously adopting the role of a devoted ally. Taipei hoped loyalty might delay abandonment. This strategy veiled an underlying and mounting distrust of the US. As the Taiwan affairs officers saw it, Taipei's suspicion "stems from the realization that the ROC no longer figures very importantly in U.S. foreign policy . . . that the ROC no longer is able to exercise much influence within the U.S. political system and, hence, is powerless significantly to affect major policy decisions relating to it." Believing that "recognition would be popular in the U.S. and could give President Nixon a needed boost . . . ROC Embassy officers have said they expect recognition within a year.[26]

Accordingly, Konsin Shah, long a close aide to CKS, became ROC consul general to New York, poised to take over as an unofficial ambassador, the Office of ROC Affairs in the State Department (Taiwan desk) speculated. Intelligence reports given to Winston Lord, Kissinger's special assistant suggested that the ROC would, if all else was lost, turn its consulates into unofficial tools for manipulating local Chinese communities to influence US public opinion. Kissinger told Zhou Enlai in November that Shah would be a useful informal contact for the US after 1976.[27]

The problem of the defense of Taiwan resonated most with the American military on the island. Since Washington did not clarify precisely what would happen in the aftermath of the Shanghai Communiqué, local forces continued to act as though nothing had changed. According to William Gleysteen, the deputy chief of mission at the embassy,

> CINCPAC [office of the commander in chief, Pacific Command] had little appreciation of what was going on in Washington, and the Seventh Fleet and Taiwan Defense Commanders had even less. They didn't want to think about withdrawals; they even spoke of beefing up forces. The JCS [Joint Chiefs of Staff] in Washington, who were closer to senior policy makers, had more than an inkling of what might happen, but they were in no hurry to issue guidance until ordered by the president. . . . As a result we sometimes had senior military personnel from the Pacific commands, including CINCPAC himself, reassuring their Taiwan counterparts that all would be well.[28]

The United States heightened misunderstanding when, confronted by a looming peace agreement with Hanoi, it supplemented weak South Vietnamese air defenses with a loan of one hundred of Taipei's F-5A aircraft. In exchange, the US temporarily boosted Taiwan's air force with more powerful F-4 Phantom jets and implemented plans for coproduction of Northrop's F-5E fighter in Taiwan. These developments ran contrary to retrenchment, bestowing hope where Washington had not intended.

Kissinger, by contrast, sought to sustain the momentum of normalization. In February 1973 he returned to Beijing with an agenda that focused on Soviet problems, the war in Cambodia, and facilitation of commercial ties. Most devastating to Taiwan was the fact that Washington and Beijing, tired of conducting routine business through high-level trips and representatives in Paris and New York, created liaison offices.

The Liaison Innovation

With the advent of these liaison offices, the two Chinas essentially changed places in the hearts and minds of America's leaders and its public. Soon China's Liaison Office far outstripped the old ROC Embassy in the business of US government agencies as well as in the life of the diplomatic community. The opening came not without criticism, from Taipei first of all, but also from others (initially including Kissinger himself) who agreed that such a representative entity should not operate in the nation's capital.[29] But Kissinger quickly became so committed that, according to the archivist and author William Burr, he manipulated Nixon into agreement. To address the risk that he might not be able to control the US office in Beijing, Kissinger set up a private communications channel to the White House and used a CIA agent to bypass State Department personnel.[30]

To Americans China was of strategic importance and Taiwan had ceased to be. As early as 1971, Kissinger had begun to quote studies that indicated the US could block any military threat from China with submarine-launched Poseidon missiles and B-52 bombers, a fact that rendered Taiwan expendable as a basing area.[31] By 1973 Kissinger no longer thought military action against China likely. Privately he told the president, "The PRC might well be closest to us in its global perception. No other world leaders have the sweep and imagination of Mao and Chou."[32] When Washington had to deal with war in the Middle East in 1973, Kissinger sought out the Chinese to brief but never considered any role for Taipei.

It was not surprising, therefore, that Kissinger could not find time to meet with Taiwan's ambassador despite Shen's repeated requests for interviews.[33] Compounding Shen's problem was US government officials' holding Beijing's representative in higher regard than Taipei's man in Washington. Shen had been an ambassador and a vice foreign minister before becoming ambassador to the US, but his career as a newspaper reporter dominated perceptions of him. Huang Zhen of the PRC had attained high military rank in the civil war. He had served in various diplomatic posts, including as ambassador to France. There he had conducted secret talks with American representatives. He also served as a member of the CCP Central Committee.

Summoned home for consultations, Shen found his government in turmoil. Beyond expressing indignation, Taipei could think of nothing to do about the new situation created by the liaison offices. Never before had Beijing agreed to open a mission in a capital where the ROC still had an embassy. During a confidential meeting with CCK, an unproductive discussion examined the sudden need directly to compete with Chinese "diplomats."[34]

This crisis in relations with the US hastened Chiang Ching-kuo's decision to take the reins of power from his ailing father and the position of premier from Yen in May 1973. The younger Chiang had begun to think about a strategy of political change, combining elections and Taiwanization, to earn his government wider public and foreign support, and to emphasize the despotism of the other China across the Strait. He briefly encouraged a free speech movement through which intellectuals and a fragment of the public demanded younger, better-educated, and more representative bureaucrats and legislators; the rule of law; a free press; and an end to secret decision making. Chiang utilized these pressures cautiously to begin to push aside hard-liners in the KMT.[35]

Despite American reliance on CCK, who even in the early 1970s clearly remained in tight control of the military and intelligence establishments, not all of Taiwan's American interlocutors admired Chiang or his government. If no longer a sinister figure commanding brutal security services, Chiang did not easily rouse enthusiasm.[36] Richard Solomon, of the NSC staff, reflected the concerns of many when he disparaged "the leadership in Taipei," which "continues to find it politically more acceptable to have us impose a future on them than to take the risks of . . . establishing a direct dialogue with Peking."[37] Few American officials sympathized with CCK's reflexive rejection of talks. They dismissed the argument that Taipei would be engaging from a position of weakness and would fatally undermine popular confidence in the government.

Americans also possessed little sympathy for or understanding of the mistrust that Taiwan's leaders felt in the wake of the Kissinger-Nixon trips and the opening of the liaison offices. Shen noted that in a meeting with the secretary of state, shortly before Kissinger's February trip to Beijing, the affable Rogers chided him: "If we have to reiterate our assurance to your country every time we have had some contact with the Chinese Communists, it would give people the impression that your country does not have much faith in us."[38]

In Beijing in November 1973, Kissinger again provided Zhou with a series of assurances about US–Taiwan relations. Kissinger notified China that F-4 Phantom jets capable of delivering nuclear bombs would be removed from Taiwan in 1974, as would half of the remaining 9,000 US military personnel. He promised to withdraw U-2 spy planes and American nuclear weapons. Further, Kissinger assured Zhou, who expressed concern about technology transfer, that the US coproduction contract with Taiwan for short-range F-5E fighter jets would supply only parts for assembly, not scientific and technological data. Once the parts stopped flowing, so would the assembly line. There would be no absolute increase in the number of planes available to the Taiwan military. Finally, in words that would have repercussions for future US–Taiwan–China relations, Kissinger told Zhou, who had labeled the F-5E CCK's lifeline, "We have no plans on this plane, on this project, beyond 1978." In Kissinger's view, normalization should be completed by mid-1976—which would entail severing all formal association with Taipei.[39]

Zhou and Mao, in turn, appeared to confirm that Kissinger had been right all along, that Beijing could be reasonable on Taiwan. China would allow the US–China relationship to flower even as significant ties continued between the US and the ROC. Kissinger told Nixon on November 19 that Zhou had hinted at substantial relations between Washington and Taipei after recognition. Seeming to draw a parallel between Taiwan and the Baltic states, Mao observed that the latter had been permitted to retain embassies in the US even after Moscow opened its embassy there. Taiwan reunification might have to wait one hundred years, but, Mao asserted, normalization with the US must not. Ten years later, Kissinger speculated: "Was it another hint that normalization could be separated from the issue of Taiwan? . . . At a minimum, it suggested that China would not attempt to swallow Taiwan quickly afterward; certainly, that the Taiwan issue would not be an obstacle to our relations, that contrary to public perception we were under no pressure with respect to it."[40]

Various sources in Washington bolstered Kissinger's complacency. The National Security Council posited a relaxed leadership group whose desire to control Taiwan had diminished so long as no other power, most especially the Soviets, took over. Beijing would be satisfied to keep Taiwan internationally isolated, assuming the world community would accept China's claim to the island, and the US would remove its forces.[41] Lord, by this time director of Policy Planning at the State Department, and Deputy Assistant Secretary Hummel argued that Beijing saw the US as a guarantor against unwelcome outcomes: a turn to the Soviets, to the Japanese, or toward independence, or collapse into chaos.[42]

By contrast, the US Liaison Office in Beijing reported mounting apprehension that united-front tactics and propaganda campaigns would not succeed. Early in 1974 Washington appointed an experienced ambassador to Taipei, rather than downgrading the post, which highlighted the slow and erratic pace of normalization. To the aging and ill leaders on both sides a Taiwan settlement seemed urgent.[43]

Yet internal Chinese political conflict undermined possible resolution. After Kissinger's 1973 visit, Mao denounced Zhou as weak in dealing with the Americans. Mao expected Zhou to dominate, since he considered Kissinger "just a funny little man . . . shuddering all over with nerves every time he comes to see me."[44] To Politburo members in late November Mao excoriated the premier for "rightist errors": that is, he suggested that Taiwan could be liberated peacefully.[45] Even as Kissinger waxed rhapsodic about his philosophical exchanges with Zhou and imagined that the Taiwan issue could be set aside, Zhou came under attack for not being more confrontational.

As for conditions in Taiwan, Americans saw quiet in the streets and attributed it to prosperity and a pragmatic acceptance of eventual US derecognition. Analysts stopped worrying about the government's ability to stay in power and even remarked favorably on the flexibility and self-assurance of officials. Reports from the island made clear that CCK would not adopt radical policies. In 1971 Kissinger had assured Ambassador Shen, "We had no intention of withdrawing recognition" from Taiwan. "They would be very foolish to commit suicide in order to avoid death." In 1973 he no longer felt compelled to do so, telling Shen little about his visit to China, scolding him for accusations that the US "compulsively" sought relations with China, and advising him to be restrained in dealing with the administration.[46]

Shen's days of dealing directly with Kissinger were, in any case, coming to a close. Before the end of the year, the State Department informally banned high-level meetings. Instead, Taiwan officials had to deal almost exclusively with the head of the Taiwan desk at the State Department. Beginning in the spring of 1973, this was Roger Sullivan, a man known in Taipei to favor normalization. Taiwan diplomats resentfully told him that they interpreted his appointment as a move to restrain them.[47]

The most fervent hopes for a solution to the impasse in the Taiwan Strait focused on direct talks. Such a dialogue, Washington believed, would extricate the US from the confrontation. Each party viewed the idea differently, however, depending on whether it believed it would prevail in negotiations and whether it expected to obtain US support. Thus, in the 1970s Taipei resisted and Beijing welcomed talks. According to Hummel, Beijing saw "the U.S. as a bridge that can encourage the GRC eventually to reintegrate itself with the mainland."[48] While Taipei armed Taiwan's consul in New York with unacceptable terms, CKS sought to bind all officials to a pledge that, even after his approaching death, no one would engage with Beijing regardless of the ferocity of US pressure.

With little maneuvering room, Taipei engaged in a brief flirtation with Moscow, hoping to gain leverage with Washington and an advantage over Beijing. For its part, Moscow looked to Taiwan to counter the Sino-American opening, and it sent a squadron of warships through the Taiwan Strait in February 1973, for the first time since 1949. Rumors circulated that the Soviet navy would lease a base in the Penghu Islands. Foreign Minister Chow Shu-kai told the newspapers that balancing the Washington-Beijing alignment made sense for Taiwan. CCK, however, grew uncomfortable. Moscow might be valuable as a threat but would not be safe as an ally. When the Soviets proposed assembling a coalition of anti-Mao governments to support Taiwan independence, CCK backed away, notifying Washington. The backlash from hard-line anticommunists ended Chow's tenure as minister.[49]

Although military protections offered by the Mutual Defense Treaty and the 1955 Formosa Resolution remained after Nixon's China trip, an undercurrent of uncertainty had been introduced into the defense relationship. Each side wondered how long the treaty would remain in force, and stories circulated that Congress intended to repeal the Formosa Resolution. State Department analysts concluded that the likelihood of an attack on Taiwan had significantly fallen, so providing weapons to Taiwan had become a political and economic gesture rather than a military necessity.[50] The US military assistance program ended in fiscal year 1973, and discussion began about terminating indirect support provided through foreign military sales credits (FMS). Washington emphasized that neither a treaty nor weapons could do more than Beijing's assurance that it would seek to liberate Taiwan peacefully. In 1973, when the US left Vietnam, officials in Taipei concluded no treaty was safe. James Shen remarked sardonically that the abandonment of Vietnam would provide Taiwan "a breathing space" because Washington would recognize that "selling one ally down the river was quite enough for one year."[51]

Taipei grasped at straws. In the spring of 1974, when Walter McConaughy left his post as ambassador, Taiwan feared, and logic dictated, that representation would be downgraded, since the administration intended to end diplomatic relations. Instead, the White House named another ambassador and Taipei celebrated, erroneously interpreting the appointment as meaningful support. Actually, by the winter of 1974, Watergate preoccupied Nixon, normalization had stalled, and maintaining the status quo in representation preserved a bargaining chip.

Kissinger, however, did not see Leonard Unger, the new ambassador, as a man of action likely to strengthen Taiwan's position, or a dominant figure whose views should be taken seriously. He explained to Deng Xiaoping, China's vice premier, that having a seasoned diplomat in place would help ease Taiwan's transition from formal relations. But he told an American official "flat out, on several occasions, that he wanted to get rid of Len Unger and wanted to stick it to the Taiwanese simultaneously." At the embassy, conviction grew that Kissinger had sent Unger because he was easily distracted by busywork and would not impede Kissinger's manipulation of Taiwan-China affairs.[52] Meanwhile, despite Taipei's displeasure with James Shen's achievements as ambassador, and Kissinger's efforts to avoid him, Shen kept his job because replacing him would emphasize the lack of progress on normalization.[53]

Military cooperation endured even as the tolerance for other activities declined. In part this reflected institutional opposition to downsizing and disengagement. US military leaders on the island, for instance, assured Unger in April 1974 that, should China attack Taiwan, the US president would authorize them to strike the mainland in coordination with the ROC military, and use US forces to defend the island. The admiral in charge of the Taiwan Defense Command, reflecting the Pentagon's anxiety about Taiwan's vulnerability, "accused the embassy of pandering to the PRC against the interests of our hosts in Taiwan." According to the prickly Deputy Chief of Mission William Gleysteen, "I warned him that . . . we would have no trouble getting Washington to order him to behave. . . . This sobered him down."[54] Local commanders found they could not disrupt the steady redeployment of men and equipment as Washington accelerated their departure.

Fearing potential reactions to cuts in US assistance, as early as 1972 Secretary of Defense Melvin Laird had heightened security around US military storage areas and added so-called permissive action links, that is, locking mechanisms, to the bombs. James Schlesinger, his successor, also worried that Chiang could be tempted, under certain circumstances, to try to seize US weapons.[55] Gleysteen, however, although acknowledging that Washington's message regarding the removal of nuclear materials had given "Chiang a jolt," thought it "implausible to imagine CCK trying to take possession of the nuclear warheads."[56] In fact, CCK did not resist removal of U-2 intelligence aircraft or nuclear warheads.

Redeploying fighter jets put Chiang in a more difficult political position.

The US planned to remove advanced F-4 Phantom fighters and replace them with less effective F-5A aircraft that Taipei had loaned to South Vietnam in 1972 at Washington's behest. These planes, now combat veterans, appeared inherently unreliable despite having been refurbished. In the interim, moreover, PRC capabilities had improved. CCK did not seek to block Washington, asking only for an evaluation of ROC defense capabilities first. He reminded Unger that he had assisted Washington unquestioningly when Nixon needed him in Vietnam.[57] Unger plaintively wrote to Hummel that CCK had gambled that the US would be grateful and he had lost.

Washington reinforced the negative message by readjusting procedures and policies to reflect its new PRC orientation. "Taiwan," officials worried, "has been buoyed by recent events"; it ought not "feel . . . that it has a new lease on life." Travel regulations quietly discouraged senior executive branch officials from going to Taiwan. Lord, Solomon, and Hummel advised Kissinger to reduce still further administration support for keeping Taiwan in international financial institutions, reasoning that Taiwan's economy could withstand expulsion and that its diplomatic status would not be unduly harmed, since everyone already expected that development. They also recommended repeal of the 1955 Formosa Resolution: the executive branch would gain favor with Beijing and in Congress, while the Mutual Defense Treaty would still protect Taiwan. Washington also had to discard plans for the 1975 replacement of deteriorating embassy facilities in Taiwan.[58]

NIXON AND KISSINGER viewed Taiwan as expendable, as less valuable than the strategic and political advantages that a new relationship with the PRC would secure. As a result, they decided to give Beijing what it wanted in order to make a deal. In the process, they misled China's rulers into believing that the US would step aside and allow Taiwan to collapse. When that did not happen, Beijing, like Taipei, felt betrayed.

In their eagerness to play the China card, Nixon and Kissinger undermined the effectiveness and durability of their initiative. They underestimated support for Taiwan and ignored Taiwan's capacity for meaningful political reform, which would provide the wherewithal for survival. Their shortsightedness, virtually guaranteed by excessive secrecy, bred mistrust everywhere. This collateral damage to US integrity, diplomacy, and democracy, at home and abroad, constitutes the most serious indictment of the policies they pursued.

FORD'S TRIBULATIONS

GERALD FORD spent his presidency under Nixon's shadow, and his foreign policy reflected it. He inherited Henry Kissinger along with his predecessor's decisions. Together Ford and Kissinger tried to save South Vietnam and rescue détente with Moscow, but they failed. They tried to ignore congressional restraints, such as the 1973 War Powers Act, but Ford, weaker than most presidents, could not win support for prolonging war in Vietnam. The greater influence of Congress during Ford's tenure also was reflected in the executive's inability to realize normalization.

Ford, a former member of the House, felt acutely the congressional and electoral pitfalls of taking bold action on China against anticommunist and pro-Chinese Nationalist opposition. Because Beijing lamented the "incomprehensible" ouster of Richard Nixon and did not appreciate Ford's political vulnerability after he pardoned the former president, Sino-American relations soured. But China also contended with tumultuous internal politics that distracted officials and impeded potential progress. In 1976 both Zhou Enlai and Mao Zedong died, the ultraradical Gang of Four landed in prison, and Deng Xiaoping began maneuvering to return to power. Deng was determined to revamp China's economic structure and open the country to international trade and investment. His goal was to regain China's place among the great powers. Although wary of American leaders, he understood that the US could be enormously useful.

CHAPTER FOUR

Collapse and Reprieve

The Watergate scandal destroyed the Nixon administration and made recognition of the PRC impossible. Nixon had less and less time to deal with China as details of the break-in at the Democratic National Committee headquarters and associated presidential abuse of power and obstruction of justice became public. He also had to hold on to support of conservative Republicans in Congress, who insisted on preserving links to Taiwan. Thus, in 1974, when much else fell apart, Taiwan enjoyed a reprieve. Discreet celebrations greeted Nixon's resignation; had his onetime vice president and friend, Spiro Agnew, taken office, relief might have become rejoicing. But Agnew had been forced out in 1973 for corruption, and Gerald Ford became president.

Ford, like Harry Truman, had a reputation as a novice in world affairs. That seemed especially striking and damning, as it had been for Truman, following a "foreign policy president." Ford resented the categorization, noting service on defense and intelligence committees in the House of Representatives (R-Mich.). Moreover, Nixon actively educated Ford, directing Kissinger and his NSC deputy director, Brent Scowcroft, to brief the vice president at least once a week on global issues. Nonetheless, few knew his intentions or how dependent he would be on Kissinger.

Ford's China record had reflected staunch Republican positions against the People's Republic and for Chiang Kai-shek. As he later told the journalist and author Patrick Tyler, Nixon's opening to Beijing stunned and scared him.[1] Nevertheless, as House Minority Leader, he went to China soon after Nixon. He returned persuaded of the need to resolve the Taiwan issue and establish relations with Beijing.[2]

For these reasons Kissinger, who remained national security adviser and secretary of state, had no trouble convincing Ford to meet privately with China's Washington representative. Through Huang Zhen, Ford could send a letter to Mao pledging to fulfill all Nixon's promises and accelerate normalization. Taiwan by contrast saw only reaffirmation of inexorable movement toward derecognition. Although the new president greeted Huang and fifty-nine other foreign envoys, only the deputy secretary of state met with the ROC ambassador.[3]

Domestic Politics

Throughout his brief presidency, Ford wrestled with Washington's Taiwan dilemma. To win election as president in his own right, he wanted a foreign policy triumph such as establishing diplomatic relations with Beijing. China's preconditions, however, remained inflexible and too formidable. For Beijing's leaders, the benefits of recognition by the US could never outweigh the threat to regime stability of jeopardizing title to Taiwan. Moreover, by the middle of 1974 strategic ties to the US had declined in value. Sino-Soviet tensions moderated just as Americans grew disillusioned with détente and anxious about Soviet aggression. Beijing believed it had leverage to demand US concessions on Taiwan. With neither side willing or able to compromise, progress proved impossible.

At the same time, the Republican right in the US used the Taiwan problem against Ford, berating him for inadequate aid to and respect for Taipei. Ronald Reagan, Barry Goldwater, and William Buckley supported Taipei's lobbying, focusing attention on issues that otherwise would not have moved Americans. Chiang Ching-kuo pressured Ford, even though he believed he could do little more than delay US recognition of the PRC and had to proceed cautiously lest he endanger his control of Taiwan.

Ford quickly became the target of conservative Republicans who sought to commandeer the presidency. Ronald Reagan, Ford's primary opponent for the party's nomination, ran to Ford's right on domestic and foreign policies; he differed sharply on issues such as the Panama Canal, Vietnam, and détente.

Probably the most surprising of Ford's campaign counselors proved to be George H. W. Bush, then serving as head of the US Liaison Office in Beijing. Bush—an old friend and rival for the vice presidency in 1973—

had accepted the China assignment with enthusiasm. He recognized, however, that distance from Washington could damage a political career and, therefore, reminded Ford often of his value. Taiwan, he and Ford agreed, would be one of the key problems the president would face and, though Ford saw it as "a political issue to manage domestically," Bush assured him that help would be forthcoming from Beijing in the run-up to the 1976 election.[4]

Bush accordingly sought to shape the political influence of Ford's interactions with China. Anticipating the president's planned visit to Beijing, he recorded in his so-called Peking Diary, "I personally believe the President can come and go without solving the Taiwan issue, but I am sure this will be in doubt as far as others go." Showing his lack of expertise but abundance of optimism as a two-month veteran, Bush added, "Of course maybe the issue will be resolved by then." In a back-channel cable to Kissinger on January 15, 1975, a wiser Bush warned that the press might judge the visit solely by achievements on Taiwan, but PRC leaders appeared unready to compromise. Moreover, he warned that the supporters Ford needed most at the Republican convention might tolerate the establishment of an embassy in China and the downgrading of representation in Taiwan, but they could not accept a "sell-out."[5]

The pro-Taiwan conservatives amply demonstrated their capacity for righteous anger when Chiang Kai-shek died on April 5, 1975. The passing of this longtime ally—a man who in many uncomfortable ways embodied the modern history of US–China relations—demanded acknowledgment with an official delegation to attend the funeral. Ford, determined to avoid antagonizing Beijing, designated Secretary of Agriculture Earl Butz to represent him, a decision that enraged US conservatives and elicited a protest from CCK. Goldwater, having organized a large congressional delegation, told the press he had warned Ford and Kissinger, "If they want to change our relationship with Taipei . . . they've got a hell of a fight on their hands." Two NSC China watchers, Richard Smyser and Richard Solomon, complained that "to humiliate an old ally by sending an obviously insulting funeral delegation will not engender respect in Peking. It will be seen as a sign of weakness." If the leaders there "will turn against us on [this] . . . symbolic matter . . . an argument can be made that our relationship with Peking is so fragile that it is no relationship at all."[6] Ford retreated and dispatched an unenthusiastic Vice President Nelson Rockefeller.

And then Vietnam collapsed. The war had been a significant variable in the US–Taiwan–China triangle. It made Washington and Beijing wary of each other and gave Taipei scope to imagine a broader war facilitating a Kuomintang return to the mainland. During the prolonged Paris peace talks, Taipei gave the south's President Nguyen Van Thieu advice on negotiating with the communist north. When southern resistance ended, Thieu fled to Taiwan, where officials gave him a warm welcome.[7]

The fall of South Vietnam—an ally and a symbol of anticommunist struggle—shook Taiwan's confidence, but it also sparked hope that Ford might be open to renewed cooperation with Taiwan. In two communications to the president in May, Chiang proposed that Ford use Taiwan as part of the US defense perimeter in Asia.[8] Washington did not reply.

In the wake of Saigon's disintegration on April 30 and with a presidential visit to China coming, George Bush also sprang into action, explaining that he felt compelled to be candid about the "pure politics" of the president's situation and Ford's "personal interests." Bush warned that Ford's trip could magnify the Taiwan problem into a "political nightmare," potentially "a major weapon for your opponents be they Republican or Democrat."[9]

Ford had been building defenses. He assured the American Society of Newspaper Editors that he viewed relations with Taiwan "a matter of very, very great importance." To a press audience on May 6 he mentioned a desire to "reaffirm our commitments to Taiwan" and ignored normalization with Beijing. A few days earlier, Defense Secretary James Schlesinger had observed that Taiwan could be defended and that the US would do so in accordance with the Mutual Defense Treaty. Normally, US officials avoided talking about the pact.[10]

Nevertheless, when Ronald Reagan gave the first foreign policy address of his campaign for the Republican nomination in June 1975, he condemned Ford for his pro-China policies and for his lack of attention to Taiwan. If the president insisted on traveling to Beijing, Reagan urged, he ought to go to Taipei as well.

Kissinger's determination to secure his China legacy was, accordingly, preempted by Ford's political ambitions. Kissinger's aides argued that normalization remained possible and that the Chinese would be accommodating because they feared growing Soviet influence in Vietnam following the end of the war. Furthermore, they reasoned a deal would be easier so long as Mao and Zhou were both alive. But at a meeting on July 6, Kissinger complained that "for political reasons it's just impossible." Even if the Chinese gave him generous terms, he would be obliged to say no thanks, he lamented, since "if there's any one thing that will trigger a conservative reaction to Ford, that's it." The campaign could not tolerate debates over arms sales to Taiwan.[11] On September 28, 1975, Kissinger had to tell the Chinese foreign minister in New York that Ford could not make a final deal in Beijing that autumn.

The Republican right believed that Ford might compromise Taipei's interests while in China, if he went at all. In October 1975 one of his closest White House confidants, Robert Hartmann, urged him to cancel the trip. Hartmann knew little about foreign policy but believed that "though dwindling, the old 'Formosa Lobby' is still potent." He suggested that if Ford had to go, he should stop in Taiwan on the way back to curtail the damage, although Hartmann conceded this might not be wise from a foreign policy perspective.[12] In November, on the eve of Ford's journey, moderates in Congress joined the right wing in reminding the president how critical Taiwan remained to the "national interest, to the security of Japan and our allies, and to the peace of East Asia."[13]

Barry Goldwater staunchly defended Taiwan's status. He and Kissinger had begun meeting privately in the wake of the July 1971 China opening, but the Arizona senator refused to be co-opted. He frequently voiced suspicion of Nixon and Kissinger and declined to go to Beijing with Nixon to provide right-wing cover. Goldwater's concern grew out of his experience training Chinese pilots in World War II and flying food over the Himalayas. He had admired Chiang Kai-shek long before their first meeting in 1967. Nevertheless, he did not denounce the Shanghai Communiqué, declaring that as long as Taiwan did not suffer, he would give Nixon's policy a chance.[14]

Ford's opponents hated détente, detested Kissinger, and found China policy a ready target. Standing up for Taiwan turned out to be a convenient way to bash the administration, even for those who knew little about the island, and Ford found it necessary to parry almost constant assaults on his foreign policies. After securing the Republican nomination, he exulted to Kissinger, "Now that we have gotten rid of that son-of-a-bitch Reagan, we can just do what is right," a remark that applied easily to a spectrum of Taiwan issues on which the right had held him captive.[15]

Taiwan's Policies

Ford did not know administration positions on China and Taiwan in any detail when he took the helm on August 9, 1974, and understood even less about Taipei's actions and expectations. A briefing paper presented to him a few days later explained the commitments that had been made. It alerted Ford to the fluctuating pressure from Beijing to resolve the Taiwan stalemate and outlined the Japanese model: severing all formal contacts with Taiwan and having only nonofficial ties.

The document also examined US treatment of Taiwan and Taipei's response, including a candid picture of US efforts to compel Taiwan's gov-

erning authorities to face reality, a critical assessment of their resistance, insatiable demand for pledges of support, and refusals to negotiate with the PRC. According to the paper, Taiwan interpreted the Shanghai Communiqué as having "*preserv[ed] Taiwan's options either to integrate with the Mainland or to decide to become a separate nation*," a position that later would be identified not with the KMT but with the opposition. Moreover, the report alerted Ford to the need for vigilance because of the "capacity of the ROC for making serious trouble."[16]

By the middle of 1974, the prevailing outlook among Taiwan's informed elite appeared to be resignation, not troublemaking. Ambassador Unger observed: "Although senior officials will only rarely discuss such matters—and then only in the most guarded terms—most of the politically sophisticated in and out of government seem now to believe US diplomatic recognition of Peking is inevitable. . . . People fervently hope . . . that when it comes, the USG will act responsibly and (in their terms) 'morally,' so that Taiwan will continue to exist distinct from the mainland."[17]

As for Taiwan's military establishment, the officer corps at least entertained no illusions. They could not reverse the drawdown of US troops, receive cutting-edge weaponry, or sustain previous levels of assistance. They acknowledged the "inevitability" of PRC military superiority.

The idea that people in Taiwan had become reconciled to the establishment of diplomatic ties between Washington and Beijing, however, raised hackles among officials at the top in Taipei. In the autumn of 1974 CCK suggested a frank and candid exchange with Ambassador Unger to communicate his views of US policy. He told Unger that US actions were "creating a 'new monster'" by seeking friendship with communists. This was "as fruitless as trying to mix gasoline with water" and was producing a "psychology of doubt" throughout the region.[18]

Chiang also penned a series of letters to Ford about Taiwan's loyalty, cooperation, and importance to the US security network in East Asia. He bluntly warned against the disastrous results should Ford establish diplomatic relations with China during his December 1975 trip. But the US did not deign to respond and Chiang could only reiterate his alarm through his own embassy in Washington.[19] At the same time, Chiang recognized the futility of angering the Americans and accommodated as much as possible. When the US ambassador asked him not to take aggressive actions against the mainland while Ford visited, Chiang complied.[20]

As for what Taiwan would do after derecognition, US embassy personnel expected more interest in separation from, than unification with, the mainland. CCK would not declare independence but "probably would decide on some less extreme formalization." Open discussion of this issue, however, remained "proscribed" in Taiwan. As a result, "even senior and knowledgeable govt officials who, occasionally, have informally discussed 'theoretical options' [such as 'two states within one nation'] with us tend to slide along . . . without precision." The majority of the population opposed negotiation or union with Beijing. To declare independence, however, would cost support from hard-line Kuomintang adherents (most dangerously in the military and security establishments), from Washington, and from the international community. Justification for mainland control on the island would also be undermined. The embassy urged Washington "discreetly but pointedly" to remind Taipei of its opposition to any attempt to alter its juridical status and that the certainty of a PRC attack in the absence of reliable US support would throw Taiwan's armed forces into disarray.[21]

Squeezed on all sides, CCK turned to covert operations. Intimidation, violence, and even assassination would be considered against American supporters of diplomatic relations with Beijing. Taipei targeted critical scholars, spying on them, barring them from entering Taiwan, and briefly discussing use of letter bombs.[22] In September 1974 CCK placed Mei Ko-wang in charge of running ROC intelligence agents in the US, hoping his background in police administration and his Michigan State University doctorate would be more useful than intelligence experience.

Mei managed an elaborate network through which US officials surreptitiously funneled classified documents to Taipei to alert CCK to developments compromising ROC interests. Arthur Hummel, deputy assistant secretary and assistant secretary for East Asian Affairs at the State Department in the mid-1970s, lamented failures of security. "The Chinese Nationalists . . . could just walk in the front door of the Pentagon and talk to their friends, who were . . . not marching to the same tune as the Executive Branch."[23]

Information gathering did not suffice. Taiwan had convinced the Nixon administration to sell it two World War II–era submarines costing slightly more than $300,000, but both came stripped of weaponry, torpedo tubes welded shut, and were intended by the US for training and underwater exploration. In 1975 CCK authorized National Security Bureau (NSB) agents working under Mei to purchase twenty torpedoes, paying roughly $100,000 for each. These torpedoes had been stolen from the US Navy, possibly at the behest of Taiwan agents and high-level officials.[24] What the NSB did not realize was that the FBI had penetrated the operation and Taiwan had been caught in a sting. Rather than prosecute, however, Washington shielded sensitive US–Taiwan–China relations, exonerated CCK, and protected joint intelligence gathering with Taiwan, insisting only that Taipei withdraw its agents.[25]

CCK, however, did not end covert operations because of one failure. Instead, he replaced Mei with Admiral Wang Hsi-ling, who had previously been deputy director of the NSB in Taipei and a naval attaché in CKS's office. He had attended school in the US and served in Washington between 1969 and 1973, amassing a wide network of friends and acquaintances who could provide access and information. Under Wang the NSB reported directly to Chiang Ching-kuo and controlled all domestic and foreign intelligence operations.[26]

Meanwhile, in Taiwan, CCK pursued nuclear research, assembling technicians, laboratories, equipment, and fuel from Europe, the US, Canada, and South Africa.[27] Although Washington anxiously sought to block a weapons program, China made its effort more difficult, insisting the International Atomic Energy Agency (IAEA), a UN subsidiary, stop dealing with Taiwan, which had been ousted from the UN. Accordingly, the IAEA could not inspect Taiwan's research reactor, which was capable of producing enough plutonium for two bombs a year. Canada, from which Taipei had bought the facility, similarly could not impose safeguards because it had switched diplomatic relations to the PRC. Simultaneously, European companies appeared poised to build a pilot reprocessing plant, which would provide Taiwan a steady and unsafeguarded plutonium supply.

Intelligence community analysts, in the first formal assessment of Taiwan's progress in November 1972, argued that it possessed no strategy for using nuclear weapons and would not test or fabricate them. State Department and CIA officials, though often quarreling, nevertheless agreed Taipei would not risk provoking China and jeopardizing US and Japanese support. The administration decided, nevertheless, to intervene.[28]

Taipei acceded readily to a US inspection of suspect facilities, claiming it did not keep "any nuclear secrets from its friends." Skeptically, Roger Sullivan told Assistant Secretary Arthur Hummel, "We are not yet persuaded that the [Nationalist] Chinese are really hearing us, let alone taking us seriously."[29] In fact, a US Atomic Energy Commission scientist found trace evidence of prohibited activities. Taiwan accordingly promised to suspend research, although Americans worried that some officials remained committed to "keep[ing] open [a] military option."[30]

In 1976, after the US had heightened local insecurity by pulling its own nuclear weapons out, CCK announced that, using computer-simulated design research, his government had developed the capability to produce nuclear weapons. US intelligence estimated that within four years Taiwan could construct a crude explosive device deliverable by airplane regardless of any sanctions. Secret reassurance from CCK on May 27 and subsequent discussions with the foreign minister appeared inadequate after new, categorical evidence surfaced that Taipei continued seeking reprocessing capabilities. Ordered to deliver a démarche, Unger stressed that military and economic assistance was at stake.[31] CCK also saw Unger and repeatedly asserted that Taiwan conducted only peaceful research. To prove it, the US could base inspectors at his nuclear sites.

Treatment of Taiwan

Given Taiwan's utter dependency, US officials tended to make policy toward the island without consultation or much warning, without excessive thought or planning, and, frequently, with the objective of curtailing the government's access, opportunities, and maneuvering room. They called this approach the "conditioning process," through which they hoped to shape Taiwan's behavior and expectations. The US embassy in Taipei advised "sugar-coating" such conditioning, since "we have seen that problems often stem more from the form and presentation than the substance of change."[32] Those who objected fundamentally to the new direction of US policy would surely have contested this conclusion about form versus substance, but there was, nonetheless, a case to be made for preserving traditional practice and the dignity of officials when feasible.

Ambassador Unger argued for better and more frequent communication: advance notice of mainland trips, access to texts of communiqués before they became public, prompt briefings and assurances, where possible, that policies had not been fundamentally altered.[33] Unger found himself too often transmitting partial or misleading information, thus undercutting his credibility. After Unger's deputy William Gleysteen assumed duties as deputy assistant secretary of state for East Asia, he reached out to Taiwan, providing better access to information when "Kissinger refused all contact with Taiwan officials, and none of my other seniors, including [Assistant Secretary Philip] Habib, wanted to hold Taiwan's hand." But, on concrete policies, Gleysteen worked as readily as anyone "to strip away all unessential functions from our civilian and military establishments in Taiwan."[34]

Taiwan's ambassador found the Ford administration no more accessible or responsive than its predecessor. James Shen's repeated requests to pay courtesy calls, deliver letters, or be briefed rarely elicited positive replies and, when they did, were almost invariably conducted at lower levels than he had proposed. Shen had no better luck befriending a new crop of diplomats or working with old-timers than he had had in previous years. Everyone knew that CCK wanted to replace him with Chow Shu-k'ai, a sophisticated man close to Taiwan's president who was able to deal more effectively with Americans. Nevertheless, when Shen sought US approval for a new ambassador, the symbolism of renewing the Taiwan link led to rejection. State Department officials recorded that "Shen was more shaken than we have ever seen him"; they expected that "although CCK may take the news with less signs of emotion, we recognize that he will be jolted."[35] A year later, even with Shen in questionable health and another inquiry made quietly by CCK's unacknowledged son, John Chang Hsiao-yen, who was then serving at the ROC's embassy, Washington still said no.[36]

Taiwan's future security requirements, more than any other question, defined the nature of continuing involvement between Washington and Taipei and the extent to which that relationship encumbered US–China reconciliation. Beijing continued to expect that establishing relations with the US would bring recovery of Taiwan because Washington would cease being an obstacle. Beginning with Kissinger's first visit in July 1971, this idea had been central to normalization for the Chinese.

Americans did not necessarily appreciate or accept this view, but they recognized the uncertain future of an entity shunned by the international community. The makers of American policy, therefore, sought to create a framework for dealing with Taiwan that would ensure growth of economic, social, and cultural ties, but minimize political and security relations and responsibility. How far this could go without causing Taipei to despair or Beijing to act rashly became the crux of Kissinger's Taiwan problem.

While preparing for his first Ford-era China trip, Kissinger called for a new study of arms sales and a possible Chinese attack on Taiwan. National Security Studies Memorandum 212 emphasized the difficulty of advancing normalization while reassuring Taipei. If China launched an invasion, the study asserted, it would succeed unless Washington intervened or Taipei used nuclear weapons. China would attain aerial dominance, sink Taiwan's fleet, blockade its ports, and land 100,000 troops, all without significant resistance. Arms purchases from the US, however, were having beneficial results, preserving political stability, deterring development of nuclear weapons, and discouraging involvement of Soviet interlopers. The study even imagined that China might accept sales so long as Washington did not provide offensive or advanced weapons, give Taiwan independent production capabilities, or transfer materiel in huge quantities.[37]

Those closest to Kissinger believed that "it is in our interest to minimize as far as possible a direct U.S. involvement in Taiwan's future security affairs (as an arms supplier, or through a public statement of some sort committing the U.S. to the future security of the island) which over the long run would very likely prove a major irritant in our dealings with Peking." They pointed to Beijing's conviction that military sales made Taiwan less disposed toward reunification.[38] ROC officials had to be made to see that they could preserve Taiwan's security by political rather than legalistic or military means. Whereas in 1974 Ambassador Unger was permitted to endorse the Mutual Defense Treaty unambiguously, by 1975 Kissinger advised the president that "reaffirmation . . . would not now be wise." Arms sales, however, could be short-term compensation for abrogating the treaty.[39] Some types of assistance had been terminated in 1973, and Kissinger believed it would be reasonably easy to discontinue others, including weapons sales. Most treacherous, given domestic politics, would be prohibiting cash transactions for defensive weapons, but this too was necessary.

In the interim the administration had to determine which weapons systems would be destabilizing and which Taiwan needed. The State Department generally prevailed: Taiwan obtained only modest increments to its capabilities. In 1974, for instance, Taiwan requested Harpoon missiles to defend against PRC patrol boats. The Harpoon, a surface-to-surface missile slated for the US Navy, had been cleared for sale to South Korea. Unger argued that "reasonable deterrent power is one of the factors which has made for peace in the Taiwan Strait area," and that "domestic confidence in ability to defend itself is very important to political stability on Taiwan."[40] State Department and White House concern for Chinese sensitivities, however, overrode Unger and undercut the Defense Department's desire to sell Harpoons.[41]

More important than struggles over specific weapons, the larger legal problems of providing security for Taiwan after derecognition remained unresolved. State Department lawyers complained that their diplomat colleagues ignored the need for clear rights and obligations. The US could be left without legal grounds to defend Taiwan amid political expectations that it do so. The question partly concerned the future of the US–ROC Mutual Defense Treaty. Only a tiny elite knew that Nixon and Kissinger had agreed to abrogation in Beijing in 1971. The rest argued over whether, if international law did not automatically terminate the treaty with a break in diplomatic relations, derecognition of Taiwan as a state would void the pact and the US ability to defend the island.[42] At the NSC, where Brent Scowcroft had become national security adviser, analysts asserted that since the US had never "explicitly recognized Taiwan as part of China," it would not infringe on China's sovereignty in coming to Taiwan's rescue.[43]

Arms sales to Taiwan after derecognition also required a formal legitimizing structure, since US law demanded that only states or international organizations could be buyers.[44] Kissinger scoffed at the idea of any legal construct, however, believing the Chinese had the right to stop sales whenever they wanted and the US could do nothing.[45]

From the field, the ambassador and other embassy officers called on Washington to deal forthrightly with the future of Taiwan. Not until late 1975, however, did planners note "that maintenance of these [security, economic, social, and cultural] relationships with Taiwan would require amendment or enactment of a considerable body of legislation by Congress." On the eve of Ford's trip they finally concluded that the vital work must begin, counting on the probability of delay in normalization to get it done in time.

The questions Policy Planning posited in its study proved to be among the most critical the Carter administration would face in making derecognition a reality. They included not simply the broad and fundamental matters of how to sustain a military balance, but also the prosaic problems of how to continue US military training, liaison, and joint defense planning. The study discussed alternative structures for representative offices and noted that the legal underpinnings for treaties, agreements, and laws regulating and facilitating nuclear cooperation, tax and tariff and patent rights, most-favored-nation trading rights, and a series of other commercial and financial practices would all vanish and have to be reconstituted through new legislation and negotiated measures. In the end, however, the Policy Planning Staff opted for delay, concluding that "while some spadework could be done beforehand, there seems no alternative to deferring Congressional consideration of the legislative underpinnings of our post-diplomatic relations with Taiwan until after the announcement of an agreement to achieve full normalization of US/PRC relations."[46]

Worry about the sensitivity of the issues and fear of leaks led executive branch officials to minimize openness with Taiwan as well as to put off decision making. Charles W. Freeman Jr., then deputy director of the Taiwan desk, learned directly about Kissinger's "unspoken instruction not to speak honestly to Taiwan representatives about what the future might hold." When he approached Ambassador Shen about accommodating the inevitable change, "I was roundly chastised for talking to him about this."[47] Leonard Unger had no better luck writing to Winston Lord in January 1975, arguing against surprise. He warned Lord that unruly military and security forces as well as a distraught public could contest Chiang's grasp on power. Potential tumult in Taiwan, however, never competed effectively with politics in Washington.[48]

Dealing with Beijing on the Taiwan Issue

Despite the elaborate choreography of Ford's first days in office, Beijing had little patience with the course of normalization and resolution of the Taiwan issue. Zhou Enlai responded to Ford's letter to Mao in an "aloof" manner and Kissinger could not elicit any enthusiasm from Beijing for the prospect of his next visit. When a congressional delegation led by Senator J. William Fulbright (D-Ark.), chairman of the Senate Foreign Relations Committee, traveled to the China in September 1974, Beijing took the opportunity to send a harsh message to the American people.

The US Liaison Office in Beijing, fearing trouble, tried to keep the members of the delegation from focusing on Taiwan, but vice foreign minister Qiao Guanhua frustrated this strategy. He immediately insisted on abrogation of the Mutual Defense Treaty and rebuffed Senator Hiram L. Fong's (R-Hawaii) favorable comments about dialogue between China and Taiwan, declaring that "peaceful reunification is an impossibility." Mao had confronted Kissinger with this view years before, but Kissinger had kept it from the now nonplussed politicians. Chairman of the House Foreign Affairs Committee Clement J. Zablocki (D-Wisc.) asked what the alternative to negotiation would be, and Qiao starkly responded, "It is simple logic. The opposite of a peaceful solution is a non-peaceful solution."[49] One angered member of the delegation later told Kissinger that he believed rapprochement was nothing more than a "ploy" for recovering Taiwan.

As Kissinger prepared to meet with Qiao the following month in New York and to travel to Beijing in November, he and his advisers remained optimistic that normalization could proceed, requiring only the modification of Chinese terms regarding Taiwan. In fact, Hummel, Lord, and Solomon argued that a short-term impasse might actually be positive. It would remind the Chinese of the importance of relations and strengthen Mao and his allies who advocated them. Further, it would demonstrate that constraints such as national interest and domestic politics really did shape Ford administration behavior.[50]

Kissinger, however, could not sell his message. His suggestions that Washington had to have terms more generous than Tokyo's and more expansive than those he had proposed in 1973, providing a liaison office or a consulate in Taiwan as well as a defense tie, proved unacceptable. The Chinese did not see a consulate in Taiwan as compatible with one China.

Deng Xiaoping, lacking Zhou Enlai's finesse and Mao's tendency to speak in indirect fragments, bluntly expressed China's dissatisfaction with US policies. Kissinger sought to explain: "To us the question of the defense commitment is primarily a question of the way it can be presented politically. It is not a question of maintaining it for an indefinite period of time." But Deng refused to bend, doubtless recalling that Zhou had been criticized in 1973 for being too flexible in talks with Kissinger.[51] Both the Mutual Defense Treaty and all vestiges of official representation should go. China would not commit to peaceful tactics and there would be no lengthy interval between American departure and China's takeover. "What reason is there," Deng asked rhetorically, "to drag the Taiwan issue [along] like . . . Vietnam . . . into such an untidy mess?!" Defeated, Kissinger affirmed Deng's three Taiwan principles (break relations, abolish the treaty, regard Taiwan as an internal matter) without any of the palliative additions he and his China specialists had envisioned. When Kissinger left Beijing, he had no face-saving Taiwan agreement, no viable draft communiqué for Ford's visit, and no clear path by which to avoid serious problems during the summit.[52]

The Chinese became less willing to compromise as the president's trip neared. In preparation, Kissinger sought interim steps that would not presuppose a break with Taiwan, but would please Beijing. He made clear that this would be the best Washington could do until after Ford's reelection. The Chinese, however, had no interest in cosmetic changes and refused to undertake substantive advances until the US had relinquished Taiwan. Deng had earlier told a group from the American Society of

Newspaper Editors that using force to eliminate the Taiwan authorities would be like "removing dust from a floor with the aid of a broom."[53]

Thus, the president began the December trip with no last-minute agreements to conclude while in Beijing, no formula on Taiwan that he could accept on the eve of an election. As the president told Deng, "We can't just cast aside old friends."[54] On the other hand, Ford undid the damage to US–China relations wrought by Kissinger's dismal 1974 visit. Ford indicated that he would abandon the idea of a liaison office in Taipei, would use the Japanese model, and would complete normalization during his first full term as president, having just learned the previous month that Nixon had privately "accepted" the one-China principle. Finally, he did not insist the Chinese renounce force even though the CIA warned that China had begun preparations to invade Taiwan within five years.[55]

On the heels of Ford's visit, domestic upheaval in China made flexibility on Sino-American relations or the Taiwan question unlikely. Zhou Enlai, who had organized and carried forward the opening to the United States, died of cancer in January 1976. He left behind Deng to tend to the relationship, but Deng's political roots were shallow, and he was purged by a coalition of radicals. Mao Zedong continued to guide policy on the US and Taiwan, but by June his infirmities overwhelmed him, and in September he was dead. As power shifted in the summer of 1976, anti-American diatribes became more common, especially regarding Taiwan.[56] Vice Premier Zhang Chunqiao, a rabid member of the so-called Gang of Four, declared a peaceful resolution of the Taiwan issue undesirable, telling Senate Minority Leader Hugh Scott, "It is more reliable to settle this question through a war." Preparations, he added, had begun and the PLA would cut off this "noose around the neck of the U.S."[57] Kissinger argued that tough talk compensated for a lack of action. Thomas Gates, former defense secretary and Bush's successor as liaison office chief, however, shared Scott's alarm that Zhang might be serious.[58]

Heightened antagonism on the Taiwan issue extended beyond the small radical grouping at the top. Other Chinese leaders were also angered at a perceived resurgence of US and Japanese interest in Taiwan's security and presumed fostering of two Chinas. PLA military exercises, planned before the leftist ascendancy, exceeded anything attempted since 1962, when CKS had been threatening to attack the mainland and Beijing feared Kennedy would assist him. Not only did the PLA mobilize the army and air force, it also mounted amphibious operations to mimic landings on Taiwan. ROC intelligence warned that Beijing might seize an indefensible target such as Pratas Reef, almost three hundred miles off Taiwan's southern coast. But US interagency estimates minimized the buildup, and Scowcroft told Ford that Taipei hoped to "excite fears of PRC intentions," possibly seeking to interfere in the outcome of the US presidential campaign.[59]

By October Kissinger had grown angry and bitter about conservative attacks. Besieged on issues such as détente, he could not even pursue his China triumph. He told his advisers that China would attack Taiwan as soon as the US relinquished its position in the Strait, and he warned, "For us to go to war with a recognized country where we have an ambassador over part of what we recognize as their country would be preposterous!"[60]

Kissinger would not have to sort it out. Ford lost the 1976 election and Taiwan's nemesis disappeared. But Kissinger's frustration and the absence of recognition of China by the United States did not alleviate anxiety, gloom, or distrust in Taipei. The Americans continued to pursue Beijing and, meanwhile, the Taiwan issue was ignored. Domestic politics in the US and China protected Taiwan's interests—by distracting Washington and Beijing—more than Taiwan itself.

MORAL IMPERATIVES;
MILITARY CHALLENGES

JIMMY CARTER entered the presidency with amorphous ideas about foreign affairs. The Soviet Union quickly took precedence. Carter and his secretary of state, Cyrus Vance, believed in the desirability and possibility of a new détente. It would be centered on arms control, which Vance pursued eagerly while Carter cut military expenditures.

Carter also sought to bring justice and equity to Washington's foreign policies. He would not support dictators just because they averred anticommunism; rather, he planned to hew to strict moral principles abroad. He emphasized the importance of reversing Teddy Roosevelt and returning the Panama Canal to Panamanians despite fervent conservative opposition focused on security of access (1977). He risked his personal prestige and influence to bring Egyptian and Israeli leaders to the US to sign an unprecedented peace accord at Camp David (1978).

The US did not fare as well elsewhere. In Nicaragua civil conflict brought the left-leaning Sandinistas to power over US opposition (1979), and in El Salvador brutal death squads and civil war spread chaos and economic ruin (1980–92). American ignorance and complacency led to missteps in Iran, where alignment with the shah produced a protracted hostage crisis at the US Embassy (1979–80). Finally, Carter's hopes for better relations with the Soviets collapsed when Moscow launched an invasion of

Afghanistan (1979). By then the anti-Soviet National Security Adviser Zbigniew Brzezinski had displaced Vance as the president's key foreign affairs adviser.

Beijing watched the new administration with chagrin because it ignored China, seemed willing to appease Moscow, and articulated a threatening human rights agenda. When Carter finally raised the issue of normalization, however, Washington allayed Chinese unease by offering military ties, most-favored-nation trade preferences, and silence on China's dissident human rights movement (Democracy Wall, 1978–79). Further, Carter not only refused to condemn China's invasion of Vietnam (1979); he rendered assistance by sharing valuable, and otherwise unobtainable, intelligence. For administration officials, recruiting China to join the anti-Soviet struggle, which had motivated Nixon and Kissinger, became increasingly important. Congress agreed, but sought simultaneously to protect Taiwan, ignoring administration opposition.

CHAPTER FIVE

Derecognition

NEITHER THE United States nor Taiwan proved ready for the events of 1978–79, even though both had had ample time to prepare. Throughout the previous decade, American leaders had focused on the challenge of establishing relations with China. They had worried about persuading the isolated and unpredictable Chinese communists that cooperation against the Soviet Union would be advantageous. They had spent countless hours calculating how to overcome real and imagined domestic resistance to a logical, beneficial, and long-overdue policy. By comparison, planning for the diminished role of Taiwan—an ally that would soon cease to be an ally, a state that would no longer be recognized by many states, and an erstwhile international player that would become peripheral to world affairs—appeared unglamorous and burdensome. Consequently it received little attention.

On the Taiwan side, by the mid-1970s leaders understood the inevitability of derecognition, although they refused to discuss it and devised no better response than delay. They endured humiliation as American diplomats sought to force acknowledgment of their hopeless situation. Critics would later say that with a willingness to change, Taiwan could have negotiated a better or, at least, less onerous future. Perhaps, but it is not clear that the opportunity existed, and the requisite mutual trust was absent.[1]

Sorting Out the China-Taiwan Issue

Jimmy Carter's campaign and his first months in office obscured his intention to establish full diplomatic relations with the PRC. On the road he insisted, "I would be reluctant to give up our relationship with the Republic of China," unless the US could safeguard the Taiwan people from coercion and oppression.[2] Moreover, after his inauguration he quickly met the PRC's Washington representative, declaring he would observe the Shanghai Communiqué, but he immediately moved on to emphasize other issues. His Asia staff had to plead for attention lest he squander his opportunity to shape the region's future.[3]

Meanwhile, the NSC and State Department sorted out what Nixon, Ford, and Kissinger had promised to, and accomplished with, China. Carter had been partly briefed by Kissinger. To sharpen the picture, Cyrus Vance, as secretary of state designate, assembled a group with Asia experience in December 1976, including Richard Holbrooke, soon to be assistant secretary for East Asia and Pacific Affairs at the State Department; Michel Oksenberg, who would become the key China specialist at the NSC; Anthony Lake, Vance's choice to head Policy Planning; and Deputy Assistant Secretary of State William Gleysteen. Partly at the urging of Mao Zedong's translator Nancy Tang Wensheng, the series of conversations between Mao, Kissinger, and Nixon were unearthed despite Kissinger's reluctance, and Oksenberg, Holbrooke, and Gleysteen studied the strategic, legal, and political problems associated with normalization.[4]

Holbrooke, an early member of Carter's foreign policy team, entered the State Department committed to rapid recognition of China. His enthusiasm for normalization drew him to Oksenberg and the White House, whereas his strong personal and bureaucratic identification with Vance and the State Department caused him to defend their views. Holbrooke's personality and style thrust him to the center of many disputes. One foreign service officer described reviewing decisions with Holbrooke: "He would often have a meeting, with two television sets going, on different channels, and while he was reading a newspaper, he would be discussing a policy issue. He had a notoriously short attention span."[5]

The conspicuous, clearly mutual bitterness between Holbrooke and Zbigniew Brzezinski, Carter's national security adviser, complicated cooperation between the NSC and State Department, but the degree to which it affected policy toward Taiwan and China remains unclear. Holbrooke's animosity toward Brzezinski surfaced even before the inauguration, which alienated Carter, who later blamed him for press leaks.[6] It also influenced the relationship between Holbrooke and Oksenberg. Oksenberg vehemently denied undue friction, asserting, "To be sure, there were . . . moments of rivalry and tension, but the main story I would stress is the pursuit of common objectives," which included "regular State, DOD, NSC consultations."

According to Gleysteen, "Brzezinski and Oksenberg . . . enjoyed . . . cutting out Holbrooke—and infuriating him." In China, "Brzezinski's behavior was outrageous, particularly his delight in humiliating Holbrooke and the State Department both in private and public—behavior that would have been unimaginable for his Chinese hosts, who of course took careful note of this gratuitous advertisement of strains within the American camp," recalled Gleysteen. "On the plane on the way home, resentments boiled over [leading to a] disgusting shouting match among all of us and the threat of a school yard physical battle between Holbrooke and Oksenberg."[7]

Brzezinski voiced no surprised. "It's like two generals wanting to lead an army in battle. They want the same victory, but each would like to be the commander in chief of the operation, and, I think, that was a little bit at stake here. The State Department wanted to have the action on it. The president felt, and I shared the view, that if we did it through the State Department we would never get it done."[8] Ironically, when writing the recognition communiqué, Oksenberg borrowed Roger Sullivan from the State Department to speed drafting, which meant that Sullivan had to call in sick so that Holbrooke would not know he was working at the White House.

Oksenberg, a political scientist from the University of Michigan, came to Washington dedicated to ending years of dithering over recognition of China. His efforts as an outsider to push the Ford administration to act had been frustrated by the president's political weakness. Now, as a member of the White House staff, he could make his knowledge, charm, and determination count. As his boss, Brzezinski, recalled, Oksenberg "play[ed] a central role in moving the American-Chinese relationship forward, in developing the conceptual framework for it."[9]

Brzezinski had his own agenda. Even though "I knew that publicly one had to make pious noises to the effect that U.S.–Chinese normalization had nothing to do with U.S.–Soviet rivalry," he wrote in his memoir, Brzezinski understood the "Soviet dimension" as the crucial reason to go forward. And, because stopping Moscow motivated him, Brzezinski, as much as if not more than Kissinger, ignored the bothersome interference of

Taiwan and its supporters. Brzezinski observed many years later, "If Taiwan had been by then a flourishing democracy, a very successful example of development, perhaps the significance of that fact might have arisen. But that was not the case."[10]

At Oksenberg's recommendation, Brzezinski urged Carter immediately to affirm "Nixon's Five Points," which had accepted Chinese terms regarding Taiwan's status. Only the strong objection of the secretary of state, rooted as much in bureaucratic rivalry as in concern about Taipei, delayed this early and unexamined decision on Taiwan policy.[11] Holbrooke, a not unbiased source, remarked, "Zbig just didn't give a goddamn about Taiwan . . . like Kissinger, Zbig was a big-nation chauvinist."[12] In fact, when meeting with Deng, Brzezinski sought to emphasize that after a "historically transitional period" of indeterminate length, "the existence of some separate Chinese entities . . . will come to an end," but that Washington expected this would happen "peacefully."[13]

Vance, by contrast, sought relations with China as an end in itself and not a bludgeon to wield against the Soviets. Absent Brzezinski's ulterior motive, he also lacked his sense of urgency. Further, temperamentally Vance could not have been more different from the irrepressible Brzezinski, whose brash intensity and toughness clashed with the secretary's subdued and gentlemanly demeanor. Vance preferred measured progress and careful planning for both normalization and the complex Taiwan question. He would later assert, "Since we were determined not to jeopardize the security of Taiwan, I did not feel we could simply accept . . . [China's] conditions. They could, however, provide a framework for our discussions."[14]

In reality, Vance's approach on Taiwan, although more deliberate, substantively proved much the same. As he wrote in his memoir, he believed relations with Taiwan ought to be unofficial and that the defense treaty needed to be terminated, though he felt that the agreement should not be cut off abruptly, but rather according to its provisions. Vance understood the importance of arms sales and the constituencies determined to preserve those sales. He wrestled with pressures from Congress—dispatching Holbrooke to work with key members—and the entreaties from Taiwan's insecure government. He also felt keenly the fears of other states such as Israel, which would judge Carter's reliability in part by this policy. Finally, Vance believed it crucial that Beijing not use "rhetoric about 'liberating' Taiwan by force," even though eliminating such language constituted a cosmetic change. The secretary claimed subsequently, "I would have to be clear and firm on those positions in internal policy discussions, for some of the president's advisers, particularly Zbig, were so anxious to move rapidly toward normalization that they seemed ready to compromise the well-being of the people of Taiwan."[15]

The record of interaction with the Chinese that Oksenberg assembled clarified the problems that previous administrations had failed to resolve but provided no easy solutions. Once the euphoria of the opening had been overtaken by domestic political disarray in the US and China, Beijing grew less patient, telling US officials that their country "owes China a debt," given its interference in the Chinese civil war. It would brook no US efforts to assist or defend Taiwan but welcomed pressure on Taipei to reach an accommodation with the PRC. Jimmy Carter, in turn, read the past exchanges and insisted that efforts to settle outstanding issues be managed so that "we should not ass-kiss them the way Nixon and Kissinger did."[16] This did not mean Carter valued the Taiwan relationship more or that he would extend himself to protect it.

Actual administration policy became clearer in the spring of 1977 with the articulation of Presidential Review Memorandum 24. It set out four options for establishing relations with Beijing: (1) a full embrace, following the Japanese model, which required renunciation of all formal ties to Taiwan; (2) a partial advance, recognizing the PRC while retaining diplomatic and military links to the ROC; (3) a unilateral effort, whereby Washington reduced ties on its own terms; or (4) a reserved relationship, which preserved the official status quo but expanded military and intelligence contacts with Beijing.

Although the presidential review committee unanimously recommended the full embrace, Brzezinski sought to move even more vigorously toward Beijing and away from Taipei.[17] Gleysteen later recalled that "at the outset, every one agreed that we had to be careful about Taiwan, since we had a lot at stake there and would have the world watching to see how we dealt with an ally. . . . I was certain Vance would not be a party to any deal undermining Taiwan."[18] Brzezinski's zeal, therefore, caused friction. But Carter shared the national security adviser's absorption in the new relationship and viewed Taiwan as an annoyance, almost an adversary. "In the absence of consistent presidential leadership," Carter wrote later, "Taiwanese lobbyists seemed to prevail in shaping United States policy." He would not let Taipei's legendary influence peddling—the giving of gifts and embarrassing favors to his friends in Plains, Georgia—derail normalization.[19]

Others in the administration felt the need to compensate Taipei, and arms sales became the point of the most contentious debates within official circles. Senior Nationalist government officials complained to the press that they had submarines without torpedoes, outdated destroyers without

Dick Wright

missiles, and an air force shockingly outnumbered by the PRC. One such official confided, "To be honest, we all feel very vulnerable."[20] Thus, the value of US military supplies provided to Taiwan surged from roughly $60 million in 1976 to $153 million in 1977. Even so, Morton I. Abramowitz, assistant secretary for international security affairs at the Department of Defense, told Michael Armacost at the NSC, "We should get off our ass and start approving the Taiwan arms cases right away." Aware of White House dynamics, he reminded Armacost, "Including this bit in any memo for the president makes the problem more complicated than it is."[21]

Controversy surrounded arms sales. No one wanted to anger the president or evoke bad memories of the final days of arms transfers to Vietnam.[22] Further, the administration could not reach consensus on the single most important weapon—a plane to replace Taiwan's aging fighter aircraft, which, the Joint Chiefs of Staff (JCS) estimated, would begin crashing in significant numbers by the end of 1981. The choice least likely to anger China, and therefore most appealing to the State Department, was to increase Taiwan's force of relatively unsophisticated and short-range Northrop F-5Es, planes that posed no threat to the mainland. The Defense Department, in favor of protecting Taiwan from the communists and safeguarding the administration from the Taiwan lobby, wanted to sell the General Dynamics F-4, a more capable, all-weather aircraft.[23] The NSC, which initially favored the F-4, reversed its position during the long debate.[24]

A third option involved purchase of a non-American plane. Taiwan considered buying sixty Israeli Kfir jets, whose capabilities fell between the two US models. General Electric would earn some $200 million in licensing fees for the plane's engines, but the US would not actually supply the aircraft. Oksenberg opposed the Kfir, however, arguing that it was too sophisticated and would alarm Beijing. Moreover, he cast doubt on the wisdom of identifying Israel with Taiwan, lest this endanger Israeli security and thereby harm the US.[25] Israel did not share his worries and claimed to have "obtained China's tacit approval."[26] But Chiang Ching-kuo opposed weakening his US connection by purchasing major weapons systems from non-American suppliers. His preference, as he told Ambassador Unger, was development of an upgraded F-5E. He may also have been nervous about a high-profile purchase from Israel, given Taiwan's dependence on Saudi Arabian oil.[27]

In the end, Carter rejected all advice regarding Taiwan's needs and China's demands. Subject to domestic political pressures as the presidential campaign heated up in the spring of 1980, he decided to allow both Northrop and General Dynamics to resume competition for design of an export aircraft that Taiwan could buy. His successor would have to make the choice Carter refused to make.

Taiwan's Reactions to Carter

From the beginning, Taipei had few options for deterring the Carter administration from its set course. Seeking to accommodate Carter's professed priorities, CCK launched a year of human rights observance in Taiwan in December 1976. Only days after the inauguration, the head of Taiwan's Central News Agency, Jimmy Wei Ching-meng, one of CCK's close friends, breakfasted with the NSC press spokesman and asserted that the fate of Taiwan's people qualified as a human rights issue and should be of concern to a man with Carter's reputation.[28]

The Taiwanese could not, however, ignore Carter's pursuit of normalization. To be sure that Washington's intentions were clear, Holbrooke visited Taiwan in April 1977 to speak directly to CCK.[29] He returned in August to brief CCK on Secretary Vance's visit to China, pointing out that, although both Beijing and Washington considered the disputes regarding representation in Taiwan a setback, the US remained committed to severing the Taiwan security treaty, withdrawing US troops, and ending recognition. CCK took the news with equanimity—to worried Americans, far too much equanimity—insisting that he also believed in the concept of one China and differed only in locating the capital in Taipei. Since the

United States would ultimately find it impossible to reach a settlement with Beijing, ROC officials had no reason to worry.

In fact, Chiang had no intention of remaining quiescent in the face of Carter's determined march toward derecognition. Most dramatically, he pushed yet again to obtain nuclear arms and missile capabilities. On January 27, 1977, shortly after Carter's inauguration, CCK announced support for the new president's ban on atomic testing and renewed earlier pledges "never [to] engage in the production of such weapons." As before, his secret orders to continue research became apparent when aerial surveillance conclusively established ongoing isotope separation activities at Taiwan's main atomic facility, the Institute of Nuclear Energy Research (INER).[30]

Carter's people decided to crack down hard, threatening not just nuclear but other cooperative programs if Taipei refused to end or redirect its atomic programs. Vice Foreign Minister Fred Ch'ien complained to a US delegation that Washington followed a double standard that allowed French and West German sales of similar reprocessing facilities to Brazil and Pakistan. He asked anxiously about penalties for ignoring US warnings, confirming Taiwan's surreptitious behavior, but also leading the US ambassador to speculate that Ch'ien sought ammunition to defeat bureaucratic advocates of weapons. Soon he would have to.[31]

Officials reluctantly signed a highly limiting agreement disrupting a variety of nuclear projects. It caused considerable discontent among some scientists and officials who blamed US accommodation of Beijing or Washington's insistence on a uranium fuel monopoly.[32] By July 1978 intelligence again suspected nuclear activities and the US confronted CCK. Clearly "annoyed and disturbed," Chiang declared he had repeatedly pledged his cooperation; he had accepted the negative effects on his scientists and avoided a public controversy, but the US continued to challenge his integrity and treat Taiwan "in a fashion which few other countries would tolerate."[33]

In Washington, meanwhile, Taiwan placed spies in government agencies to gather information and, if possible, disrupt US–China normalization. William Gleysteen described Taiwan's operations under the guiding hand of Wang Hsi-ling as "an aggressive, out-of-channel attempt to jump the White House." Michel Oksenberg similarly believed Taiwan would find out most everything because "they had a lot of friends." In 1977, accordingly, the administration placed Taiwan on its "criteria list" of hostile foreign intelligence services that required monitoring, making it the first friendly government to be treated that way. Its diplomats also came under surveillance that included use of national security wiretaps.[34]

At the same time US rules almost completely isolated James Shen from senior officials in the US government, depriving him of the ability to deliver Taipei's message and undermining his authority. Within his own embassy, Shen had to cope with competitors for CCK's ear in a pattern reminiscent of the 1940s, when Madame Chiang Kai-shek regularly interfered with the work of the ROC ambassador. One deputy had a direct avenue to the president's office, and the men in charge of military and intelligence affairs used their private channels to devalue Shen's reporting and advice in Taipei.

Brzezinski in particular avoided Shen. Oksenberg obtained Brzezinski's agreement for a briefing to follow his China trip—a minimal gesture since he had arranged to arrive in Beijing on the day of Chiang Ching-kuo's inauguration as president and made no effort to correct the error or alleviate the insult. But Brzezinski refused to follow up, rebuffing pleas and reminders despite Oksenberg's awareness that culturally he had disgraced and discredited Shen. In his disdain for Shen and Taipei, however, Brzezinski was not alone. Even while admonishing him, Oksenberg noted that seeing Shen was "unpleasant . . . for all of us." Later Brzezinski would say that he had nothing to offer Taiwan and wanted to avoid lying to Shen.[35]

When Brzezinski embarked on his Beijing journey, Taipei remained without a useful plan of action for response to the inexorable progress toward derecognition. CCK had his America expert, Fred Ch'ien, analyze the mission and outline policy alternatives. What, Chiang wanted to know, might the government do if Brzezinski's trip was successful, and what actions ought he take if Washington decided to break relations. Informal advice from the US side insistently called on the ROC to adjust to a new and lesser status.

John Chang Hsiao-yen had transmitted this message from Washington in 1977 after State Department officers Burton Levin and Chas Freeman warned him that "the storm was gathering," and Taipei must prepare. Chang had cultivated and been cultivated by young US diplomats who knew him to be CCK's illegitimate son as well as a capable official and hoped that messages entrusted to him would find their way to the president. No one knew for sure: virtually all ROC officials denied that Chang had contact with CCK, but Chang himself occasionally hinted that a memo or a telephone call might get through.

Chang, like everyone else, found Taiwan's Foreign Minister Shen Chang-huan unresponsive, someone who preferred to ignore bad news from Washington. Even though Shen spoke excellent English, he had not lived abroad, rarely traveled, and displayed noticeable anti-Americanism. Critics thought him incompetent, obsequious, and opinionated, like overcooked food you "cannot chew . . . cannot swallow . . . and cannot cut."

Unsurprisingly, warnings from self-described young Turks in the embassy (like Chang and C. J. Chen) did not persuade him.

Similarly, his tradition-bound ministry denied the seriousness of Taiwan's situation and the need to talk to the US government about the future. James Soong Chu-yu later lamented that traditionalists like Shen ignored inevitable trouble, declaiming, "If you don't see the coffin, you can hold back your tears" (bujian wan tsai, buren liu li).[36]

In Washington and Taipei, those whom CCK actually relied on remained unclear. Chang described Shen as CCK's close confidant who, as foreign minister and secretary general of the president's office, strongly influenced the president's perceptions. Mark Pratt, the embassy's political counselor, disagreed, arguing that Shen's residual loyalties to CCK's nemesis, Madame Chiang Kai-shek, had led CCK to trust Ch'ien and Soong more.[37]

The problem went beyond resistance in one ministry. Roger Sullivan, who had been involved with Nixon's China opening, arrived in Taipei in June 1977 as deputy chief of mission with a mandate discreetly to initiate conversations about future developments. At this he signally failed. Looking back, he remarked that after Holbrooke's frustrating trip to Taipei, "I don't think anybody actually said this was a waste of time . . . but we discussed . . . that they just had their heads in the sand and . . . when things began to move very fast after the Brzezinski trip . . . not only wasn't it useful to talk to them, but it was probably dangerous." Even American-educated Chinese scholars and overseas Chinese found that the local press resisted publishing articles and letters addressing Taiwan's fate and necessary change.[38]

CCK and his inner circle had entrusted their long-term survival to a policy of delay. In part Chiang saw this as a practical decision to build the economy and initiate political reforms so that there would be as much progress as possible before the United States acted on normalization. At the same time, Chiang and his advisers feared they could accelerate normalization by seeming to accept it. Officials in the US might feel freer to compromise Taiwan's interests in negotiations with Beijing, and friends of Taiwan might be disillusioned enough to end their resistance against recognition.

American officials understood these tactics. Richard Holbrooke recalled thinking, "When you start planning for something you are totally opposed to, you are admitting it is going to happen, so that is why some people don't get life insurance." Cynics suspected that, because of encouragement from the ROC lobby in Congress, CCK may have believed that recognition could actually be stopped. In Taipei people clung to the hope that whatever the Americans might want to do, in the end they would not just abandon Taiwan.[39]

If delay was the key, distrust also played a role. Holbrooke's offers to work with Taiwan officials to plan for the future clashed with his clear preference for recognition of China as soon as possible. Rumors that Sullivan had been put in place to take over from Unger when the US downgraded the embassy in Taiwan discredited Sullivan. As a known advocate for relations with Beijing, he found that "the more I tried [to discuss the future], the worse it got. I tried it at all sorts of levels. Tried it with some of the military people. Tried it with Fred Ch'ien, but every time I would bring up anything, Fred would say . . . you are not going to establish diplomatic relations with the communists so forget about it. There is nothing to discuss. . . . By February 1978 or so we were . . . talking nice-nice to each other and not communicating."[40]

On the other side, the policy of restraint and compliance left US officials free to pay little attention to Taiwan. After Brzezinski's trip to Beijing, Unger met with CCK, who reiterated that, despite Washington's misguided policy, he sought to sustain US–Taiwan relations largely unaltered. Chiang had in times past broken ties with untrustworthy associates who flirted with the communists, but here the stakes were too high, and in July 1978 the CIA told the White House that CCK would be accommodating so long as he could count on trade, investment, and arms sales.[41] James Lilley, the national intelligence officer for East Asia, who considered the Carter administration's "policy making . . . akin to a steamroller," sought through a National Security Study Memorandum to urge "more examination of the terrain [that] would allow us to chart a wiser path through complicated issues"; he got nowhere.[42]

The small circle of Americans privy to the prolonged progress of negotiations believed that secrecy remained absolute. Recalling the strict regimen surrounding the talks and the last-minute breakthroughs, J. Stapleton Roy, the deputy in Beijing, asserted, "Strategically they saw it coming. Tactically they weren't able to get the advance information they needed in order to use it." Ambassador Shen reinforced that assessment in his memoir when he laid out the reasoning at the embassy and presumably in Taipei. Analysts had concluded Carter would not establish relations in the immediate future for a number of reasons: (1) negotiation of the Strategic Arms Limitation Treaty (SALT) took priority; (2) Vance was preoccupied with Middle Eastern affairs; (3) there had been no consultation with the Senate, as required by the so-called Dole-Stone amendment to the International Security Assistance Act of 1978, which although nonbinding seemed an important milestone; (4) Congress was in recess; and (5) Carter's religiosity precluded action during the Christmas season. In retrospect, Brzezinski added, "That this was the trend was quite clear, but that this was about to happen I don't think that that was clear, because it was quite tightly held. My goodness, even the assistant secretary of state for East Asian Affairs was pretty much kept out of it."[43]

Yet in October US clandestine services discovered that Taiwan intelligence expected US recognition of China before February 1979—Carter aimed for January 1.[44] In November these same sources found that the Ministry of National Defense had, for what appeared to be the first time, briefed its officers on the impending shift in relations. They were told little would change since in effect the U.S. Embassy in Taiwan had already been downgraded and the liaison offices had long been operating as embassies. US military units remaining in Taiwan had no real defense role, so the island would not be more vulnerable as a result.[45]

THOSE WHO guarded the precise details of recognition did so assuming that there was a useful secret to be discovered. If Taipei knew the precise sequence of events, ROC officials, working with anticommunists in the US Congress, could somehow prevent progress. This was an American article of faith at the time and has been repeated regularly since.

In reality, there was no such secret. Everyone knew recognition was coming, and whether that happened in December or March was largely irrelevant. Taipei had enough support in the Congress to protect it against abandonment, but not enough to stand in the way of diplomatic relations with China. If it could have mounted a formidable campaign to stop recognition, it would have done so in the closing days of 1978. Given existing signals and suspicions rife in Taipei and Washington, whatever forces could be rallied were already in place.

Taiwan's machinations, moreover, meant less to Deng than the Taiwan bargain that had been negotiated. Taiwan could prevent recognition only if it could cause a revolt in Congress, which it could not, or block Beijing. Deng Xiaoping had, reluctantly and with caveats, proved willing to acquiesce on arms sales, the issue most distasteful to him and most likely to jeopardize his bargain. Taiwan lobbying, though potentially irksome, would have been unlikely to scare him away.

CHAPTER SIX

Final Act

INDECISIVENESS CHARACTERIZED the Carter administration's first efforts at negotiation with Beijing. The president's domestic vulnerability and the political risk of appearing to undermine Taiwan reduced the appeal even of a policy that would weaken Moscow and make it more compliant. When on July 30, 1977, Carter astonished his advisers by instructing Vance to reach an agreement on establishing relations during his August visit to Beijing, the president had not decided the terms of a viable accord or what he would need to protect himself on the Taiwan issue. Almost as soon as Vance had left Washington, Carter regretted his impulsiveness, given Vice President Walter Mondale's warning that, in Congress, progress on China could jeopardize support for ratification of the Panama Canal Treaties.

Vance's Taiwan Trouble in Beijing

As a result, Vance's negotiating posture became contradictory and ultimately angered the Chinese. Vance later described it as a politically driven "maximum position."[1] He told Foreign Minister Huang Hua that once relations had been established, "the [Mutual Defense] Treaty would lapse, all U.S. military installations, advisors and other forces would be withdrawn, and all military credits would come to an end." On the other hand, in a move that Beijing denounced for violating agreements authorized by Nixon and Ford, he asserted that Washington's many responsibilities necessitated "as a practical matter" that "U.S. Government personnel . . . remain on Taiwan under an informal arrangements [*sic*]," in an institution that "would not be diplomatic in character": no flags flying, "no Government Seal would be on the door, and no names would appear in diplomatic lists."[2]

Vance's visit swiftly deteriorated. Even before he spoke, the Chinese had taken a "confrontational rather than an accommodating stance," according to Michel Oksenberg, so the unwelcome US backtracking was not the trigger.[3] Huang Hua harshly condemned US aggression against China and asserted that Americans only paid "lip-service" to fulfilling China's conditions for normalization.[4] Deng Xiaoping compared Vance to Kissinger, who had been more accommodating. As recently as 1974, Kissinger had acknowledged concessions to Mao and Zhou—Washington's withdrawal from Taiwan, its abrogation of relations with the ROC, and its nullification of the Mutual Defense Treaty (MDT)—without expecting anything in return. Deng reminded Vance that Ford too had accepted the Japanese formula for establishing relations.

Deng also appeared deliberately to misunderstand Vance, pointedly rejecting any expectation that China would renounce force. Deng sarcastically noted, "We Chinese do have the ability to solve our own issues. There is no need whatever for American friends to worry themselves." As for a semidiplomatic US mission in Taiwan, Deng dismissed the thought, commenting acerbically, "You want an embassy that does not have a sign on its door."[5]

Any thought of presenting the Chinese with the draft communiqué that had resulted from hours of deliberations between Vance, Carter, and Brzezinski at Camp David vanished. Vance's priorities, in any case, precluded a breakthrough on relations with China, since the administration had too much at stake on Panama and SALT.[6]

The confrontational demeanor of the Chinese that Oksenberg noted reflected leadership instability in the wake of Mao's death. Deng had been rehabilitated only the month before, and his commitment to support Hua Guofeng as party chairman and head of state seemed unlikely to endure. He did not want to be perceived as pandering to Washington, and he saw advantages in insisting publicly that the US take China's views more seriously. A newspaper story suggesting the NSC appreciated Chinese flexibility on Taiwan elicited an angry denial by Deng to an American press delegation.[7]

The failure of the secretary's trip and Taiwan's plight in no way diminished Brzezinski's enthusiasm for the Chinese connection, stimulated by heightening tensions with the Soviets and the intensifying struggle with Vance. Whereas Oksenberg feared it had become politically impossible for Carter to settle for anything other than a liaison office, Brzezinski's special assistant, Rick Inderfurth, saw the development as evidence that "we're obviously not 'crawling away' . . . from Taiwan."[8] Having established friendly relations with the acting head of the Chinese Liaison Office, Han Xu, a bright and affable diplomat with excellent English, Brzezinski relentlessly pressed Carter to send him to Beijing to accomplish what Vance had been unable to do. Oksenberg and Armacost encouraged his interest, planning a series of moves that they hoped would yield recognition by the middle of 1979.

To this end, the Oksenberg-Armacost recommendation sought to "recreate a sense of the inevitability of normalization, partly to make Taiwan aware of our resolve." They called for public education on the importance of relations with China. They proposed that a "respected, knowledgeable, discreet lawyer" be brought in to "critique and assist" the State Department Legal Bureau in studying arrangements for future relations with Taipei because "it is essential that the legal work be invulnerable to Congressional probing." Particularly given the problems that later befell the administration's Taiwan omnibus bill and Brzezinski's assertion that a shortage of time and need for secrecy made it impossible fully to protect Taiwan, this early planning suggests opportunities existed to do more.

Oksenberg and Armacost also called for more troop withdrawals, redistribution of personnel to different Asian locations, and reevaluation of intelligence collaboration. They even urged announcement of a package of "major arms sales to the ROC" to shield Carter from charges of abandoning Taipei as disentanglement moved forward.[9]

Finally, in the spring of 1978, Brzezinski set out for China with a mandate from Carter to accelerate normalization. A May 10 memo to the president from Vance, Brzezinski, and Secretary of Defense Harold Brown proposed a unified negotiating posture, recanting the liaison-consulate office initiative rejected by Beijing and explicitly affirming Nixon's so-called Five Points.[10] Brzezinski assured Vice Premier Deng that the Carter administration would treat Taiwan as Beijing's problem, asking only that China's leaders neither embarrass the US nor mar its reputation for reliability in Asia. Brzezinski made clear that he saw the period between normalization and reunification as "historically transitional," and that his efforts to clarify the terms of US–Taiwan interaction applied only to that relatively brief interlude.[11]

Brzezinski returned to Washington with a far more favorable result than had Vance the previous year, but also with a dilemma. A deal seemed within reach, but, as Brzezinski saw it, the terms included a trade-off. Beijing was willing to ignore US arms sales to Taiwan, but it would then refuse to make a statement regarding peaceful liberation. It would speak publicly about a peaceful changeover if, and only if, the US stopped selling weapons. Hua Guofeng was blunt: "We think that if Chiang Ching-kuo of Taiwan did not get U.S. equipment and weapons there might have been a quicker and better settlement of this issue."[12]

Carter saw a way out. The solution was not to address the issue directly, but instead to launch highly secret negotiations. The president insisted that developments be known only to a small circle, including Brzezinski, Vance, Brown, Mondale, Ambassador Leonard Woodcock, Oksenberg, and Holbrooke, along with staff members Roger Sullivan (detailed to the White House from State), William Gleysteen at State, the CIA station chief, and J. Stapleton Roy, Woodcock's deputy in Beijing. Carter warned Vance against leaks, observing, "I don't trust (1) Congress, (2) White House, (3) State, or (4) Defense to keep a secret." Fearing "concerted opposition from Taiwan's supporters," Carter sought to frustrate Taipei's sympathizers and spies in his government.[13] Brzezinski worried less about Taiwan per se than about anticommunist sentiment that he thought could derail negotiations. Thus, Vance's admonition that the administration would be well advised to consult with Congress, as well as Taiwan and Japan, met silence from Carter.[14]

As a December deadline loomed, the talks became more focused and methodical. The president participated personally in drawing up instructions and solving problems. The American team toiled to sustain informal US–Taiwan ties without incongruous vestiges of the old era.

Among the hurdles to surmount was dissolution of the 1954 US–ROC Mutual Defense Treaty. Nixon and Kissinger had conceded this as one of the basic preconditions to establishment of diplomatic relations with Beijing, but the question remained when and how this would happen. According to Article 10 of the treaty, either side could give the other one year's notice of its intention to terminate. Beijing initially demanded faster action, and some US officials argued that derecognition would kill the treaty. Meanwhile, in August 1978 Brzezinski discovered from the new Chinese Liaison Office chief, Chai Zemin, and his deputy, Han Xu, that Beijing coincidentally had ended its friendship treaty with the Soviet Union with one year's notice, in accord with treaty language, which provided the perfect precedent.[15]

Key to the process at home would be bipartisan political cover. To secure this, the administration turned to a highly visible, esteemed Republican lawyer for advice. Herbert Brownell had served as attorney general under Dwight Eisenhower. Brownell recommended that the MDT be terminated in compliance with treaty provisions to keep complaints from the Taiwan lobby at a minimum. Thus, well before the actual shift in relations, a decision had been reached regarding the management of the treaty.

The future of arms sales remained far more problematic. Beijing regarded such sales as inflammatory and illegitimate, while Taipei saw them as symbolically and functionally decisive. In the US they remained politically, morally, and strategically indispensable. Members of the Nixon and Ford administrations had continued weapons sales while trying to limit the quantities and qualities of the items made available. As derecognition of Taiwan drew closer, officials sought to sell advanced equipment to Taiwan to leave its defenses in the best repair possible and to structure some continuing supply links in the context of commercial sales and informal relations. Beijing objected. As Han Xu observed repeatedly, these efforts ran counter to commitments under the Shanghai Communiqué and appeared out of step with Carter's alleged desire to move rapidly toward final normalization. US "obstinacy" in insisting on supplying the "Chiang clique" would preclude normalization. Nevertheless, Oksenberg, always the optimist, evaluated Holbrooke's September 7 exchange with Han Xu and concluded that the Chinese position could have been much tougher. "A careful reading," he told Brzezinski, "reveals the Chinese have not ruled out arms sales following normalization categorically as a barrier to normalization."[16]

Ultimately, although Beijing's views would be allowed to govern many decisions on specific weapons systems, the Carter administration insisted that China "tolerate continued U.S. arms sales to Taiwan and must not contradict our statement that we are confident the Taiwan issue would be settled peacefully by the Chinese themselves."[17] The president took pains to make this clear to Chai Zemin at an important meeting on September 19, 1978, explaining that these policies would work in the interests of both Washington and Beijing by deterring Taipei from developing nuclear weapons or turning to a third party for assistance against China.[18]

What the Americans were saying "implicitly," according to Oksenberg, "was that the quantity and quality of sales would be linked to Beijing's posture on the Taiwan issue. The Shanghai Communiqué had linked the size of the American military presence on Taiwan to the level of tension in the region. . . . Though this point was never made in any discussions with the Chinese, a logical extension of this principle would suggest that arms sales would diminish as tension continued to diminish."[19]

As the final negotiating sessions played out, Deng and Woodcock reached several agreements regarding US–Taiwan relations. On December 13 Deng accepted the one-year treaty termination, asking only that "during this period of one year the U.S. will refrain from selling weapons to Taiwan because it would cause a lot of trouble." It should not appear that Washington continued to implement provisions of the treaty. Further, Deng did not take issue with a four-month lag in withdrawal of remaining troops after relations had been established.[20]

Everything appeared to be on track. Then, just hours before an announcement of formal ties, it became apparent to the Americans that a clear understanding on arms sales did not, after all, exist. Holbrooke had, on December 12, unsuccessfully attempted to point out to Brzezinski the lack of evidence that Deng fully appreciated Washington's plan to resume defensive weapons sales after the one-year moratorium. On December 14 Chai, the PRC Liaison Office chief, confirmed Holbrooke's fears, remarking to Brzezinski how smoothly everything had gone since Washington had abandoned the idea of continuing arms sales to Taiwan. This may have been genuine misunderstanding or, as the China analyst Alan Romberg posits, manipulation designed to make Washington accommodate.[21] Either way, Carter suddenly faced the prospect of taking an accord to Congress that could not be defended politically.

The president, therefore, insisted Woodcock meet again with Deng and confront him directly on resumption of arms sales after December 31, 1979. Deng fulminated against Carter and upbraided Woodcock for more than an hour, insisting, "If that is the case, we cannot agree to it, because this actually would prevent . . . a peaceful solution of the Taiwan issue"; it gave CCK the wherewithal to refuse to discuss reunification. Woodcock and Roy had ample evidence that Deng had either missed signals or hoped a crisis might carry the day. Eventually, Deng yielded, unwilling to allow normalization to collapse, particularly since he intended to invade Vietnam as soon as US recognition provided a buffer against Soviet reprisals. Nevertheless, Deng made clear he would raise the issue of arms sales again.[22]

The other complex Taiwan question, inherited from the Shanghai Communiqué, pertained to the relationship between China and Taiwan. PRC officials repeatedly sought to commit their American interlocutors to language that determined, and diminished, the standing of Taiwan's government. Their draft of the impending normalization accord labeled Taiwan a province of China—a formulation Carter had warned Woodcock to guard against—and had to be discarded. The negotiations proceeded in English and both agreed the English text would be authoritative. The Chinese translators, however, persuaded their American counterpart, J. Stapleton Roy, to agree to a modification of the Chinese text to convey more accurately US *acknowledgment* of the position of all Chinese on cross-Strait relations, switching from *renshidao,* used in 1972, to *chengren.* The alteration thereafter led the Chinese to assert sporadically that US policy now *recognized* the point rather than just *noting* it. No matter how often Washington disclaimed any change, analysts reading the Chinese rather than the English text rejected American denials. Furthermore, Washington dropped the arduously fashioned 1972 phrase "all Chinese on either side of the Taiwan Strait" for the imprecise "Chinese position."[23]

Carter and Deng followed up on Taiwan issues when Deng marked diplomatic relations with a celebratory trip to Washington in January 1979. The president asked Deng to use the words "patience" and "peaceful" when discussing Taiwan with Americans. To this Deng responded that he hoped Washington, as well as Tokyo, would encourage Taipei to enter into talks with the PRC: Beijing's patience would run out if Taiwan delayed too long. Chinese leaders thereafter rarely mentioned delay as a reason to use force against Taiwan until the 1990s, when they became increasingly worried about the Taiwanization and political activism of people on the island. In turn, Deng urged Carter to be "prudent" in the matter of arms sales, even as he objected to the fact of these sales. To *Time* magazine he would observe that such sales spoiled chances for a peaceful resolution of the Taiwan issue because "Chiang Ching-kuo will think he has nothing to fear."[24]

Implementation

In his memoir, Jimmy Carter remarked, "We had been fair and honest with the people of Taiwan—even though at the time they did not agree with this assessment."[25] Indeed, Taipei seethed with demonstrations, many of them targeting Carter. Twenty years later, people on the island still resented him. When he visited in 1999 and unapologetically declared himself to have been right and to have helped build Taiwan's economy and democracy, Foreign Minister Jason Hu dismissed his claims. Taiwan's success, he asserted, flowed from Taiwan's actions; the "severance of relations could have devastated us." Former political prisoners charged Carter with responsibility for a wave of brutal political repression.[26]

A backlash also developed in the early months of 1979 in the United States. Taiwan's advocates in the US Congress sought to frustrate the shift of diplomatic relations and termination of the MDT. Those who protested did not include just long-term friends of the ROC. Taipei attracted a broader constituency, compelling the administration to commit to more far-reaching protections and guarantees than it had desired.

Michel Oksenberg had predicted some of these problems in an early 1977 report to Brzezinski on the Taiwan lobby. As Brzezinski repeated to Carter, a relatively quiescent lobby had over the previous six months revived and begun a program to obstruct normalization. Oksenberg lamented its efforts to manipulate the US government, to court states and localities, and to win over members of Congress. Nevertheless, he asserted that the power of the lobby ought not to be exaggerated.[27] Throughout his tenure at the White House, Oksenberg tried to reassure groups such as the Committee for a Free China, hoping to blunt their activities.

As negotiations between Woodcock and Deng reached the final stage, splits developed in the administration. Vance wanted Congress to be brought into the last phase of the process because of the 1978 Dole-Stone amendment. The White House had tried to derail the initiative by Senators Robert Dole (R-Kans.) and Richard Stone (D-Fla.) even as the ROC Embassy assisted Senate staff in refining wording and gathering signatures among those who feared that the Carter team, like the Nixon White House, would move secretly on Taiwan policy. Although the amendment passed 94 to 0, Oksenberg believed that he and the NSC congressional relations specialist Madeleine Albright had substantially weakened it. Vance, Holbrooke, and Warren Christopher, deputy secretary of state, worried that Senate leadership, if excluded from the process, would balk. Brzezinski and Oksenberg, on the other hand, did not see the value in a dialogue with Congress and easily convinced the president to opt for secrecy.[28]

Not only did the administration not fully inform Congress, but the president chose to make his announcement about normalization during the Christmas recess, when he could be sure that opponents of the policy would not be in Washington. Even the secretary of state had gone to Egypt. Only a rather brusque cable from Brzezinski reached Vance, who cut short his trip and hurriedly returned, taking a helicopter directly from Andrews Air Force Base to the White House for the ceremony. Carter's remarks announcing his diplomatic triumph to the nation addressed the Taiwan issue in only the most general terms, making no clear statement regarding US plans to protect the island. Ironically, Brzezinski later told the *Washington Post* that some of the negative response from Taiwan sympathizers could have been stanched "if we had beefed up that section" of the speech.[29]

The administration also worsened the situation by the way it notified Chiang Ching-kuo. Having decided to keep negotiations with Beijing a closely held secret, the White House had complete discretion over when and how the several concerned parties would be told. How much time to give CCK before a public announcement had been debated for months at lower levels of the government. During an October visit to Washington, Ambassador Unger, in consultation with Harvey Feldman at the ROC desk, believed he had gotten a commitment that Taipei would be allowed two weeks to prepare. Those more closely invested in the normalization process, however, never intended to give Taiwan that much time to "scuttle it." Concern about the potential for a leak, in fact, moved the announcement from January to mid-December, surprising even Woodcock and Roy in Beijing.[30] Finally, at Brzezinski's behest, Carter directed that CCK be given just two hours' warning, though State Department intercession added a few more hours.

Notice to Unger came late in the evening on December 16, Taipei time. Administration officials subsequently insisted that Unger had violated proper procedures and gone to a Christmas party without leaving contact information. The Carter appointees, who did not regard Unger highly in any case, declared him "missing in action." Unavailable at the crucial moment, he critically delayed receipt of the message, so that CCK had to be awakened in the early morning hours.

Even then Unger had trouble reaching Chiang. CCK's biographer Jay Taylor blamed the bureaucratic cordon surrounding Chiang rather than the ambassador. Perhaps because the officials closest to CCK realized that the US ambassador would not try to make contact at such an hour unless he intended to break relations, they sought to shield Chiang. Unger finally spoke to Chiang's aide James Soong Chu-yu, bypassing the Foreign Ministry, at about three o'clock in the morning, and Soong set up an appointment for nine that same morning.

Unger and his political counselor, Mark Pratt, seeking to maximize Chiang's warning time, would not wait. Stressing urgency, they had Soong rouse the sleeping president to hold an immediate meeting. Soong had by then consulted Vice Foreign Minister Fred Ch'ien, who reported that ROC Embassy staff in Washington did not expect derecognition. But when CCK, flanked by Soong and Ch'ien, met with Unger, he did rupture relations. CCK observed that Washington would eventually come to lament the choice of China. A committed ally had been tossed aside for a flirtation with a bandit regime.[31]

Chiang immediately initiated a series of meetings to devise a rejoinder to Carter's announcement. Foreign Minister Shen, at one gathering of the inner circle, offered to take responsibility and step down, but CCK demurred. Instead, CCK examined ministry contingency plans to construct the official response. Later that morning CCK also met with the KMT Standing Committee. Foremost, everyone agreed, he had to reassure the public to preserve stability on the island. CCK therefore went on the air that evening and denounced US perfidy toward Taiwan and the free world. He also asked people to remain confident and assured them he would neither negotiate with communists nor abandon the mainland. Chiang permitted demonstrations in front of the US Embassy, but initially he kept the violence under control.[32]

Carter, foolishly self-righteous, dispatched a delegation to Taipei to mollify CCK, instead providing a target for more dramatic protests. The gesture reflected the degree to which the White House was out of touch with the workings of the ROC government and sentiment on the island. David Dean, who would later head the American Institute in Taiwan (AIT) and befriend CCK, judged it a quite "ill-considered move."[33]

The American group, led by Warren Christopher and including Michael Armacost, Roger Sullivan, and Herbert Hansell, encountered a mob of some ten thousand at the airport, assembled, they believed, by ROC authorities. Vice Foreign Minister Fred Ch'ien's "welcoming" remarks set the tone as he challenged them to take "the first step in your government's efforts to mitigate the disastrous damage wrought by this mistake." Ch'ien later insisted that CCK and Foreign Minister Shen dictated a tough reception and belligerent language. At the US Embassy officials believed that General Wang Sheng, CCK's enforcer, not Ch'ien, orchestrated the subsequent riot, but that Ch'ien knew and approved. Ch'ien's later indignation and claims that he could not warn the Americans mollified none of those caught in the motorcade when the crowd struck.

The assault began immediately. As Christopher recalled twenty years later, "eggs and ripe tomatoes began to fly at us . . . cans and rocks encased in mud. . . . Within three or four minutes, every window in the car was shattered. . . . Some held bamboo poles that they jammed through the car's broken windows. . . . Next . . . hands grabbed at us through the windows, attempting to pull us into the mob." To reporter James Mann, Christopher would assert, "It wasn't just a demonstration, it was an attack. . . . Frankly, it was not a pleasant experience." As the police and military forces followed orders to stand aside, the crowd injured Christopher and Unger, the former sustaining cuts while the latter's eyeglasses were smashed.[34]

The scale and ferocity of the violence surprised the Americans and came close to disrupting the mission. The delegation, out of touch with Washington for hours, bypassed its hotel and sought refuge in the hills outside Taipei. Finally, Carter reached Christopher and offered to extract him, but the deputy secretary, after polling the group, decided to stay. The next day anti-American demonstrations continued, and students crushed peanuts to signal their antipathy toward the US president, who had been a Georgia peanut grower. Christopher insisted on a session with Chiang Ching-kuo, to whom he described the mob violence and the absence of police assistance. Christopher observed that Chiang "fidgeted, seeming to know the story before I told it," and then the American asked quite stiffly "if we could expect to be treated in a civilized and diplomatic way." To Christopher, CCK's assurances seemed "grudging," and his apology "perfunctory."[35]

Meanwhile, privately and publicly the ROC government refused to entertain any thought of an unofficial relationship. According to James Soong, Chiang told Christopher that the "international status and personality of the Republic of China" would not change simply because Washington had chosen to recognize the PRC. Chiang demanded "assurances of a legal nature" to legitimize promises of arms sales, even as he pledged to help preserve peace and stability in the region. Finally, he asserted that five principles, a formulation created by Soong, must shape any ongoing links between Washington and Taipei: "reality, continuity, security, legality, and governmentality." This meant roughly that Washington must not ignore its continuing responsibilities to and ties with the ROC, including treaties, agreements, and defense obligations. Further, the US had to establish a government-to-government mechanism for carrying out such relations, a contention Christopher rebuffed.[36]

During the working talks that accompanied Christopher's exchange with CCK, Taiwan's lead negotiator, Fred Ch'ien, again emphasized government-to-government relations and insisted that the US acknowledge de facto ROC control over Taiwan, Penghu, and the offshore islands by granting local recognition. Not only would this affirm facts on the ground, it would give Taipei legal standing in US courts to defend assets and agreements against PRC claims. But these arguments contravened Carter's normalization package, and the Americans rebuffed Taipei. Soong later asserted that the delegation had come without authorization to negotiate, their trip simply a result of pressure from Congress and a poorly managed goodwill gesture.

In fact, the effort had been worse than a failure. Christopher fled the island, he recalled, "on such short notice that some of my party had to leave personal belongings in the hotel."[37] David Dean reflected later: "I think that this riot had a profound impression on the victims. Christopher and the others who came with him became sour about Taiwan and the relationship. It was foolish of us to have sent a mission to Taipei at that particular time because we should have anticipated some public outrage. We should have met in Guam or Hawaii."[38] Americans remaining on the island braced for a repeat of the melee on January 1, 1979. Taiwan's government, however, recognized that further demonstrations would be counter-productive and not only banned them but also provided protection for people and property.

Taipei's position could hardly have been more difficult. The leadership—angered by Washington, frightened by Beijing, and disturbed by the potential for internal upheaval—did not have the freedom to indulge emotions, lest residual American support be jeopardized. As Senator Dole wrote to CCK, "The shock and dismay of your people . . . is certainly understandable," but riots "do not reflect favorably upon the Republic of China."[39] Thus, although the government lobbied in Washington to protect its interests, CCK sought to moderate the actions of Taiwan's staunchest supporters and keep firm control over formal discussions with the American authorities.

Freelancing, he knew, would challenge his efforts. Madame Chiang Kai-shek, who had been living in the US, rallied her family to fight Carter. She summoned Vice Foreign Minister Yang Hsi-k'un, designated by CCK to negotiate with the US government, to her New York home and tried to push him aside in favor of her nephew David Kung Ling-kan.[40] Yang fended her off, bolstered by CCK's animosity toward the scion of the wealthy Kung family, which had often meddled in ROC overseas affairs under her direction. Madame Chiang was not to be thwarted, however, and, finding CCK's caution incomprehensible, she surreptitiously continued agitating among members of Congress.

Uncertainty regarding their future status, and mistrust of US intentions, led members of the ROC diplomatic corps to take several hasty defensive measures. Not only did they destroy files as though going to war, they financed street protests and wrote newspaper articles. The ROC's chief information officer, Loh I-cheng, attacked the United States in the *New York Daily News* and its affiliates, which led Vance—with Carter's blessing—to demand his immediate recall. Commenting on the confrontation, the *Wall Street Journal* complained, "His real offense was being too eloquent a spokesman for the State Department bureaucracy to tolerate. This is, we submit, not the way a great power should behave." Loh guessed, probably correctly, that the administration banished him to prevent his leadership of demonstrations during Deng Xiaoping's impending visit.[41]

ROC officials also scrambled to protect assets from seizure by the PRC. They turned over cars and bank accounts to individuals. The most visible property, the elegant twenty-six-room Victorian mansion Twin Oaks, home to nine of China's ambassadors, was "sold" for ten dollars to the

Friends of Free China, an organization cochaired by Barry Goldwater and Thomas Corcoran, a political operative since the Franklin Roosevelt administration who had long aided Nationalist China's legal affairs and lobbying. The conveyance of the embassy residence provoked an outcry from Beijing. Indeed, Beijing concluded that the administration's desire to announce recognition two weeks early had somehow helped Taiwan protect the property.

In fact, the Twin Oaks sale was legally flawed because of errors in the rushed transfer of documents. The State Department urged Beijing to file suit in US courts; Holbrooke, who felt Taipei had stolen the estate, contemplated securing a private attorney for the inexperienced Chinese diplomats.[42] When the PRC took no legal action, Deputy Secretary Christopher specifically voiced surprise to Ambassador Chai Zemin. The Chinese, however, believed the US government should handle the problem for them: in Deng's words, "U.S. law doesn't govern China," and it was undignified to go to court.[43]

Looking back at the disarray, David Lee Ta-wei, subsequently foreign minister and representative to Washington, observed, "Perhaps the only feeling shared by US and ROC officials was a distinct lack of trust." He recalled, "Many State Department officials suspected the ROC would try every measure to muster support to unravel or disrupt the new agreement with the PRC. . . . To ROC officials . . . the way the ROC was treated . . . [was] utterly beyond belief."[44]

Domestically, meanwhile, CCK tightened his control, suspending legislative elections scheduled for December 1978. Popular voting, he insisted, would be too risky in the aftermath of the derecognition announcement. Chiang might genuinely have feared instability, or he may have welcomed an excuse to undermine opposition politicians who were using derecognition to rally supporters. The Carter administration, which had accelerated the timetable for declaring its new policy without taking Taiwan's elections into account—indeed, the relevant officials probably did not even know they were to take place—forced the Taiwan public to pay a high price. This accorded with a long history of American policy emphasizing stability over human rights, security rather than freedom in Taiwan. That the "human rights president" should be dismissive of Taiwan citizens' rights dismayed those in Taiwan who hoped that one result of derecognition might be a weakening of KMT domination.

Chiang's broader intentions remained unclear. Despite implementing limited reforms for several years, particularly ones designed to bring Taiwanese into government, his habitual authoritarianism rendered him highly cautious and readily brutal. At the end of January 1979 Chiang established a small, elite unit in the government, which he called the Liu Shao K'ang (LSK) designed to rejuvenate policy formulation and implementation. The LSK comprised two levels, a central leadership group and a lower echelon of bright staffers. At the top CCK drew together his confidant Ma Chi-chuang, KMT Secretary General Tsiang Yien-si, Premier Sun Yun-suan, Defense Minister Kao Kuei-yuan, and Wang Sheng to meet with him regularly to deliberate and to govern when his health problems prevented his own participation. Day-to-day operations came under Wang's direction. He recruited thirty well-educated young officials from political and security agencies to work in absolute secrecy on LSK projects. Reflecting the wider political indecision of Chiang and his circle, however, the LSK not only engaged in overt efforts to repair and reform a troubled system, but also mounted clandestine initiatives using violence and intimidation to hold on to power and to oppose Beijing through a "united front offensive."[45]

The outpouring of support for Taiwan from highly visible Americans immediately following the recognition announcement buoyed spirits in Taipei. Senator Richard Stone called it "a slap in the face of a staunch friend and ally," and Representative Lester Wolff (D-N.Y.), chairman of the Asian and Pacific Subcommittee, quickly assembled a delegation and traveled to the island over State Department protests. The columnist George Will chided the human rights president for hazarding the freedoms of Taiwan's millions, and the presidential aspirant and former head of the Beijing Liaison Office, George Bush, denounced Carter for caving in to the Chinese.[46] The *Wall Street Journal* also felt Carter had given too much to the PRC, since it needed the US more than the US needed China. In fact, the Department of State press survey staff noted that, although sentiment overall favored recognition, both proponents and opponents focused on Taiwan's sudden vulnerability and the absence of security guarantees.[47]

Dole, encouraged by the ROC premier, extended an invitation to CCK on behalf of the Coalition for Peace through Strength to come to Washington to confront Carter before relations ended. Although Chiang welcomed Dole's gesture, he refused, believing that he must not leave Taiwan at such a fraught moment. Challenging Carter directly, moreover, would fail and have harmful consequences.[48]

In reality, few of the critics actually opposed normalization with China. Many objected to the form of the final decision. Republicans and even some Democrats saw Carter's deal as capitulation, an unseemly rush to accept terms that had previously been too unsavory to countenance.

Nixon, ironically, wrote to Carter in confidence, complaining that Carter's failure to secure a clear pledge from Beijing not to use force endangered Taiwan. Although Nixon noted that China did not have the means to attack, he urged Carter to use the possibility to justify arms sales. Almost sympathetically, he reminded Carter of Taipei's "fanatical core of support in the nation and the Congress," and he observed, "There are those who contend that the pro-Taiwan forces are stupid, short-sighted and reckless. Assuming for the sake of agrument [*sic*] this to be true, they are a fact of American political life and they are effective. Unless their opposition is mitigated . . . the fall-out on future foreign and defense policy battles . . . will make the Panama Canal controversy look like a Sunday school picnic." Indeed, Nixon urged Carter, even as he guarded the executive prerogative over treaty making, to seek Congress's cooperation in the future. Carter must have questioned Nixon's sincerity, given Nixon's own behavior toward Congress. He also may have laughed when he read the declaration that "the stakes for America and the world are too high for partisanship as usual."[49] Carter's own partisan approach and his disdain for Congress would cause him considerable trouble in the months ahead.

On January 1, 1979, the US established diplomatic relations with the PRC and ended them with the ROC, culminating a decade of changing loyalties and disintegrating ties. That the end came under a Democratic president but had been instigated by a Republican demonstrated the universal agreement on the initiative. American officials had become entranced by the benefits, real and imagined, that Beijing could impart, and rejected the authoritarian regime in Taipei.

Rejection, however, did not equal abandonment. As disillusioned as some Americans might have become with the authoritarian and corrupt KMT government, many economic, cultural, and security ties bound Taiwan to the United States. Americans in Congress, the broader citizenry, and even officials in the executive branch of the government suspected that the Carter administration had no plans to protect Taiwan. This distrust would produce some very concrete responses in the weeks that followed.

CHAPTER SEVEN

The Taiwan Relations Act

WITH US RECOGNITION of the PRC a fait accompli, the formal trappings of diplomacy no longer applied to Taiwan. Suddenly, a myriad of political, economic, cultural, social, and security ties threatened to unravel. Beijing's superior legal standing made Taiwan vulnerable. Although it had had considerable preparation time, the Carter administration entered this new era ill equipped. It may have been too much caught up in the China opening and the national security issues involved to think about Taiwan.

Zbigniew Brzezinski reflected on the flaws in the Carter administration's arrangements, insisting that "normalization had come with such suddenness, and the circle of people involved had been kept so tight, that adequate preparations for the various issues cascading upon the bureaucracy could not have been undertaken earlier . . . . Perhaps some of our subsequent problems, such as the ambiguities and disagreements with China over the Taiwan Relations Act, can be attributed to the lack of planning, but it must be remembered that under very trying circumstances the State Department did extremely well."[1] In reality, this view is a myth the administration sought to propagate. Brzezinski excused the failings of US policy at a time when secrecy, as it had in the Nixon-Kissinger years, allowed preoccupation with a single goal to dominate decision making. In fact, how to make the new relationships with China and Taiwan function had engaged lawyers and diplomats beginning in 1972 but especially during 1978. The documents, as well as recollections of key officials, make this clear.[2] If the text of specific legislation had yet to be written, much of the wording existed, vetted by the bureaucracy and approved at higher levels.

In April, before Brzezinski's crucial trip to Beijing, but at a time when key people saw normalization as certain to occur during Carter's first term, State Department lawyers predicted legal hazards and looked for remedies. In particular, it appeared clear that Senator Barry Goldwater would use the Senate floor and the courts to contest the president's right to terminate the Mutual Defense Treaty. Accordingly, Holbrooke believed the administration needed a security package to offset Goldwater's threats of impeachment.[3]

The administration considered three approaches for dealing with Congress when it came to diplomatic relations. Holbrooke summarized the possibilities on April 11, 1978, to an interagency group: (1) the Woodcock proposal, whereby the president would announce that relations had been established and then expect Congress to set up appropriate mechanisms for dealing with Taiwan; (2) a timed proposal, whereby the president would give Congress as many as sixty days to pass legislation protecting Taiwan and then establish relations regardless; or (3) a contingent proposal, whereby the president would establish relations only after Congress had made provisions for Taiwan.[4] The White House, refusing to give control of the matter to Congress, opted for an expanded Woodcock alternative. This would entail a public announcement of recognition and administration-sponsored legislation to frame the new relationship with Taipei.

Crafting an acceptable and comprehensive Taiwan bill was complex and controversial, given the multiple audiences and conflicting goals. At every juncture, the constraint of Beijing's sensitivities loomed over executive branch drafters, enjoining them to emphasize function over symbols. As careful as government officials had been in phrasing the Shanghai Communiqué so that the US only *acknowledged* a Chinese view of "one China," the lawyers believed "we have apparently accepted" that principle. At the same time, "our laws already deal in some ways with two entities," so "it is possible that the omnibus statute will have to provide that Taiwan shall not be treated as a political subdivision of any country, even though the PRC could legitimately argue that such a law was inconsistent with 'one China.'"[5]

Federal legislation designed to cover routine business with foreign states would no longer pertain to Taiwan after derecognition, which would create banking, immigration, and other problems. Under the watchful eye of Herbert Hansell, the State Department's legal adviser, a three-month study looked at options. Hansell and his team assumed that what was necessary was a laborious rewrite of every regulation specifically to include Taiwan. Dreading that, they instead concluded that an umbrella statute would suffice. Accordingly, the heart of the Taiwan Enabling Act became the declaration that wherever US laws referred to foreign states, nations, countries, or governments they would also pertain to Taiwan. Hansell later admitted that in the weeks between promulgation of the initial executive order and passage of the Taiwan Relations Act (TRA) in April 1979 he expected a challenge from business interests to this creative concept. "I was saying a little prayer. It could obviously have been a source of real embarrassment."[6]

The Security Gap

As hard as Taiwan worked to consolidate economic ties, the sudden vulnerability of the island demanded that the leadership focus its most diligent efforts on remedying the defense gap in the new US–Taiwan relationship. Even before Congress reconvened, when committee and senatorial staffers contacted the ROC Embassy's congressional liaison team about what needed to be done, they were told: provide for security.[7]

During December the Senate Foreign Relations Committee (SFRC) set to work studying Taiwan's security dilemma and the crucial issue of arms sales, as well as prosaic areas of law, economics, and logistics to facilitate continuing contacts. As one novice staffer named Stanley Roth noticed, "The [administration's] legislation was completely contemptuous of the Congress and in some respects almost completely contemptuous of Taiwan . . . . It almost read, and I use the word *almost* because I don't think you can say it definitively, as if they expected Taiwan to vanish." Observers at the White House watched developments apprehensively, knowing that even friends of normalization took exception to the way diplomatic relations had been established and to the scope of the president's remarks regarding Taiwan's future. Therefore, while NSC and State Department China specialists became "consumed" with preparations for Deng Xiaoping's January visit, they reluctantly found themselves forced to deal with unrest in Congress and in Taiwan.[8]

The absence of adequate security guarantees in the legislation preferred by the White House stood out both at the time and subsequently as the most obvious flaw in administration thinking. No one in a position of authority should have doubted that this anomaly would draw attention and invite criticism. Detractors such as Richard Allen, a Reagan Republican, recalled concluding that after a few years there would be a crisis and the Carter people "would say well, my gosh, I can't do anything about it, it's too late." Instead, such opponents "met and conspired" and targeted the Hill.[9]

There were reasons for the Carter White House's failure to make protection of Taiwan a high priority, given the political ramifications, but nothing adequately accounts for this miscalculation. First, as Brzezinski contended, the drafters, working against a strict deadline, attended only to the most vital issues, which for them did not include defense. Members of the administration argued that, although Beijing had not renounced the use of force, it had declared its desire to solve the Taiwan question peacefully. Furthermore, the PRC lacked the capabilities for an attack—particularly amphibious lift. Taiwan's armed forces, although smaller, were "far more modern and are deployed in strong defensive positions."[10] For the foreseeable future, therefore, the island would be safe. Carter planned to raise the question of defense in his transmittal remarks, and the White House deemed that approach adequate.

Time pressure, however, came only at the end of a long process of discussion. Hansell asserted, "I don't think that things were omitted because we didn't have time to deal with them because we had months and months to fuss" with the Enabling Act.[11] As to the salience of defense issues, the assistant secretary for International Security Affairs at Defense, David E. McGiffert, argued in January 1979, "Where we confront issues that involve a trade-off between Taiwan's future security and possibly arousing PRC sensitivities, I believe we should opt in favor of the former." Trusting to China's declarations of peaceful intent would do little to reassure Taiwan or alleviate doubts among allies in Asia or critics at home.[12]

A second explanation relates to the administration's preoccupation with the China opening and celebration of the triumph with Deng in Washington. By 1978, though the details remained secret, NSC and Department of State personnel focused exclusively on normalization. Tending to the Taiwan relationship was distinctly secondary, as the thinness of the proposed legislation attests. "We were not as Taiwan oriented as the Senate Foreign Relations Committee," observed Hansell many years later, "so a lot of provisions that were cranked into the bill once it got there were . . . Taiwan-favoring positions. That wasn't where we were in the Department of State. I don't mean to say there was any hostility, but we weren't looking out for the interests of Taiwan nearly so much as we were trying to build the relationship with the PRC."[13]

Michel Oksenberg, who played a central role in crafting the approach to Congress, insisted on a third version, asserting that the administration intentionally made the enabling act weak. Members of Congress would "have criticized, amended, and amplified any legislation" sent by the White House, so this bill, Oksenberg declared, served as "the vehicle for Congress to make its contribution," without causing distress to the White House.[14]

The administration's commitment to deter measures that threatened compromises with and promises to the PRC suggests a fourth possibility. Key figures in the Carter administration did not expect Taiwan to survive as a discrete regime once Washington recognized the PRC as the only legitimate government of China. In that case, they wished neither to support independence for Taiwan nor to get in the way of unification if a fight ensued.

Finally, officials in the White House may also have wanted to use the Congress to accomplish a goal that the administration could not seek directly. Thus, they omitted defense arrangements from the bill, certain that members would add the necessary details. A high-level Taiwan official noted privately that he had been urged by a low-ranking State Department officer to mobilize friends in Congress to fill a gaping hole in the omnibus bill. The administration could deflect Beijing's anger onto elected representatives whom the White House would say it could not control. This version would most annoy Beijing. It would, at the same time, go furthest to exonerate the Carter team from domestic accusations of abandoning an erstwhile ally. But in all the years since 1979 and despite everything that has been written, no member of the Carter administration has presented this as justification.

Faced with objections to the administration's posture on the defense of Taiwan, the NSC and the State Department worked, although not always in unison, to contain the reaction. State Department officers also tried to forestall further complaints about lack of consultation by discussing the pending omnibus bill with both the SFRC and the House International Affairs Committee. Even Holbrooke got results, in spite of his image as "high-handed, arrogant, and egoistic" as well as a "PRC Zionist" unconcerned by Taiwan's dilemma. Efforts to collaborate with Senate Democrats such as Ted Kennedy (D-Mass.), Alan Cranston (D-Calif.), Frank Church (D-Idaho), and Robert Byrd (D-W.Va.) prevented the most objectionable resolutions from being passed. Some members continued to consult with Taiwan on provisions of the legislation, actually calling Fred Ch'ien in the hospital in Taipei to check details with him.[15]

The State Department generally appeared more realistic and conciliatory than the White House, as it recognized that language regarding security had become inevitable. Vance vigorously fought provisions such as one from Senator John Danforth (R-Mo.) threatening to break relations in the event of a Chinese attack on Taiwan, but he also urged Carter to accept a Democratic formula that emphasized peaceful resolution and arms sales.[16] Carter, however, opposed all measures, proclaiming that nothing was needed. Angered, he threatened a veto, "leaving it illegal to deal with Taiwan in any effective way."[17]

Carter's motives are difficult to establish, given the certainty of defeat, the potential political embarrassment, and the costs for subsequent work with Congress. Possibly he acted because the NSC staff insisted that a show of obduracy would mollify Beijing. Perhaps the president resented desertion by fellow Democrats, especially Church, chairman of the SFRC, who planned to run against him in the 1980 presidential primaries. Whatever the reasons, his stance did not serve him well.

Congress rebuffed Carter and inserted security language in the legislation. The crucial passages asserted that "any effort to determine the future of Taiwan by other than peaceful means, including by boycotts and embargoes," would be of "grave concern" to the US, that defensive weapons in appropriate quantities would be made available to Taipei, and that Washington would "maintain the capacity of the United States to resist any resort to force or other forms of coercion that would jeopardize the security, or the social or economic system, of the people on Taiwan."[18]

Congress ignored Carter's objections and said explicitly that Taiwan required support from the United States to ensure its security, refusing to entrust the island's future to the goodwill of Washington or Beijing. Congress did not, however, compel specific US actions as a defense alliance would, nor did it retain powers of initiative. On arms sales, for instance, members could not agree to dictate which weapons should be sold, how often, or in what volume. Instead, they allowed the president to determine what to sell. They preserved only the power to block his decisions.[19]

Provisions pertaining to legal and commercial affairs passed muster easily. Both the administration and Congress sought to protect Taiwan's property interests, right to appear in court, and participation in treaties, international agreements, and international organizations. The TRA aided US business in Taiwan by extending loan guarantees (the Overseas Private Investment Corporation) and it eased continuing informal contacts by creating a detailed framework for a nongovernmental representative entity.

China, as expected, voiced alarm and anger, questioning the administration's sincerity. Its officials insisted that several provisions in the TRA undermined commitments made during normalization. But despite administration fears, Beijing made no move toward rupturing relations.[20]

Making the New Order Work

Passage of the TRA did not end the struggle with Taiwan's supporters over the conduct of relations. A suit by Senator Goldwater, six of his senatorial colleagues, and eight congressmen asserted that Carter had exceeded his constitutional authority in unilaterally terminating the Mutual Defense Treaty. The White House charged that Goldwater wanted to disrupt normalization, whereas the senator claimed he wished only to protect congressional prerogatives. Justice Department lawyers fought the case throughout the rest of 1979, until the Supreme Court finally held it a nonjusticiable political question that coequal branches of the government had to decide themselves.

The following year, as the arms sales moratorium expired, the executive branch and Congress clashed again when senators asked to see Taiwan's shopping list and the administration refused. Holbrooke, summoned to explain to the SFRC, asserted that, as in all foreign sales relationships, Congress could veto only a completed package. Church, Javits, and other authors of the TRA rejected his position, arguing that to protect sales from Chinese interference there had to be full disclosure. They prevailed in 1980, but for the following twenty years oversight lagged as interest and initiative waned.[21]

Suspicion continued to characterize many aspects of the relationship between Washington and Taipei after December 1978; the US government was convinced Taiwan would try to contest normalization; that Taipei barely contained its indignation. Taiwan's agents clearly relished undermining US–China relations, mounting anti-China rallies and seeking to spread doubts in Beijing about US commitment. In October 1979, for instance, the FBI discovered that Admiral Wang Hsi-ling had obtained American contingency war plans, which revealed that in the event of conflict with Moscow, Washington intended to abandon China to protect Western Europe. The revelation was embarrassing and potentially damaging to fragile ties with Beijing. Taipei happily saw the information published, though there was no particular benefit to its own position vis-à-vis the US.

Agents in the US primarily sought to bolster the island's security. To do this, they cajoled, flattered, bribed, and bullied. Roger Sullivan found that as he negotiated the details of Taiwan's future, his embassy interlocutors already had his official instructions, provided by a sympathizer from the State Department.[22]

Vice Foreign Minister Yang Hsi-k'un, Sullivan's counterpart, rendered "an extraordinarily skilled performance," according to one US participant, "on the level of rhetoric, tugging at the heartstrings; at the level of practicality, devising solutions; at the level of tactics, integrating intelligence with negotiation." When necessary, Yang could muster support from Congress. Further, there appeared to be a "Taiwan . . . mole in the Situation Room at the White House." Thus, on one occasion Senator Richard Stone telephoned to complain about something Carter had ordered Sullivan to say to Yang. The Yang-Sullivan meeting had been postponed, however, so Stone's protest came before the offending remark had been delivered.[23]

Nonetheless, the Americans pressed the Taiwan delegation hard. Hansell and his legal team started with a general Japanese model and organized a private nonprofit corporation, registered officially January 16, 1979, to which US foreign service officers could be detailed and government funds sent. To end resistance to dealing with this American Institute in Taiwan (AIT) and to launching a corresponding private organization, Sullivan notified Yang that US Embassy personnel would begin leaving Taiwan in mid-February and operations would cease March 1. Loh I-cheng, the discredited information officer, believed that his expulsion, announced January 15, was meant to induce cooperation.[24]

Taiwan finally set up its non-embassy, non-consulate, non–liaison office on February 15, 1979. Its name, the Coordination Council for North American Affairs, or CCNAA, lacked referents to China, Taiwan, or the United States. Fred Ch'ien mockingly complained it could be confused for Chevy Chase National Alcoholics Association. Carter, meanwhile, having warned the US side "to live up strictly to our PRC agreements," nevertheless allowed Taiwan officials to characterize relations as having "certain overtones of an official character" even as Washington called them "unofficial."[25]

AIT immediately became the vehicle for all transactions between Washington and Taipei. Its staff worked without pay for four long months because funding had not been authorized. High-level official visits, already rare, ceased, with the exception of trips by the national intelligence officer for East Asia. Taiwan's representatives' access to government offices in Washington ended; meetings were held in hotels and restaurants. When one NSC director unfamiliar with Taiwan affairs welcomed someone from CCNAA to the White House, Taipei seized the opportunity to publicize the event, heightening administration distrust. The NSC reduced the visibility of military assistance and supported State against Defense to curb training programs; it favored aid for specific weapons rather than comprehensive assistance. Some in the trenches, such as AIT's first Taipei-based director, Charles T. Cross, felt that "the extreme political sensitivity of the subject, the strong feelings about China and Taiwan in America, and the certainty of leaks precluded any genuine policy discussion at this early stage . . . . It led to incoherence in our treatment of Taiwan and failed to take into full account the importance to the United States of the de facto independent island."[26]

In Taiwan, AIT avoided the media and reduced contacts with officials and highly placed friends. The US government moved facilities out of downtown locations, selling prime land at great profit. AIT personnel, particularly the director, rejected formal titles and invitations to functions for the diplomatic corps. No active-duty US military personnel could serve on the island, and diplomats had to resign temporarily from the foreign service. As in Washington, business could not be conducted in government offices, a fact that made restaurants and golf courses familiar venues for meetings.

In the early days, until he was dispatched to Washington as head of CCNAA, Fred Ch'ien became the primary interlocutor for Charles Cross in Taipei. As an experienced America specialist, "he was expected by his colleagues to show hurt pride over how the United States was treating Taiwan"; at the same time, "he needed to underline Taiwan's friendship with the United States and its hopes for the future without attacking any American politicians—or AIT—personally." Cross recalled, "We saw him masterfully walk this thin line many times." In fact, Ch'ien developed a reputation for histrionics, turning his temper on and off at will. On one occasion, he became so irascible that Cross told him, "It's a good thing I'm not an ambassador, Fred, because no *real* American ambassador would sit through this kind of thing."[27]

Perhaps surprisingly, CCK projected understanding. David Dean, the new chairman and managing director of AIT in Washington, who had established a friendship with the president in years past, visited Taipei in the spring of 1979. "[CCK] saw relations with the U.S. as vital to Taiwan's security, although a lot [of] his countrymen and high officials were livid. . . . He himself calmed them down and tried to rebuild the relationship."[28]

Although the fundamental nature of the US–Taiwan relationship established at the end of the Carter administration could not have been altered significantly, US attitudes and Taiwan's responses worsened conditions. Beijing did not, after all, prepare a list of "best practices" for dealing with Taiwan; any effort to dictate behavior would have been rebuffed. Nevertheless, Washington proved more restrictive than even Tokyo when applying procedures modeled on Japanese regulations. Cross recalled, "The more . . . Taiwan officials [became irritated by the rules], the more they tried to test them; the more the rules were noticed, the fewer opportunities there were to change them." Washington's distrust of Taiwan and sensitivity to China rigidified positions.[29]

While Chiang had to adjust external relations during 1979, he also confronted unprecedented domestic political pressures. Opposition elements, newly organized into a *dangwai* movement (people outside *the* party), promoted peaceful efforts to organize and publish, using US derecognition as a reason to challenge KMT legitimacy. Simultaneously, Taiwan independence advocates staged violent attacks on KMT institutions, including party offices in New York and Washington. CCK became caught between KMT moderates who argued that survival depended on opening up Taiwan's political system and conservatives who emphasized rigorous suppression of dissent. In December 1979 pro-democracy forces numbering in the tens of thousands gathered in the southern city of Kaohsiung to mark international human rights day; they soon clashed with police forces.

US officials, initially distrustful of CCK's intentions, concluded that he did want to liberalize and needed support against KMT hard-liners and independence extremists. Thus, Americans secretly tried to deter the Kaohsiung demonstration and, when that proved impossible, pressured Chiang not to crack down. But the KMT used force anyway and, in crushing the opposition, sending leaders to jail, and suppressing political activism, created a group of martyrs who went on to shape Taiwan's politics in the 1990s and beyond. They included Annette Lu Hsiu-lien (a future vice president), Lin Yi-hsiung (a future party chairman), and Shih Ming-te (a future legislator and party chairman), all of whom received substantial prison terms, and those who unsuccessfully defended them in court, particularly Chen Shui-bian (a future president), Frank Hsieh Chang-ting (a future premier and potential president), and Su Tseng-chang (a future Taipei county magistrate, party leader, and presidential aspirant).[30]

As brutal as the suppression became, Americans took minimal notice; they were focused more on Beijing than Taipei and preoccupied by the Iranian hostage crisis, the Soviet invasion of Afghanistan, and the assassination of South Korea's president. David Dean, the chairman of AIT, did meet with CCK to press for public trials in civilian courts without death sentences for *dangwai* leaders. He also met with relatives of jailed dissidents and promised to try to secure early releases. Meanwhile, Chiang sought to mitigate the damage to his reputation among old friends, showing Dean pictures to demonstrate that neither the police nor the military had used excessive force.[31] The Congress thereafter monitored the course of protest and reform more actively to reinforce the idea that democratization rather than strengthening martial law would safeguard Taiwan.

IN SUM, the restrictions built into the new US–Taiwan relationship were self-imposed and incremental, designed on the US side to convert normalization understandings into reality and on the Taiwan side to preserve a measure of dignity. The Carter administration sought to alleviate Beijing's suspicions of US backsliding, aroused by the TRA in particular. Wary of Taipei, it sought to prevent Taiwan from circumventing poorly defined limitations. Taipei hoped to exacerbate China's anxieties through the TRA and expand undefined boundaries. Mistrusting Washington, Taipei struggled to commit the US to as many aspects of an official relationship as possible. Ultimately, these rules guided American officials as they eased China in and locked Taiwan out of the formal diplomatic community, completing the process begun in the Nixon era.

RECOGNIZING YOUR
FRIENDS AND ENEMIES

THE CONSERVATIVE revolution launched by Ronald Reagan produced an aggressively anticommunist foreign affairs agenda reminiscent of the early cold war. Reagan talked about a Soviet "evil empire" (1983) and significantly escalated military expenditures, building on, but far exceeding, Carter's rearmament program. Reagan's team supported dictatorships and so-called freedom fighters if they pledged to battle communism. They undertook an ill-starred arms-for-hostages deal that linked Central America and the Middle East in a financial bargain and nearly wrecked Reagan's presidency as he sought to overthrow Nicaragua's leftist Sandinista leader, Daniel Ortega (1987).

Reagan eventually abandoned his harshly anti-Soviet stance in service to his dream of ending the possibility of nuclear war. He engaged Mikhail Gorbachev on arms control and promoted an antinuclear shield called the Strategic Defense Initiative—Star Wars—which he insisted could protect Soviets as well as Americans (1983–86).

Reagan's shift on China came earlier, when he was still fixated on recruiting allies in his anti-Soviet crusade. The president, a longtime critic of China, accepted the idea that Beijing would help restrain Moscow, and he agreed to improved relations and arms sales. His real awakening, however, followed his 1984 China trip, when he apparently concluded that the Chinese were not real communists. Relations between Washington and Beijing entered a golden age of presumably firm, stable, and enduring friendship. There were some nagging irritants, such as China's export of missiles to the Middle East, but these were not allowed to blur the rosy picture of Sino-American amity. In fact, Congress spent much of Reagan's tenure highly critical of Taiwan, not China. Members deplored Taipei's human rights abuses and pressed for political change. Taiwanese Americans organized and called on Washington to demand freedom from repression in Taiwan. The Sino-American idyll would not be disrupted until after Reagan left office.

CHAPTER EIGHT

The Reagan Difference

R ONALD REAGAN presented himself as the vigorous and principled answer for an America bereft of purposeful and visionary leadership. He would restore pride and dignity to a nation humiliated by Carter's Iranian hostage crisis, the Panama Canal giveaway, and defeat in the Vietnam War. He promised to destroy the Soviet Union and vanquish communism. In his run for the presidency, Reagan vilified Red China and pledged to re-recognize Taiwan. More than any president before him, Reagan expressed sympathy for the plight of the Nationalist Chinese and held out hope that he would right wrongs perpetrated against them. As late as December 1983, he pledged not to "retreat from our alliance with . . . the Chinese on Taiwan," even though that alliance had been abrogated almost five years before. Reagan's sometimes passionate oratory made Taipei and friends of Taiwan happy and spread anxiety in Beijing as well as among Americans who had labored to normalize relations with the PRC.

But Reagan did not significantly change Taiwan's place in the world. He employed rhetoric and symbols, not conviction or plans for action. He never curtailed ties to Beijing, nor did he elevate diplomatic links to Taipei. On the contrary, this self-declared champion of Taiwan's interests presided over the most significant step toward ending arms sales to Taiwan of any president before or since.

Reagan's Taiwan and Taiwan's Reagan

The Reagan record on Taiwan derived from the peculiar place Taiwan held in Reagan's world order. Reagan never appreciated Taiwan as a particular place with indigenous problems and opportunities. He had traveled there and remembered fondly the people who had entertained, flattered, and indulged him. Nevertheless, Taiwan was simply Reagan's anticommunist pawn.[1] He favored Taipei because it aligned itself with the free world, supported the United States internationally, and refused to succumb to communist antagonists. In contrast to other Taiwan advocates like Henry Luce or Walter Judd, Reagan did not admire Chinese culture, traditional arts, and philosophy, or have a commitment to protecting its values. He had neither studied its history of modern turmoil nor grasped the complexities of the stand-off between it and China. Although analysts of Reagan's presidency might note that the man displayed similar lapses of attention and awareness regarding other international topics, the Taiwan issue was not thrust on him as were others.[2] Despite his superficial grasp of Taiwan's reality, Reagan made it a contentious question among foreign policy conflicts of the early 1980s.

The advent of Reagan as the conservative voice of the Republican Party in the 1970s inspired some in Taiwan to believe that abandonment by both the GOP and the Democrats, as they rushed to Beijing, was not necessarily universal or eternal. Repeatedly during his years as governor of California, his radio commentaries spoke of Beijing's nefarious plans for Taiwan and the stellar qualities of the free Chinese, of agreements made naively by Americans that left Taipei vulnerable to communist attack. His 1976 convention challenge to the Republican incumbent, Gerald Ford, raised the Taiwan issue amid heavy lobbying by Taipei's supporters. Reagan dismissed Carter's decision to recognize the PRC as a surrender "to Peking's demands," not a triumph of diplomacy. Carter's move, Reagan complained, would undermine the international fight against communists since "the nations of the world have seen us cold bloodedly betray a friend for political expediency."[3]

Reagan himself had been to Taiwan twice, although he disliked foreign travel and embarked on such trips reluctantly. He went first as an emissary for Richard Nixon, fulfilling an uncomfortable mission to reassure Chiang Kai-shek when Kissinger "opened" China in 1971. Reagan rationalized Nixon's initiative as recruitment of Beijing against the larger communist threat from Moscow, but he nevertheless felt used by the president. His own small part rendered him complicit in the betrayal of Taiwan, damaging his credibility with domestic conservatives and creating a lingering sense of obligation to the potential victims of community oppression.

The second visit, in 1978, better served Reagan's political purposes. On a trip to establish a presidential hopeful's requisite international profile, he stopped in Taipei at the urging of his campaign advisers Richard Allen and Peter Hannaford, both of whom had long-standing Taiwan business ties. His visit included a high-profile series of meetings with ROC foreign and economic ministers as well as Chiang Ching-kuo. Those agreeable sessions and his travels across the island left him with vivid images of free-market prosperity and friendship for the US. Publicly, he declared in Taipei, "It is hard for me to believe that any sensible American who believes in individual liberty and self-determination would stand by and let his government abandon an ally whose only 'sins' are that it is small and loves freedom." Privately, according to Allen, CCK asked Reagan to watch out for Taiwan's interests if he once again became politically active, and Reagan responded, "Of course I will." Not being one to ask a lot of questions and fundamentally uninterested in Taiwan's domestic affairs, Reagan never noted that his freedom-loving friends ruled through an authoritarian government using martial-law statutes.[4]

In the campaign for the Republican nomination in 1980, as he had earlier against Ford, Reagan voiced strong sympathies for Taipei and equally strong antagonism toward Beijing. In 1976 he had spoken of forcing Beijing to accept Taiwan's independence in exchange for diplomatic relations with the US. By 1980, Carter having preempted that plan, Reagan insisted that if elected he would reestablish official relations with what he persistently called "the free Republic of China." On many occasions, having fired up the crowd, his parting words would be: "There's one message I want to deliver more than anything in the world as president—no more Taiwans, no more Vietnams, no more betrayal of friends and allies by the U.S. government."[5]

Thus, by the time that Reagan emerged as the Republican presidential hopeful, many in Taiwan saw him as a promising source of better opportunities. That these expectations far exceeded genuine possibilities stemmed from desperation on the island and the drumbeat of Reagan's words as they echoed in the media. Reagan might have been offering dual recognition or, at the very least, a liaison office for Taiwan.

Whether Taiwan officials acted to further their hopes is not clear. Anna Chennault, a prominent Republican fund-raiser, contended that Reagan's stance favoring Taiwan arose partly from illicit campaign contributions, given in expectation of favorable policies once Reagan entered the White House. Taiwan's government had awarded a multiyear contract to the

public relations specialists Michael Deaver and Peter Hannaford in November 1977, a time when the Los Angeles headquarters of their firm,
Deaver & Hannaford, served also as Reagan's office. Given the close association, they solicited his approval before taking the Taiwan account, from
which they earned some $50,000 in the first year.[6]

Reagan's decision to run had been shaped, in part, by several wealthy
southern Californians who were also active backers of the American Security Council (ASC), an organization that loudly lobbied for arms sales to
Taiwan in the wake of derecognition. Reagan subsequently assured a supporter that "through a roundabout way, our friends in Taiwan are keeping
in touch with me, and they have expressed their confidence in me and my
friendship for them."[7] Whether through Deaver and Hannaford, the ASC,
Richard Allen (who traveled to Taiwan during the presidential campaign),
or another route, Reagan believed his links to Taiwan were strong.

Across the Taiwan Strait, Reagan's mainland China audience had become singularly alarmed by the summer of 1980. The Republican candidate's advisers, accordingly, dispatched a special delegation to mollify Beijing and minimize Taiwan and China as factors in the election. In a move
that symbolized the importance of this endeavor, George Bush, the vice
presidential candidate, undertook the mission, although it meant traveling
overseas in the midst of the campaign. Bush, having been head of the US
Liaison Office in Beijing during 1974 and 1975, imagined he had the personal relationships to resolve the contretemps. He might, in fact, have
been successful had it not been for Reagan's undiscriminating anticommunism, which did not distinguish the PRC from the Soviet Union and did
not allow for attempts to conciliate the Red Chinese. As Bush departed,
Reagan called for upgrading the American Institute in Taiwan to the status
of a liaison office, although Beijing had ruled that out. Bush had to appeal
to the Chinese Embassy not to let these remarks spoil his trip.

In Beijing, Bush and his travel companions, Richard Allen and Jim Lilley,
his erstwhile China adviser then ensconced at the NSC, met with Deng
Xiaoping and Foreign Minister Huang Hua. Bush sought to explain Rea-
gan to the Chinese and reassure them that he would not backtrack on
China policy. Reagan's words about official relations with Taipei were,
Bush contended, habit rather than presumptive policy. To Allen, however,
Bush seemed to be appeasing Deng. Bush generally appeared too moderate
politically and too weak on China for Allen, who had shared Joseph Mc-
Carthy's worries about communists in the US government and had been
skeptical that a Sino-Soviet split existed until the Cuban Missile Crisis. Allen had been responsible for that portion of the Republican platform that
"deplore[d] the Carter Administration's treatment of Taiwan," convinced

that dual recognition would have been possible had the president been tougher. Furthermore, Allen saw himself, rightly, as far closer to Reagan on Taiwan. So, rather than leaving it to the vice presidential candidate to deliver Reagan's message, Allen independently asserted that Beijing would have to accept the prospect that a Reagan White House would treat Taiwan better than had its predecessors. Allen thought this a reasonable concession for the added security that alignment with the US gave China against the Soviet threat.[8]

Richard Allen's abrasive remarks had barely concluded when the news that Reagan had reiterated his pledge to reestablish diplomatic relations with Taiwan disrupted the meeting. Deng exclaimed to Bush, "He did it again!" Clearly Reagan continued to favor a two-Chinas policy and Bush, however much a friend to the PRC, could not control him. The New China News Agency proclaimed that this was "absolutely not a slip of the tongue" and that Reagan had "insulted one billion Chinese people."[9]

Deng attributed some of Reagan's misguided views to Ray Cline, the CIA operative and friend of Chiang Ching-kuo who had become a Republican campaign adviser. Beijing feared Cline would be named assistant secretary of state for East Asia, and, although it soon became apparent that Cline would not enter the administration, the Chinese continued to be alarmed about him and others like him.[10]

Reagan may have delighted Taipei, but his rhetoric worried supporters at home. Rejection of the consensus reached by Republican and Democratic presidents on the need to work with Beijing and maintain only an informal tie with the Nationalists might give Democrats an opportunity to portray him as uninformed, irresponsible, or even dangerous. As a result, his campaign promoters, including Allen, came gradually to understand that the Taiwan question could hurt him and that he must disavow drastic changes in policy on Taiwan should he become president. Although Reagan persisted in disparaging China and lauding Taiwan, he actually did little more than alter "the petty practices of the Carter Administration, which are inappropriate and demeaning to our Chinese friends on Taiwan."[11]

Even minor alterations seemed significant in context. Reagan's staff invited representatives of the Republic of China's government to attend the presidential inauguration, including the governor of Taiwan province, the mayor of Taipei, and the secretary general of the Kuomintang. Delighted by this symbolic affirmation of their new status, officials in Taiwan rushed to capitalize on the opportunity, announcing a delegation of fifty people, including one of CCK's sons and the former ambassador James Shen. As soon as the press publicized the story, however, China's ambassador, Chai

Zemin, announced that if a Taiwan delegation came, he would not. Thus, before the new administration was installed, relations with Taiwan had already threatened a crisis.

Allen, Deaver, Ed Meese, and perhaps Reagan himself would have dispensed with the mainlanders in favor of the island Chinese. Those who had worked on normalization, however, rallied to stop a potential inauguration debacle. John Holdridge, the assistant secretary for East Asian Affairs designate, collaborating with Lilley and pushed by Alexander Haig, the incoming secretary of state, acted immediately. They prevailed on Chennault, who had been instrumental in arranging the invitation, to communicate Washington's dismay to her KMT contacts. Holdridge used his booming voice to tell the Taipei director of the American Institute in Taiwan, Charles T. Cross, over an ordinary, unscrambled telephone line that it would be unwise for the ROC government to embarrass Reagan. Cross also went to Fred Ch'ien, who was then serving as vice foreign minister, and in an "emotional" session continued what he called the "pounding" on Taiwan officials. One problem remained. The KMT secretary general had already arrived in Washington and had to be disposed of. Whether by his own initiative or with encouragement, he feigned illness, was hospitalized, and could not participate in any of the festivities.[12]

The Arms Sales Issue

Taipei swallowed the humiliation because a far more important issue loomed: arms sales. Taiwan officials faced two different questions: protection and expansion of routine procurement; and acquisition of a far-from-routine advanced fighter aircraft. In both cases, reasons to be optimistic existed, but past experience warned of undependability of even favorably disposed Washington decision makers. Furthermore, Taipei did not know how and when the China factor would complicate the process.

Weapons sales had resumed in January 1980, during the last year of the Carter administration, after expiration of the one-year freeze built into the recognition package with the PRC. Although equipment ordered before the moratorium had been delivered during the freeze, new deals had not been contracted. Pent-up demand ought to have meant a flood of business, since the Ministry of National Defense had the money budgeted and the rubber-stamp legislature of the time did not interfere with defense questions. Trouble arose, nevertheless, because, as AIT reported, Taipei officials "are reluctant to make commitments for lower priority items until they receive definite assurances that they will be able to purchase their high cost priorities, such as the FX [an experimental fighter aircraft] and the Harpoon missile."[13] Finally, in June, because of his reelection difficulties, Carter sought business community votes by authorizing Northrop and General Dynamics to compete to build an airplane with advanced capabilities. This meant a revival of Northrop's hopes for its F-5G program (later redesignated F-20) and General Dynamics' comparable F-16/J79.

When Carter left the White House, however, the choice of aircraft remained undetermined on political and technological grounds. Washington questioned Taiwan's requirements and feared Beijing's response. Taipei, in turn, mistrusted US decision making and worried about choosing between General Dynamics and Northrop, constituents respectively of Jim Wright, Democratic House Majority Leader, and Ronald Reagan, who was becoming president. For neither the first nor the last time Taiwan felt caught between the competing pressures of supportive friends.[14]

Thus, at the beginning of the Reagan administration, in January 1981, Taiwan needed to institutionalize an arms purchasing procedure, and it also wanted finally to secure the elusive FX. Along with US aircraft manufacturers and members of Congress, Taipei began to press the Reagan White House, not knowing how hard members of the new administration could be pushed. Fred Ch'ien, for instance, rejected advice from Cross at AIT that he temper his weekly complaints, asserting that forbearance would mean defeat. If the PRC could actively oppose granting Taipei the FX, Ch'ien argued, Taiwan should be no less vigorous in seeking it.[15]

CCK did not have the inflated expectations of Reagan that some in his government held. He had not imagined that the new president would reverse derecognition. Instead, he focused on defense and Reagan's support of that. Chiang made up his own mind on relations with the US after conferring with Fred Ch'ien and his confidants Wang Shao-yu, who was serving as general secretary of the Executive Yuan, and Foreign Minister Shen Ch'ang-huan. The fact that these close aides were often highly critical of US failings and enraged by US treatment of Taiwan surely colored his views. Nevertheless, he stayed surprisingly calm in the midst of great instability. Restraint, not forceful action, remained his policy.[16]

A similarly contentious atmosphere surrounded Reagan. Reagan, however, proved unwilling to choose among competing factions. Divisions that would cause serious problems for the White House in its Central America policy and characterize decision making on Middle East issues also had a significant effect on choices regarding Asia.

Those who wanted to improve Taiwan's status clashed with those who feared doing anything that might jeopardize fragile relations with the PRC and those who, although not exceptionally sympathetic toward Taipei, found a pro-Taiwan approach a convenient instrument for striking at Beijing. The advocates of a friendlier Taiwan policy included Richard Allen, Secretary of Defense Caspar Weinberger, and NSC staffer Jim Lilley. Opponents appeared primarily among China specialists in Washington and Beijing, strongly supported by Secretary of State Alexander Haig, who had participated in the Nixon opening, and Vice President George Bush. More ideological and vociferously anticommunist were individuals such as Paul Wolfowitz, head of Policy Planning at State, and Reagan himself.

Personal animosities, an early and insidious feature of the administration, aggravated these divisions. Richard Allen, the national security adviser, enjoyed neither the power nor the intimate access to the president of his predecessors, Kissinger and Brzezinski. Allied with Meese, who brought him into the White House, he had no protectors actually suited to factional in-fighting; but he made some powerful enemies, including Deaver, Weinberger, Chief of Staff James Baker, and Haig.[17]

Haig also had many opponents. Reagan appointed him to please moderate Republicans wary of the president's inexperience and conservative credentials. Haig's stints as supreme commander of NATO and aide to Kissinger qualified him for the post but never offset his outsider status. Moreover, he sought to keep Allen, George Bush, and even the president out of foreign policy making. Reagan would later describe this behavior as "utterly paranoid."

Further, in an administration with a notable Taiwan bias, Haig insisted that gestures to Taipei did not serve national interests. Instead, he maneuvered to protect Kissinger's China policy. "China was among the most important strategic questions of our time," Haig contended. "It simply did not make sense to lose the People's Republic of China in exchange for the personal or ideological pleasure of having a Taiwanese in for a nonsubstantive chat."[18] In fact, some Reagan officials had done just that and it was precisely the sort of thing that candidate Reagan had called for. Haig curbed the practice several months into the administration in just one of many gestures Reagan disliked. The president bridled at Haig's efforts to get him to abandon "a loyal, democratic, longtime ally. . . . I felt we had an obligation to the people of Taiwan, and no one was going to keep us from meeting it." Haig's ouster proceeded from complex policy disagreements and personality clashes as well as distrust of his ambitions and independence, but Taiwan lurked just below the surface.[19]

One contributing factor early in 1981 became a dispute over arms sales to Taiwan. Reagan inadvertently triggered the conflict by approving foreign marketing of an aircraft built by General Dynamics, the F-16. This decision undermined Northrop's $300 million investment in developing the F-5G made-for-export airplane that suddenly lacked a market. Taiwan remained one of the few potential buyers because it could not purchase the F-16.

Intense lobbying began by Northrop, a major California employer with old ties to Reagan's California aides and the onetime California governor. Thomas V. Jones, the board chairman, had already been charged by the Securities and Exchange Commission with using a secret fund of more than $475,000 for illegal political contributions.[20] At the Pentagon, those who had argued for air force modernization in the Carter years quietly supported Allen and Northrop. Allen optimistically encouraged Taipei to believe it would get the aircraft. Reagan personally wanted to sell Taiwan the FX, and he interpreted the TRA not simply as justification, but also as dictating the sale.

Several developments intervened to derail the effort, however. Before the FX debate within the administration had been resolved, a Japan-related controversy eliminated Allen. Meanwhile, the State Department argued that the president needed Beijing's cooperation in dealing with egregious Soviet expansionist behavior going on in Poland. Other officials considered sale of the FX too provocative. The TRA called for weapons sales to Taiwan, but it did not require Washington to provide the controversial plane. And even though decisions by the president and Congress of what to sell were to be based "solely upon their judgment of the needs of Taiwan," in fact the Chinese reaction played a critical role.[21]

Jim Lilley at the NSC favored enhancing Taiwan's capacity for self-defense, but he opposed an advanced aircraft, given the backwardness of China's air force. Even Lilley, therefore, calculated the effect on China versus Taiwan's need. Accordingly, he asked the Department of Defense to investigate Taiwan's actual defense requirements and asked the Defense Intelligence Agency to look at the consequences for Deng Xiaoping and the reform process in the PRC. Lilley decided to use the DOD for this work rather than the CIA, he subsequently asserted, because he believed certain former colleagues would dismiss the idea of supplying the FX without weighing all the factors. The agency had come to view Taiwan as an obstacle, circulating a weekly intelligence report that, he said, "highlighted Taiwan's transgressions and infractions, often in inflammatory and accusatory language." It was so biased, he believed, that he had been forced to quash it.[22]

The CIA had a lot at stake. In 1979 it had begun to operate signals-gathering facilities in western China, and in 1980 it launched routine intelligence sharing with Beijing. Everyone knew that the Netherlands had paid a big price for its decision to sell submarines to Taiwan in February

1981: Beijing had downgraded relations and warned Washington the same would happen if arms sales to Taiwan continued, a threat the administration took seriously.[23]

Alexander Haig had a different set of objectives. Although chroniclers of the period have emphasized Haig's motive as "selling weapons to China so that we can sell weapons to Taiwan," Haig, in fact, cared little about Taiwan. What Haig wanted was to promote the military relationship with China, an idea that had been broached first in the mid-1970s and quietly pursued thereafter through Republican and Democratic administrations. In the Carter years, the US had edged toward arms sales but stopped short. The provision of weapons to Beijing fit comfortably with Haig's views on the utility of an anti-Soviet alignment between Washington and Beijing. But Haig dealt with two skeptical audiences. First he had to convince a suspicious president, and his closest advisers, to approve selling arms to a communist country. Haig argued that sales to China would make sales to Taiwan easier, particularly since the arms would be defensive and could do no harm to Taiwan. Haig succeeded in getting a National Security Decision Directive authorizing this position through the White House before his June 1981 trip to Beijing.

Haig also had to convince China. Chinese leaders initially welcomed the idea of buying weapons from the US. Even though he complained about administration policy to Haig on June 16, Deng appeared eager enough to modernize his military that Haig thought he might accept the FX sale to Taiwan. Haig urged Deng not to "drive Taiwan into a state of desperation" that could lead authorities there to "attempt development of a separate nuclear capability."[24]

But Haig made a mistake that undermined his grand strategy. While still in Beijing, he indulged his ego by declaring to the press that the US and China had embarked on a new era of cooperation that would allow for weapons sales. As Arthur Hummel, then ambassador designate to China, later observed, "Al is pretty much of an unguided missile." Jim Lilley and Richard Armitage, both part of the delegation, both aware that Haig had exceeded his authority, and both sensitive to what sounded like criticism of the president, alerted Washington. Reagan dealt with this insubordination by contradicting Haig. The president warned Beijing, "We have an act, a law called the Taiwan Relations Act, that provides for defense equipment being sold to Taiwan. I intend to live up to the Taiwan Relations Act." And, he added pointedly, "I have not changed my feelings about Taiwan." Forced to acknowledge that Haig's approach had been attempted bribery, the Chinese rejected the initiative and refused to follow up on US weapons sales.[25]

Taipei must have watched Haig's performance in horror and confusion. Its officials had long complained that virtually any weapons sold to China endangered Taiwan, and his remarks caught them by surprise. Whereas Haig personally had never been mistaken for a friend, he did represent the Reagan administration, and as such his remarks were shocking.

Nevertheless, the president's immediate reaffirmation of friendship for Taiwan allayed CCK's suspicions. The following month his patience appeared to have been rewarded when he received a private message from Reagan through Singapore's Prime Minister Lee Kuan Yew. Lee had just met with Reagan, Bush, and Weinberger in Washington. In a secret pledge scripted by Richard Allen without Haig's knowledge, Reagan urged patience but guaranteed an acceptable advanced aircraft. Lee had long served as a confidential intermediary among leaders in Taipei, Washington, and Beijing and often met quietly with CCK. His ties with Chiang were both personal and rooted in Taipei's training of Singapore's army and air force after it gained independence in 1965.

Lee's mission, however, may not have been simply a White House effort to deliver assurances. Months earlier, Fred Ch'ien and the AIT's Taipei director, Charles Cross, had discussed Lee's potential as an emissary to Reagan on the important FX issue. In June, just before his arrival in Taipei, Ch'ien confided in Cross that he had asked Lee to intervene and the prime minister had promised to help.[26]

So Chiang, despite continuing, widespread distress generated by Haig, used his routine speech to the KMT Standing Committee on July 15 to call for patience and express his personal confidence in the US. CCK instructed Fred Ch'ien and James Soong, a government spokesman, to disseminate it broadly and emphasize its significance to US officials. The two men actually invited Cross for a family weekend away from Taipei to underscore Chiang's thoughts. Calling Reagan a staunch anticommunist and a true friend to Taiwan, Chiang declared that even if support sometimes might be slow in coming, his government would not complain.[27]

Beijing, however, did not drop the arms sales issue. Following the establishment of diplomatic relations with the US, Beijing pursued a conciliatory cross-Strait policy, expecting that without US recognition Taiwan would not be able to sustain its separate existence. Thus, seduction replaced intimidation in, for example, the "Message to Taiwan Compatriots," an appeal for peaceful unification released in January 1979. China stopped shelling the offshore islands and proposed trade and travel links. Finally, in September 1981, Ye Jianying, the chairman of the Standing Committee of the National People's Congress (NPC), announced a "Nine-Point Plan" for Taiwan's autonomy within the PRC, which would allow the island to sustain independent foreign relations, a capitalist economic system, and a military establishment. From Beijing's point of view, discord across the Strait had been reduced significantly, making arms sales to Taiwan unnecessary.

The Chinese found themselves able to recruit powerful supporters. Jimmy Carter visited China and wrote to Reagan in September that selling more advanced arms to Taiwan than to China would damage relations with Beijing. Chinese leaders had "pointed out [to him] that a substantial portion of the military threat against Taiwan has been removed during the last three years, that efforts are being continued to resolve the differences with Taiwan amicably and with patience, and that the United States should not interfere in this process." Zbigniew Brzezinski concurred: "While the United States explicitly reserved to itself the right to continue providing arms to Taiwan . . . it was also clearly understood at the time that prevailing circumstances would be taken fully into account. There is nothing today to indicate either a heightened threat to Taiwan or a growing air-power imbalance in favor of Communist China."[28]

At the same time, Chinese leaders believed they had acquired leverage over Washington because of mounting friction between the US and USSR. Beijing had grown stronger ideologically and strategically vis-à-vis Moscow while Washington had been in decline militarily and economically. Further, China had recovered from its domestic political upheavals. Beijing, accordingly, concluded a weakening US leadership should meet its demands regarding Taiwan.

Foreign Minister Huang Hua forcefully articulated China's arms sales position to Haig at a heads-of-state meeting in Cancun, Mexico, in October 1981, and Beijing kept up the pressure relentlessly thereafter. DOD's views on the proposed FX sale had by then been aired in the press. On October 16 Leslie Gelb of the *New York Times* revealed the secret study initiated by Jim Lilley that examined whether Taiwan needed the plane, noting that "the preliminary finding of the experts is that it does not." Further, according to Gelb, a well-placed Pentagon official, "echoing military and State Department judgments" told him, "'If the FX is sold to Taiwan, it will be strictly for political reasons, not military ones.'"[29]

This conclusion came as a surprise to proponents of the FX. During the Carter administration, the Pentagon had advocated a plane with capabilities greater than those of the FX, the Joint Chiefs of Staff insisting that diplomacy should not be allowed to interfere with Taiwan's security. Now, less than four years later, the reasoning inside the military contradicted the earlier Pentagon assessments, even though objective conditions had not improved for Taiwan's air force. The CIA, in fact, had already questioned Taiwan's ability to dominate the skies over the Strait.[30] A representative of Taiwan's Defense Ministry told reporters, "We're maybe equal with the mainland," in terms of the quality of the two air forces, but "their quantity is much larger." Taiwan, under such circumstances, had to stay ahead technologically, since "we must control superiority of the air or we cannot maintain our security."[31] Vice President George Bush, pleased by the Defense Intelligence Agency result but aware of its unexpected nature, asked Lilley about its soundness. Lilley surprised him by recommending he accept the conclusion. Of course, "Haig loved it," recalled Lilley.[32] In sharp contrast, at the Pentagon dissenters argued that the FX should not have been thrown away unilaterally when good negotiators could have gotten concessions on Taiwan from Beijing.

When dialogue resumed between Haig and Huang on October 29, both sides understood that the administration had Defense Department cover for a decision not to offer the FX to Taipei and that momentum behind an affirmative choice had diminished significantly. Gelb had noted in the *Times,* "The State Department has been trying to calm Peking by holding up signing about $500 million in new arms sales contracts to Taiwan, excluding the FX." If, as Lilley supposed, Haig himself had leaked the study, then the secretary had freed his hand to reach a compromise with China.[33]

At the meeting, moreover, Haig promised that total arms sales would neither rise above the maximum dollar amount sold under Carter nor augment in "quality or quantity" what Taiwan possessed, providing Huang, before negotiations, much of what Beijing wanted. Reagan had authorized Haig to do so when the secretary circumvented those who would have advised against presidential approval. Haig rebuffed Huang's charges that the US sought to create two Chinas and refused to accept a termination date for sales, but serious damage had nevertheless been done to Taiwan's interests.[34]

Reagan still resisted pressure from Haig and Beijing and did not actually rule out the FX for Taiwan until an early January 1982 NSC meeting. There Haig emphasized that keeping the plane sale alive had cost PRC participation in the December 1981 international denunciation of martial law in Poland. In reality, Beijing's view of spontaneous political movements meant that China would not have cooperated anyway. Believing he had to choose between fighting Moscow and aiding Taipei, however, Reagan sacrificed Taiwan. As a result, Haig's views on China's primacy, for the moment at least, trumped Taiwan's interests.[35]

Talks based on a draft paper presented by John Holdridge in Beijing in January filled the next several months. The initial US document spoke of selling only defensive weapons, of linking sales to Beijing's nonuse of force, but not of cessation. Beijing insisted that all arms sales must end and that a fixed date had to be the goal of a new communiqué.

The gap between interlocutors became clear immediately when Holdridge announced the administration's decision not to provide the FX to Taipei, but simply continue the F-5E coproduction contract. This appeared an ideal compromise since Taiwan already flew the airplane, so no technological upgrade would be involved. Beijing's unanticipated and vociferous objections surprised the NSC, which had expected not only to take "some flak from Taiwan supporters," but also to "quietly work to consolidate our position with the PRC." Chinese protests shocked Holdridge, whose sympathies rarely put him at odds with Beijing. Washington officials did not realize that eight years earlier Kissinger had promised Zhou Enlai that the US would not continue F-5E coproduction upon expiration of the original contract. Kissinger's willingness to deprive Taiwan of the main foundation of its air force to please Zhou in 1974, however, was no longer acceptable in 1982, so, in spite of Chinese outrage, the F-5E deal survived.[36]

The long arms sales negotiations nevertheless taxed Taiwan's patience. First, Taipei suffered anxiety bred by ignorance. To avert leaks and minimize opposition, Haig sharply reduced the number of people privy to information from Beijing. Holdridge, Bill Rope, head of the China desk, and L. Paul (Jerry) Bremer, his special assistant, restricted distribution of memos, cables, and conversation transcripts. The secretary also banned regular briefings of ROC officials. Taipei learned of the FX decision after Beijing had been told. Although Jim Lilley, by this time head of AIT in Taipei, had begun meeting with Fred Ch'ien and the director general of the Government Information Office about the impending agreement, Lilley himself did not know its content, since Haig had ordered desk officers not to tell him. The first official notice of the arms sales communiqué talks did not come until May 19, 1982, and Ch'ien asserts that he first learned of its wording on June 22 in West Germany from Roger Fontaine, Ray Cline's son-in-law and a *Washington Times* columnist.[37]

Taipei also faced an extended arms procurement drought. The TRA had explicitly sought to keep China from impeding Taiwan's defense, but relationships in the real world worked differently. Beijing had delivered a clear message that sales during the period of negotiations would lead to a downgrading of relations, and the administration refused to take the risk. Washington did not release Taipei's 1981 allotment of spare parts until the year was nearly over. Even then, as Tsai Wei-ping, head of CCNAA, complained, no action was taken on weapons promised in the annual August sales meeting, including missiles, helicopters, and armored personnel carriers. Hummel, who shepherded the talks in Beijing, recalled, "We decided on a unilateral moratorium," noting that it was "greatly to Al Haig's credit that he was able to persuade Reagan on the issue. His clinching argument with Reagan was, 'We Republicans cannot have, in our first year in office, a foreign policy disaster like a rupture with the PRC. . . . ' It was the domestic aspect, then, which caught Reagan's attention."[38]

Taiwan labored under one final significant handicap in this critical period—the illness of Chiang Ching-kuo. Afflicted with severe diabetes, CCK required eye surgery at the end of 1981 and his ability to concentrate during long hours of work declined. CCK's conciliatory approach shaped US–Taiwan relations. He stressed progress toward democracy to Americans and offered use of airfields and ports should Reagan need help. He would, he said, go "slowly . . . in relations with the U.S., moving like a fish under water, preserving maximum confidentiality."[39]

The US watched uneasily as the LSK, a kind of kitchen cabinet established to support CCK's decision making, increasingly substituted for his personal rule. External policies appeared unchanged, but under Wang Sheng, the head of the widely feared Political Warfare Department, progress on domestic reforms stalled. Suspicion that Wang aspired to succeed Chiang aroused an increasingly active opposition. Evidence of anti-Americanism—he had organized the frenzied "welcome" for the Christopher delegation in 1978—boded ill. The CIA brought him to the US in 1983 to overcome his dislike for and ignorance of Americans, but Wang used the trip to intimate that the US wanted him to take power. "Alarmed by Wang's political ambition," Chiang disbanded the LSK and sent Wang abroad.[40]

Meanwhile, in Washington, Haig pushed Beijing's demand for a cutoff date for arms sales. In his determination he was not alone; Bush too sympathized with Beijing's perspective, as AIT's Lilley discovered during a trip to Washington: "You have got to realize," Bush told his protégé, "where the big relationship is. It is with China, not Taiwan." Lilley, nevertheless, did not approach CCK to get his agreement to a termination date. Aware that he was disappointing not only Haig but also Bush, Lilley explained that he could not jeopardize Taiwan's security or violate the TRA.[41] He also doubtless worried about preserving his credibility in Taipei.

In April 1982, with belligerent warnings continuing from Beijing and negotiations stalled, Haig convinced Reagan to write to China's leaders professing support for a one-China policy. Early drafts from the State Department exasperated Reagan because, he wrote, of "the note of almost apology to the P.R.C." National Security Adviser William P. Clark and the NSC reworked them, but the letters still reflected Haig's sense of urgency more than Reagan's convictions. One of them told Deng Xiaoping, "We will not permit the unofficial relations between the American people and the people of Taiwan to weaken our commitment to this principle [of one China]." A second assured Premier Zhao Ziyang that "in the context of progress toward a peaceful solution, there would naturally be a decrease in the need for arms by Taiwan." A third similarly reassured the general secretary of the CCP, Hu Yaobang.[42]

Both the fact of the letters and their content dismayed Taipei. Washington, continuing an old habit of ignoring Taiwan, did not bother to forewarn the leadership. Tsai cautioned that CCK's "prestige and credibility are on the line" for failing to manage the US. CCK, barely able to walk and suffering debilitating headaches, should not be faced with US betrayal. Fred Ch'ien berated Lilley for Washington's zeal. Why send three letters when one would have sufficed? Ch'ien, a man whose temper and biting rhetoric had flayed any number of Americans, heaped scorn on Lilley, an old friend with whom he, and many others in Taipei, felt they could be outspoken and blunt.[43]

When George Bush arrived in Beijing in May to influence the long-stalemated arms talks, he similarly discovered the limits of *guanxi* (personal relationships). According to sometime intelligence officer Donald Gregg, who accompanied the vice president, Foreign Minister Huang "battered Bush" for promoting two Chinas and rebuffed protestations of simple "loyalty to our friends." Furthermore, Huang denigrated all the concessions already made to China, including the FX decision, the agreement on quality and quantity limits, the commitment to observe a maximum dollar figure, and even pledges from Reagan to reduce sales if peace prevailed in the Strait.[44] Although US officials were alarmed, talks inched forward. Both the US ambassador, Arthur Hummel, and his deputy, Chas Freeman, believed that some agreement had to be concluded regardless of Chinese attitudes. Hummel blamed "Reagan's personal proclivities" regarding Taiwan for the crisis and the months of arduous talks he had endured.[45]

Lilley in Taipei, meanwhile, reassured CCK that Bush had done nothing in Beijing to harm Taiwan's defenses. CCK, in turn, declared himself not worried, saying he had confidence in Reagan, who had reassured him in both March and May of the US's compliance with the TRA and its determination to protect Taiwan's free choice regarding the future. But, of course, the administration, as Gregg lamented, "has been . . . try[ing] to satisfy Beijing first and worry about Taipei later. I have told them that I do not think this will fly."[46]

By June the acrimonious negotiations finally reached the point where State Department officers could prepare text for a joint communiqué. Hummel concluded that the final tipping point came as the summer deadline for signing the F-5E contract and sustaining the coproduction line approached. US representatives "persuaded PRC leaders that, if we did not have an agreement on their ultimatum, the terms of which were public knowledge, we would . . . make these sales to Taiwan, and the whole world would believe that we were just spitting in the eye of the PRC."[47]

When the final drafting process began, Taiwan's Washington representative, Tsai Wei-ping, alerted Taipei. There a public rumor rapidly spread that AIT would be closing, and officials privately believed arms sales would be phased out.[48] Tsai urged David Dean, chairman of AIT, to inform Taiwan about the document as it evolved.

Tsai also secured a meeting with National Security Adviser William Clark on June 15, at which he explained that any end to weapons sales would allow Beijing to coerce Taipei into talks. Clark had been "a total stranger" to Taipei upon assuming office, so Tsai emphasized in his follow-up letter that discussions "on their terms . . . would be tantamount to our surrender." The TRA "obligated" the US to sell Taiwan arms, meaning that Clark must take steps to "forestall any adverse development."[49] One of Reagan's old California friends, Clark filled a series of uncomfortable foreign policy posts. As national security adviser, according to one NSC staff member, Colin Powell, Clark occupied "a job for which he had little bent or taste." Clark's priority, however, was to serve Reagan's interests, and thus on Taiwan he offered support where the president wanted to give support.[50]

Reagan rejected an arms cutoff date. Indeed, he balked at the quality and quantity restrictions he had accepted the previous autumn when he confronted them anew in June 1982. Reagan told Goldwater in a June 18 White House meeting that he would not acquiesce on the termination of sales. Goldwater had just publicly declared in Taipei Reagan's staunch friendship for Taiwan and called for the ouster of uncooperative members of the administration. Further, Goldwater had privately buoyed CCK's spirits with a promise he attributed to Reagan that advanced fighter aircraft were still coming.[51]

NEVERTHELESS, concern in Taiwan mounted and engendered discontent in the US among those who had begun to doubt the president. Clark pledged to thirteen conservative members of Congress on June 23 that the "president will not abandon our moral and legal commitments to Taiwan." Reagan personally wrote to one of his most conservative supporters, the publisher of the *Manchester Union Leader,* "It just isn't true. I'm not turning my back on Taiwan, and other than a few State Department types, no one is trying to push me that way." At the beginning of July, a coalition of twenty-eight conservative political leaders urged Reagan not to approve Haig's communiqué, which they termed an "ultimate and humiliating blow to Taiwan." According to the New Right activist Paul Weyrich of the Coalition for America, "There is a sense of anger over this that I haven't seen on any other issue." Members of Congress, still irritated that the White House had not consulted them before deciding against selling the FX, warned Reagan's national security adviser against ignoring them a second time. The chairman of the Senate Foreign Relations Committee, Charles H. Percy (R-Ill.), wrote to Clark, reminding him that limitation or abandonment of arms sales would violate the TRA and cause the administration significant difficulties in Congress.[52]

CCK took a pragmatic stand despite the anxiety of the moment. When his advisers recommended turning to France for fighter aircraft, he demurred lest this provide Reagan with an excuse not to fulfill his promise to provide one. The commitment appeared more valuable to Chiang than any pressure US arms manufacturers or the American military could bring to bear.[53]

The growing chorus of alarm about the impending communiqué with China did not derail the agreement, although it disturbed and even surprised Reagan. Pressure from Beijing to end sales had grown so intense that by mid-1981 some response had seemed necessary. Reagan had accepted Haig's arguments because he wanted China's cooperation against the USSR, and, once having delegated authority on the issue, he paid no attention to details. According to Gaston Sigur, his National Security Council senior Asia adviser, the president signed the agreement believing that the "Chinese [had] accept[ed] that there would be no use of force." Thus, he did not expect the feeling of betrayal among his political allies or the distrust the whole process had generated in Taiwan. To fulfill his "dual-track policy" that would provide good relations with both Beijing and Taipei under such circumstances, he decided to balance China's arms accord by giving Taiwan a commitment of equal importance and durability, known as the Six Assurances.[54]

CHAPTER NINE

American Assurances

In July 1982 Ronald Reagan made six secret pledges to Taiwan that in different ways affirmed Washington's commitments to Taiwan, regardless of the arms sales communiqué being signed with Beijing. The specific points were:

1. The United States had not agreed to set a date for ending arms sales to Taiwan;
2. The United States had not agreed to hold prior consultations with the Chinese on arms sales to Taiwan;
3. The United States would not play any mediation role between Taiwan and Beijing;
4. The United States had not agreed to revise the Taiwan Relations Act;
5. The United States had not altered its position regarding sovereignty over Taiwan; and
6. The United States would not exert pressure on Taiwan to enter into negotiations with the Chinese.

To the surprise and dismay of China and critics in the US, they became lasting policy statements. Although four points referred to past actions, time transformed all six into promises about future behavior.

The precise origin of the Six Assurances has remained a mystery. Its author(s) labored in secret, and many of the key actors died before anyone sought to establish provenance; relevant documents, if they exist, remain classified. Crucial, too, has been the politicization of the issue, both by those who want credit and by those who argue that Taipei foisted the assurances on unsuspecting Americans. The latter even assert the package began to be called the Six Assurances only later by Taiwan, although the *Washington Post* called them the "six confidential assurances" as early as August 18, 1982.[1]

Further, over time more claimants to a role in having conceived or drafted a part of the document have emerged. Many precursors did exist. In June 1982, as State Department officers wrestled with language for the China communiqué, Mark Mohr, deputy director of the Taiwan desk, received orders to put together a statement that would be transmitted from Reagan to CCK. Lacking precise guidelines for his task, he did have a broad range of ideas from which to choose, given the persistent discussion of Taiwan's status and vulnerabilities that had been a subtext of the entire arms sales imbroglio. Mohr remembers compiling a list of five points quickly and alone.

David Dean, on the other hand, recalls working with Mohr and injecting thoughts culled from Washington and Taipei. He had, shortly before this collaboration, addressed a Georgetown University group and emphasized similar points, asserting the US would not agree to a termination date for arms sales, would not consult Beijing regarding weapons, would not mediate, and would not pressure Taipei to talk. He wanted Tsai Wei-ping, head of the Washington Taiwan office who was in attendance, to send this message home.[2]

In Taipei diplomats had long been wondering how to get Washington to bolster Taiwan's security. John Chang Hsiao-yen, at that time head of the North American desk at the Foreign Ministry, asserted in a later interview that he had been urging Taipei to demand compensation for the impending communiqué and that the Six Assurances constituted the response. Further, Chang said he contributed one of the critical ideas, which Dean separately identified as the sovereignty item. That claim would account for the sixth assurance that Mohr did not recall writing. In any case, the draft most probably was discussed confidentially with diplomats at CCNAA and may have been vetted in Taipei. Fred Ch'ien, present when Lilley first discussed the assurances with CCK, insisted that he and Chiang were surprised. Lilley recalls, by contrast, "the distinct feeling" that the contents were not new to Chiang and that someone at the State Department had probably leaked them. Assistant Secretary John Holdridge's version, that Taipei imposed the assurances on Washington, at least can be dismissed. Taiwan did not have the influence. Similarly unpersuasive is Special Assistant to the Secretary of State Charles Hill's account that Reagan drafted them personally: Reagan had not followed the debates closely enough.[3]

A final element in the mix of forces that yielded the Six Assurances appears to have been Haig's relentless effort to manipulate Reagan. As one participant attested: "The assurances in fact were intended as something of a sham because as [Bill] Rope [head of the China desk] explained to me many, many times, the general idea was to screw Taiwan and get as close to the PRC formulation of a date certain to stop all arms sales to Taiwan as possible. But this would have to be sold to Reagan and that's where the assurances were supposed to come in."[4]

As had been the case with Haig's scheme to use arms transfers to Taiwan to convince the president to accept a military relationship with Beijing, so too did the Six Assurances work in the mind of the secretary as a circuitous route to better US–China relations. Haig never expected vigorous adherence to the assurances and did not foresee that a new constellation of officials at the State Department would use them to offset a communiqué they did not like and would not fully implement.

The composite product, having been massaged by many hands, bypassed AIT Washington to go directly to Lilley for personal delivery to CCK on July 14, 1982. In a cloak-and-dagger operation befitting a CIA veteran, Lilley changed cars at the venerable Grand Hotel and was spirited away by Fred Ch'ien to sneak unnoticed into a meeting with CCK. Chiang voiced dismay at the quantity and quality restrictions of the impending communiqué but remarked also on his relief that Reagan had resisted a sales termination date. Chiang wrote to the American president on July 16, hailing the six points that would bolster Taiwan's security, but asking Reagan to avoid a joint statement with Beijing. At the least, Washington could issue an independent declaration, which would do less harm to Taiwan's morale and its future. Imagining that Reagan would not comply, however, on the following day Chiang called together the top officials of his government to warn them.[5]

Less than two weeks later Lilley returned with a so-called nonpaper that detailed additional administration policies. This document, intentionally lacking the official markings of US government correspondence, empowered Lilley to say that Reagan's willingness to go along with the China communiqué rested entirely on the maintenance of peace in the Taiwan Strait. "The U.S. will not only pay attention to what the PRC says, but also will use all methods to achieve surveillance of PRC military production and military deployment," it asserted. The White House obligated US intelligence agencies to share with the ROC information gathered while monitoring PRC forces. If at any time Beijing did challenge the peace,

"U.S. commitments would become invalidated."[6] More concretely, the US would extend the F-5E contract set to expire in August and provide Taipei F-104 aircraft discarded by West Germany when Bonn acquired more advanced planes. These aircraft had become symbols of endorsement demanded by Taipei, even though U.S. military pilots called them "flying coffins."

Reagan's discomfort with and confusion about his contradictory policies of befriending China and protecting Taiwan contributed to authorization of yet another nonpaper that August. Only hours before the communiqué was announced, CCK heard from Reagan that Washington would adjust Taiwan's defense requirements on the basis of "all indicators of Beijing's intentions toward Taiwan." For the first time, the PRC had allowed a connection to be established between arms sales and Chinese behavior.[7]

Washington hoped these private pledges would reassure Chiang, but CCK did not find secret promises adequate. Sustaining his own confidence in the Reagan administration was difficult enough, but for the average resident of Taiwan or the staunch member of the KMT it would be far harder. On August 16 Ch'ien noted to Lilley Chiang's alarm and his decision to publicize the Six Assurances if the US did not. Further, CCK wanted immediate notification to Congress of the F-5E joint production agreement. The White House thereupon authorized Taipei to announce the Six Assurances just ahead of the August 17 communiqué.[8]

Reagan found that the agreement with China provoked very mixed reactions. Those who had feared a rupture in relations with Beijing celebrated, but they were not Reagan's natural allies. Despite the Six Assurances, many others worried about Taiwan's future and questioned Reagan's commitment. To William Rusher, publisher of the *National Review,* the president asserted, "You can tell your friends there I have not changed my mind one damn bit about Taiwan. Whatever weapons they need to defend themselves against attacks or invasion by Red China, they will get from the United States." When Dan Rather on the *CBS Evening News* commented that Reagan had backed away from Taiwan, the president telephoned the journalist to tell him, "There has been no retreat by me. . . . We will continue to arm Taiwan."[9] Not surprisingly, such comments alarmed Beijing. The New China News Agency, responding to the dialogue in Washington, insisted that arms sales to Taiwan and peaceful resolution of the Taiwan issue were "two separate questions of an entirely different nature."[10]

Reagan also made one other top-secret effort, probably orchestrated by Gaston Sigur, to provide for Taiwan's survival.[11] From his NSC perch, Sigur had written or coordinated most of the papers and statements related to the communiqué crisis. Now he captured Reagan's discontent with the negotiations and his suspicion of Beijing's intentions in a sensitive one-page memo drafted in William Clark's presence. Sigur wrote: "The U.S. willingness to reduce its arms sales to Taiwan is conditioned absolutely upon the continued commitment of China to the peaceful solution of the Taiwan–PRC differences. It should be clearly understood that the linkage between these two matters is a permanent imperative of U.S. foreign policy." Reagan would say much the same about the relationship of peace to arms sales in an interview published in *Human Events* the following February.[12]

Having asserted the linkage of arms sales to peace, the memo specified that "both in quantitative and qualitative terms, Taiwan's defense capability relative to that of the PRC will be maintained." This constituted a personal commitment that Reagan wanted his successors to follow. Revolutionary in conception, the idea of preserving a military balance across the Strait also would ultimately be unworkable, given the disparity in size and resources between the contenders. Nevertheless, it had an enormous influence on US–Taiwan relations.

In the near term, the very existence of the memo remained a closely guarded secret. Few in the US government learned of it, even those handling Taiwan and China affairs, although it apparently served to allay concerns among crucial congressional critics. According to Secretary of State George Shultz, its existence, once revealed to Taipei, made a big difference in the level of anxiety there. The paper, however, disappeared into carefully guarded National Security Council files, emerging only when challenges arose to arms sales. Then the theory underlying it would be used to defeat them.

This, as it turned out, represented only one of several ways in which the August Communiqué's effect was diminished. Negotiation of the communiqué had been prolonged and arduous. China had won significant concessions regarding US support for Taiwan. But Chinese leaders had not thought of everything, nor could they compel the Americans to accept all demands. It quickly became apparent that loopholes existed in the agreement that could be exploited in Taiwan's behalf. These gaps included technology transfer, commercial sales, weapons replacement, and, of greatest significance, financial transactions. In each of these areas, a sympathetic government in Washington would have adhered more closely to China's preferences. Certain ideas might not have been broached at all. As it happened, the administration wanted to protect Taiwan more than it wished to please Beijing, and so creative interpretation of the August Communiqué took over.

Shultz Arrives

When Alexander Haig left the State Department, Reagan named George Shultz as his secretary of state. The historian Ronald Steel observed that Shultz's "stolid reasonableness" proved to be exactly what Reagan needed to "reassure Americans and calm foreigners," which, most especially, included the Taiwanese and their friends in the US.[13] Taipei saw Haig's elimination as a signal of better times to come and welcomed the appointment of an old friend. Shultz, moreover, brought in a new cast of characters after July 16, 1982, some closer to him personally, others more congenial in point of view. For instance, he preferred Paul Wolfowitz, erstwhile chief of the Policy Planning Staff, as the new assistant secretary for East Asia, removing John Holdridge, who had been particularly supportive of Beijing. Soon Rope would be out, too—ten years later Taipei would block his appointment as AIT head in Taipei. From Taiwan's point of view, these were auspicious changes.

Skepticism regarding the need to align Beijing with Washington in the struggle against Moscow and distaste for pandering to China characterized this Reagan team. Shultz later wrote that his "attitude was a marked departure from the so-called China-card policy." He contended that "when the geostrategic importance of China became the conceptual prism through which Sino-American relations were viewed, it was almost inevitable that American policymakers became overly solicitous of Chinese interests, concerns, and sensitivities." He disapproved equally of Nixon and Kissinger's approach and Carter's willingness to permit Beijing to dictate "'obstacles'—such as Taiwan . . . that the United States had been tasked to overcome in order to preserve the overall relationship."[14] Indeed, Shultz emphasized in an interview, "these old China hands, all they talk about is the relationship. We ought to turn that around and say, what we are concerned with is the substance. And if we can have progress in dealing with the substance, in dealing with problems, and taking advantage of opportunities, then that will result in a good relationship."[15]

Shultz arrived too late to disrupt the August Communiqué process, but he disliked it. He reserved special ire for Beijing's insistence that sales of arms to Taiwan be ended. Haig had contended that Washington had to capitulate. Shultz saw this as "unacceptable." As president of the Bechtel Corporation, an engineering and construction firm with extensive business interests in Taiwan rather than the mainland, Shultz emphasized that Asia offered much to Americans that China couldn't supply. Just before his appointment Shultz had traveled to the region, stopping in Taiwan, where he met with CCK and Fred Ch'ien, who eagerly sought time with a man rumored to be the next secretary of state.[16] Shultz, nevertheless, did not shun China, recognizing the significance of its markets and its military potential.

Paul Wolfowitz expressed similar ideas. He had disparaged Carter's 1979–80 arms moratorium as catering unnecessarily to China. According to the writer James Mann, Wolfowitz "felt that the notion of China's global strategic importance had been largely manufactured by Kissinger to make himself look smart and to help justify the opening to China."[17] The new assistant secretary believed Beijing needed US help against Moscow far more than Washington needed the Chinese. In Haig's State Department, he had been one of the few high-level figures who had dared directly to oppose the secretary's tilt toward China as well as his position on the August Communiqué. As a result, Haig had treated him as an adversary, shutting him out of the arms negotiations and threatening to fire him.[18]

Gaston Sigur also considered the US government to have been "mesmerized" by China; friends and allies in the region had been neglected as a result. A specialist on Japan who had lived there for years working with the Asia Foundation, he shared not only Reagan's anticommunist convictions, but also Japanese cynicism about China and sympathies for Taiwan. Sigur's ability to exert influence was greater than most National Security Council staffers or assistant secretaries of state, given his assiduously cultivated network of interagency and international contacts.[19]

Richard Armitage, who held the post of assistant secretary of Defense for International Security Affairs, had, like Sigur, developed a strong Japanese expertise and a philosophical commitment to alliances: willingness to be brash and provocative made him a critical member of the Reagan team. When particularly difficult issues arose he was always centrally involved; an entry on his personal calendar noting "haircut" told his staff he was closeted somewhere with Sigur and Wolfowitz, since Armitage was nearly bald.[20]

This triumvirate of Wolfowitz, Sigur, and Armitage became especially important in translating ideas into policy and action. Armitage's pragmatism diverged significantly from Wolfowitz's ideological approach and Sigur's analytical bent, just as his muscular build and gravelly voice contrasted with Wolfowitz's scholarly demeanor and Sigur cherubic appearance; they made for an odd but effective coalition. Given the fierce competition between Shultz and Defense Secretary Weinberger as well as the clash over power and access to the president that developed between Shultz and National Security Adviser Clark, Wolfowitz, Armitage, and Sigur played a crucial mediating function without which many issues could not have been resolved.[21]

It was not surprising under these circumstances that one of the first major studies to be done after Shultz moved into the State Department in July 1982 recommended that China's significance in the country's Asian policy be reduced. China, it argued, continued to gain more from their relations than America did, so Washington should focus on Japan and other friends and allies. China would simply have to accept the new dispensation.[22]

One man high in the administration who did not share the orientation of the Reagan team was Vice President George Bush. Although he had been point man for Taiwan's case at the UN in 1971, he tended to be far more sympathetic to Beijing than others in the White House or the Pentagon. But Bush did not challenge the administration's Taiwan policy. Arthur Hummel, who shared his views on Beijing, recalled that Bush was "very much out of it. . . . [He] simply didn't want to have to argue with Ronald Reagan about China policy."[23] The vice president remained so successful in keeping his contrary opinions from the president that in 1983 Reagan thought about sending him to Taiwan on a goodwill mission.[24]

Given these dynamics, several largely unanticipated developments modified the damage that the August 17 Communiqué could have done to Taiwan. Technology transfer allowed Taiwan to continue to deploy more and better equipment in its own defense, its modest arms industry rather than the communiqué being the primary limitation. As Washington sought to reduce its shipments to Taiwan, providing expertise and blueprints appeared a comparatively low-cost and low-profile alternative. Technology could also be transferred by private industry, which would decrease the government's responsibility even more. Sales of weapons through commercial channels expanded greatly, as the government reduced its foreign military sales (FMS), thereby allowing restrictions on quality and quantity to be stretched by American companies.

The idea of Taiwan's self-reliance became more appealing to Washington, although it seemed a mixed blessing to Taipei: local production strengthened island defenses but reduced the value of weapons as political trophies attesting to US commitment. The most significant technology transfer program supported the 1970s decision to build an indigenous fighter aircraft (IDF), but other important projects moved ahead as well. General Dynamics, for instance, facilitated construction of Perry-class fast frigates to replace World War II–vintage ships.[25] On the eve of the fourth anniversary of the August Communiqué, China denounced technology transfer as a devious evasion of the communiqué, but Washington flatly rejected the complaint. An unnamed US official declared, "We don't want to reopen negotiations with the Chinese on this score. The text is very clear. It talks of arms sales and not technology."[26]

Quality restrictions had been a crucial component of the communiqué negotiations, conceded early by Haig and written into the final text. Nevertheless, even at the time of the talks, Americans recognized that it would not always be possible to replace failing equipment with exactly the same models. Inventories would be depleted and production lines closed. Instead, Washington reserved the right to provide newer versions of old items. Invariably, prohibitions against enhancing quality standards would be violated over time.

Surreptitious enhancement of Taiwan's inventory also proceeded through sales of civilian hardware and spare parts. Taipei, for instance, might purchase a helicopter outfitted for civilian use but separately order special radar and seawater coating. Suddenly, Taiwan would have an antisubmarine warfare platform. Similarly, "spare parts" could be reconstituted in Taiwan to yield needed weaponry.[27]

The financial side of the communiqué, however, provided the broadest area for redefinition. The communiqué did not specify formulas to calculate the ceiling from which reductions would begin; the levels of annual reductions; the role of inflation; the prices of goods and services; or the amount of money Taiwan could spend in any given year (the "bucket," as it was nicknamed). Thus, interpretation played a pivotal role, and, with changes in the administration, those filling in the details favored a more generous approach to Taiwan than had those who gave the initial American assurances to Beijing.

In practice several things happened. Reagan officials set an artificially elevated budget ceiling from which to begin calculating annual reductions in arms sales to Taiwan. They devised the figures by taking the maximum Carter administration expenditure and adjusting that figure upward for inflation. Then they arbitrarily decreased the amount in increments of roughly $20 million each year, but permitted less in some years and small increases for occasional large purchases. Fred Ch'ien, who had taken the helm of Taiwan's representative office in Washington at the beginning of 1983, claimed some success in undermining the August Communiqué by using parallels to cost-of-living adjustments to take account of the continually rising prices of military goods. Use of commercial channels in place of government-operated FMS further interfered. FMS sales could be tracked, added up, and reported at the end of any predetermined period by fiat. Commercial sales, in contrast, generated documentation according to business practices, not congressional calendars and bucket limitations, so DOD personnel complied with regulations by fabricating numbers.[28]

The scope of transactions that would fall into the bucket provided the best opportunity to bend the agreement in Taiwan's favor. Those who supplied arms to Taiwan concluded that the communiqué would have a serious effect not only on arms sales, but also on defense capabilities. As a result, they made a decision, camouflaged in the intricate bookkeeping of the defense establishment, to take some expenditures out of the bucket so that there would be more room for additional sales. A minor adjustment when first conceived, it would eventually become a huge, clandestine change.[29]

The August Communiqué, then, had not altered US policy as much as had been expected, but the advent of George Shultz had reshaped the Reagan administration's approach to Asia. Creative interpretation of the communiqué left Beijing's leaders such as Hu Yaobang convinced that they had been lied to, and Shultz's tough demeanor demonstrated that Washington would not accede to China's bullying. Although the US wanted good relations with Beijing, Shultz would carry out the Taiwan Relations Act with as much energy as the August Communiqué. Thus, when a dejected arms procurement delegation arrived from Taipei immediately after the communiqué's signing, its members were surprised and delighted to find that the Pentagon stood primed to sell a large package of weapons.

Shultz, moreover, at his first meeting with a senior Chinese official, insisted on close adherence to the TRA. In a "testy exchange" on October 1, 1982, he put Foreign Minister Huang Hua on notice that he, the president, and Congress all supported it. Shultz recorded in his memoir that just five months into his tenure as secretary he was already "fed up" with Chinese complaints on the Taiwan issue. He pointed out to the Chinese that "frustrations and problems" in the relationship between Washington and Beijing were "inevitable" because of political differences, but he would not seek "progress . . . at the expense of . . . our close unofficial relationship with the people of Taiwan."[30]

A good example of the administration's refusal to capitulate to Beijing's demands came in 1983, when the PRC insisted on joining the Asian Development Bank (ADB) and ousting Taiwan in the process. Beijing argued that according to the ADB charter, only UN members could participate and that Washington had no choice but to support its position. Paul Wolfowitz and Treasury Secretary Donald Regan rejected this view, insisting that Taiwan's founding role in 1966 had not been as representative of mainland China but was based on the resources and population of Taiwan. Congress, too, had protested the idea of ejecting Taiwan as early as

1980, threatening an end to US funding for and participation in the bank. In the midst of the controversy, Regan raised the stakes by talking about US friendship with the Republic of China while visiting Japan.[31] Ultimately, Taiwan resolved the confrontation by accepting the designation "Taipei, China," but the administration had made its position clear.

Taipei adjusted to the August Communiqué by intensifying its search for defense weaponry. In a January 1983 meeting with his top advisers, Chiang emphasized the importance of pushing hard on institutionalization of the arms sales process and focusing persistently on key weapons purchases. Hau Pei-tsun, chief of the General Staff, had been worrying for many months that US arms negotiators in Washington were trying to satisfy TRA obligations with outdated, unwanted, unnecessary, or overpriced equipment, squandering Taiwan's resources and undermining security. CCK emphasized quality over quantity and welcomed technology transfer.[32]

In Washington CCNAA had a different perspective. Fred Ch'ien, appointed director after the August Communiqué, agonized about retaining the favor of US arms makers. His messages home argued that Taiwan did not have the luxury of being selective. A talented networker and astute analyst of congressional politics, Ch'ien believed that orders had to keep flowing so that Taipei could count on a large pool of companies willing to lobby for it on Capitol Hill.[33] Americans both marveled and fretted at Ch'ien's ability to ensure that Taiwan "enjoyed a level of influence in Washington that many countries enjoying formal ties would envy."[34] Cynics ascribed his success to a large budget and a lack of scruples.

What Taipei wanted most Ch'ien had trouble securing through networking—the F-16. General Hau felt that in the arms talks Taiwan remained at a disadvantage because of its total dependence on the US. He had no leverage and relied on the goodwill of his interlocutors.[35] Nevertheless, Taipei hoped that Reagan had been sincere in his confidential pledges to CCK regarding provision of an advanced plane. At every opportunity Nationalist officials argued that the F-16 constituted necessary defensive air power. Washington, however, seemed to have found a solution that did not require a controversial sale but would fulfill Reagan's promise.

Development of the IDF had been discussed and studied in the US and Taiwan for years, but in the wake of Reagan's ruling against the FX, Pentagon officials began to reexamine Taiwan's air defenses and opportunities for US assistance to a Taiwan project. The IDF would have to be limited in design and execution, but DOD concluded that, regardless of Beijing's objections, Taiwan must have a successor aircraft by 1992, when the F-5E would no longer adequately protect the island. Moreover, Washington preferred that the plane be built in Taiwan with US assistance rather than bought from foreign sources.[36] That preference touched precisely on the sensitive issue that divided officials in Taipei as they argued over funds.

Taiwan's government announced it would move forward with the IDF in 1982 over the objection of the ROC Air Force, which considered the need too urgent to wait for a domestic aircraft. The Aero Industry Development Center (AIDC), a subsidiary of the government's most important research center, the Chung Shan Institute of Science and Technology, accordingly got an annual budget of roughly $350 million to do the primary construction and coordination, which cut out the air force entirely and heightened its subsequent lack of interest.[37]

Design and production became a process of complex coordination. The Taiwan government secretly approached General Dynamics for technical assistance, assuming that by consulting the company that manufactured the F-16, it would end up with a similar aircraft. In doing so, it strained relations with Northrop, which was working closely with the Taiwan air force. Other US companies, including Lear, Garrett, and General Electric, provided components and help in testing IDF capabilities as well as training for Taiwan's engineers in North American facilities. Throughout the complicated process, US officials insisted that they exercised no management or control. US companies required licensing authority from Washington to provide equipment and expertise, however, and Washington also determined the specifics of design and capability. Looking back on the process, many officials have acknowledged playing a role in determining the aircraft's capabilities when they really didn't understand enough about technical issues like weight, thrust, and compatibility. Moreover, there were grueling arguments over engine size, wingspan, and other features that differentiated the IDF from the F-16.[38]

Several more months passed before Shultz gave final approval to transfer the IDF's systems integration technology and avionics. Although usually sensitive to political and personal dynamics, Taipei sought to influence Shultz through Defense Secretary Weinberger and National Security Adviser Clark, both chronically at odds with the secretary of state. Bill Brown, deputy to Assistant Secretary of State Paul Wolfowitz, better served Taiwan's interests. He and his counterparts, Jim Kelly at DOD and David Laux from the NSC, prompted Wolfowitz, Armitage, and Sigur to support the IDF at a critical meeting with Shultz, in opposition to China hands at the State Department, who argued that IDF development violated the August Communiqué, and that the aircraft would not be viable. Word ultimately came in early July 1985 that the US would support the project and approve General Dynamics' involvement.[39] According to Chief of the General Staff Hau, CCK considered the decision "a great achievement for our military diplomacy": he had provided support of US operations in Nicaragua (see the section "Central American Leverage," below), believing it would secure the IDF.[40]

In 1984 Peace Pearl—an advanced avionics program—further complicated the IDF story. As part of anti–USSR Sino-American military cooperation, Washington offered Beijing sophisticated radar, inertial navigation equipment, and computers to refit roughly fifty-five Chinese F-8 aircraft, giving them all-weather capability. Horrified Taiwan officials got the story wrong and thought the US was selling China the F-16s that Taipei had been denied. General Hau protested and David Dean immediately explained that the US would refurbish, not replace, the Chinese aircraft. Even this angered Taipei, since any modernization of China's air force or navy would disturb the existing military balance and thus threaten Taiwan.[41]

Peace Pearl proceeded nevertheless and seemed to some Americans an opportunity for simultaneous transfer of high-tech devices to Taipei. Senator Jesse Helms (R-N.C.), among others, dropped his opposition to the China project in order to supply Taiwan a duplicate system. Various State Department officers, distrustful of Taiwan and convinced that China would not tolerate the transfer, strongly opposed the idea. In the end, Peace Pearl with China collapsed because of the events at Tiananmen Square and huge cost overruns, but Taiwan got the avionics package anyway.[42]

Reagan's China Trip

Reagan's China trip, in April 1984, became a critical milestone for Taiwan and the allegedly pro-Taiwan president. Reagan found he quite liked the Chinese and their "so-called Communist" country.[43] Reagan's anti–Chinese communist barbs subsided and a China euphoria gripped Americans.

Reagan had actually visited Asia in 1983, and his political advisers had called for a stop in China as a dramatic gesture. Both the NSC and State Department, however, insisted that Reagan not appear eager to visit Beijing, a posture that had given the Chinese too much leverage over his predecessors. A Washington summit, forcing a Chinese leader to come to the US, should happen first. It occurred in 1984, when the PRC concluded that Reagan would be reelected and that his muscular approach toward Moscow served Chinese interests. Reagan and Premier Zhao Ziyang discussed the Soviets, of course, but, according to Secretary Shultz, the president also set aside "constructive ambiguity" to deliver a steely message on Taiwan, remarking that the TRA should be strengthened, not weakened as Zhao urged. Further, Reagan told his diary, he warned Zhao that "any use of force would change our relationship beyond repair."[44]

Reagan's journey nevertheless angered Taiwan's supporters. En route, Reagan met Barry Goldwater in Hawaii, the senator having been to Taipei possibly to reassure CCK at the president's behest, just as Nixon had dispatched Reagan himself to placate Chiang in 1972. In his memoir Reagan noted, "Barry was upset about my visiting China and made little attempt to hide it." Goldwater "suspected I was getting ready to give up on Taiwan, and I don't think I convinced him otherwise." Gary Jarmin of the American Council for a Free Asia warned that conservatives would not tolerate compromise of Taiwan's interests. Without their "enthusiastic support," he forecast, "the president's re-election chances will be severely undermined."[45]

To Taipei the trip suggested eroding support and an occasion for bargains that would undermine Taiwan's security. Preemptively, Fred Ch'ien gave Clark a list of concessions that Reagan must resist, including a new communiqué, compromise of the TRA, or ending of arms sales before peaceful unification. The administration, in turn, used AIT representative Lilley to reassure Chiang, emphasizing Lilley's access in Washington, giving CCK a copy of what Reagan planned to say in Beijing, and reiterating the Six Assurances as well as a pledge to brief Taiwan's leader soon after Reagan left China. In striking contrast to the silence of the Carter years and Haig's stonewalling, openness about conversations with the PRC characterized the final years of the Reagan presidency.[46]

Still, as John Chang Hsiao-yen observed, "It is very painful to see Mr. Reagan shaking hands and hugging our enemies," a TV image that Taipei's leadership showed uncensored to the Taiwan public.[47] More disturbing, Reagan discussed arms sales and nuclear cooperation, and China pressed for accelerated annual reductions in sales to Taiwan. The US and China initialed a nuclear reactor deal—later nullified by Congress—which made Taipei imagine that its interests had been compromised in exchange for a package worth some $20 billion to private companies. Soong complained, "President Reagan once said that 'communism will end up on the ash heap of history.' We wonder if someday we'll end up on the ash heap of nuclear destruction."[48]

Washington's willingness to undertake military cooperation with China disheartened Taiwan. The perception of Beijing as a comrade-in-arms fighting the threat from Moscow had facilitated normalization and become the crucial factor in persuading Reagan to cooperate with the PRC.

During the mid-1980s Washington and Beijing worked together to thwart Moscow's advances in Afghanistan. They shared intelligence, and China permitted the US to establish monitoring stations on Chinese soil. Moreover, during the Reagan era policy makers concluded that the US should sell China military equipment, making Beijing eligible for FMS, that is, official US financing. That the US saw these weapons as useful for border defense against the Soviets did not placate Taipei, which objected that every weapon sold endangered the island.

Taiwan also faced the possibility that its own arms purchases could be curtailed because of continuing human rights abuses. Not only had there been violent repression of dissent at the end of the 1970s, but in the early 1980s evidence emerged of spying and intimidation against activists in the United States. Members of Congress, most prominently Representative Stephen Solarz (D-N.Y.), chairman of the Asia Subcommittee of the House Foreign Affairs Committee, sought to make sales eligibility contingent on White House guarantees that harassment had stopped.[49] The late 1984 assassination of the journalist and spy Henry Liu in California escalated outrage and sparked more hearings. The discovery that the killing had been ordered from the very top in Taiwan, possibly by one of CCK's sons, might well have been devastating for relations with Taipei.[50]

CCK, expecting serious damage to the positive ties Taipei had cultivated with Washington during the Reagan years, first vigorously denied culpability and suppressed news of the murder in Taiwan. With mounting evidence secured by the FBI that tied Admiral Wang Hsi-ling, an embassy official and director of the Intelligence Bureau of the Ministry of National Defense (MND), to the affair and to CCK, the cover-up began to unravel. Reluctantly, Chiang conceded that some of his underlings had been complicit, and various individuals served short jail sentences, although their military careers were not unduly harmed. CCK's biographer, Jay Taylor, believes Chiang did not authorize Liu's slaying but felt guilty because he had sanctioned other executions. Chiang confided to one of his secretaries (a future president), Ma Ying-jeou, that martial law in Taiwan sent the world a negative message. Publicly he expressed shock and remorse.[51]

In the end, although indignant about operations in the US, especially the killing of an American citizen, the Reagan White House did not denounce Taipei, giving Free China more leeway than Washington would have accorded Red China. Reagan had appointed Jeane Kirkpatrick to her post as US ambassador to the UN and later considered making her his national security adviser, precisely because he admired her argument that friendly authoritarian governments, such as that in Taiwan, were more acceptable than hostile, revolutionary, totalitarian regimes, such as the one that governed China.[52] Officers at AIT concluded that the Reagan administration "did not want to come down hard on Ching-kuo," and although the dynamics of the cold war and human rights put pressure on Taiwan, both Taipei's requests for assistance and the Reagan administration's support were undiminished.[53]

Neither arms sales nor Washington's nuclear umbrella allayed fears in Taiwan about vulnerability to nuclear as well as conventional attack. Suspicion that the US could be distracted or "bought" led to continuing experimentation with an independent nuclear capability. In the early Reagan years, officials such as Jim Lilley repeatedly emphasized the unacceptability of a Taiwan nuclear arsenal.

After Reagan's trip to China and the apparent signing of a US–China nuclear deal, CIA espionage found that Taiwan had revived its nuclear program. Evidence that Taipei was untrustworthy led US inspectors to intervene, reminding Taipei that these activities violated signed mutual agreements negotiated before the Reagan administration. Taipei grumbled about American imperialism as CCK and his fiercely loyal military chief, General Hau Pei-tsun, considered recanting a restrictive accord the implications of which, they argued, had not been fully understood.[54]

In 1987 the deputy director of Taiwan's Institute of Nuclear Energy Research, Colonel Chang Hsien-yi, confirming satellite surveillance, alerted Washington to significant progress toward weapons whose development China had said would trigger an attack. Chang, who had been a CIA asset since the 1960s, defected with reams of documents, and early in 1988 pressure on Taiwan began in earnest. David Dean arrived from Washington, followed shortly by a second mission that insisted that Taipei shutter both its hot-cell complex and the island's largest research reactor, which would end plutonium production and preempt separation of plutonium from spent fuel. Washington offered no quid pro quo; it simply insisted that experimentation stop.[55]

Taiwan's top officials initially denied sponsoring nuclear research. Under pressure, however, General Hau took responsibility, probably shielding CCK. More than a decade later, Hau indignantly recalled that Taipei had had the data, the plans, and the technicians and could easily have gone nuclear. The US "didn't have any evidence that we were producing nuclear weapons, and should have trusted us." Did the Americans want us to "kill all the scientists"? On March 21, 1988, with no real alternatives, Taiwan notified the IAEA that activities were being suspended and facilities dismantled.[56]

Central American Leverage

CCK understood that the role of a dependent state sometimes required support for the overseas adventures of its patron and that this could accrue to the dependent's international standing. Central America met both imperatives in the 1980s, as had Vietnam in an earlier era.

Washington first proposed involving Taipei in Reagan's Central American crusades to get around the Boland amendments of 1982 and 1984, which prohibited the Pentagon, the CIA, and all other intelligence agencies from giving aid to the Nicaraguan contras in their campaign to oust the left-leaning Sandinista government. Reagan, however, did not intend to be constrained. In 1984 he ordered his NSC to circumvent Boland restrictions through alternative sources of funding.

Taiwan emerged as an attractive potential source of support. Major General John K. Singlaub had extensive contacts on the island, including Chiang Wei-kuo, the president's brother, with whom he had attended the US Command General Staff College. Initially, Singlaub approached Fred Ch'ien on behalf of the White House; late in 1984 he went to Taiwan to solicit funds from the foreign minister. For Taiwan the issue involved a serious diplomatic risk, since Nicaragua was one of only a few states with which it continued to have diplomatic relations. Moreover, Taipei worried about defying Congress, whose goodwill was essential to survival.

Singlaub, however, was unrelenting and stressed the confidentiality of contributions, suggesting a letter of credit or use of third parties such as a Panamanian bank deposit, or an inflated purchase price for forty American-built torpedoes that Taiwan wanted to buy from Israel. The overpayment, $10 million above an agreed-on price, would then be diverted to the contras in a maneuver that closely previewed the Iran-Contra fiasco. To the few privy to the money scheme, such as CIA Director William Casey, Taiwan appeared a likely candidate for contributions because of its anticommunist history. Nevertheless, Taipei remained undecided, neither refusing nor agreeing to the plan.[57]

Meanwhile, Oliver North, the NSC's key link for the Central American contra campaign, approached the PRC, with Gaston Sigur's assistance, for help in facilitating a shipment of much-needed weapons. North then used that arrangement to put renewed pressure on Taipei. Sending Singlaub back to what the sanitized NSC documents call "a senior Taiwanese official"—almost certainly Fred Ch'ien—the White House declared to Singlaub's interlocutor that the administration had been forced to recruit the PRC because of Taiwan's lack of cooperation. The official responded immediately that this was now a "considerably different situation," and it might produce a more favorable reaction from decision makers in Taiwan.[58] At about this same time, Sigur met with Ch'ien to emphasize that the initiative had been authorized from the top and was not a freelance operation. Indeed, early in 1985 Ronald Reagan made his feelings about the contras crystal clear: he called them "the moral equal of the Founding Fathers." Reagan, moreover, did know of Taiwan's involvment. North weighed in with Taipei soon after, telling the Taiwanese defense attaché that a new contra government would have diplomatic relations with the ROC—a promise he also made to the PRC.[59]

Singlaub apparently intended to follow up by seeking an appointment with CCK through his erstwhile friend Chiang Wei-kuo. During the trial of Oliver North, Singlaub testified to the US District Court that Elliott Abrams, then assistant secretary of state, called him off because "someone at the highest level" had approached CCK directly with the request. Evidence does exist that NSC, CIA, and State Department officials met and decided to stop Singlaub, but the reasons remain unclear.[60]

In any case, Taiwan did contribute, sending money and light weapons as well as training personnel. The arms went through private channels arranged by the CIA station chief in Taipei.[61] The funds, transferred in two payments of $1 million each through the KMT's World Anti-Communist League, went into a Swiss bank account maintained by North. On December 17, 1985, the Sandinista government broke diplomatic relations with Taiwan and turned instead to the PRC for support.

But Taiwan's role in Central America did not end with the Nicaraguan contras. Taiwan had also established a long-running relationship with Manuel Noriega, Panama's ruthless president. Noriega had traveled to Taiwan early in his career for military and intelligence training, where he became friends with Admiral Sung Ch'ang-chih. Sung subsequently became chief of the General Staff and defense minister; between 1987 and 1991 he served as ambassador to Panama. There he sought to exploit the country's most appealing features, including opportunities for trade and investment, access to the Panama Canal, diplomatic recognition, and assistance in various clandestine enterprises aimed at the PRC. Washington, meanwhile, had also trained and worked with Noriega: the CIA had maintained him on its payroll and Casey had used him to funnel arms to the contras.

When Washington finally turned against Noriega in the late 1980s because of his criminal enterprises, Taiwan decided to break ranks. Indeed, in 1988, when Washington maneuvered to buy Noriega's resignation by dropping drug indictments and paying a substantial bribe, the Panamanian leader suggested Taiwan as a source of the requisite financing. Washington did, in fact, approach Taipei as one of several potential donors and secured its agreement, although the deal collapsed for other reasons.[62] Meanwhile, Taiwan increased its weapons sales to Panama, making up for the shortfall caused by a US ban. Fred Ch'ien sought to prevent the government from taking such a risky action, but he proved unable to undermine the infectious enthusiasm of Chen Li-an, the minister of economics, who argued that the benefits of Taiwanese-Panamanian relations were significant. In 1989 Taipei created a $1 billion fund for development projects in Panama. As Mario Rognoni, a close adviser to Noriega, saw it, "The Taiwanese were the ringleaders of those helping us. The others followed."[63]

Caution in the Strait

Taking risks in Central America was one thing, in the Taiwan Strait another. Although Washington repeatedly called for improving relations with China, until the late 1980s Taipei was unresponsive to initiatives. Efforts even by friendly Americans to bridge the divide between Taipei and Beijing failed. Ray Cline, for instance, ventured into this hazardous territory with the blessings of the future CIA chief William Casey, then running Reagan's campaign. When CCK refused to see him, however, he also lost his entrée into the Reagan administration.[64]

PRC offers fared no better. Taipei firmly rebuffed the September 1981 Nine-Point Proposal of Ye Jianying, deemed conciliatory by many Americans because it treated Taipei as a regional authority. No one in Taiwan's leadership, however, believed the PRC could be trusted to grant promised rights and privileges.[65] Similarly, Deng Xiaoping's 1983 articulation of the concept of "one country, two systems" fell flat. Deng explained that China would not interfere in Taiwan's domestic affairs, nor would it send officials or military personnel to the island; but it would reserve the rights to represent Taiwan internationally and to defend it militarily. Taiwan's leaders, however, remained suspicious. As Premier Sun Yun-suan had said in February, Beijing's "peace talk is merely another form of war, we shall never fall into their trap."[66] Thus, on his 1984 trip to China, Reagan firmly rejected entreaties from Deng that he press Taipei to discuss "one country, two systems." Subsequent lobbying for the concept by Kissinger and others struck Wolfowitz as misguided and a clear violation of the Six Assurances. Shultz concurred, and the effort stalled.[67]

CCK nevertheless decided he could accelerate domestic political reform and simultaneously undertake cautious improvement of relations across the Strait in 1986. He began to democratize his government and permitted unprecedented, if modest, contact with the PRC. Feeling acutely that his illness—which often confined him to bed and made it impossible to read state papers—left him little time to cement his legacy, Chiang lifted martial law, permitted an opposition political party to operate, and freed the press. Having made Lee Teng-hui, a Taiwanese, his vice president, he struggled to ensure Lee's right of succession. And, when a pilot hijacked a cargo plane to the mainland, he authorized the first official contacts since 1949 to resolve the episode.

Chiang acted because he saw reform as critical to the survival of his government, not because he had experienced a democratic epiphany. He had been pushed by democracy advocates and a rising middle class at home, goaded by international pressure and embarrassment, and disturbed by the loss of US official support and mounting congressional pressure.

Thus, he persevered in the face of resistance from his longtime supporters in the military and in the right wing of the Nationalist Party, recognizing that Taipei could no longer deny improvement in US–China relations or rely on unrealistic hopes for Beijing's collapse. Chiang tasked his advisers to study lifting martial law, which foreign governments insisted on. They concluded that martial law, as practiced in Taiwan, could be lifted in name while most of the restrictions Chiang required could be retained. He conspicuously announced his intention first not to a domestic audience but to an influential American publisher, Katherine Graham of the *Washington Post,* whom he could, and needed to, impress.[68]

In response, the Reagan administration tentatively sought to advance cross-Strait reconciliation. Indeed, in October 1986 George Bush told Fred Ch'ien that China's modernization warranted an entirely new approach to relations.[69] George Shultz, during a 1987 visit to Shanghai, "welcome[d] developments, including indirect trade and increasing people-to-people interchange, which have contributed to a relaxation of tensions in the Taiwan Strait." Lauding the "evolutionary process toward peaceful resolution of the Taiwan question," he maintained that Washington wished to "foster an environment within which such developments can continue to take place."[70]

For Taipei, Washington went too far. David Dean had been approached before the trip and asked that Shultz refrain from just this sort of speech, understood by Fred Ch'ien as pressure to negotiate. According to Martin Lasater of the Heritage Foundation, who was visiting Taiwan, Shultz's remarks appeared to advocate abandonment of CCK's official position of "no negotiations, no compromise and no contact" with the PRC. Whatever Chiang might do personally, he wanted Washington to respect his Three Nos and instructed General Hau to emphasize this point during his October 1987 visit to the US.[71]

The desire to encourage better relations between China and Taiwan did not lessen Washington's interest in intelligence cooperation with Taiwan. Intelligence from Taiwan's agents had a reputation for unreliability, and the US often segregated it lest false leads cause policy misadventures. Washington nevertheless sought access to such data to protect itself from surprise and protested when Taipei refused to share. Americans put more faith in the parallel universe of high-tech signals collection. Eventually, Taiwan's location led the US to build a massive electronic-listening post at the cost of hundreds of millions of dollars. Although Washington and Beijing no longer contended as cold war antagonists, the station, operated by a cadre of US civilian defense contractors and retired military personnel, continued to provide extremely valuable data about China in the 1980s and beyond.[72]

AFTER THE first years of his administration, Reagan said little about Taiwan. Problems in the Middle East and Central America became more volatile and embarrassing. His preoccupation with protecting the US against nuclear attack, his desire to advance arms control, and his determination to end the cold war and liberate Eastern Europe took clear precedence. When he looked east, he saw China not as the adversary he had once imagined, but as a partner in defeating the Soviet Union. Thus, Ronald Reagan went to Communist China and, like Nixon and Kissinger, he did not let Taiwan get in the way. Reagan's second term became a golden era in Sino-American relations.

It can be argued that simultaneously opportunities developed in cross-Strait relations partly because of good US–China relations. Deng Xiaoping promoted a nonconfrontational approach designed to further peaceful unification, and Chiang Ching-kuo relaxed his Three Nos to permit travel and economic exchange. Lee Teng-hui's assumption of the presidency in 1988 reinforced this trend, given his adherence to a one-China policy. But Taiwan needed strong US support to risk negotiations, and Sino-American harmony undermined Taipei's fragile trust in Washington.

Ironically, these years also proved a crucial time for democracy in both Taiwan and China. In Taiwan CCK, albeit reluctantly, recognized that he needed to nurture political change in his government and party for them to survive international isolation, internal volatility, and his impending death. Chinese leaders, who allowed an unprecedented period of intellectual openness in the mid-1980s, chose a different path, turning away from the challenge of democracy. Indeed, both feared the undisciplined American model. But as Taipei tentatively began to trust its people, Beijing decided it could not.

THE END OF THE COLD WAR

THE ENDING of the cold war and the collapse of the Soviet Union posed enormous challenges to George H. W. Bush, a man whose career had been rooted in caution and political calculation. He expected to be a foreign policy president, but rapid change demanded imagination and courage, not conventionality and prudence. As he said himself, he lacked the "vision thing." Thus, he approached Soviet reform gingerly, distrusting new realities. Moreover the public expected a "peace dividend" that drained resources from defense and diplomacy, narrow his options, dismay the Pentagon, and worry critics in Congress.

Bush seemed at his best building a coalition to fight the Persian Gulf War (1991). Using his carefully honed networking skills, he cajoled world leaders into contributing forces or funds—or both—to save Kuwait's independence from Iraq, thereby assuring US dominance over the region and access to oil.

Bush tried a variation on personal diplomacy after violence erupted in China in 1989, but far less successfully. The student protests and China's brutal suppression of them undermined the president's plans to build closer and stronger relations with China. Outraged Americans demanded that Beijing be isolated, loans and trade be frozen, and human rights become central in Sino-American relations. Congress and human rights groups condemned Chinese leaders. Bush, however, ignored their censure and labored to maintain ties, encountering heavy criticism after public disclosure of his efforts.

As the broad consensus that had sustained Sino-American relations since 1971 broke down, Bush found himself repeatedly at odds with Congress and the public. Renewal of China's most-favored-nation trade treatment evolved into a wrenching and taxing annual congressional ordeal. Disputes materialized over arms sales and prison labor. The president, however, barely criticized China, convinced US national interests demanded repairing the Tiananmen rift. In this he proved less tentative and wary than in most other aspects of his foreign policy.

CHAPTER TEN

Shifting Ground

TAIWAN PLAYED a peculiar role in the political career of George H. W. Bush, a man who never wanted to be identified with its interests or to help it achieve its most crucial objectives. He unintentionally assisted it when Richard Nixon appointed him ambassador to the United Nations. He fleetingly railed against the Carter administration for jettisoning it to establish relations with Beijing. And then he turned to it one final time to stave off defeat at what proved to be the abrupt termination of his political life. Otherwise, he paid little attention to Taipei. His White House responsibilities focused most of his attention on the Soviet Union and Eastern Europe as European communism imploded, and then on the Middle East, to fight the Gulf War. His desire to build strong ties with China tilted him away from Taipei. And, even after the June 1989 Tiananmen massacre eviscerated that desire, he did not join other Americans in developing a new interest in Taiwan.

Bush's entanglement with Taiwan could not have been predicted. He had little understanding of the island and worked with its UN mission in 1971 not out of dedication to the China representation issue, but because his responsibility as UN ambassador required leading the fight to save the ROC's seats in the Security Council and General Assembly. Bush threw himself into the campaign zealously, eager to build a credible foreign policy record and prove that his appointment had not been a sign of disrespect to the organization, as some skeptics suggested. Using his wide network of friends, he labored vigorously to preserve space for America's ally, knowing that the PRC could not be prevented from entering the institution. Over time the battle became personal. He felt misled by instructions from Washington and betrayed by Kissinger's trip to China. On the other hand, he never made it an issue; Nixon had already told him that he sought "not brains but loyalty" from Bush.[1]

Whatever anger Bush may have felt over the debacle did not carry over to his interaction with the Chinese on either side. Bush displayed no conscious ill will toward the Nationalist Chinese, even though their insistence on waging a losing fight taxed his energies, resources, and contacts. He subsequently wrote that he had admired the quiet fortitude with which Taipei's representative endured the ordeal. Yet Bush did not allow bonds forged in the heat of battle to color his views of China. Diplomatic relations might not yet exist between Washington and Beijing, but it was clear that the White House wanted the incoming PRC mission treated well and that there was no professional or political reason for a continuing relationship with Taipei.

George Bush, in fact, would soon become a self-styled mainland China hand. In 1974 Gerald Ford offered him a choice of ambassadorial posts in London, Paris, or Beijing, and, to the surprise of many, he elected to serve at the liaison office in China. He wrote in his diary at the time that "everybody in the United States wants to go to China," and it seemed that he shared that enthusiasm for the exotic communist east. More important, the China Liaison Office gave him the chance to establish credentials in a new field where his lack of background might be less of a handicap. Bush relished the fact that "the professors don't know a hell of a lot more about what's going to happen in China than the politicians or the military."[2] (Of course, he could more easily make that assertion because he did not read their writings, just as he failed to exploit much of the State Department material provided before his departure.)[3] Once he returned from the field, his frustration and boredom quickly forgotten, he considered himself an authority on China and Sino–US relations. When he became president, both admirers and critics characterized him as his own China desk officer, and he sought to fill the role, sometimes to the detriment of national policy.

In reality, although Bush knew more about the PRC than any previous president, everyone exaggerated his expertise. During his tenure as head of the liaison office, China policy continued to be made and conducted primarily in Washington. When Kissinger visited Beijing, the secretary largely ignored the liaison office, and Bush often complained that information from Washington about decision making was hard to come by. He knew he was "playing in Kissinger's sandbox," with little choice but to cede "the high-level, substantive dealings with the Chinese power-wielders" to the secretary. His feelings on the matter may explain why he never sought a meeting with Mao Zedong during his fourteen months in Beijing, although the Chinese leader told him, "Why don't you come and look me up?"[4]

Bush's commitment to China mixed domestic politics with the cold war utility of the link to Beijing as he understood it. The political motive seemed clearest in 1978–79, when Jimmy Carter established diplomatic relations with the PRC and Bush condemned him. Bush, of course, favored relations; his supposed outrage focused on the compromises that Carter had made—in contrast to Republican integrity. "By the administration's own admission," Bush complained, "it never received—or even asked for—specific assurances from Peking about a peaceful solution to the Taiwanese question." Unlike his Republican predecessors, who resisted such an unprincipled deal, Carter had demonstrated to Beijing "just how easily we can be pushed around."[5]

Days later, however, Bush assured Deng Xiaoping that his opinion essay had been intended only as a political jab at Carter. He understood the "one China and Taiwan" problem from his months living in Beijing and said, "My only reservation is I would like to codify this 'peaceful' problem." According to Jim Lilley, who was present as an adviser to Bush, Deng responded, "We will try to solve Taiwan by peaceful means but not tie the other hand. Can you persuade Taiwan to negotiate with us?" Bush, who had a reputation at the NSC for being "swayed by personal relationships with foreign leaders," agreed. "If I can ever be helpful, I will—I will help get them to negotiations."[6]

Taipei understood that Bush's attack on Carter did not reflect a retreat from his overriding desire to build relations with China. The common UN fight, Taipei's only bond with Bush, had receded into the distant past. Taiwan could not trust this man to protect its interests. Books such as Theodore White's *Thunder Out of China* and Barbara Tuchman's *Stilwell and the American Experience in China*, which he read as liaison office chief, drew devastating portraits of Nationalist Chinese abuse of power, incompetence, and corruption when they ruled the mainland.[7] He had also been impressed by the popular passion he encountered on the Taiwan issue. "I remember," he recalled, "in the early days how Chinese workmen refused to hang a map of Asia on my office wall because it showed Taiwan in a different color from the mainland."[8]

Bush sought to purvey the image of a man close to China's leaders, an old friend of the Chinese people, and someone dedicated to good US–China relations. Beijing gladly bolstered that impression. Thus, Bush preserved his China connections during his years as vice president in an administration more concerned about Taiwan than he was. An inveterate networker, he had entertained the heads of Taiwan's Washington mission, Tsai Wei-ping and Fred Ch'ien, as well as important businessmen such as Koo Chen-fu, but this occurred very privately and drew no notice. The US Information Agency published two versions of Bush's biography shortly before his inauguration: the one disseminated in Taiwan included a pledge to uphold the TRA, but the one distributed on the mainland did not.[9] Taipei could only hope that Bush's friendship with Deng Xiaoping would not tempt him to act as a mediator between Beijing and Taipei.

President Bush sought to strengthen relations with China and appointed individuals to government posts who agreed with that goal. His national security adviser, Brent Scowcroft, with whom he enjoyed close personal as well as professional ties, had been involved in Nixon's China initiative. Lacking independent political ambitions, Scowcroft appeared to Bush more trustworthy than others in his administration. Indeed, after their twenty years of collaboration, people said that "they share[d] a brain"; upon leaving office, they wrote a joint memoir, *A World Transformed*.[10]

Scowcroft had been part of the "small cadre of men serving under [Kissinger] . . . who were to guide American policy toward China for the next quarter-century," motivated by the assumption of China's "surpassing strategic importance."[11] Deputy Secretary of State Lawrence Eagleburger also had been with that cadre. He would travel with Scowcroft on the summer 1989 secret trip to China that later embarrassed Bush.

Nearly as important, Bush appointed James Baker secretary of state though, or maybe because, he remained a neophyte in the realm of foreign relations: the president cared more about his consummate political skills and their thirty-five years of friendship. Baker gladly deferred to the president on China policy, happy to avoid a complicated issue fraught with hazardous political penalties. Baker's dislike and distrust of the Chinese paralleled his only slightly less intense estrangement from specialists in his own agency. He isolated himself from working-level diplomats, creating a small inner circle of confidants to guard the ramparts and thoroughly alienating much of the foreign service.[12] Baker did not push State Department interests at the White House or make efforts to include the diplomats' perspectives on China, much less on Taiwan issues.

No one at high levels in the government gave Taiwan useful support. J. Danforth Quayle, Bush's young, conservative running mate, sympathized with Taipei. Even before the Republican National Convention ended, however, Bush perceived Quayle as a liability, less agile and intelligent than had been imagined.[13] Quayle's self-destruction rendered his pro-Taiwan sympathies useless to Taipei, although he occasionally acted as the administration's interface with the island.

And instead of familiar figures sympathetic to Taiwan (such as Richard Armitage and James Lilley), Bush chose Richard Solomon as State Department East Asian assistant secretary. Solomon, whose apprenticeship with Kissinger might have made him particularly sensitive to China's concerns, focused instead on Cambodia. Thus, his easy access to Baker and Bush, which could have been advantageous to his more forceful predecessors, made less of a difference for China-Taiwan policy during his tenure. In any case, Baker had no interest and Bush saw no reason to consult anyone at State.

Overall, the Bush administration strikingly minimized the ideological undercurrent of politics in Washington to Taiwan's disadvantage. Bush cast foreign policy debates in pragmatic rather than value-laden terms, which caused Reagan loyalists, who had never trusted Bush, to conclude that he had ordered "a systematic purge."[14] Even though Reagan's support had proved fickle, Taiwan continued to see him as favorable to the island's interests. Now, at the beginning of 1989, Taiwan could not identify anyone in an important policy-making post who considered US–Taiwan relations as important as improving ties to China.

In fact, as Bush's presidency started, the prospect for rapid progress with China looked very good. During Reagan's term reform accelerated in China and friction between Washington and Beijing diminished. Bush's election appeared to herald even better times. The president met with China's gregarious Ambassador Han Xu even before the inauguration and, when the death of Japan's Emperor Hirohito provided the opportunity for a February trip to Asia, Bush decided to stop in China. The unexpected and unusually early visit distressed Taipei and its sympathizers in the US, all of whom feared that Bush would be vulnerable to Chinese blandishments.[15] Li Zhaoxing, spokesman for the PRC Foreign Ministry, aggravated tension by stressing that Beijing hoped to convince Bush to promote the "one country, two systems" formula.

Within months, however, an ugly dispute over human rights marred Bush's China "homecoming." On February 26, 1989, security forces excluded a prominent dissident, Fang Lizhi, from a banquet during Bush's visit, an incident widely publicized in the US and deeply embarrassing to Bush. In June Fang sought and received asylum at the US Embassy and remained a "guest" until June 1990, when the Chinese agreed to let him leave the country.

Tiananmen

Fang's need for sanctuary derived from the massive demonstrations in June 1989 calling for political reform that erupted in Tiananmen Square, the heart of China's capital. The American media—present because Deng Xiaoping was celebrating his victory in repairing the decades-long Sino-Soviet rift by welcoming Mikhail Gorbachev to Beijing—broadcast horrific pictures worldwide as troops used guns and tanks against young, unarmed protesters. Tiananmen generated popular revulsion across Europe and Asia, and it shattered the American consensus promoting good US–China relations.

The anger of Americans and the intransigence of the Chinese instantly destabilized the relationship with China. Bush instinctively tightened his grip, centralizing decision making within a small circle, which he controlled. The president concentrated on sustaining dialogue, minimizing sanctions, and persuading Beijing to conciliate American opinion through positive gestures. Bush remained convinced that for reasons of strategic location, economic potential, population size, and environmental impact, China warranted presidential attention and American cooperation.[16]

In the aftermath of Tiananmen Square, Taiwan's political reform and economic modernization suddenly attracted the attention of other Americans. They found that Taiwan's ruling party had been gradually relinquishing power since the mid-1980s and that a lively political opposition had propelled the democratic transformation of domestic politics. Meanwhile, with the communist bloc dissolving, the Soviet Union collapsing, and the cold war ending, China's strategic importance disappeared. In the spring of 1990, a year after communist authorities had crushed protesters across China, Taiwan's president, Lee Teng-hui, met with student leaders, whose 30,000 compatriots massed in central Taipei, and promised a national conference on political reform. As he told an American official, he had been a graduate student at Cornell University in 1968 and expected the United States to fragment amid the violence and turmoil of that year. When it did not collapse on the first day, or the next, he realized that democracy was not "luan" (chaos); it was an extraordinarily strong and stable system. By 1990 he was in a position to facilitate its growth in Taiwan.[17]

Officials in Taiwan sought to take advantage of the disaster in China, but this was not the 1950s or 1960s, when Chiang Kai-shek would have appealed for support to mount an attack. Financial assistance flowed to

dissidents who fled repression. With some trepidation, Taiwan joined in US–sponsored sanctions and boycotts and suspended new investment. Deputy Foreign Minister John Chang Hsiao-yen reminded the press, "We are concerned Beijing might create an encounter with us to provide an excuse for their own domestic unity."[18] Taiwan welcomed the prospect that Tiananmen had damaged US–China relations, but it warily greeted speculation by Americans that Beijing's brutal leadership could not stay in power, its hopes held in check by the island's vulnerability.[19]

The determination of Taiwan's business community not to let the crackdown on the democracy movement interrupt commerce for too long may have been as potent in speeding a revival of cross-Strait relations as it was in avoiding trouble. Taiwan government officials explained to AIT's David Dean that this desire to restore links to the mainland had to be understood in context. "The U.S. didn't realize the true nature of the communists and now they were seeing it for themselves." In Taiwan, on the other hand, "we knew it all along and we weren't taken aback by this."[20]

Supporters in the US, although disturbed that Taiwan so rapidly returned to business as usual, saw the aftermath of Tiananmen as an opportunity to promote its interests. At one extreme, Senator Jesse Helms sought to end contacts with "Red China" and treat Taiwan as the real China. Others simply acknowledged the great strides Taiwan had been making while the world had been entranced by China. The White House found that Taiwan's emergence as a morally superior and clearly democratic society complicated restoration of ties with Beijing.

Taiwan's New Appeal

Taiwan's attractiveness also had a lot to do with the success of its economy. By 1992 Taiwan had accumulated the largest foreign exchange reserves in the world. In 1990 it announced a Six-Year National Development Plan on which it proposed to spend some $300 billion, virtually inviting a US government appeal for financial support of military operations in the Persian Gulf. Taiwan's uneasiness about Bush's views and his old ties to Richard Armitage, who was acting as a special envoy, secured a commitment of $300 million, a sum exceeding amounts pledged by more populous and powerful, but not more eager, friends of Washington's.

Taiwan relished the opportunity publicly and privately to lend support to Washington and to Armitage, whom political and military leaders liked and respected. Foreign Minister Fred Ch'ien boasted to the media that "the United States was looking to us to openly declare our position. This shows that the United States takes us seriously."

Taipei had its own reasons to support the war. Taiwan depended on the Middle East for 60 percent of its oil, which gave it a direct interest in removing Iraq from Kuwait, its second-largest supplier. Further, officials sought to separate Taiwan from countries like Libya, which had been charged with helping Iraq violate UN sanctions.

Instead of expressing gratitude, Washington ultimately declined the promised funds, much to Taiwan's dismay. That the decision came after money had been solicited proved embarrassing, but not unprecedented, and may have been due in part to Chinese objections. The White House clearly sought to avoid a retaliatory Chinese veto of UN action in the Gulf. For neither the first nor the last time, Washington may have followed an impulse to check with Beijing on Taiwan issues.[21]

Adding to Taipei's bitterness over the incident, Beijing maneuvered the administration into a meeting between Foreign Minister Qian Qichen and Bush in the White House, even though it abstained rather than vote with Washington at the UN. Thus, Beijing erased a major Tiananmen sanction without performing, whereas Taipei, with cash in hand, could not break out of its isolation.

Overall, Taiwan had greater success promoting its visibility through domestic transformation than by international competition. From the mid-1980s it advanced political reform, lifting martial law and legitimizing a multiparty system and free speech, including an aggressive press. Taiwan's January 1990 application to enter the General Agreement on Tariffs and

Trade, accordingly, received serious consideration. Ironically, Bush even tried using good feeling toward Taiwan to help preserve China's most-favored-nation trade status against attacks by prominent Democrats. Beijing did not make it easy. In 1991 it ran a $13 billion trade surplus, threw up fresh trade barriers, and persisted in missile exports to Syria and Pakistan in spite of US opposition. Recognizing his dilemma, Bush wrote a conciliatory letter to Senator Max Baucus, chairman of the Subcommittee on International Trade of the Senate Finance Committee, delineating actions to be taken to deal with China on technology transfer, human rights, and trade abuses. He promised to promote Taiwan's membership in the GATT as a "customs territory" and, in a significant departure for his administration, said that if Taiwan qualified first it should enter GATT first and not have to wait for China.[22]

By the autumn the burgeoning economic integration of China's southeastern provinces with Hong Kong and Taiwan to form a "natural economic territory" began to take on potential political significance.[23] Secretary of State Baker appeared to be hinting in the pages of *Foreign Affairs* that if China did not act more responsibly on issues such as arms sales, the administration might have to resort to an "ultimate sanction—a threat to the territorial integrity of the Middle Kingdom." As Leslie Gelb interpreted this in the *New York Times,* "instead of China eventually absorbing Taiwan and Hong Kong . . . the exact opposite could happen—Taiwan and Hong Kong . . . could absorb the southern tier of China."[24]

Prosperity and the beginnings of democratization in Taiwan, then, generated enthusiasm in Washington among those who believed developments on the island might serve as either a threat or an example to China. Lee Teng-hui spoke along similar lines when, two days after his May 20, 1990, inauguration, he told the press that he hoped Taiwan would become a model for the mainland, and he created a National Unification Council (NUC), a Mainland Affairs Council (MAC) and a Straits Exchange Foundation (SEF) to that end. According to Jim Lilley, Lee also asked him to carry a message to China's president, Jiang Zemin, in 1990 that he, Lee, would not declare independence.[25] In February 1991 Lee's administration promulgated guidelines to encourage progress toward unification through development of human rights, democracy, and prosperity in parallel political entities on both sides of the Strait. Lee appeared to identify better cross-Strait relations and a generally peaceful environment as vital to political change in Taiwan.[26] In May, moreover, Lee ended the period of "national mobilization for suppression of the Communist rebellion," repealing "temporary" measures that for more than forty years had sustained

KMT oppression and reinforced hostile views of the mainland. To Washington's relief, Lee's rhetoric and actions reduced the likelihood that Americans would end up fighting the PRC over Taiwan.

Democracy in Taiwan

Democratization in Taiwan engendered a wider audience and unprecedented freedom for those who advocated independence. Furthermore, the dissolution of the Soviet empire inspired activists to make invidious comparisons. "If the three Baltic republics can become independent, why can't Taiwan?" asked a member of the Legislative Yuan. "Taiwan is economically more powerful than they are, it has more people, and it has a military. If Taiwan is stronger than they are and China is weaker than the Soviet Union, then why can't Taiwan submit a vote to the people to declare independence?"[27]

Lee Teng-hui's rise spurred radical politics and split the KMT, first figuratively and, in 1993, literally. Initially, Lee co-opted the popular elements of the agenda of the Democratic Progressive Party (DPP) as he fought KMT conservatives and military figures who opposed political change. They (the so-called non-mainstream faction) had been strong enough to force an inexperienced, Taiwanese Lee to accept a reliable and conservative mainlander as premier, General Hau Pei-tsun, in 1990. They kept Lee on the defensive while they maneuvered to recapture leadership of the party. In early 1993 there were even rumors of an impending coup.[28] Ultimately, Lee prevailed, ousting Hau, shedding obstructionists, and provoking formation of an oppositionist, pro-unification Chinese New Party.

Meanwhile, the DPP also struck out in a new direction. Domestic reformism, Soviet collapse, the end of the cold war, and the sudden flourishing of democracy inspired militant elements in the DPP to revamp the party charter. Under the influence of the New Tide faction, the DPP endorsed creation of an independent Republic of Taiwan, and Chen Shuibian, of the usually more moderate Justice Alliance, added the requirement that independence be decided by referendum. Over the next few years the DPP would follow a consistently disruptive and unelectable course.[29]

For the United States, Taiwan's more volatile domestic politics and its newly assertive international posture challenged assumptions and established practices. A democratic Taiwan turned out to be more complicated than an authoritarian elite. Lee's flexible, or pragmatic, diplomacy compelled Washington to negotiate with a Taiwan not content to stay at home or remain outside important governmental and nongovernmental organizations. Lee and other officials traveled wherever they could, joined whichever groups would have them, and sought vigorously to integrate Taiwan into the world community to make it more difficult for the PRC to isolate the island or to coerce it into unification on Beijing's terms.

Managing this thrust challenged Washington throughout the 1990s, particularly when Washington's orientation remained so heavily China-focused. Bush appointed his old friend, Jim Lilley, as ambassador to China, knowing Lilley's sometimes acerbic views of Chinese politics and leadership, but clearly believing that the man's personal loyalty and commitment to Sino-American relations would be paramount. Indeed, Lilley weathered the difficult days of Tiananmen and remained Bush's bridge to China's leaders until June 1991.

Not long after stepping down, however, Lilley struck out at the Chinese, whose behavior during and after Tiananmen he abhorred. He denounced the very men with whom he had been dealing in Beijing. Then he broadened his critique, telling a public gathering that Beijing must rethink its nineteenth-century ideas of sovereignty, particularly its "anachronistic" claim to Taiwan. Lilley asserted that the US government had been "locked for too long into the three communiqués. . . . You can't just stand still." The increasingly prosperous and democratic Taiwan of the present, he stressed subsequently, had become a Taiwan of the Taiwanese and no longer could be bound by an agreement that asserted "all Chinese on either side of the Taiwan Strait" believed in one China.[30] This new Taiwan deserved greater US aid. To Beijing's consternation and to Taipei's clear delight, not only did Bush fail to chastise Lilley for his outspokenness, but the president made him assistant secretary of defense for international security affairs.[31] Lilley, therefore, proved to be in a pivotal spot when the decision on selling Taiwan an advanced fighter aircraft arose in 1992.

The Lure of Arms Sales

For an administration that did not intend to pay much attention to the island, let alone revolutionize US–Taiwan relations, the new departure in weapons sales caught many by surprise. Initially, the arms trade process continued as it had in the Reagan years. Washington leased several Knox-class frigates to Taipei, licensed Taiwan to build a series of smaller Oliver Hazard Perry–class frigates (minus some key equipment), sold antisubmarine helicopters and SM-1 Standard naval surface-to-air missiles, and approved E-2T airborne early-warning aircraft as well as components for Patriot antimissile systems. Some of these deals moved slowly because, despite the admonitions of the TRA, US officials worried about Beijing's re-actions. One Pentagon official recalled that "the big debate through all those years was what straw would break the camel's back . . . and there were those of us who argued that you needed a pretty large telephone pole to break the camel's back. A lot of things that people argued were the end of the world just were not the end of the world. A lot of the time . . . it wasn't the Chinese who were the problem; it was those in the government who felt the Chinese were the problem." Thus, as another official recalled, Taipei was allowed to purchase the E-2T only after a cosmetic change that made it less effective and more expensive.[32]

But Chinese opposition proved less potent than might have been ex-pected, given George Bush's orientation. The TRA called on government agencies to make defense equipment available to Taiwan, and US indus-try agitated to get official approval for weapons systems, lamenting that "business for us is shrinking in the U.S., so we have to start looking over-seas." The Bush administration, heeding this distress, explicitly rejected even the pretense of shunning arms manufacturers and instructed am-bassadors to assist defense contractors in securing foreign deals. During 1991 aggressive marketing made the US the world's leading arms exporter: American companies sold more than half of all arms purchased in world markets.[33]

The disaster at Tiananmen, moreover, meant that Chinese objections did not have the same weight after June 4, 1989, that they had had before June 3. Other conditions specific to Taiwan had changed as well. During the Reagan administration Taiwan's military had acquired more sophisticated equipment, and the need for expertise finally eroded opposition to the idea of active-duty US military personnel traveling to Taiwan. Beginning in 1991, American military officers could provide assistance in Taiwan so long as they were camouflaged in larger teams and civilian clothes. Hei Youlong, a businessman, observed, "Before, Taiwan could never pay bil-lions of dollars for weapons. . . . Now, Taiwan has money and when it talks, people start listening." Taipei, for instance, could approach a Maine shipyard to assist with construction of Perry-class frigates, thereby ingrati-ating itself with Senate Majority Leader George Mitchell (D-Maine).[34] At the same time, France sold several Lafayette-class frigates to Taiwan for $2.5 billion and also improved its chances of securing contracts for infra-structure projects and a jet fighter deal.[35] Taiwan even came close to ac-quiring submarines. Surprisingly, the United States gave serious, if brief, consideration to a project in which an American company would perform the overall systems integration for a European consortium.

More secret still were the changes made in financing arms sales. By

1990–91 the cost of spare parts for Taiwan's aging military equipment consumed virtually the entire annual arms sales budget. Without readjustment, either Taiwan's military would obtain no new weapons or existing inventories would quickly fall into disrepair.

To a small contingent of officials, a flexible answer seemed obvious—redefine the contents of the so-called bucket. In other words, beginning in 1992 the budget devoted to Taiwan arms purchases, which under the August Communiqué had to be reduced annually, would cover a new range of goods that would no longer include spare parts. Once the White House and Congress could be convinced of the advantages of the policy rewrite, this revolutionized Taiwan's ability to purchase weapons while also sustaining its existing army, navy, and air force capabilities.

The item most eagerly sought by Taiwan remained an advanced fighter aircraft. Like its predecessors, the Bush administration rebuffed these requests on the grounds that the F-16 was an offensive, not defensive, plane. Even reports that the People's Liberation Army Air Force had purchased sophisticated Sukhoi-27 fighters from Moscow did not change Washington's position. AIT's Chairman and Managing Director Natale (Nat) Bellocchi told Defense Minister Chen Li-an on March 7, 1991, that officials in Washington were "skeptical that such a sale had taken place" and convinced there would be no "fighter gap." In other words, Washington calculated no Sukhoi-27s could arrive in China before Taiwan deployed its IDFs in 1996 or 1997.[36]

Administration opposition remained intact in the last round of arms sales talks before the 1992 US presidential election. When Defense Minister Chen appealed for a reconsideration of the decision, warning that Taiwan would have to seek a fighter "elsewhere," Bellocchi rebuffed him: "He should not anticipate any change this year."[37] Nevertheless, by September 1992, with two months to go till the balloting, Bush had reversed his position.

Clearly, whatever good technical reasons existed for approving the sale of the F-16 to Taiwan, the president acted on the basis of political imperatives. By the summer of 1992, George Bush faced an enormous problem. Despite the popular acclaim he had earned as leader of the victorious Gulf War coalition, a faltering economy had soured the electorate and polls showed him falling significantly behind his Democratic challenger, Bill Clinton, and the third party candidate H. Ross Perot was threatening further to diminish his vote count. Capturing a majority in a key state like Texas suddenly took on overwhelming importance, particularly given Bush's identification with Texas as his adopted home and the embarrassing possibility that he might forfeit its thirty-five electoral college ballots.

Bush believed he had a single option to try to win the Texas vote, and he used the prerogatives of office to bypass bureaucratic resistance to foreign sale of America's most advanced aircraft. Whether the idea for this initiative originated with Bush, his campaign advisers, or Texas businessmen and politicians, its value for winning votes did not need a lot of elaboration. Taiwan's CCNAA representatives and General Dynamics certainly missed no opportunities to promote it, lobbying with Republican and Democratic politicians in Texas and in Congress to appeal to the administration. As early as mid-July, the White House deputy chief of staff privately told Representative Joseph Barton (R-TX) that a "quick and dirty" examination of the matter had determined that the idea "had a lot of merit."[38]

On July 30 Bush informed reporters that his administration had begun to review the idea of an F-16 sale to Taiwan. At roughly the same moment, General Dynamics announced an impending layoff and Democratic Governor Ann Richards, Senator Lloyd Bentsen, and two hundred congressmen appealed to the president to reverse himself on the F-16. Bush directed the Defense Department to undertake something more than a cursory study and yet, presumably, reach a result that would facilitate the sale. As Robert Suettinger, then National Intelligence officer for East Asia, recalled, "Several interagency work groups were held in August at which the Defense Department presented its case to a rather skeptical audience of State Department, Commerce Department, and intelligence community representatives."[39] At the White House, no one took the review very seriously, since the choice had already been made. State Department officers, recognizing that the exercise was pro forma, busied themselves looking for ways to implement the president's order while staving off the worst of China's fury. When Bush went to the General Dynamics plant in Forth Worth, Texas, on September 2 to announce a massive sale of 150 planes to Taiwan, he knowingly ignored commitments to China and objections from within his administration. Cynics noted that the $4 billion contract and 5,800 jobs saved would buy a lot of votes in Texas.

The simultaneous sale of 72 McDonnell-Douglas F-15 aircraft manufactured in California and Missouri to Saudi Arabia for $5 billion reinforced this impression. In fact, the sales were explicitly linked within the administration. The F-15 deal involved even more complex political maneuvering, requiring that Israel acquiesce in the transfer, that Congress waive a mandatory consultation and notification period, and that potential regional proliferation be ignored.[40]

Despite the transparently political motives that dominated all other considerations, a case can be made that approving the F-16 for Taipei had other roots as well. Jim Lilley waged the fight vigorously from his new post as assistant secretary for international security affairs at DOD, lobbying Undersecretary of Defense Paul Wolfowitz and Douglas Paal at the NSC. He also capitalized on an opportunity to educate Defense Secretary Richard Cheney while traveling with him in Asia. Lilley prompted a request for a memo Cheney could use to review the question with his cabinet colleagues. But even Cheney later conceded that without the election Bush would not have sold the planes.[41]

Several new factors militated in favor of an advanced fighter deal in the early 1990s. First, the Pentagon had long since estimated that the Taiwan air force would begin to deteriorate sharply around 1992, and, as if on schedule, F-104s and growing numbers of F-5Es began crashing. Not only did this demonstrate the unreliability and obsolescence of the planes, it also significantly reduced Taiwan's ability to recruit pilots and the number of aircraft that could be flown in the event of an emergency. Actual "in-commission rates" for the air fleet varied from 51 to 67 percent, depending on the model. President Lee Teng-hui recalled that his visits to families of downed pilots became unnervingly frequent.[42]

At the same time, Taiwan's indigenous fighter plane, through which the Reagan administration substituted technology transfer for supply of an advanced aircraft, had run into problems. In Taiwan critics quipped that IDF actually stood for "It Don't Fly." But even had it been on schedule and reliable, one DOD official dismissed it as "an underpowered, Mattel version of the F-16."[43] Given this serious decline in the Taiwan air force and the resulting vulnerability, even those administration analysts who usually disregarded Taiwan's interests in favor of good relations with China warned that Beijing could be tempted to attack.

Second, the cold war had ended and the Soviet Union as well as the communist bloc had ceased to exist. With the threat of Moscow's expansionism and nuclear belligerence gone, China's strategic importance virtually evaporated. Especially after Tiananmen, only a few Americans could argue a coherent justification for strong US–China relations and even fewer could make the case that Beijing's cooperation had to be secured at the risk of jeopardizing Taiwan's interests.

Third, the collapse of the Soviet Union had initiated a great arms bazaar that sold high-tech weaponry at cut-rate prices to earn capital for the new Russia. Although Washington doubted early reports, Beijing did, in fact, purchase two dozen sophisticated Sukhoi-27 (or SU-27) aircraft. China had previously begun to upgrade its own F-8s, but post-Tiananmen sanctions had thrown US–China cooperation in the so-called Peace Pearl program into disarray. Subsequently, mounting costs and export controls led Beijing to abort the project.

Acquisition of the SU-27 altered the dynamic across the Taiwan Strait much more thoroughly than an improved F-8 would have. Taiwan's air force did not have a comparable plane, and as Beijing put this aircraft into service, the military balance changed appreciably. Under such circumstances, Washington was virtually required to invoke Reagan's secret memo and take action, especially since the SU-27 purchase appeared to be part of a larger Chinese assertion of power in Asia, which disturbed its neighbors. Evidence had emerged of Chinese efforts to buy an aircraft carrier from Ukraine as well as surface-to-air missiles and KILO-class submarines from Russia. Within the administration an informal interagency discussion group, which had begun to meet in 1991 and encompassed people from the NSC, the vice president's office, DOD, the State Department, and the CIA, began to focus on the Chinese problem. In the winter of 1991–92, it prepared a paper that pointed beyond air power to PRC naval expansion and interference in the Spratly Islands, in the South China Sea, as evidence of an increasingly activist China. The paper recommended more frequent interaction between the Pentagon and the Taiwan military as well as new sales to remedy weaknesses in air defense and technology. These conclusions did not signal a major commitment to Taiwan by the agencies themselves, but foretold shifting opinions in these units as imbalances escalated.[44]

Fourth, Taiwan had entered into negotiations with France for an alternative advanced fighter aircraft. The Mirage 2000-5 compared well with the F-16 and, although the logistics of servicing an American-made plane would be easier given Taiwan's almost total dependence on the US for equipment, spare parts, and expertise, a new source of supply had its virtues.

Negotiating with the French, at least initially, could also have been leverage to facilitate an F-16 sale. The Mirage's manufacturer, Dassault, actually encouraged this idea to draw Taipei into negotiations.[45] President Lee Teng-hui later contended that "it was not until negotiations for the purchase of Mirage fighter aircraft from France made progress that the United States ceased its reluctance to discuss exporting F-16s to Taiwan."[46]

The State Department, however, remained unmoved. In fact, according to AIT Director Bellocchi, the attitude among those who counted was: "Fine. Let the French share some of the burden. Let them share in taking all this heat from the Chinese." Therefore, at the June arms sales talks, having once again denied Taipei the aircraft, officials specifically suggested that the Mirage might make a good alternative.[47]

Word in the press that the White House was encouraging Taipei to spend its money in France instead of Texas, however, could be disastrous for the Bush campaign. Bellocchi, who had established a friendship with James Soong Chu-yu, secretary general of the KMT, was dispatched abruptly to waylay him in Houston and deliver word that the F-16 would be available after all. The Bush administration wanted a clear indication that Taipei would buy the plane before the president announced his offer publicly.

At the same time, Bellocchi urged Taiwan to scrap the Mirage deal. Delighted but discomfited, Soong warned that Taipei could not extricate itself from the French contract. In fact, Taiwan both bought the F-16 and signed with France. Chief of the General Staff General Liu Ho-chien spent his routine fall 1992 visit to the US assuring Americans that Taipei's Mirage entanglement would not subtract money and manpower from the F-16 program.[48]

Ironically, the deal also stirred controversy in Taiwan. Members of the legislature grilled Fred Ch'ien, then foreign minister, on why Taiwan needed both planes. Among other reasons, the government used the F-16 deal to drive a harder bargain with France, extracting a better price for the Mirage even as it canceled its option to purchase sixty additional planes. Nevertheless, Wei Yung, chairman of the Foreign Affairs Committee, complained, "The Mirage is a beautiful aircraft. But it is too expensive. . . . For every aircraft, you could start a new university."[49]

Finally, Taiwan's prosperity helped ensure the fighter deal. It had become a significant market and investment destination. Arms sales suddenly qualified not just as money earners, but also as admission tickets to broader transactions. Moreover, with the end of the cold war and the disappearance of immediate security threats, the western alliance was beginning to fragment. US allies, facing the same decline in domestic military procurement that bedeviled American contractors, looked increasingly to Taiwan as a new market. European cabinet- and subcabinet-level officials flocked to Taipei, promoting both military and commercial contracts. Only the US business community, stymied by the continued ban on official trips, could not count on government assistance.

To some complacent Americans in the US government it appeared that Taiwan "can't screw around too much with an old, vital friend, to make new friends who don't care about the Pacific." But among senior KMT and elected officials, trust in Washington's support declined in the early 1990s. Ting Shou-chung, a KMT legislator serving on the National Defense Committee and a son of an army general, lamented that "the U.S. government values mainland China more heavily than its friends on Taiwan" and has been "neglecting our security needs."[50] Ting led fifty-three of his colleagues in the Legislative Yuan in proposing a resolution barring Americans from bidding on projects in the six-year public works program as payback for the government's unwillingness to sell F-16s to Taipei.[51] Taipei split between those who wanted to use the situation as leverage against Washington and those who were satisfied to cut the US out and bestow contracts on non-American companies.

One example of the way Europe sought to bundle business deals to displace US dominance involved the linkage of Lafayette-class frigates, the Mirage transaction, and potential contracts for Taiwan's fourth nuclear power plant. Taiwan's coastal defense plan for the 1990s envisioned the purchase of a fleet of small frigates to supplement larger ships already on hand. The new craft were to be bought from South Korean manufacturers. In the midst of negotiations, however, the Ministry of National Defense unexpectedly signed a contract with the French company Thomson-CSF for significantly larger and more costly Lafayette-class frigates. Hau Pei-tsun, who was chief of the General Staff at the time, later observed that "without the Lafayette deal, Taiwan would not have been able to get the Mirage 2000-5 fighter planes. Without the Mirage deal, Taiwan would not have been able to get the F-16s from the US."[52] Korean ships could not provide the same stimulus as French ships.

France in 1992 made half of all its overseas weapons sales in Taiwan, and French interests hoped this would provide access to infrastructure projects. So significant had the profits become that the French government ignored Chinese threats. Eventually the Lafayette deal, or Operation Bravo, involved enormous bribes in Taipei, Paris, and Beijing.[53] These machinations did not develop into a scandal until after voters had swept Bush from office.

George Bush fought his political demise vigorously. Faced with the possibility that he might lose to Clinton, he stopped worrying about Beijing. After years of denial, political calculations produced a stunning reversal, and the US agreed to sell Taiwan F-16 fighter aircraft. The president told his Fort Worth audience that peace in the Taiwan Strait and stability in the region had been a direct result of past arms sales and that the F-16 transfers would "sustain the confidence . . . [in Taiwan] to reduce . . . tensions."[54]

Aftermath

Predictably, the Bush administration denied that approving the F-16 departed from the strictures of the August Communiqué signed with Beijing in 1982 or the defense posture consistently followed by the US government. Acting Secretary of State Lawrence Eagleburger, who had initially declared that the sale would be made over his dead body, argued to the press that transfer of the planes would do no more than restore Taipei's ability to protect the island at the same level as had existed at the time of derecognition, given how many aircraft Taiwan had lost.[55] The administration also noted the provisions of the TRA that enjoined it to arm Taiwan, and since the US no longer manufactured the requisite spare parts for the F-104 or the F-5s in the Taiwan inventory, it had no choice but to provide Taipei a more capable aircraft. But, in line with the 1982 communiqué, it had chosen the least sophisticated model, the F-16 A/B.[56]

Bush sought to soften the blow by inviting China's Ambassador Zhu Qizhen and the visiting foreign ministry director of the North American and Oceanian Affairs Department, Yang Jiechi, to an informal session at the White House on July 31. Yang had accompanied Bush on a trip to Tibet in 1977, and Bush had befriended him. Building on their personal relationship, Bush hoped to clarify his motives to the young man he nicknamed "Tiger Yang." "This is going ahead. It's political. Tell Deng Xiaoping that this is something I have to do."[57] Subsequently, Bush allegedly promised, either to Yang or to others, that upon reelection he would somehow rectify the situation created by the sale.[58]

To Beijing the US action appeared to necessitate retaliation, although reassurances from Bush moderated its response. Vice Foreign Minister Liu Huaqiu called Ambassador J. Stapleton Roy to the Foreign Ministry after the Fort Worth announcement, protesting that "the Chinese side is shocked and outraged by this decision. . . . This will lead to a major retrocession in Sino–U.S. relations."[59] According to a variety of Hong Kong sources, whose reliability is difficult to judge, the military pressed relentlessly for a tougher "anti-hegemonist" approach.[60] China withdrew from talks on proliferation and human rights and resumed sales of M-11 missiles to Pakistan despite an agreement with the US not to do so. Thereafter, Beijing repeatedly sought to link its proliferation to US arms sales to Taiwan, citing the F-16 specifically because, the Chinese argued, it could deliver nuclear payloads—just like a missile. But Beijing did not do more because it faced pending commercial disputes with the US, which threatened its most-favored-nation trade status and entry into GATT. And Chinese leaders preferred to see Bush reelected: creating a serious crisis could only help put Bill Clinton in the White House.

As for cross-Strait relations, China complained that it had deescalated tensions in the 1980s, but the US and Taipei had spurned its peaceful posture. In actuality, China had never relinquished the threat of war, and it had resumed military exercises in 1990. Beijing sought to discourage growing Taiwanization of the island's politics and to retaliate against Taiwan for its support of the Tiananmen demonstrations of 1989. After the F-16 debacle, according to Robert Suettinger, a Clinton NSC staffer, China ensured that "no arms sale would go uncontested, no visit unprotested, no hint of change in the procedures for U.S.–Taiwan relations unchallenged. Beijing had a grievance, and it would . . . extract every ounce of leverage it could from what it called Bush's 'mistaken decision.' "[61]

Dialogue did not stop, however.[62] Despite the heated rhetoric of their disputes, Taiwan and China demonstrated in 1992 and 1993 that when they wanted to talk they could find a way. During the autumn of 1992, the two sides came to an understanding regarding the principle of one China to facilitate a meeting between Wang Daohan, head of China's newly created Association for Relations across the Taiwan Strait (ARATS), and Koo Chen-fu, chairman of the SEF, both men elderly intimates of their respective leaders.[63] Beijing asserted that "in routine cross-Strait consultations, the political meaning of 'One China' will not be involved." By contrast, Taipei stated that "each side has its own understanding of the meaning of One China." Subsequently, Taiwan proposed a formula known as "one China, different interpretations" to denote these two versions; later they would be labeled the "1992 consensus" by the Taiwan official and scholar Su Chi.[64] In 1992 and 1993 both sides accepted these parallel statements as a basis for talks. Optimism rose so high in some quarters in Taipei before the April 1993 Singapore session that Chiu Cheyne, a member of the KMT standing committee and confidant of the president, who was serving as secretary general of SEF, declared his intention to "tear down the Berlin Wall between Taiwan and the mainland."[65]

Notwithstanding this cross-Strait contact, Taiwan never seriously considered turning down the F-16. Ding Mou-shih, head of CCNAA, met for the first time with the recently appointed assistant secretary of state for East Asian Affairs, William Clark Jr. (not related to Judge William P. Clark), to discuss Bush's July 30 remarks on an F-16 sale. Clark described the pending review as impartial and "without preordained conclusions," but Taipei knew the president would not have gone public so soon before the election if the decision might be negative.[66] The customarily reticent Ding proved the perfect interlocutor. A consummate professional, Ding carried out orders cautiously and in this sensitive period patiently awaited word that the deal would go public. From Taipei, AIT reported more obvious enthusiasm, noting that "in almost every recent conversation with Taiwan authorities of every stripe, a possible F-16 sale comes quickly to their lips. Expectations are high."[67]

Taiwan authorities saw the plane as enhancing security and deepening ties to the United States. Lee Teng-hui, delighted with Bush's reversal, insisted it had been a military decision, not the result of domestic political calculations, no doubt because that enhanced its significance for Taipei. Ding found it impossible to dissuade him, and David Dean had no better luck. Chen Li-an, the defense minister, declared the sale "a major political breakthrough" for the US–Taiwan relationship. Beijing's fury at the news heightened the pleasure. Carl Ford, a Defense Department official at the time, reflected that "our willingness to show support . . . is really more important than the military requirements and if China doesn't get mad it's not any good."[68]

Not everyone in Taipei greeted the news with enthusiasm, however, given the enormous cost of the new purchases. Air Force Commanding General Lin Wen-li disparaged the F-16 model that the US offered to sell (F-16 A/B), making clear that Taiwan needed the more sophisticated version being used by the US Air Force (F-16 C/D) rather than a design intentionally underpowered and wired for air-to-air defensive operations without an air-to-ground bombing capability. The DPP shared these objections, but the KMT government took them less seriously. Others saw the package not just as a strain on the national budget, but also as a diversion of funds from IDF development at a time when continuing difficulties threatened a decade of effort. Minister Chen pledged that the IDF would not be adversely affected, but plans were already being made to acquire navigation, ground-attack, and communications capabilities of the more advanced F-16 in an expensive add-on package called a midlife upgrade.[69]

Indeed, the huge commitment for the F-16s, as well as the Mirage aircraft and the IDF, highlighted complaints about the secretive procurement practices of the Taiwan military. Politicians and manufacturers objected that the process prevented competitive bidding, raised costs, and channeled projects and technology to favored companies. In 1992 Defense Minister Chen was forced to admit that bypassing weapons experts meant "different arms purchases were handled by different military units, sometimes leading to confusions [sic] and an unnecessarily large expenditure of time."[70]

Taiwan's peculiar status made it an ideal experimental theater as well. As Kurt Campbell, deputy assistant secretary of defense for Asia and Pacific Affairs in the Clinton administration, told Congress, at a time when Aegis (an advanced combat, control, and information system) had become a centerpiece of Taipei defense requests, "We actually agreed and urged Taiwan, in 1992, to purchase Aegis . . . and they decided not to go ahead with it." But the 1992 version was more primitive and small enough to be mounted on ships other than the formidable Arleigh Burke–class frigates the US used. American contractors viewed the potential Taiwan purchase as a test of the reliability of the "mini-Aegis" system and of its attractiveness for other likely markets in Greece, Spain, and Portugal. Moreover, Taiwan was expected to shoulder some of the development costs. The Taiwan military did not want another problematic IDF-style program.[71]

Within the Department of State reverberations of the F-16 decision produced uncertainty about the direction of future relations with Taiwan. Clark, whose assistant secretary appointment came in the waning days of the Bush presidency, concluded that a reexamination of Taiwan policy should be one of several end-of-term studies undertaken during his brief tenure. A Japan specialist, Clark approached Taiwan more sympathetically than many at State and sought to rectify cumbersome procedures complicating relations with Taipei. His initiative, however, remained low-key, promising no important reformulations; when time ran out on the Bush presidency, the report had made little headway. Clark would subsequently push the idea in the *International Herald Tribune*, urging Bush's successor to "move ahead with all possible speed."[72]

THE REAGAN and Bush administrations effectively demonstrated lessons of national and personal self-interest when it came to US–Taiwan relations. Ronald Reagan signed the August Communiqué, which, despite subsequent efforts at modification, served as a significant restraint on arms sales to Taiwan. George Bush, on the other hand, undermined it fatally just a decade later to solve his personal political crisis. The sale of F-16s to Taipei liberated Taiwan from virtually all the constraints imposed by Reagan, and the greater sophistication of weaponry transferred laid the groundwork for a broader and deeper military relationship between the US and Taiwan. By that time, China's Tiananmen massacre had ended the American love affair with China and Taiwan's accelerating democratization and Taiwanization brought the kind of positive attention that had been absent for two decades. In Taipei reservations remained regarding American trustworthiness and reliability. But officials, even the shrewd Lee Teng-hui, tried to think of the shift as basic: the F-16 decision became a hopeful symbol that Taiwan could trust Washington more and not find that it had simply been caught in politics as usual.

SEARCH FOR A NEW
WORLD ORDER

BILL CLINTON headed a sprawling, uncoordinated administration that faced a multiplicity of post–cold war problems without clear foreign policy priorities. Strong emphasis on trade promotion and overseas investment led to an early push to ratify NAFTA (the North American Free Trade Agreement, 1992), and secure liberalized trade terms from Japan (1993). Simultaneously, concern over human rights abuses produced action in Haiti against a military junta (1994) and in Somalia to restore order. But the death of American soldiers in the streets of Mogadishu (1993) discredited humanitarian intervention and Washington thereafter was unconscionably slow to react to atrocities in Bosnia (1992–95) and failed to respond to genocide in Rwanda (1994). To some, involvement in Haiti and Somalia smacked of international social work, and critics urged focus on the political and economic transformation of Russia and NATO expansion (1993–94).

The post–cold war world order produced new as well as old dilemmas. Terrorists struck in New York, bombing the World Trade Center (1993), in Saudi Arabia, killing Americans at the Khobar Towers (1996), at US embassies in both Kenya and Tanzania (1998), and against the USS *Cole* at anchor in Yemen (2000). Clinton opened diplomatic relations with Vietnam (1995), sponsored a fragile plan for governing Northern Ireland

(1998), and tried unsuccessfully to bring Palestinians and Israelis to agreement at Camp David (2000). North Korea's nuclear weapons program took Washington to the brink of war before officials negotiated the Agreed Framework to derail it (1994). Critics, however, called inducements for Pyongyang bribery and Congress impeded delivery of economic aid.

In fact, after the 1994 congressional elections, the new Republican Congress obstructed Clinton's domestic and foreign initiatives. It proved tougher on China and more supportive of Taiwan than Clinton, energized by those who believed the China challenge was becoming a new cold war. Congress hesitated on China's entry into the World Trade Organization (WTO), making permanent normal trade relations with Beijing a high hurdle (1999). The following month, Congress's Cox Committee accused China of stealing US nuclear weapons secrets.

Intelligence errors also plagued Chinese–American relations. In 1993 the US intelligence community concluded that a PRC freighter en route to Iran carried chemical weapons components. The US Navy's search of the *Yinhe* sparked Chinese anger and uncovered no chemicals. Worse, in May 1999 American bombers flying on behalf of NATO forces over Kosovo struck the Chinese Embassy in Belgrade. The Chinese, officials and ordinary citizens, believed the American strike to have been intentional, and violent demonstrations shook Beijing. Even apart from disagreement over Taiwan, Sino-American relations were frequently troubled in the 1990s.

CHAPTER ELEVEN

Change and Continuity

TAIWAN'S LEADERS watched the passing of the Bush era with mixed emotions. The president had not been a friend to Taiwan, but he had, nevertheless, provided handsomely for Taiwan's security and enhanced its international profile. William Jefferson Clinton arrived in the White House with promising credentials—he had campaigned against "coddling tyrants" in Beijing and had been a repeated visitor to Taiwan—but he also evinced little interest in foreign affairs. Relying on him to remember one small island in Asia, when he emphasized the importance of restoring the US economy to the exclusion of virtually everything else, appeared entirely unrealistic. Would Taipei be able to count on his surrogates to watch over the island's concerns, or would it have to build, once again, from the outside in to try to shape policies for a post-Tiananmen world? This time at least, it did not appear that Taipei would be struggling against the strong pro-China tilt that had characterized the Bush era.

Quite the contrary. Friction with China marked the early months of the administration. The Chinese leadership approached it defiantly, having hoped for the reelection of George Bush and being angered by threats to impose sanctions if human rights practices did not change. Although the greatest pressure for curbing China's trade privileges (most-favored-nation treatment, MFN) came from Congress, Clinton had embraced the idea during his campaign, encouraged by foreign affairs advisers who saw logic in promoting justice through market access. Thus, Clinton's national security adviser, his secretary of state, and the assistant secretary for East Asian Affairs argued that relations with China could not be seen solely through the lens of business interests, but, to be healthy and stable, must simultaneously emphasize a values dimension. These men, however, did not represent the most important dynamic within the administration. They soon found their agenda undermined and their personal power weakened by those promoting development, growth, and job creation.

Anthony Lake stood at the core of the group endorsing a humanitarian vision for the new administration. Lake had signed on as a Clinton foreign affairs specialist early, and, as national security adviser for a president who paid little attention to foreign relations, he became more vital than many of his predecessors. If Lake willed it, a subject could escape Clinton's consideration entirely. At the same time, Lake, a veteran of bureaucratic infighting, sought to avoid the combat he had witnessed between Kissinger and Rogers or Brzezinski and Vance. He talked often of playing an honest broker rather than promoting his views or accruing power. A newspaper profile described him as "by design the most obscure member of the Clinton foreign policy team," declaring him "surely the only national security adviser ever to stand beside the President in a *New York Times* photograph and be described as an 'unidentified' man."[1]

Lake's self-effacing manner did not prevent him from vigorously promoting the concept of democratic enlargement. In September 1993 he struck a neo-Wilsonian posture, arguing that by nurturing new democratic governments, Washington would simultaneously make the world safer and more prosperous because these societies would shun war, terrorism, human rights abuses, and disruptive trade barriers. He went on, whether out of conviction or poor NSC staff work, to lump China with authoritarian "backlash" states like North Korea. Chinese government claims that the lives of average citizens had been bettered might be true, but Lake held that it was not enough to be Mother Teresa; there must be political reform as well. This would be good for China, for the United States, and, had he thought about it, for Taiwan. Taiwan, however, was not an important variable for Lake, despite its accelerating democratization.[2]

Warren Christopher had said much the same thing during his confirmation hearing as secretary of state in January 1993. Aware that many critics of China would want reassurance, he affirmed that the new administration intended to "facilitate a peaceful evolution of China from communism to democracy by encouraging the forces of economic and political liberalization."[3] To Christopher, emphasizing human rights had been a lifelong preoccupation, beginning with civil rights work in the Johnson years and as second in command at the State Department during the Carter administra-

tion. As secretary, he sought to recenter human rights in foreign policy after the drift of the Reagan and Bush years. Particularly, Christopher later
wrote, "I wanted to send an unambiguous message to states like China . . .
that they could not hide behind . . . claims of cultural exceptionalism."
This would not be, he told the June 1993 World Conference on Human
Rights, "the last refuge of repression."[4]

But the human rights coloration of his initial policy soured Christopher
on China. Not only did the Chinese disregard the moral argument that
treating their own citizens better was the right thing to do, but they also refused to accommodate minimal White House targets on human rights,
which triggered a domestic backlash against Clinton. During his March
1994 trip to Beijing, Christopher endured a "brutal diplomatic meeting"
and described Chinese leaders to Clinton as "rough, somber, sometimes
bordering on the insolent." Bruised and angry and receiving no support
from Clinton, he contemplated resigning.[5] Thereafter, he had no enthusiasm for things Chinese. The newspapers may have caricatured the point by
frequently contrasting his multiple trips to the Middle East to his two
China visits, and he met with Chinese diplomats whenever events required, but he clearly distanced himself as much as possible.

This did not translate into an advantage for Taiwan, however. Christopher may have been outraged by Chinese rudeness, but no one on the
mainland assaulted or injured him. It had been more than fifteen years, but
he still had fresh memories of the 1978 Taiwan protestors against derecognition who had surrounded his car, "jumped on the bumpers and fenders,
violently rocking the vehicle," while "Taiwan police in the vicinity did
nothing more than stand quietly, staring impassively." Once back in Washington, he faced "prolonged, rancorous negotiations" with Congress over
the Taiwan Relations Act.[6] His schedule as secretary was hectic, but Christopher's aversion to Taiwan, rooted in experience and not alleviated by
time, made more difference in the attention he gave to the island.

Finally, the third exponent of a human rights initiative, Winston Lord,
became assistant secretary. He had gone to China with Kissinger and been
Reagan's ambassador, but Tiananmen had changed his priorities and, although a lifelong Republican, he had denounced the Bush administration
for not caring sufficiently about human rights abuses. Lord now sought to
hold Beijing to a higher standard. He thus became a central figure in pursuing a policy of linkage between MFN and improvement in human rights
behavior in China. He would be a prime casualty when it failed. Already
lacking effective support from a weak and uninterested secretary, Lord
found White House political operatives undermining him, distrusting his
Republican roots. After mid-1994, moreover, his discretion on China nar-

rowed further because of competition from economic agencies. Those, such as Commerce Secretary Ron Brown, who wanted to open new markets in China to strengthen the domestic economy ignored the rest of the administration, disregarding efforts to pursue a unified American approach to Beijing. Having been a victim of internecine struggles in the Bush era, Lord did not engage the stronger adversaries who monopolized Clinton.

Lord's problems regarding China, like Christopher's, failed to give Taiwan an advantage. Lord's perception of Taiwan did not reflect the disdain of his mentor in diplomatic service, Henry Kissinger, but, he nevertheless approached the island with extreme caution. He had never traveled to Taiwan, and his career path led away from the island. Indeed, the fact that his wife's family had strong Taiwan ties—he had been married in the historic Victorian mansion at Twin Oaks, used by Taiwan representatives as their official residence in Washington—inclined him to maintain a discreet distance from its people and problems. As Kissinger's aide and a presence at the negotiations that produced rapprochement, he had a basic commitment to the one-China policy and saw no reason to tamper with it. His position as assistant secretary reinforced his voluntary detachment and inaccessibility.

As the Clinton administration assumed office, Taiwan's first hurdle was just to be noticed. The White House quickly became swept up in crises in Somalia and Haiti. In the East it had China problems, but Taiwan constituted a bright spot, democratizing, prospering, and enjoying a markedly improved human rights record since the mid-1980s. Agitation for change in US policy accrued more sympathy because of Taipei's success, the demeaning and awkward practices imposed since derecognition in 1979 appearing less and less tolerable to government and business. Nevertheless, lacking urgency, these problems lingered through the Bush years, and initially Clinton administration officials avoided them as well.

The Taiwan Policy Review that finally addressed them proved a much discussed and disparaged exercise as it dragged toward a conclusion in September 1994. It began unremarkably as one of many foreign policy studies for Democrats who had been out of power for twelve years. The review drew on David Keegan's unfinished study, interrupted by the end of the Bush administration, and its main focus remained process: facilitating contact, defining travel rules, and reducing barriers to economic and political interaction. Assistant Secretary Lord and his deputy, Peter Tomsen, went over it on several occasions with Deputy National Security Adviser Samuel R. "Sandy" Berger, NSC Senior Asia Director Kent Wiedemann, also a Lord protégé, and Wiedemann's deputy, Sandra Kristoff, making few changes to a document that had been vetted and reworked repeatedly by two generations of officials. Lord forwarded it to the National Security Council for approval along with a China policy review in July 1993.

At the White House the China review moved forward—it would become the foundation for the administration's policy of engagement—and the Taiwan study stalled. Even after its existence became known throughout Washington, Taipei, and Beijing, nothing happened, which made it the subject of exaggeration, speculation, controversy, and intrigue. At the Chinese Embassy officials worried; at the Washington office of CCNAA expectations began to rise.

The delay of eighteen months between the review's initiation and approval eventually became more significant, and more interesting, than the study itself. Explanations have ranged from the personal and bureaucratic through the political and international. Inefficiency and inertia as well as weak and colliding bureaucracies played a role. Lake had not yet wrested China policy from the State Department in the summer of 1993, and no one paid attention to Taiwan at the NSC. State, at the same time, could not or would not argue to dislodge the review.[7]

Most important was timing. Both NSC and State Department officials had more insistent problems to handle and preferred to sidestep the Taiwan review. The struggle over MFN for China and the nuclear crisis on the Korean peninsula and the death of Kim Il Song, as well as the battle with Congress over Taiwan arms sales, claimed higher priorities. Allowing the Taiwan Policy Review to languish became embarrassing, but little could be gained from completing and releasing it.

Lee Teng-Hui Asserts Himself

Lee Teng-hui, already looking ahead to the 1996 Taiwanese presidential election, knew that minor adjustments in arms sales provisions or contacts with American officials yielded by the Taiwan Policy Review would not galvanize voters. In this first round of fully democratic direct balloting, something more dramatic would be needed. The KMT remained the dominant party, but DPP appeal had grown more rapidly than expected, and popular sovereignty defined the future. Lee would have to run harder, even though Beijing would doubtless become more nervous and belligerent.

Disregarding risks, Lee began to transform the KMT from a mainlander to a Taiwanese party. A notorious interview by the Japanese writer Ryotaro Shiba in the weekly *Shokan Asahi* in 1994 set the tone: Lee likened himself to Moses leading his people out of oppression by an "alien regime." Lee's words referred to the harsh rule of KMT mainlanders over Taiwan, but Beijing assumed that "Egypt" meant China and that Lee advocated independence. Lee recognized the significance of indigenization and had chosen to foster what the international relations specialist Benedict Anderson termed an imagined community based on Taiwanese rather than Chinese symbols. The state would teach Taiwan history and geography in the schools and encourage the use of the Taiwan dialect rather than Mandarin.[8] It did not hurt that his initiatives co-opted the DPP's most attractive issues.

He also adopted a strategy of "pragmatic diplomacy." This meant, said Foreign Minister Fred Ch'ien, "we do not pretend to be what we are not." Thus, Taipei would no longer automatically sever relations with governments that recognized the PRC, since Taiwan finally acknowledged that it no longer governed the mainland and that another political entity did.[9] Lee mounted a hopeless campaign to enter the United Nations after the DPP demonstrated the popularity of the proposal, asserting that the Republic of China should be able to rejoin under the divided states formula that had admitted two Germanies and two Koreas.[10]

Lee used the island's growing prosperity to try to break out of China's policy of isolating Taiwan. Not only did he tempt the UN with a promise of $1 billion if Taiwan was voted in, but Taipei also offered huge grants of developmental aid to small states that would switch diplomatic recognition from China back to Taiwan. He would secure both a diplomatic victory thereby and support in the UN. An example of "successful" dollar diplomacy came when Haiti's recently exiled president, Jean-Bertrand Aristide, surprised the UN General Assembly by crediting "particularly . . . the Republic of China, Taiwan," among those who deserved thanks for putting him back in power. "It is our hope, [Taiwan] will regain its place in the great family of the United Nations."[11]

Further, Lee pursued an itinerary of overseas travel designed to boost Taiwan's international reputation and his own domestic standing. He played golf throughout Southeast Asia and met with heads of state during these "informal" visits. He sought full participation in international organizations and yearned to visit the US. Lee's request to attend the November 1993 Asia-Pacific Economic Cooperation (APEC) meeting in Seattle, after Clinton had raised it to a head-of-state level, however, was predictably denied. Accordingly, State Department analysts braced for the day that Lee would try to use a visit to his allies in Latin America to justify a layover on US soil. The moment came with an invitation to Costa Rica in March 1994 to attend an inauguration ceremony.

China's ambassador Li Daoyu, informed that a refueling stop for Lee might be contemplated, escalated efforts to deter even a brief stay. A 1993 Chinese White Paper entitled "The Taiwan Question and the Reunification of China" had argued that people in the US "have cooked up various pretexts and exerted influence to obstruct the settlement of the Taiwan question." Now Taipei's actions, with US help, would further internationalize the independence issue.[12]

Lord's deputy, Peter Tomsen, opposed concessions to Lee. Tomsen reasoned that angering China on such a highly sensitive question when so many other issues had to be resolved would not advance US national interests. Some suspicion existed, moreover, that Lee had purposefully timed his request to undermine US trade talks with China. Arguing that precedent still constrained the department since the Taiwan Policy Review had not been approved, Tomsen directed the East Asia Bureau to rebuff the idea of a landing in California or Hawaii.

As the NSC China specialist Robert Suettinger tells it, when the démarche arrived in the White House for final approval, he could immediately see the potential for trouble in a curt rejection. He urged Lake to work out a more tactfully crafted approach to avoid enraging Foreign Minister Fred Ch'ien, a customarily volatile official.[13] Lake, however, still not convinced that the White House should engage China-Taiwan policy, preferred not to challenge State Department drafting.

The mistake became apparent immediately. Lynn Pascoe, the head of AIT in Taiwan, elicited instant fury from Ch'ien, who denounced the Americans as "spineless jellyfish" for allowing themselves to be bullied by Beijing.[14] Ch'ien may not simply have been engaged in histrionics; he may have recognized that his own difficult relationship with President Lee would not be strengthened by failure on an issue so dear to the president's heart. In the end, the White House and State Department backed down and agreed to let Lee land in Honolulu.

Eager to get past the incident quickly but determined to avoid a media circus, the administration set strict rules for the transit. Lee would not be allowed to spend the night or play golf. He could disembark and be received in a VIP lounge, but at Hickam Air Force Base rather than the commercial airport, where crowds and cameras could not be controlled.

Had the US government decided to welcome Lee graciously or had Lee concluded that he had achieved everything he wanted simply by coming to the United States, a precedent would have been set but only a minor change in policy made. Relations between Washington and Taipei would have been improved. There would certainly have been harsh words exchanged between Washington and Beijing, but the affair probably would have ended there. Nothing proved that simple.

Neither Washington nor Taipei handled Hawaii well. US officials, having been manipulated into hosting Lee, saw the event as an imposition and a trap. Determined to create conditions under which Lee would be distanced from television, the press, and Chinese Americans, they did not extend themselves further to ensure that the president of Taiwan would receive treatment appropriate to his status. Nat Bellocchi, who as head of AIT's Washington office was sent to Honolulu to meet Lee, found facilities at Hickam not simply substandard but unsafe. Local military personnel, he noted, expected Lee to enter a crowded terminal and traverse open areas through throngs of people awaiting arriving aircraft. Pro-independence activists had attempted to assassinate Chiang Ching-kuo in 1970, so Bellocchi found the inadequate precautions alarming. Obviously, no one intended harm to come to Lee, but low-level officials with no background knowledge had been put in charge of the event. And VIP quarters at Hickam were spare, providing some comfort for the president but no amenities for his staff. Taiwan's Washington representative, Ding Mou-shih, contacted Lee on the plane to describe the situation.[15]

Lee Teng-hui's decision not to disembark, therefore, surely reflected the circumstances that would have confronted him at Hickam's terminal, but it may also have been motivated by his personal political agenda. A low-key visit to a tiny lounge would generate little election publicity, whereas the insult of being trapped on a refueling plane yielded far more politically both in Taipei and among supporters in the US Congress. Stories of the president, controlling his righteous indignation at the attack on the dignity of his government and his people, receiving Bellocchi on the aircraft, and joking about not falling down the boarding ramp lest he touch US soil, gained wide currency. Interviewed a decade later, Lee denied, with mock surprise, that he had been angry and said the episode and his response had been part of a normal day's work.[16]

Winston Lord fumed that Taiwan should have been "grateful that for the first time its president . . . [could have] set foot on American soil." Instead, "Lee decided that he would play up this incident and magnify it . . . [by putting] out a statement that we wouldn't let Lee off the plane. . . . We never caught up with that allegation. I was blue in the face, telling every newsman on the record, and every congressman and senator" that this was not true. Tomsen concluded cynically that Lee decided not to disembark, independent of local conditions, but for the political effect.[17] In any case, not only did the State Department fail to squelch the Hawaii stories, but the incident allowed Lee to stimulate sentiment for a compensatory trip. His supporters had been seeking an invitation from Cornell University for many months to no avail. After the landing in Hawaii, things changed.

Repercussions from that event quickly merged with the fallout from the long-awaited Taiwan Policy Review. By September 1994 the Clinton administration had weathered a series of clashes with Beijing over China's failed bid for the Olympic games, alleged illicit chemical shipments, and linkage of human rights to trade. China's escalating complaints about the Taiwan Review had people worried. Thus, the Taiwan Interagency Working Group completed its labors with Beijing's sensitivities very much in mind. Whatever the reason, the Taiwan Policy Review revolutionized no aspect of Taiwan's status, altered few rules of behavior, and pleased no one. Stanley Roth, senior director for Asia at the NSC by the time the Taiwan Policy Review came out, remarked later that "it might have been wiser not to do it. . . . It came down to an incredible series of nits."[18]

Under provisions of the review, Taiwan gained somewhat higher visibility and greater access. To make it easier to identify and locate the representative office, Washington permitted substitution of Taipei Economic and Cultural Representative Office (TECRO) for the meaningless label Coordination Council of North American Affairs. US officials could enter government offices in Taiwan and Taiwan's representatives could do the same in Washington, except at the White House, the adjacent Old Executive Office Building, and the State Department. At the Defense Department, meetings could occur at ranks below Taiwan's chief of the General Staff (until 2002 Taiwan's most powerful military officeholder) and the US Defense secretary. The review permitted transit stops by officials when deemed necessary that were "consistent with security, comfort and convenience." This would open up travel, or not, depending on which Americans interpreted conditions at any given time. Only the president, vice president, premier, and vice premier were explicitly barred from visiting the US. The foreign and defense ministers, who would be allowed in, could not come to Washington.

Finally, to improve economic interaction, the review authorized a subcabinet economic dialogue and efforts by State Department officials, up to undersecretary level, to advance US business prospects with the US's sixth-largest trading partner. The US would support Taiwan's right to be heard in international organizations apart from the UN, particularly those with economic agendas. Where such organizations did not require members to be states, the US would "more actively" seek to help Taiwan gain membership.[19]

Taipei's unhappy reaction made clear that eighteen months of effort had been expected to produce more. In Washington the head of Taiwan's representative office noted that the US government had taken the least innovative route, even on the choice of a new name for that office, having rejected preferred alternatives solicited from him and discussed at great length. In Taipei the foreign minister asserted that although he would now enjoy official visits from the AIT head in Taiwan, important gaps remained. In fact, Taipei felt most keenly the absence of any declared willingness to secure entry into critical organizations such as the UN, the International Monetary Fund, and the International Bank for Reconstruction and Development. Further, it did not increase political dialogue at higher levels. Lee Teng-hui complained that Washington paid too much attention to Chinese communist demands, throwing into doubt "the reputation of the United States as the vanguard of the world's democracies."[20]

Annoyed that the administration had released the long-awaited review on Labor Day, when Congress was not in Washington, various House and Senate members criticized it publicly. Clinton's friend Senator Charles Robb (D-Va.), chairman of the SFRC Subcommittee on East Asian and Pacific Affairs, declared it "unseemly as well as unfortunate" that the administration had not allowed Taiwan's representative mission to take an appropriate name that would "truthfully describe their duties here." The reason, sadly, was that "Beijing [might] take offense." Senator Hank Brown (R-Colo.) more bluntly declared the Taiwan Policy Review a "slap in the face to Taiwan."[21]

But the most pointed criticism emanated from Jim Lilley, who, having served as head of AIT, felt he understood what had been conceded, what remained the same, and what had been "a step backward" in the new arrangement. He criticized the Clinton administration for not pledging to support Taiwan's admission into international organizations. He asserted that an economic dialogue had been under way for more than a decade and that US officials had regularly traveled to Taiwan. Lilley saw major regression in the restriction of visits to the US by figures such as the vice president, who had frequently come in the past. And finally, he denounced the lack of courage in Washington's insistence on the name Taipei Economic and Cultural Representative Office rather than the simpler and more accurate Taipei Representative Office, declaring this "is not creative ambiguity, it is preemptive concession." How was it, Lilley wondered, that small nations in the shadow of China could behave better toward Taiwan than the US?[22]

So as a result of delay and disappointed expectations, the Taiwan Policy Review, which might have been deemed an advance in US–Taiwan relations, won the Clinton administration little praise. Lord insisted to the press, "We believe we have struck just the right balance and that both Beijing and Taipei should be ecstatic."[23] Instead, just a month after the release of the review, Congress passed an amendment to the Immigration and Nationality Technical Corrections Act that allowed Taiwan's president or another high official to come to the US to discuss problems, including nuclear proliferation, the environment, and trade. Clinton immediately countermanded it, but Congress had made its dissatisfaction with administration preferences clear.

Other influences in the Congress also militated against the administration's efforts to keep the balance it preferred on China-Taiwan issues. Trade and investment friction naturally preoccupied American business leaders. In 1994 they helped force the White House into an embarrassing retreat on linkage between human rights and MFN for China. But Taiwan bought more than twice as much from the US as China did, and some parts of the business community exerted pressure in behalf of Taipei. When in November the Democrats lost leadership of both houses of Congress to the Republican Party, Taiwan issues became part of a broader condemnation of Clinton's foreign policy. By the beginning of 1995, Lord found himself under siege by advocates of granting Lee Teng-hui a visa for a visit to, not a transit through, the country.[24]

Lee Seeks a Visa

The fulcrum for crisis became an invitation to Lee to deliver the Olin Lecture at an alumni reunion at Cornell University, where he had earned a doctorate in agricultural economics in 1968. Cornell's president had repeatedly visited Taipei, eliciting several Lee Teng-hui fellowships to support studies in international relations. These were followed by a gift of $2.5 million to endow a professorship in world affairs in Lee's name. The idea of an appearance at Cornell or at any other of several universities that had invited him predated the Hawaii debacle, and Cornell's president had approached the State Department about inviting Lee as early as the spring of 1993. Cornell had been asked to wait for the Taiwan Policy Review's travel adjustments.

Lee did not want to wait and, after Hawaii, escalated his visa campaign by hiring Cassidy & Associates, a well-known public relations firm with strong ties to the Democratic Party. In so doing, Lee circumvented those in his government and party who opposed angering Washington and who counseled against provoking Beijing, key among them his foreign minister, Fred Ch'ien. Lee often bypassed his formal advisory structure to consult individuals he trusted. In this instance he believed Cassidy would energize the lackluster lobbying operation of the official representative office in the US. That may have been why the president ignored TECRO's questions and concerns about Cassidy's past performance and collateral damage to other Taiwan lobbying efforts. Taiwan's diplomats discovered from newspapers that Lee, through the auspices of the Taiwan Research Institute (TRI), had engaged Cassidy. Not surprisingly, they resented it.[25]

Lee's tactics, however unorthodox, benefited from the image that he could project in Washington of himself and Taiwan's politics. Although the shift to democracy had begun in the 1980s, and Tiananmen had brought the news to Americans that a truly free China existed in Taiwan, Lee's upcoming run for the presidency in a direct, freely contested election—the first in Chinese history—garnered considerable attention. Anyone who did not look too closely at his ruling style—as opposed to his rhetoric—could see Lee as an embodiment of American values.

During the winter and early spring of 1995, Clinton found pressure building to grant Lee a visa. Cassidy & Associates, working hard to earn its $4.5 million fee, generated growing demands in Congress to give democracy its due. Richard Bush, then a staff aide on the Hill, deemed it "the most sophisticated effort I ever saw, far and away. . . . They pushed all the buttons. I knew the administration was sunk." Representatives of the Taiwan government and paid consultants traveled through congressional districts, making commerce deals and funding education. Some thirty state legislatures passed resolutions favoring Lee's trip. The TRI, run by Lee's close associate and fellow Cornell alumnus Liu Tai-ying, would later be charged with buying Lee's visa using payments from an illegal National Security Bureau slush fund of $100 million. Members of the 104th Congress, as unaware of the dynamics of the Taiwan-China relationship as they were of the source of the money, appreciated the largesse.[26]

On the other hand, members of Congress didn't really need to be bought when upholding democracy could be cast in simple terms. Large numbers of legislators were unusually inexperienced, having been brought to office by the midterm upset of 1994, and they had a particularly meager grasp of international affairs. But how much did they need to know? If Clinton could welcome the controversial Gerry Adams, leader of the political wing of the Irish Republican Army, to the White House in the spring of 1995, over London's protests, why would they want to turn away an elected head of government because Beijing said no? State Department priorities "as usual" seemed wrong. Stanley Roth, who watched the developments from his perch at the NSC but had decades of staff experience on the Hill, asserted in a later interview that "Taiwan had enormous support in the U.S. Congress. . . . The nature of the event, combined with the perception of Taiwan as good, as a role model, I think was more than enough to shore up congressional support, and I would say Cassidy's role in the Congress was marginal."[27]

The final important factor also involved Congress. The tidal wave of Republican victory in the autumn of 1994 placed the leadership and key committees in the hands of Taiwan sympathizers and bitter critics of China. Thus, Newt Gingrich (R-Ga.) promptly went on record as favoring Taiwan's admission to the UN as he took up his responsibilities as House Speaker. Taiwan could also expect support from Ben Gilman (R-N.Y.), who was chairing the House International Relations Committee, and Jesse Helms (R-N.C.), who dominated the Senate Foreign Relations Committee. Helms invited Taiwan's representative to be his first formal visitor after he became the committee's chairman.[28]

The Chinese, in contrast, proved unable to persuade Congress or the public of their alarm or the lengths to which they would go in reprisal. Americans, unwilling to believe a confrontation could be looming, assumed that Beijing's dependence on the US market would prevent serious visa-related problems. Later, many in Congress remarked that the crisis following their vote came as a surprise and that they might have voted differently had they understood what the outcome would be.[29]

Beijing did not help its case by seeking to deliver multiple messages, forgetting each would be heard by unintended audiences. Chinese leaders sought to reach out to the US and put Tiananmen behind them. China called repeatedly for Clinton to invite Jiang Zemin to the United States.

The fact that Congress pushed so hard for a Lee visa when Jiang could not get his invitation rankled. But threats over Taiwan did nothing to eradicate negative images that lingered from 1989.

At the same time, China hoped to divide Washington and Taipei. Jiang had just prevailed in a lengthy internal debate in the Taiwan Affairs Leading Small Group, the paramount government-party unit for deliberation, coordination, and decision making on Taiwan. He immediately implemented a conciliatory approach toward Lee Teng-hui. His Eight Points (Jiang Ba Dian), delivered as part of a speech on January 30, 1995, were heralded as the new fundamental framework for engagement leading to unification. Jiang acknowledged that the status quo would endure for an extended period, during which trade, investment, and visits would draw the two sides together. Stability would be the objective. China watchers welcomed the new policy as "highly conciliatory."[30]

But, Jiang's remarks also had a sharp edge—a reminder that Taiwan's people should turn away from domestic radicalism and foreign interference. He excluded DPP hard-liners from benefits and warned against dependence on the US. "We do not promise not to use force," he warned. "If used, force will not be directed against our compatriots in Taiwan, but against the foreign forces who intervene in China's reunification and go in for 'the independence of Taiwan.'" Taiwan's salvation would be to affirm one China and cease pushing for "expanding its living space internationally." More directly to shake up Americans, China canceled a visit by the transportation secretary in reprisal for the trip he had previously made to Taiwan under the auspices of the 1994 Taiwan Policy Review.

Chinese leaders clearly hoped either to seduce or discipline Lee and discourage Washington from interfering. Lee's counterproposal and the US action on his visa quickly disabused them of these notions. Lee waited three months before responding, during which his advisers sought to determine whether Jiang had a unified government behind him and where the PLA stood on the cross-Strait initiative. Then Lee delivered a six-point rebuttal on April 8 that angered Chinese leaders. Repeating themes he had employed before, Lee posited a relationship in which Taiwan would use its economic know-how to help China solve its internal problems and work with China to cultivate Hong Kong and Macao after reversion. More significantly, Lee premised any advances in the relationship on Beijing's renunciation of the use of force, which Jiang's Eight Points had clearly rejected. Lee insisted that Taiwan would behave as, and had to be treated as, an equal, whereas Jiang had demanded that Taiwan be subordinate to China. And Lee asserted the right to join international organizations alongside China and meet with PRC leaders in the context of those international gatherings, even as Jiang wanted pragmatic diplomacy ended and Lee to stay at home. In spite of the obvious contradictions, some of Lee's advisers insisted the two declarations had laid the basis for dialogue.[31]

The fact of these exchanges and the fairly moderate tone they took made Beijing's rumblings about the dire consequences of Lee's attending a simple reunion at Cornell seem harsh and, perhaps, implausible to nonspecialists in the US. Chinese leaders were wrong to think the president and Congress understood the gravity of their words. They overestimated the influence of the American China-watching community in interpreting their concerns.

On the other hand, the nonspecialists at the top of the Chinese government appear to have been equally misguided in their appreciation of the US system. They accepted assurances—in particular those from Secretary of State Warren Christopher to Foreign Minister Qian Qichen on April 17, 1995—that Clinton would not grant Lee a visa because that would be inconsistent with unofficial relations. But Chinese officials did not hear Christopher hedge with the observation that the legislative branch could thwart a US president. This caveat made little impression on leaders who did not wish to hear it and may not have believed it. The warning failed, even though China had America specialists who could have explained it. Besides, the leadership had been told before, the caution having been delivered to the PRC Embassy and the Foreign Ministry earlier by lower-level US officials. The NSC's Robert Suettinger has noted, "If their embassy was going back to Beijing and saying don't worry, everything is going to be fine, then they were deceiving themselves. They had to know. But did they report back honestly? Probably not."[32]

As the debate over the Lee visa escalated, it finally captured Clinton's attention, and the president found that he did not like his official position. Although he understood China's distress, he did not sympathize with the idea of barring Lee from a private visit to his alma mater. Clinton's nostalgia for Georgetown and other universities he had attended played a role. Having condemned Beijing's repressive system, moreover, it seemed wrong to side with autocrats against the leader of a representative democracy. He would later remark to newsmen that all Americans had "the constitutional right to travel"—a dubious proposition—and Lee as a "citizen of the world" should also be able to "travel around our country." According to a senior official, Clinton remained irritated with Chinese attitudes and angry at the embarrassment of his misguided linkage policy; he insisted, "Just as the Chinese demand to be respected in their way, they have to respect our way."[33]

Clinton's sympathies may also have been aroused by his exposure to

Taiwan and its people. As part of his gubernatorial duties as a promoter of commercial deals for his state, Clinton had taken the first Arkansas trade mission to the Far East. He made additional trips to Taiwan, more than to any other overseas destination, and his efforts in seeking business ties for local companies produced an array of contracts. In his memoir he asserted that in 1986, as he prepared a speech challenging Taiwan to reduce trade barriers and increase investment in the United States, he refined his views on international economics, advancing a constellation of ideas that would make him a New Democrat by the end of the year.[34] Thus, Taiwan became for him a marker in his political development—one factor that shaped his perception of foreign relations as a mechanism for enhancing domestic economic opportunity. Doubtless, he also recalled the continuous banqueting, lavish entertainment, and shameless flattery.

So Taiwan's foreign minister, eager to remind Clinton of those happy occasions, told the *New York Times* early in 1993 that the president-elect "is one of the few leaders in the U.S. who has extensive knowledge of us." Clever officials hung a picture of Clinton posing in Taiwan in the Foreign Ministry.[35] Although they were chastened somewhat by their experience with Ronald Reagan, who had not lived up to elevated expectations, there appeared to be positive signs. Their hopes had been buoyed during the campaign by Clinton's support for selling the F-16 fighter aircraft to Taiwan, even before George Bush made public his decision to do so. Of course, Taipei knew Clinton's enthusiasm, like Bush's, stemmed not from a desire to protect Taiwan but from a need for votes. He too advocated protecting jobs in defense industries in Texas, refusing to let it be seen as a Republican cause. Nevertheless, for Taiwan this was good news.[36]

None of this history prepared Clinton for the crisis that he would trigger by adopting what he believed to be an honorable stance on the Lee visa. The same could not be said for those around him. Various people struggled to find ways out of the difficult situation. Stanley Roth, at the NSC, apparently explored the possibility of recreating the Hawaii visit that Lee had originally requested in 1994, with golfing and a hotel stay. The US ambassador to China, J. Stapleton Roy, thought that Washington was long overdue in telling Chinese leaders of the probable trip and should offer Jiang Zemin the state visit he coveted to soften the blow. Berger and Suettinger at the NSC as well as Jim Steinberg and Alan Romberg at the State Department adamantly insisted that the visa be denied. According to a *Washington Post* reporter, Steinberg, head of the policy planning staff, "was apoplectic" as he tried to get Christopher to act. But, although an architect of unofficial relations with Taiwan, the secretary remained passive, neither a confidant of Clinton nor one who relished plunging into the fray. A disgruntled senior official complained that Lake believed Chinese threats were being exaggerated. Rather than alert Clinton to the risks, he reinforced Clinton's leanings, understating the likely repercussions and arguing that Lee's trip would be "perfectly lawful."[37]

By May 17, 1995, when Lake, Christopher, and Secretary of Defense William J. Perry gathered for their regular breakfast meeting, each had decided that Lee must be allowed to come. Perry's support for this view was most surprising, since he had long cultivated a relationship with the mainland Chinese, particularly those in the PLA. In 1980, while serving as undersecretary of defense, he had been leader of the first US military delegation to visit the PRC, and he had continued visits in subsequent years as a Stanford University defense industry specialist.[38] Now, in 1995, he associated himself with the others, although his links to Beijing were far stronger than theirs.

The NSC Asia staff discovered their pro-visa decision the next day. Roth and Suettinger nevertheless proposed delaying until Congress made further postponement impossible. The intervening time could be used to negotiate compromise arrangements with both Taipei and Beijing. They hoped to devise an acceptable Lee visit. Lake, however, insisted on immediate action.

On May 18, as the NSC finished its implementing memorandum, Clinton attended a meeting with Democratic Leadership Council members, including Robb (who had accompanied him on a Taiwan trip in 1985), Joseph Lieberman (D-Conn.), Sam Nunn (D-Ga.), and John Breaux (D-La.), during which the senators raised the Lee dilemma. Commiserating with Clinton, these powerful Democrats made clear that if the president stood against the tide on Capitol Hill, he risked damage to his entire legislative agenda. The House had voted 396–0 for a nonbinding resolution favoring a Lee trip; in the Senate, despite administration pressure, a similar measure carried 97–1. Neither house saw "legitimate grounds for excluding President Lee Teng-hui from paying private visits" to the United States. In passing, the resolutions demonstrated the potential for damaging changes to the TRA. A pending amendment (H.R. 1460) prohibited the secretary of state from preventing any elected Taiwan official from entering the US on the grounds of "adverse foreign policy consequences." Clinton could stop it, but he was loath to have his "first veto to be in support of the People's Republic of China," particularly since Congress would effortlessly override him.[39]

Clinton shifted his position swiftly and suddenly. Neither Taipei nor

Beijing received more than twenty-four hours' notice. Taipei's jubilation and Beijing's rage echoed across Washington.

THE CLINTON administration had been manipulated by a weak client state that had, not for the first time, used the American system against itself. The modest adjustments in Taiwan's status immediately became overshadowed by Lee's larger ambitions and deep pockets. But Lee's effectiveness in securing his visa was not just a function of money politics. To Americans in and out of government Taiwan's democratization seemed a great achievement, all the better because the US had played a role in advancing it. Welcoming a democratic leader to the US over the objections of a communist government responsible for the Tiananmen massacre made sense. Although there would be regrets and recriminations later, initially many in Washington thought they had done the right thing, even if they were troubled by the intense lobbying that had forced the decision.

Lee Teng-hui, on the other hand, having triumphed in his struggle to get to the US, had become increasingly cynical about American policy. His memoir, written several years later, would portray his relations with Washington as almost always difficult. Although this exaggerated friction for dramatic effect and ignored his respect for elements of American society and certain individuals, it did reflect his accumulating problems and growing distrust after his brief visits to Hawaii and Cornell.[40]

CHAPTER TWELVE

Taiwan Strait Crisis

A s soon as Clinton authorized Lee's visit, a major crisis in relations among Washington, Taipei, and Beijing appeared inevitable. The visa comprised an irritant to the US, which Lee aggravated rather than minimized, and a challenge to Beijing that the leadership could not overlook. Nevertheless, Lee Teng-hui, Jiang Zemin, and Bill Clinton never imagined that a military confrontation would develop in the spring of 1996. The depth of their mutual ignorance and mistrust, their cynical maneuvering, and their competing political and cultural imperatives virtually guaranteed misfortune.

The State Department worked with TECRO to ensure that Lee would undertake a modest, private visit. Lee and his entourage could stop in Los Angeles, but not in New York, with its large Chinese American community and UN headquarters. Senior officials would not meet him. The AIT staff and a Taiwan Coordination Office minder, assigned by Assistant Secretary Lord, would "keep Lee under control . . . and make sure that he didn't do something that would be awkward."[1] The East Asia Bureau also sought to minimize press coverage and ceremonial receptions by local governments and Chinese-American organizations.

Events departed significantly from their plans. Lee wanted the greatest exposure with the highest degree of "officiality" he could get. Hundreds welcomed him in California on June 7, and the Los Angeles mayor as well as the governor's representative turned out. Members of Congress ignored the White House and traveled to upstate New York to meet him.

The heart of the trip, however, according to Winston Lord, became Lee's speech. Lord repeatedly asked Benjamin Lu Chao-chung, head of TECRO, for the text as Lee's intimates and a senior diplomat, Ding Mou-shih, drafted it. When Lord read it, he found the remarks chauvinistic and inflammatory, in no way a nonpolitical reminiscence about Cornell. By then, however, the press corps had copies. Lee referred to the Republic of China fifteen times, repeatedly talked about nation and country, and urged China to follow Taiwan's model of political development. To Lord, and to others in the administration, such as Defense Secretary Perry, the speech precluded any hope for tolerance from Beijing.

In truth, the speech was neither so offensive nor so decisive. Lee's political goals in traveling to the United States could not have been satisfied with much less. Moreover, although Lee did introduce two new points in his speech, he had said similar things in previous ones. First, he emphasized that popular elections imbued the ROC with sovereignty, not just its status as the successor state to the Qing Dynasty. Second, he asserted that Taiwan's democracy should be a model for China and the world. But Lee's success in securing a visa and becoming the first Taiwanese president to travel in the US was enough to infuriate the Chinese. Looking back, China's Foreign Minister Qian Qichen acknowledged the efficacy of US limitations on Lee, declaring that Taipei's hopes had not been fulfilled.[2]

That Lee's trip triggered a crisis derived from more than his speech. Because it followed the Bush F-16 sale and Clinton's Taiwan Policy Review, it appeared to China's leaders to be yet another rejection of an agreement with Beijing never to support Taiwan independence. Jiang Zemin, in the early stages of a succession struggle, had to restore the credibility of his threats in Taipei and his decisions to his colleagues. *Xinhua*'s commentary condemned Lee as "swollen with arrogance" as he postured for domestic political gain.[3]

For Lord, Lu's deceptive behavior as representative became the final intolerable act in his unsatisfactory tenure. Americans insisted that Lu had leaked confidential information to the press, harangued officials at meetings, and occasionally misrepresented facts to his interlocutors. Lu had been unwilling to report bad news to Lee and, as a result, did not convey everything that the US government told him, frustrating American officials and leaving Taipei unprepared to deal with important problems. Preoccupied with outreach to Chinese Americans, Lu chose to ignore the mounting confrontation in the Strait in 1995 and 1996, even when missiles were falling near Taiwan.

After Lee's visit to Cornell, the assistant secretary refused to see Lu, and when Lu realized Lord's door had closed, he prevented his deputy at TECRO from dealing directly with Lord's deputy at State. In Taipei, by orders from Washington, AIT's Lynn Pascoe had to curtail his contacts with the Foreign Ministry. Communication devolved on able, but still lower-level, officials. Lu may finally have left Washington before his tour of duty ended, according to Lord, who subsequently remarked, "I would like to think that I had something to do with it."[4]

Repercussions

As for the broader aftermath of Lee's Cornell adventure, once the leaders in Beijing decided how to react, the toll proved steep. As Qian wrote later, they dismissed Christopher's explanation as "mere sophistry, meant to conceal the administration's insincerity." Believing Lee planned to seize independence, they concluded that Washington intended to use Taiwan to keep China weak economically and politically. Granting the visa had been a US test for Beijing to see if the Chinese would submit.[5] China disrupted the recently resumed cross-Strait dialogue, ending low-level commercial and legal talks as well as those between Koo and Wang. Beijing postponed meetings with the US on arms control, canceled a Washington visit by its defense minister, and withdrew its ambassador on June 17. Although relations were not suspended or broken, China refused to accept a new US ambassador, which left both capitals without top diplomatic representation.

More dramatically, Chinese leaders launched military exercises to intimidate Taiwan and unnerve the Americans. State Department China specialists had tried to alert senior officials that maneuvers of this sort might be undertaken in the wake of a Lee visit. According to the CIA, China stepped up its military activity appreciably in the mid-1990s, reversing a multiyear trend of redeployments away from the Strait. In September 1994 Beijing staged what Lord characterized to Congress as "the most expensive exercise . . . in 40 or 50 years." But unwilling to alarm the president, Lord removed warnings about potential military action from a study sent to the White House before the visa approval.[6] Now China followed through, sending warships and airplanes on threatening drills and ordering its rocket force, the Second Artillery, to fire four nuclear-capable M-9 missiles into the waters north of Taiwan.

China's readiness and Taiwan's relative lack of preparedness in 1995 stemmed from contrasting assumptions about the future that the two sides had made years earlier. Lee Teng-hui, having ended the "period of mobilization against communist rebellion" in 1991, had renounced the ROC's long-held goal of recapturing the mainland. Taiwan then altered its military doctrine, emphasizing defense of the island over an offensive-defense in which military attacks on China were theoretically possible.[7]

Beijing, on the other hand, had undertaken intelligence analyses in 1994, examining Lee Teng-hui's intentions and concluding not only that Lee should be regarded as a separatist, but that pro-unification KMT leaders were losing influence, that the DPP's strength was growing, and that conditions were likely to worsen rather than improve. Jiang Zemin won the subsequent debate with hard-liners, which resulted in his relatively moderate eight-point approach to Lee. Unbeknown to Taipei and Washington, Jiang simultaneously approved a military buildup along China's southeast coast.[8] Thus, in 1995 and 1996, when the crisis unfolded, the PLA had the strength at least to make a show of force in response to Beijing's demands.

On Taiwan the immediate effects of Lee's trip varied. Polls showed a surge in Lee's popularity following his journey to Cornell, as well as a decline in sentiment favoring unification. On the other hand, once Chinese missiles began to fly, the stock market and currency values plummeted; as much as $4 billion fled the island within four weeks in midsummer 1995. Emigration increased conspicuously. But careful examination of the distribution of economic loss demonstrated that the pain remained localized in the north, around Taipei. Elsewhere life stayed normal, and widespread fear reminiscent of the 1950s did not arise.[9]

Lee, meanwhile, felt vindicated in his campaign for the visa and affirmed in his tight control over policy making. Nay-saying at the Foreign Ministry further soured his views of the diplomatic corps. Following his natural inclinations, he handled more and more problems among a small group of people he knew well and whose loyalty and discretion he trusted.

In the United States that summer of 1995, the Clinton administration sought ways to repair the damage caused by Lee's actions and Beijing's anger. Lee had demonstrated his willingness to jeopardize US security to serve his political priorities. US officials shaped policy with this constantly in mind. Even those who believed that Lee's visit had been right in principle agreed that Taipei had to be reined in. The approach became an issue for discussion among Lake, Christopher, and Perry at the regular meetings on US–China relations that had begun earlier that year. They favored not simply a statement that Washington would not make a habit of hosting Lee, but a broader reiteration of US policy. Thus, in August 1995 Clinton sent a letter to Jiang through Christopher setting out policy in stronger terms than usual.

The Clinton letter has been the subject of attention and speculation because it may have set forth an important policy departure and because the letter's text remains classified. The controversy has revolved around the so-called Three Nos: did the letter say merely that the US would not support Taiwan independence, two Chinas, and Taiwan's membership in the UN, or did it actually use the stronger word *oppose*—the US would *oppose* independence. Even one of the letter's NSC drafters claims uncertainty. If Clinton employed the latter, as Qian Qichen has written and the Hong Kong newspaper *Ta Kung Pao* alleged in publishing a copy leaked from Beijing, then he significantly altered the terms of previous written policy declarations.[10] At least one member of the administration who read the letter, however, has claimed that the word *oppose* referred to forces seeking independence rather than to independence directly. Thus, the *Ta Kung Pao* mistranslated or misrepresented Clinton's opposition, which was to the behavior of people in the movement, not the concept of independence per se.[11]

This formulation, however, similarly declared the administration's unwillingness further to jeopardize Sino-American relations. That message had also been delivered by Washington's passivity in the wake of missile firings into waters close to Taiwan during July and August. After subdued expressions of concern from Clinton and Christopher, nothing followed.

Lake thought the response too weak but, preoccupied with his non-Asian agenda in Haiti, Bosnia, and Ireland, he did not push for more. Later some would look back and wonder if Beijing interpreted this as a virtual invitation to further action.[12]

In Taiwan, by contrast, the tension escalated with the militarization of the standoff. China's early-summer exercises resumed in the autumn, including an amphibious invasion of an offshore island and an assault on a simulation of Taiwan's international airport. Threats to seize a small, uninhabited island elicited official disdain but some unofficial worry. In an election season in which being strong but judicious promised votes, Lee Teng-hui publicized demands for the development of nuclear weapons but pledged that he would not take such a step.[13]

Meanwhile, after Christopher met with Qian Qichen in August, US officials assured Taiwan representatives that no fourth communiqué curbing Taipei's interests would be forthcoming. Briefers did not mention the president's letter and its promises. In negotiations that autumn for a US–China summit, the State Department refused to make Taiwan central to the agenda because the US position "is not going to change." China had to understand that the time had come to "get beyond" the Taiwan issue if it wanted a summit. "The stage is over in the relationship" for pacifying Beijing.[14] In fact, the Clinton administration had already made large concessions in the Three Nos. Like Henry Kissinger and Richard Nixon, however, it preferred to imagine a conciliatory China wanting to deal with issues other than Taiwan rather than believe the US had promised too much.

Beijing quietly kept the pressure on through the autumn. While traveling in China during October 1995, Chas W. Freeman Jr., formerly an assistant secretary of defense, met with Lieutenant General Xiong Guangkai, chief of intelligence and deputy chief of the General Staff. Xiong recalled how in the Eisenhower era the US had been able to threaten China with the use of nuclear weapons. Beijing, he repeatedly observed, no longer needed to back down as it had over the offshore islands, and it could respond in kind, so "you will not sacrifice Los Angeles to protect Taiwan." Civilian analysts in Washington greeted Freeman's story skeptically. At the Pentagon, uniformed officers seemed more impressed, although Defense Secretary William Perry dismissed it. The episode might have passed almost unnoticed had not Patrick Tyler of the *New York Times* given it wide coverage, which forced National Security Adviser Tony Lake to raise it with the Chinese and made it a China community legend.[15]

The US similarly employed a touch of coercion when on December 19 the aircraft carrier USS *Nimitz* and its accompanying battle group sailed through the Taiwan Strait en route to Hong Kong rather than follow its intended course east of Taiwan. At the time, and subsequently, questions arose about whether this had been a demonstration of American might, a statement regarding international naval practice, or simply an effort to avoid bad weather. Defense Secretary Perry contended later that the US Navy regularly, if randomly, demonstrates the right of free passage through international waterways worldwide. Sending the *Nimitz* into the Strait had been at the discretion of the Pacific commander in chief and was neither coincidental nor a result of weather.[16] It probably also was not entirely fortuitous, though Perry did not say that, since in the midst of growing Sino-American tensions, it provided the auxiliary benefit of reminding China that the TRA enjoined US forces to watch developments in the Strait closely. But the sailing of the *Nimitz* proved too little, too late, since preparations for further military exercises were already well advanced.

Lee Teng-hui that winter faced challengers from the DPP and the small, pro-unification New Party in his presidential race. Although Beijing recognized Lee's popularity, leaders there sought to reduce his margin of victory and thereby curb his post-election freedom to pursue a "splittist" agenda. They sought to frighten voters, misreading the results of Taiwan's December legislative elections, in which the pro-unification New Party scored well, as testimony that coercion worked when, in fact, local issues had determined the results.[17] Thus, Beijing scheduled massive military exercises involving 150,000 troops for late February and early March. China fired M-9 missiles into international shipping lanes close to Taiwan's major ports at Kaohsiung, in the south, and Keelung, near Taipei, again driving the stock market down and causing a new run on the banks. Chinese leaders believed they could convince the electorate to be prudent.

Instead, Beijing's actions completely changed the balance of force in the Strait and challenged Washington's decades-long adherence to a policy of strategic ambiguity that had emerged under Eisenhower. The US military, increasingly troubled by China's military maneuvers and threats, unnerved the president at a February meeting by listing an array of triggers that could bring near-term war with China. Chairman of the Joint Chiefs of Staff John Shalikashvili made clear to Clinton, Lake, Berger, Christopher, and Perry that inherent in the escalating discord was an enormous risk of misunderstanding and accident. In the end, the confrontation could produce a nuclear exchange.

Government acted. Washington instructed the Pacific Command in Hawaii quietly to ready advisers and technicians as well as stocks of ammunition, spare parts, and Patriot missiles for shipment to Taiwan in case of attack by the Chinese. Admiral Joseph Prueher, just taking up his position as CINCPAC that winter, initiated contingency defense planning, having discovered that no one had wanted to prepare for a Strait crisis lest word of war-gaming or stockpiling leak.[18] Both the State Department and the intelligence community created special task forces to collect information, and the latter provided daily updates to leaders. Shalikashvili, meanwhile, reasserted military control over operational planning, excluding the NSC from force deployment deliberations.[19]

Perry found Chinese missile firings into waters near Taiwan's two largest ports in the north and the south on March 7 particularly irresponsible and dangerous. Known as bracketing, the practice could establish the proper range for a barrage aimed directly at Taiwan's bases or cities. Perry angrily pointed this out to Liu Huaqiu, director of the Foreign Affairs Office of China's State Council, who arrived in Washington as those missiles crashed into the sea. At a tense dinner, Perry told Liu that he "believed that aggressive military actions directed against Taiwan could be seen as a threat to American interests, and . . . 'the United States has more than enough military capability to protect its vital national security interests in the region, and is prepared to demonstrate that.'"[20]

The next morning Perry advised a Pentagon gathering of Lake, Christopher, Shalikashvili, Lord, and CIA Director John M. Deutch that the US ought to send two aircraft carrier groups to force the PRC to back down and restore confidence in Taiwan and among other friends in the region. Although Shalikashvili and Pacific Commander Prueher thought one carrier a sufficient signal to Beijing, Perry insisted on tougher, and unexpected, action. Indeed, he even argued for stationing the ships close to the island or sailing them through the Strait, perhaps adding an intimidating aircraft launching en route. Only Shalikashvili's strong argument that this would be too dangerous dissuaded Perry. Taipei also objected to putting American ships in the Strait, but its views carried less weight.[21]

Dispatch of the *Nimitz* from the Persian Gulf as well as the USS *Independence* from its home port in Japan did catch China by surprise and make a strong statement. Even those Chinese who feared US intervention had not expected such a powerful deployment. In fact, PLA surveillance equipment remained so modest in 1996 that, essentially "deaf and blind," Beijing discovered the location of the American armada from newspapers rather than from its own observation.[22] US officials used the press to alert China and the region to the American presence, transporting reporters to the *Independence*—clearly east of the island—where they overheard pilots bragging that they could reach the Strait in less than thirty minutes. The Chinese also took note of the name of the ship, which, Prueher averred later, he had overlooked. The USS *Bunker Hill,* outfitted with Aegis radar capabilities, meanwhile, positioned itself at the southern end of the Strait, where it could monitor missile launches and other Chinese military movements.[23] As for the *Nimitz,* although it did not arrive in the vicinity until the crisis was largely over, just announcing that it would stop enforcing the no-fly zone in Iraq testified forcefully to Washington's agitation.

As effective as the US ships may have been—China launched only one further missile after the deployment—and as much as Taiwan officials wanted Washington's support, they also had ambivalent views of the deployment of such visible and significant elements of the US Navy to the area.[24] First of all, there had been ample evidence over the previous months that China's belligerence would be demonstrated within carefully circumscribed boundaries. In each instance Beijing had announced its missile firings well ahead of time and, until March, had staged its military exercises in zones to the west of the imaginary but tacitly agreed-on median line through the Taiwan Strait. Although President Lee and his aides sketched out multiple scenarios for conflict, the Taiwan military did not expect escalation to war, a judgment shared by the US intelligence community.[25] Accordingly, some worried the US might cause an unnecessary heightening of friction.[26]

Second, Taiwan espionage in China had established that the missiles menacing the island carried no warheads. This meant that although China's missile firings terrified people and proved disruptive economically, destruction would have been limited had one hit. Governing authorities revealed this information during the crisis to reduce panic, and in doing so sacrificed a high-level military spy ring, whose members were executed by China. Subsequently, other intelligence networks suspended operations for an extended period as Beijing hunted spies. The US found itself without proper intelligence coverage, especially when Taipei refused to trust Americans with some of what it did collect. US intelligence agencies, as usual, disparaged Taiwan's capabilities, but they nonetheless regretted the absence of information.[27]

Third, the addition of US vessels to the local scene meant that Taiwan lost control of a portion of its front line. How much latitude the US demanded and to what extent Taiwan air and naval units were pushed aside under relatively peaceful circumstances troubled military leaders. What they could expect if conditions worsened would be sure to cause friction. Moreover, since communications between US and Taiwan forces remained fragmentary, anxiety regarding friendly fire accidents could not be allayed.

Finally, throughout the winter and spring before Taiwan's presidential elections, unbeknown to the Americans, secret cross-Strait meetings had occurred in Hong Kong, Singapore, and even the US. This apparently was just one act in a long drama of surreptitious contacts begun in the 1950s and continued by Lee Teng-hui when he became president in 1988. Many clandestine conversations transpired in Hong Kong, initiated by Chinese military officials but conducted under the guiding hand of the historian and Buddhist scholar Nan Huai-chin between 1988 and 1992. Lee used this venue early in his presidency to explain his policies and argue that he did not plan to push for independence.[28]

After 1992 the emissaries and venue fluctuated. By 1994 the talks encompassed the KMT financier Liu Tai-ying, who reported directly to Lee Teng-hui, and, perhaps more important, Zeng Qinghong, at that time general office director of the CCP and already a close confidant of Jiang Zemin, who apparently met with Lee's key interlocutor, Su Chih-cheng, in Zhuhai. In March 1996, when missiles were flying in China's third round of "tests" and Liu Huaqiu was having his confrontational meetings with members of the Clinton administration, he may also have had "quiet and cooperative talks" in the US with Lee Yuan-tse, then president of Taiwan's Academia Sinica and a confidant of Lee Teng-hui.[29]

The fact that Taiwan excluded Washington from this channel both facilitated and protected it. Taipei felt Americans would seek to dictate agendas, interfere with negotiating tactics, and demand to know results. US officials had sometimes tried to control Taiwan's behavior; for example, a high-level Pentagon official instructed Taiwan to ground its planes lest Americans target them accidentally. In reality, Washington distrusted the government, fearing it would launch provocative raids and harass PRC aircraft. As recently as 1994, Taiwan air force fighters had repeatedly challenged a US battle group performing routine exercises in the Strait after it identified itself.

As anxiety on the island mounted, Taipei's temptation to act preemptively grew, and Washington worried its support might be interpreted as permitting strikes against China.[30] Alterations made in Taiwan defense policy at the height of the crisis, for instance, seemed ominous. Lee adopted a new concept called "resolute defense, effective deterrence" (*fangwei gushou, youxiao hezu*), which required the acquisition of offensive weapons to hold every inch of land controlled by Taipei.[31] Misgivings Taiwan might have had regarding US intervention, therefore, paled in comparison to American dread that Taipei might misunderstand it.

Indeed, Washington saw deployment of the carriers principally as a message to the PRC about US resolve and US rights. Reflecting on possible command conflicts that troubled the Taiwan military, Secretary Perry subsequently remarked that he didn't recall any complaints. If there had been, he asserted, "it would not have influenced me."[32]

In the end, China failed to convince Taiwan's electorate that voting for

Lee Teng-hui was too dangerous. He won by a landslide. On the other hand, the DPP's candidate, Peng Ming-min, captured just 21 percent of the ballots, partly because he sought an explicit declaration of independence. So anger against China damaged any prospect of unification in the near future.

The 1995–96 crisis yielded other significant changes in the East Asian landscape. The interplay among the US, Taiwan, and China—which in the 1950s had embraced military confrontation and in the 1980s had been primarily a political contest—became militarized once again. Of course, even between 1987 and 1994, when friction across the Strait had largely subsided, Beijing issued some sixty warnings that it might use force. It also pursued PLA improvements aimed at deterring Taiwan from independence.[33]

After 1996, however, China accelerated a military modernization program that gave priority to a Taiwan contingency. Beijing began to shift from deterrent to coercive strategy and, although still unable to invade, made great strides with ballistic and cruise missiles. It increased purchases of Russian combat aircraft, destroyers, and submarines. It also hastened development of its information warfare capabilities.

Similarly, the United States committed to rebuilding an inadequate Taiwan military establishment. US arms sales to Taiwan grew and became more sophisticated in hopes that strengthening Taiwan would accomplish two crucial goals: make Taiwan better able to defend itself and thereby deter an attack, and make Taipei feel sufficiently confident to engage in talks with Beijing.

At the same time, Americans understood that the US would never be able to sell enough weapons to Taiwan. Admiral Prueher lamented the turn to arms in Beijing and Taipei, observing, "If the only tool you have is a hammer, every problem looks like a nail." Two analysts of Taiwan's political decision making, Bruce Dickson and Philip Yang, have pointed out that the result mimicked a classic security dilemma, in that Taiwan's increased vulnerability after 1996 caused it to embrace the US more tightly, seeking more advanced arms and inclusion in theater missile defense (TMD). China's ability to threaten Taiwan thereupon diminished, which prompted it to increase missile deployments and escalate its menacing rhetoric, thus raising the stakes yet again.[34]

China also suffered a setback in its relations with Japan. As a result of China's belligerence in the Strait, Tokyo opted to sign a tough military agreement with the United States, one that was more explicit and comprehensive than it had been prepared to adhere to several months earlier. Washington and Tokyo had coincidentally been in the process of renegotiating their defense guidelines as a result of a 1994 nuclear confrontation on the Korean peninsula. The accord had been completed in the autumn of 1995, but domestic economic problems had kept Clinton home. By the time of the rescheduled summit, Tokyo agreed to include an ambiguous yet noteworthy statement about cooperation in areas surrounding Japan, alluding to a concern about Taiwan not present in the original agreement.[35] Further, Tokyo entered into secret trilateral talks on security issues with Washington and Taipei at the semiofficial level.

Having been forced to bend American interests and extend American power for Taipei twice in relatively quick succession, the Clinton administration had no intention of becoming involved in similar situations again. Two fundamental changes followed: the administration addressed poor communications with Beijing and Taipei, and it attempted to undertake constructive cooperation with Taiwan.

Reaching out to China seemed most important and most sensitive. The administration invited Jiang Zemin to the United States in 1997, and Clinton went to China in 1998, hoping to alter mutual perceptions and erase the bitterness triggered by Tiananmen. The administration exceeded the tolerance of many Americans, however, when it replaced its policy of engagement with building a strategic partnership with China for the twenty-first century. The new initiative alarmed Taipei and sent an erroneous message to Beijing, exaggerating China's significance and raising false expectations about accommodating Beijing's Taiwan demands. As Lake later observed, "It create[d] illusions, and disillusion is very dangerous."[36]

US officials also decided to deal more closely with Taiwan. Robert Suettinger, preparing at the NSC for strategic talks with China, argued convincingly that a parallel dialogue should be launched with Taipei. As Jeff Bader, a foreign service veteran, later remarked, "We hadn't had any high-level discussion with Taiwan leaders in political and security areas from 1979 on. It's really quite extraordinary. It was a good decision and, in retrospect, it seems like an obvious one, but it was kind of a big deal at the time."[37]

On the Taiwan side, Lee had entrusted presentation of his views to Ding Mou-shih, the former head of TECRO's Washington office and secretary general of Taiwan's National Security Council. American confidence in Ding had developed during his extended tour of duty in the US. His unfailing restraint, serious demeanor, and faultless professionalism contrasted reassuringly with Fred Ch'ien's volatility. Given his English fluency and grasp of the issues, moreover, he could debate matters of concern and react to problems at a level of sophistication far surpassing what US officials could expect at the time from PRC representatives. It appeared reasonably certain he would communicate accurately to Taipei. What was less certain was how fully Lee trusted or listened to Ding. Although apparently respected by the president, Ding was not a member of his inner circle.[38]

The White House insisted the US–Taiwan dialogue be kept so secret that neither TECRO nor AIT would be notified. At the first meeting, on March 11, 1996, in New York, the Americans talked about US plans and exchanges with the PRC, while warning against rash actions. Washington needed to understand Taipei's intentions and explain US objectives. It did not want the authorities in Taiwan to misread the rescue as giving them license to challenge Beijing with risky pro-independence behavior. Sandy Berger and Undersecretary of State Peter Tarnoff called for cross-Strait talks and pledges of cooperation from Lee Teng-hui.

The initial New York encounter led to regular, though not frequent, meetings that convened once or twice a year. Berger, replacing Lake as national security adviser late in 1996, passed the responsibility of the Taiwan talks—and Taiwan affairs—to his deputy James Steinberg, as he began weekly meetings with Chinese Embassy representatives. Steinberg, in conjunction with Thomas Pickering, the undersecretary of state for political affairs, sustained contact with Ding and others who had accompanied him from Taipei. Despite circuitous routing and the US government's decision not to involve TECRO in visa arrangements, all efforts to keep the dialogue secret failed. Nevertheless, the channel allowed unprecedented discussion of global trends, regional security and relationships, military exercises, deployments, and stability of the situation across the Strait. Reports circulated to select readers on each side, including Clinton and Lee.

During these same years a group of current and former officials met regularly and informally in Hawaii. The dialogue originated with the Japanese Diet member Shiina Motoo, whose interest in Taiwan reflected his father's portfolio as foreign minister and granduncle's experience as the first governor general of colonial Taiwan. Lee Teng-hui sent Lin Bih-jaw from his presidential staff, and Secretary of Defense William Cohen agreed that Deputy Assistant Secretary for Asia and Pacific Affairs Kurt Campbell should attend alongside former and future officials Richard Armitage and James Kelly. Through some twelve meetings this influential group examined strategic regional issues; it was underwritten by Lee from his controversial National Security Bureau (NSB) slush fund.[39]

The administration, however, undermined efforts to improve communication by failing to remove a key obstacle to cooperation. The White House had used its top Taiwan post for political patronage, appointing James C. Wood Jr., an Arkansas fund-raiser. Wood's lack of qualifications outraged the AIT board of directors—two of whom resigned—and State

Department officers, who slowed his paperwork. Wood immediately began soliciting illegal campaign contributions for Clinton among business interests in Taiwan, apparently suggesting that the 1996 US carrier deployment required financial gratitude.

Wood's appointment and behavior alarmed officials in Taiwan. Twice in the past they had refused to accept designated representatives, Thomas Shoesmith, because they considered him a Japan hand, and William Rope, because of his identification with the August 1982 arms sales communiqué. Rejecting Wood, however, risked insulting Clinton, who enjoyed personal ties to the Arkansas operative. Instead, officials surreptitiously used the press to disclose his activities.[40] Wood's exposure paralleled that of other notorious fund-raisers, John Huang, Charlie Trie, and Mark E. Middleton. Middleton and Trie arranged a meeting between Liu Tai-ying and Clinton in San Francisco in 1995, and there were allegations that Liu offered Middleton $15 million for Clinton's 1996 presidential campaign.

Taiwan sought to sidestep the Wood disruption and overcome doubts about its intentions by sending Jason Hu Chih-chiang to Washington. A bright, energetic, and engaging man, he set about rebuilding TECRO's reputation and influence. Hu also promoted two transformative initiatives. Taipei had instructed him to broaden the definition of one China so that Washington would view China as an entity larger than the PRC. The new characterization might be one China and two governments or two entities, but always equality between Taipei and Beijing. Simultaneously, he promoted "parallel engagement." Recognizing that "Taipei could not expect equal engagement and . . . that Washington would pursue constructive or enhanced engagement with Beijing," Hu argued, "the US [nevertheless] had to keep its balance." Thus, he urged, when the secretary of state traveled to China, an assistant secretary of state should go to Taiwan. This would remedy the estrangement between the upper reaches of the US and Taiwan governments, restoring personal relationships so crucial to Chinese sensibilities. These had long been absent for Taipei, even as Beijing reinforced such ties with Washington. Hu, however, understood the US political system well enough to recognize that the policies had little chance of adoption. Nevertheless, he believed advocating them improved his relationship with Winston Lord.[41]

Another major effort during Hu's tenure passed without notice by American officials. TECRO and the Foreign Ministry carried out a full-scale reevaluation of the Taiwan Relations Act over many months; their review was driven by the disparity in support for Taiwan between the executive and legislative branches of the US government. So long as Congress seemed disposed to do more for Taiwan, perhaps Taiwan ought to ask

Congress for more. Hu completed the study after returning to Taipei as foreign minister, and the timing, in retrospect, seems suggestively close to the genesis of the controversial Taiwan Security Enhancement Act, which addressed Taiwan's security situation, although any clear link remains elusive.[42]

Hu's replacement, Stephen Chen Hsi-fan, had less success. Chen's warm relations with Lee Teng-hui, and even closer ties to Lien Chan, did not ease his way with Americans. Despite his fluent English, cultural differences made Chen an unfortunate choice. Eager to avoid confrontations, he presented talking points without embellishment and shrank from challenges, preferring to review settled ground. His relaxed and amiable nature, along with his penchant for correcting their grammar, irritated impatient American interlocutors. It quickly became apparent that for serious business he would be bypassed.

The weakness of Taiwan's diplomatic arm in Washington became less important with the appointment of Richard C. Bush to head AIT. Bush, with his many years of experience staffing the House International Relations Committee and as National Intelligence Officer for East Asia, brought expertise and authority unusual for the post. Both the White House and State Department involved him in decision making from which AIT directors were customarily excluded, further increasing his stature, credibility, and value in dealing with Taipei.

Military Relations

Another reason that the weakness of Taiwan's diplomatic representation did not cause great anxiety was the rising importance of military-to-military relations. The Pentagon had criticized too narrow and inadequate interaction for years, deeming use of retired US military personnel or defense industry representatives insufficient to make up for a lack of contact with the active US military. In 1994 the White House launched a review that led to exchanges on logistics, joint force integration, and defense planning.[43] After the Strait crisis, however, those at DOD who sought to spur reform of the Taiwan military, arms sales, and military cooperation gained enormous leverage by evoking images of US and Taiwan ships and aircraft inadvertently firing on each other. A Pentagon official remarked that at the time of the crisis, "we were looking at overhead pictures of the PLA," but realized "we didn't know what [the Taiwanese] were doing."[44]

The so-called software initiative that emerged from postcrisis soul-searching entailed an effort to spend less time selling the latest expensive, glitzy gizmo and work instead on strategic planning, training, coordination, logistics, and passive defense. Several strands flowed together to point in this new direction. Randall Schriver, senior policy director for China in the Office of the Secretary of Defense (OSD), working with the OSD's primary Taiwan hand, Mark Stokes, framed an approach designed to transform military interaction from changing the "culture" of the arms sales talks to altering assessments of Taiwan's military readiness and scientific sophistication. In the early 1990s, when the subject of refocusing programs on training and logistics had been raised, the purpose had been conciliating Beijing. Software in that context constituted a replacement for arms sales. After 1996 DOD's Campbell, working with Schriver and Stokes, saw software as a way to "reduce the sense of isolation in Taiwan, giving its military leaders a greater confidence in their ties with the United States . . . [which would allow] the Pentagon to gain better information about the thinking and plans of Taiwan's armed forces . . . [and] respond to the Republican-led Congress, which has been strongly supportive of Taiwan." All this could be done "without providing hardware to Taiwan that would offend China."[45]

The selling of weapons had, by 1996, deteriorated into a ritualized practice in which representatives of Taiwan's services jockeyed for priority admission to the US superstore, with shopping lists in hand, where they would be told what they could buy. Since they never knew what would be approved in subsequent years from among their most desired but highly sensitive choices, budgeting became an exercise in futility. Critics complained that US defense contractors with Taipei offices wielded enormous influence: they sought to sell the most expensive items to Taiwan officials, who had no options since China's pressure had closed global markets. Moreover, in their efforts to counter China's far higher inventories, military officers felt compelled to seek the latest high-tech solutions, arguing that these cutting-edge items were more devastating as well as easier and less expensive to maintain than older, low-tech equipment. On the other hand, Defense Department officials conceded, "We didn't care whether they could use the stuff or not, and they didn't much care either because it was all about 'symbology.'" Similarly, Richard Bush reflected that the systems "were as much political trophies as they were weapons of war."[46]

The Taiwan side put it differently. Confronted with the uncertainty of US approvals, Taipei bought everything available rather than wait for what might be appropriate. A very senior Taiwan official pointed to the indigenous aircraft program as a disastrous example. Initially denied the F-16, Taipei had spent as much to develop less effective IDFs in the 1980s as the 150 F-16s cost Taiwan in 1992.[47]

In the new world created by the Campbell-Schriver program, moreover, "discussions . . . turned from procurement to the policy level," recounted a Taiwanese participant. "It's things like: 'What are your aims? What do you think? What do you see happening in the next five years?' We never had that sort of conversation before."[48] This more serious exchange became a sometimes annual, sometimes biannual event at Monterey, California, in the wake of the Strait crisis. Suggested spontaneously by Campbell to General Luo Pen-li during a routine April 1997 visit, the idea developed into a broadly gauged, multiagency dialogue that expanded the exposure and raised the status of Taiwan's civilian security analysts. Certain this discussion would anger Beijing, however, the State Department and the NSC insisted the DOD postpone the first session until after the October Clinton-Jiang summit, judging the potential harm to Sino-American relations more important than any reassurance it might provide Taiwan.[49]

Reform of Taiwan's armed forces became a critical part of the software package, even though some officials worried that training would obligate the US to ensure that Taiwan had an effective military. Years of isolation from modern trends in strategic thinking and military management had handicapped the military, which remained a party rather than a national force, one burdened with internecine squabbling among its service branches. Providing weapons and demonstrating use had for years been the extent of aid. Little responsibility attached if Taiwan's soldiers, seamen, and fliers failed to function effectively. The Pentagon's sudden willingness to bring new concepts of strategy, logistics, and organization to bear promised to improve performance and undermine resistance to change. During 1998, at the request of Chief of the General Staff Tang Fei, DOD personnel sought to promote civilian involvement in military planning and development of a coordinated national military strategy. Representatives of the Pentagon's Office of Net Assessment assisted in establishing a threat assessment analysis unit. The following year military survey teams looked at Taiwan's air, land, and naval defenses to establish the government's needs and capabilities.[50]

Within Taiwan's armed forces the Strait crisis and China's military modernization compelled leaders to recognize that Taiwan risked losing its edge to the mainland. Before 1995–96 China's lack of amphibious capabilities had produced complacency in Taiwan. After 1996 ballistic missile attacks, electronic warfare, and submarine blockades all became real threats that required serious responses.

THE EVENTS of 1995–96 may have been an instance of foolhardy risk taking by Taiwan and the United States. China subsequently claimed victory. In fact, China demonstrated the intensity of its concern about Taiwan, but it lost in other ways. The crisis furthered US–Japan ties and encouraged a slowly growing willingness in Tokyo to admit to its support of Taiwan. China's bellicosity frightened governments throughout the region. Lee's presidency grew stronger, and the election prospects of the pro-independence DPP were enhanced.

Taiwan's Lee Teng-hui put the security of the island in jeopardy for domestic political gain and against Beijing's harassment. In the process, he not only highlighted democracy and free elections but demonstrated the contempt of Chinese leaders for these newly won popular rights. The island's economy experienced no lasting damage, and prospects for unification declined noticeably.

The United States, meanwhile, refused to be coerced into abandoning Taiwan. Officials mistrusted Lee more, but they drew Taipei closer to try to understand and monitor it better, agreeing to greater diplomatic contact and intimate military ties. Lee had lobbied effectively not out of diabolical genius, but because Taiwan's democratization made congressional support readily available. Lee understood that; some Americans did not.

CHAPTER THIRTEEN

Setting the Record Straight

I N THE aftermath of the 1996 crisis, mutual mistrust across the Strait and across the Pacific ensured that problems festered and solutions remained out of reach. China worried that the confrontation had not curtailed pro-independence activities. Washington braced for the next unwelcome surprise from Taiwan, convinced that Taipei would again assert political priorities without concern about negative repercussions for the US. Taiwan's policy makers, whatever their immediate intentions, saw the dynamics of triangular relations as threatening and, ignoring Sino-American apprehensions, acted to assert their principles and interests.

Americans charged with putting relations back on track turned to China with reassurances regarding the formula originated in the summer of 1995 and subsequently called the Three Nos. A secret guarantee from Clinton to Jiang pledged no support for two Chinas (or one China and one Taiwan), for Taiwan's independence, or for its entry into international organizations that required statehood. Before Jiang's trip to Washington in 1997, Beijing pressed for a public written statement refining these ideas, but the administration agreed only to Clinton's oral reiteration of the pledges in private; the State Department's press spokesman, Jamie Rubin, would explicitly affirm them after the Chinese had left Washington. This became the first public and official declaration that the US did not support Taiwan independence.

Washington had previously been ambiguous. Joseph Nye, assistant secretary of defense, for instance, told Chinese military officers in Beijing in November 1995 that "nobody knows" what the United States might do in the event of a military clash in the Taiwan Strait. Nye's reminder that Washington had reversed its policies at the outbreak of the Korean War echoed generations of policy makers on the realities of US behavior and its preference for uncertainty.[1] After the 1996 crisis, however, the administration promoted clarity, articulating the Three Nos repeatedly.

Each recitation aimed at reining in Taiwan as well as mollifying Beijing. Taiwan complained, but Lee Teng-hui did not accommodate. In November 1997, in fact, Lee emphasized his position to Keith Richburg of the *Washington Post*. "Taiwan is already independent," he said. "No need to say so." Lee spoke purposefully, just days after the summit and Rubin's remarks, and added to another interviewer, in Chinese, "Taiwan is an independent, sovereign country. Just like Britain or France."[2]

On these as on previous occasions, Lee put both the US and China on notice that Taiwan had several critical requirements regarding its status. Lee had begun speaking of the ROC as "an independent sovereign state" as early as 1988, echoing a formulation that both Chiangs had also employed. Beijing had to accept that the ROC and PRC constituted equal political entities and not seek to treat Taiwan as a subordinate part of the People's Republic. The one country, two systems, concept might work with a British colony, but it did not apply to Taiwan. Its people had made this clear at the time of Hong Kong's reversion 1997 by holding large "Say No to China" rallies. Second, Taiwan demanded participation in international affairs and would be flexible regarding the terms of that participation. Finally, China had to renounce the use of force against Taiwan. Lee insisted that speaking of "an independent sovereign state" did not necessarily imply permanent separation, but rather that Beijing must acknowledge the sovereignty of a historical ROC as well as a government chosen by a free and democratic electorate.

Lee delivered his observations on cross-Strait relations as a new Clinton administration took office. Members of Clinton's second-term national security team, with the exception of holdovers Richard Bush at AIT and Kurt Campbell at Defense, proved no more attuned to Lee's thinking than their predecessors. Madeleine Albright at State and Sandy Berger at the NSC, for instance, largely ignored Taiwan. Albright focused on Eastern Europe. She did not share Christopher's aversion to the island, but although Taiwan resembled small orphan European entities whose fate resonated with her, Taiwan's fate did not. Further, it had an annoying way of complicating diplomatic exchanges with China. Thus, she willingly de-

ferred to the NSC on China-Taiwan issues, especially given China's preference for dealing with Berger.

Berger, closer to and more trusted by the president, replaced Lake as national security adviser. Some credited him with great influence; one col-
league observed that he "wants to be accepted as a kind of Sandy Kissinger." Detractors, including Kissinger, scoffed, "You can't expect a trade
lawyer to be a global strategist." Ironically, Berger, like Kissinger, lavished
attention on Beijing, spending more time on China than on any other
issue. His priorities crowded out Taiwan affairs, which devolved to his
deputy.[3]

The Three Nos

For US–Taiwan relations, the major developments during Clinton's second
term revolved around Clinton's China trip and Lee's response. The China
visit, in June 1998, threatened Taiwan because the White House so badly
needed positive results. The administration had to pacify critics angered
that Clinton would "give face to" Chinese leaders still unrepentant about
the Tiananmen massacre. At the same time, Chinese ballistic missile sales
to Iran (and Pakistan) had to be constrained. Preliminary discussions focused on a Chinese pledge to stop missile transfers. Washington argued
that sales to Iran endangered Beijing, given its swiftly expanding need for
oil. China instead saw an opportunity to force Clinton not to sell anti-
ballistic missile systems to Taipei, systems that undercut China's deterrent
against movement toward independence. Thus, Beijing insisted on linking
Taiwan and Iran.

Washington rejected Beijing's linkage and introduced its own formula.
China had to commit to halting missiles sales to Iran. The US separately
would confirm existing policy: no decision had been made on antiballistic
missile system sales to Taiwan. Taipei's expected alarm posed no deterrent;
however, China's insistence that Washington renounce sales of nascent systems, thereby creating a permanent vulnerability and removing incentives
for freezing its own deployments, killed the deal.[4]

Meanwhile, Taipei fixated on the idea that Clinton would sign a fourth
communiqué ending arms sales. Jason Hu later privately acknowledged
that Taipei worried about a new communiqué all the time; it remained "a
shadow in the sky." Following Ding Mou-shih's March 1998 dialogue
with James Steinberg, cross-ministry meetings in Taipei examined the likelihood that Washington would trade Taiwan's interests for better US–

China relations. Albright aggravated fears by carelessly remarking, "Those are . . . issues we are working on." Beijing, unsurprisingly, encouraged such rumors, relishing Taipei's discomfort as it did. Koo Chen-fu, chairman of Taiwan's Straits Exchange Foundation, cautioned that any signed statement would "put fire into the Taiwan independence movement."[5] So Taipei tried to influence Washington. It postponed scheduled military exercises, and Lee Teng-hui told *Time* magazine that Clinton should tell Jiang Zemin to "invite President Lee to Beijing."[6]

There would not be a fourth communiqué, but Clinton's advisers insisted on sending a message of restraint to Taipei as well as meeting Beijing's expectations by having the president reiterate the Three Nos orally in China. To avoid surprising Taipei, they tried warning that a verbal declaration might occur. But neither a large delegation of visiting legislators nor TECRO's head, Stephen Chen, raised questions; perhaps they missed the signal, were forewarned by a leak, or were so focused on a specific kind of joint message that nothing else registered. Similarly, Taiwan had not protested strongly when Albright had raised the Three Nos in China.

Administration officials, accordingly, thought they could satisfy China, rein in Lee, and yet avoid a crisis. Clinton adopted a low profile, speaking in Shanghai, not Beijing, among scholars rather than officials, and in a private roundtable forum instead of a public venue. Afterward, the president's advisers believed that the administration had accomplished its purpose. A feeling of relief pervaded the presidential entourage.

Taiwan's officials, although rejecting Clinton's right to decide their future, at first denied that the Three Nos signified anything disturbing. They knew the rhetoric and were eager to minimize the effect of the president's words. A twenty-four-hour situation room at the Foreign Ministry and an interagency task force had monitored Clinton's progress through China, watching for three developments: remarks on sovereignty, pressure for a dialogue, and a bargain on arms sales. After the president spoke and American officials insisted no policy had changed, Taipei's reaction was measured. Lee himself dismissed the Three Nos as insignificant, and Washington happily circulated his words. There was no démarche, and Lee's national security adviser stated that Clinton could have done no less.[7]

But after American journalists sharply criticized him, the Hong Kong and mainland press celebrated, and Beijing authorities urged Taiwan to "get a clear understanding of the situation, face reality," and yield on unification, Taipei could not maintain its indifference.[8] Cooperation with Washington abruptly ceased. As one senior official acknowledged later, the initial silence that had greeted reiteration of the Three Nos by Rubin,

Albright, and Deputy Assistant Secretary of State Susan Shirk had misled them. "Hey, for some of us policy is policy, what's the big deal? But when the president said it, rockets went off."[9]

The degree of outrage and consternation that greeted the Three Nos varied. Although advocates insisted all three echoed existing policies, many critics, especially the DPP leadership, believed Clinton had jettisoned a two-decade-old policy of imprecision designed to preserve the right of Taiwan's people to self-determination. At the same time, Clinton had not underlined Beijing's responsibility for peaceful resolution of the cross-Strait issue—the so-called fourth No. As the China scholar Andrew Nathan observed: "What was novel . . . was the manner and context of their articulation—on Chinese soil, clustered together as a package of negatives directed at Taiwan, framed as a reassurance to China, devoid of the other elements of U.S. policy that were favorable to Taiwan, and given canonical status by public presidential utterance. It was, therefore, correct for politicians on both sides of the Taiwan Strait to interpret the statement as an intentional tilt toward Beijing."[10]

Moreover, the Shanghai statement followed by only a day Clinton's televised remarks at Peking University, where, recounting the history of the one-China policy, he said, "We also reached agreement that the reunification would occur by peaceful means, and we have encouraged the cross-strait dialogue to achieve that." It seemed that Clinton had abruptly altered US policy to favor a specific outcome—reunification—rather than remaining uncommitted and encouraging peaceful resolution of the problem. A slip quickly corrected by his staff, in context it unnerved mistrustful observers in Taipei.[11]

Shortly after Clinton's return from China, American officials emphasized policy continuity even as their sense of well-being unraveled. AIT's Washington director, Richard Bush, delivered a message of consistency and balance directly to Lee Teng-hui and to the Taiwanese people. He pledged that the US would observe the TRA, continue arms sales, and abide by Reagan's Six Assurances even as it complied with the Three Nos and the three communiqués. Bush later noted that he tried to help Lee's government, whose cooperative policies the local press and political opposition attacked in the wake of the Clinton trip. He even consciously employed the term Six Assurances, although American officials did not customarily designate US policies with Taiwanese labels.[12]

Lee used the occasion to underline Taiwan's sovereignty. He chided Bush publicly and privately, declaring, "In the future, your country should negotiate directly with us about any matters involving Taiwan." He added,

"You should not have to—and should not—hold bilateral talks with the Chinese Communists" regarding Taiwan.[13] Lee focused on the third of the Three Nos, which rejected Taiwan's right to join international organizations that required statehood, thereby undermining claims to sovereignty. He might also have objected, though he did not, to the altered tone of the US position. The 1994 Taiwan Policy Review pledged affirmatively that the US would support Taiwan's efforts to join international organizations that did not require statehood. The 1997–98 formulation (and probably the initial 1995 letter as well) said negatively that the US would "not support" its joining organizations "that did require statehood," a small but meaningful change in attitude and approach.[14]

Taiwan's irritation and alarm engendered other developments. TECRO pressured members of Congress to berate the administration about the Three Nos throughout the summer of 1998. The policy of US "strategic partnership" with China, originated in 1997 and subsequently ignored by Taipei, suddenly required resistance lest it be realized at Taiwan's expense. Lee wrote in the *Wall Street Journal* that neither China nor Taiwan "can represent the other, much less all of China," and he told the *New York Times* that Taiwan's population enjoyed a separate Taiwanese identity. Nicholas Kristof recalled that when Lee was "asked why Taiwan is so reluctant to become engaged with the mainland, when it claims to intend to get married," he replied, "Why get engaged if engagement is equivalent to becoming a local government and making ourselves slaves?"[15]

Nevertheless, Taipei and Beijing made progress toward renewed cross-Strait dialogue, proving that the crucial ingredient for talks was the will to hold them. Koo Chen-fu traveled to the mainland in October 1998 and met with Wang Daohan and Jiang Zemin. Although no substantive agreements resulted, Wang resolved to visit Taiwan to pursue political and economic discussions even though Taiwan had not met Beijing's minimum requirement—soon an inflexible condition for all negotiations—of declaring adherence to the one-China principle.

Theater Missile Defense

Taiwan's security dilemma worsened after the 1996 Strait crisis as China regrouped, dedicating its military modernization to a Taiwan contingency. Although Taiwan still had advanced weapons, arms flowing from the US, and expectations of American support, TMD attracted renewed attention. Taiwan had purchased three Patriot surface-to-air batteries such as those used in the 1991 Gulf War (Pac-2) to meet this need. In fact, studies revealed that the Pentagon had exaggerated Patriot accuracy against Iraqi Scud missiles. In any event, the first delivery occurred only after the Strait crisis ended.[16]

In the fiscal year 1999 National Defense Authorization Act, the US Congress instructed the secretary of defense to study requirements for creating and operating a more sophisticated TMD system in East Asia and directed specifically that Taiwan be included. Interest in a network drew impetus from the launch, in August 1998, of a North Korean three-stage rocket that flew over Japan, which presaged a device that might soon be able to hit the US. China objected to the idea of TMD in Asia and particularly to a ship-borne system that could protect Taiwan. DOD's study, however, estimated a fleet of eleven Aegis destroyers equipped with battle-management radar and surface-to-air missiles would be needed to defend the whole island, at a cost of $11 billion. Even then, it warned, the shield would not be impenetrable. Moreover, Taiwan could not possibly afford more than four ships, and it would be easy for China to overwhelm such a system.[17]

In fact, TMD remained widely unpopular in Taiwan for financial, technological, and security reasons. Financially, part of Taiwan's military doubted Aegis and TMD were the best uses of limited resources. Furthermore, because of existing technological problems, even some advocates of TMD argued that Taiwan should wait until the US could supply a tested and proven system. The island's proximity to the mainland and the complexity of intercepting missiles with so little warning challenged the best system. Similarly, China's rapidly expanding missile inventory and the increasing accuracy and mobility of its missiles added problems (although to some these factors magnified the necessity of a defensive capability).

Finally, the issue of security played a role. A Taiwan TMD system, even in rudimentary form, could increase the likelihood of a Chinese attack, because threats from Beijing would no longer suffice to maintain the status quo. China had specifically cited TMD as one of several reasons to use force against Taiwan. Then, too, the existence of TMD coverage could tempt Taiwanese politicians into foolhardy behavior, such as a declaration of independence. A TMD system created a false confidence; the population might panic should the system fail. Finally, a TMD shield, even if illusory, might give the US an excuse not to come to the rescue if Taiwan got in trouble.

But Lee Teng-hui wanted to involve Taiwan in TMD for political rather than military reasons. Domestically, he sought to counter DPP support for TMD and thereby defend his defense record. Abroad, TMD would sig-

nificantly strengthen ties with the US and integrate Taiwan into a defense network in the region that included Japan and South Korea. Thus, a succession of defense ministers who shared reservations about the utility of TMD nevertheless asked Washington to include Taipei in TMD planning. Tang Fei, the defense minister whom Americans found sensible, solid, and admirable, asserted in August 2000 that TMD stood for Taiwan missile defense and was "vital to Taiwan's security."[18]

Taiwan's vulnerabilities encouraged consideration of a still more sensitive option: offensive capabilities. Proponents maintained offensive arms would be cheaper, as effective, and more reliable than the US. They would either deter Beijing by permitting targeting of mainland cities (countervalue tactics) or would complicate PLA defense planning and waste its resources (counterforce operations). In July 1999 Tang Fei openly asserted the necessity of "counterattack weapons" for the first time. Competing candidates in the island's 2000 presidential election all eventually advocated offensive measures. The DPP contender, Chen Shui-bian, insisted that the key would be "keeping the war away from Taiwan as far as possible," meaning an offshore defense.[19] Washington strongly objected, having committed itself to provide only defensive weaponry. Moreover, many

Americans urged Taiwan to do more to fortify itself, such as buffering facilities with concrete and burying critical infrastructure, measures that
wouldn't provoke China or give Taiwan the ability to strike the mainland.[20]

State-to-State Relations

Taiwan's predicament remained chiefly political. Lee Teng-hui focused on
that part of the equation, taking the opportunity of a July 1999 interview
with a German journalist from *Deutsche Welle* radio to clarify his views
on Taiwan's status and relationship with Beijing. Startling members of
his own government whom, as usual, he had not consulted, he used a question previously submitted by the reporter to assert that relations between
China and Taiwan ought to be conducted on a "special state-to-state"
basis.[21]

Lee acted out of mixed motives. He wanted most of all to assert parity
with China. When Koo Chen-fu had traveled to the mainland and resumed
the disrupted cross-Strait dialogue, Wang Daohan had agreed to a return
visit. Lee considered it of surpassing importance to establish Taiwan's
equality at the negotiating table before Wang arrived, so that Beijing could
not treat Taipei as a provincial capital. In fact, Taiwan's NSB reported that
Jiang Zemin planned to underline Taiwan's subordinate status in his October 1 commemoration of the PRC's fiftieth anniversary just before Wang's
trip. That Lee took this intelligence seriously seems especially likely since
Yin Tsung-wen, the secretary general of his National Security Council at
this time, had been head of the NSB from 1993 to 1999. Lee may have desired equality, or he may simply have wanted to prevent a Wang trip.

Another motive for the president was the opportunity to entrench his
political ideals before he stepped down from twelve years in office, uncertain who his successor would be. He had discovered long before that, by
co-opting DPP positions and playing to popular sentiment, he won elections. In the wake of his "two-state" declaration, his popularity soared to
87 percent.

Finally, Lee and his closest advisers believed it crucial to tell Washington
publicly that—in the Three Nos and in its carelessness about the way it
thought and spoke about one China—the US had gone too far in placating
Beijing. Clinton, Lee asserted, lacked a proper view of history and failed to
think through the issues carefully enough. Lee had not said so explicitly
before this, neither in July 1998 nor in his book *The Road to Democracy*,

in which he denied that Clinton had changed direction. But he praised congressional criticism of Clinton's policy, saying it "demonstrated the candor and soundness of American diplomacy."[22]

In the *Deutsche Velle* interview, however, Lee responded directly with his so-called two-state theory. His rejoinder had been carefully planned. Shortly after Clinton spoke of the Three Nos in 1998, Lee assembled a team of ten academic, legal, and personal advisers headed by the lawyer and trade expert Tsai Ing-wen to examine the question of Taiwan's sovereignty and cross-Strait relations.

The study group quickly concluded that Taiwan had put itself in an untenable position. By accepting identification as a "political entity," Taiwan had conceded to the PRC the legitimacy of statehood, thereby eroding the international standing of the Republic of China. If it did not immediately alter its inadvertent loss of status, there would soon be nothing left to save. Taipei should abandon terms like "one China" and "one China each with its own interpretation"; it should even abolish the National Unification Guidelines. Instead, Taiwan had to assert its legitimacy as a state, alongside the PRC, within one future nation called China and carry on special state-to-state relations.[23]

When the German reporter alluded to Taiwan as a "renegade province," his cliché angered the president. On the morning of July 9, Lee told Tsai and the project director Chang Jung-feng that he intended to announce the state-to-state formula. Chang maintains that he tried to persuade the president that the timing was wrong. The members of the study group believed that both Beijing and Washington should be forewarned, and that Taiwan should raise the issue with Wang Daohan rather than surprise China. MAC Chairman Su Chi, on the other hand, stressed that the task force, and especially Tsai, wanted to advance a separatist agenda and happily sacrificed Wang's visit. In any case, Lee pressed ahead, asserting that if one is always too cautious, "he'll never accomplish anything great."[24]

US officials felt blindsided by the two-states concept. Not only had there been no consultation, but Taipei had not bothered to notify the US, even though Su Chi had been in Washington immediately before Lee's announcement. Such discourtesy, at the least, gave the impression that Washington had lost control of Taiwan policy, and some feared Beijing would conclude that the US could not manage this increasingly dangerous situation. Su insisted that he had had no warning himself and, therefore, could not have given any. But Su did know about the *Deutsche Welle* interview, if not its exact intent, and did know about the study; so did vice president Lien Chan and Foreign Minister Jason Hu.[25]

Su provoked an even larger crisis when he faced the Taipei press. After hasty briefings he later dismissed as inadequate because of the president's absence, he declared on July 12, "We have shown our good will by calling ourselves a political entity under a one-China policy. But the Chinese Communists have used this policy to squeeze us internationally. We feel there is no need to continue using the one-China term."[26] Widely and understandably interpreted as a blanket rejection of one China, Su's words were as incendiary as Lee's original statement, even though what he meant to say, and ordinarily did say, was that Taiwan could not accept the PRC's definition of one China. Lee claimed that Washington demanded Su's ouster but that he thought this unreasonable.[27]

Washington, bracing for an explosive reaction from Beijing, sought to make Taiwan accountable and demonstrate US blamelessness to China. Kenneth Lieberthal from the NSC and Assistant Secretary of State Stanley Roth flew to Beijing to calm the Chinese, deny US involvement, and avert retaliation. Although Clinton's trip to China in the summer of 1998 had been deemed successful, subsequent events derailed relations. Not only had charges of campaign finance irregularities against Beijing arisen, but Congress began investigating alleged Chinese espionage at nuclear laboratories. Premier Zhu Rongji's World Trade Organization mission to Washington in April 1999 failed to resolve PRC accession, which embarrassed him. Washington and Beijing disagreed over the war in Kosovo, and in May the US accidentally bombed the Chinese Embassy in Belgrade, which prompted attacks on the American Embassy in Beijing, and both sides were aggrieved.

Lee had knowingly leapt into that fraught situation, worsening it and virtually guaranteeing that Beijing would assume US complicity. Clinton phoned Jiang Zemin on July 18 and, in a thirty-minute call, stressed US support for one China and expressed surprise at Lee's move. Nevertheless, aware that PLA units had begun holding large-scale military attack exercises that menaced Taiwan and potentially threatened US forces, Clinton pressed Beijing not to use force in response to Lee's rhetoric. Jiang resisted, declaring that China would not abandon force to prevent separation.[28]

At the same time, tensions between Taipei and Washington ran high. Lee, uncertain about the desirability of sending an emissary to Washington, was told not to. Darryl Johnson, AIT's Taipei director, on the eve of departure called on Lee to express US displeasure and provoked a "testy" exchange. Lee held a grudge, later describing Johnson as someone who would "come to the presidential office and interrogate me like he would a criminal. I always ignored him."[29]

As Lee awaited a Washington envoy, he might well have wondered about the Lieberthal-Roth mission. Months before, Kenneth Lieberthal had proposed a fifty-year "freeze," during which Taiwan would not seek independence and Beijing would not use force for unification. Economic, cultural, and political integration would occur throughout the freeze, facilitating a peaceful resolution. Lieberthal, long perceived by Taiwan as a foe and a China sympathizer, had taken the idea to Taipei in 1998, lighting a firestorm not just among independence advocates, but among skeptics who viewed the idea as undemocratic. Lee described Lieberthal's joining the NSC staff as "adding frost to snow." During Lieberthal's tenure at the University of Michigan, Taipei had withdrawn a $450,000 contribution because he signed a report endorsing the US's one-China policy in 1996. Now a possibly hostile official had the power to implement a dangerous proposal.[30]

The administration meanwhile sent Richard Bush to Taiwan to find the proximate rationales for "two states" and to emphasize Washington's irritation. Lee, though fond of Bush personally, later complained that the US government should have sent someone of higher status—although that objection was hardly compatible with his refusal to concede that he had caused a serious problem. He argued that the state-to-state idea, like the Three Nos, was not new, only a different formulation. Bush assured Lee the US would sustain the TRA, Reagan's Six Assurances, and arms sales. There had to be, however, more consultation and greater consideration of US interests. Lee responded that he had not conferred with Washington because it could not stop him and should not have to bear responsibility for his actions.

The price Lee paid for "two states" proved limited, a fact that confirmed Lee's view that "even when Washington indicates no support for Taiwan, it does not mean that it opposes the policies held by Taipei."[31] Albright delivered caustic remarks about him, and Washington, he claimed, urged him to accommodate China in situations such as Wang Daohan's eighty-six character statement on one China and unification that autumn.[32] DOD canceled a task force visit intended to recommend improvements for Taiwan's air defenses, but it rescheduled the trip in September. When Clinton met Jiang Zemin at a summit of APEC leaders in mid-September, he remarked that Lee "had made things more difficult for both China and the United States." Indeed, by then virtually everyone in the executive branch dealing with Taiwan and China affairs had come to think ill of Lee. For the rest of his tenure he would be seen and treated as irresponsible.[33]

The administration's tougher message emerged at the UN too, where Ambassador Richard Holbrooke, shortly after taking up the post in 1999, opposed admission of Taiwan for the first time. The decision to do so easily gained support from Albright, who as UN ambassador had wanted to take the same position. Taipei, however, discounted Holbrooke's initiative, coming as it did from someone labeled an adversary as far back as the Carter years.

Probably the most serious cost of Lee's two-state declaration was the disruption of secret high-level communications between Washington and Taipei. In the aftermath of the 1996 Strait crisis, the Clinton administration had conducted various quiet dialogues, including the Ding-Steinberg talks. At an even higher level of confidentiality, according to senior Taiwan and American officials, a trusted former senior official traveled regularly to meet with Lee to try to prevent misunderstandings and surprises. When Lee failed to use the channel to give advance notice of "two states," the direct contact ended.[34] Rather than break down mistrust, the secret channel probably contributed to it.

Otherwise, US–Taiwan relations did not change radically. No one demanded a recantation from Lee. Two aircraft carriers remained in the vicinity of Taiwan until it seemed clear that Beijing would not retaliate. The US government did not rush its new head of AIT to Taipei, as an emergency would have required, nor did it withhold his arrival to express disapproval, as many in Taiwan's government believed to be the case. The new appointee, Ray Burghardt, subsequently expressed surprise that anyone had reached that conclusion, having used the time for personal affairs. Lee himself wrote in his book *Asia's Wisdom and Strategy* that by the end of the year Burghardt appeared "to have understood what we did."[35] Sales of military equipment, including early-warning radar aircraft, were barely interrupted.

When Clinton told reporters, during a July 21, 1999, press conference, that three pillars defined his China-Taiwan policy, most observers thought he was warning Taiwan against pursuing the two-state initiative further. But two of the three pillars cautioned China, not Taiwan, calling on Beijing not to use force and not to disrupt Wang Daohan's mission to the island to resume a dialogue: "The one-China policy is right, the cross-straight dialogue is right, the peaceful approach is right." Clinton even added the Fourth No, which he had been censured for not saying in Beijing in 1998. If China used force, "under the Taiwan Relations Act, we would be required to view it with the gravest concern."[36]

As though on cue, aircraft from China and Taiwan flew provocative sorties above the Strait over the ensuing weeks, daring each other to strike out. Problems with military preparedness in Taiwan accordingly became of ever greater concern to US officials. Those who retained faith in residual effects from the old alliance with US forces reluctantly acknowledged that a twenty-year gap had taken a significant toll. By the summer of 1999, the US found a military resisting reform, a legislature unwilling to appropriate funds for modernization, and a population unmindful of Chinese threats. Taiwan's defense budget had been declining for years, and the army still dominated the Ministry of National Defense, demanding that ground forces receive the greatest proportion of budget allocations and first priority on weapons purchases. Similarly, of troops drafted the largest numbers went into the army, even though the air force and navy would do the critical fighting if a conflict erupted. Taiwan might want Aegis, but it lacked trained personnel to keep the ships afloat, just as the air force repeatedly had been compelled to ground its F-16s for lack of qualified pilots. Friction among the services over money and privileges made joint planning difficult and all-service war-gaming impossible.[37]

The source of many of these problems, Americans concluded, lay in the political rather than security motives for fielding a military. Critics insisted that Lee Teng-hui wanted strong forces for promoting relations with the US rather than for fighting or deterring the PLA, since he did not believe that China would attack, but he did assume the United States would bail Taiwan out if it did. One very senior US military official lamented: "I find there are pockets of Taiwanese military officers . . . who understand what modern warfare really is and who are good professional military officers. Then there are just military dilettantes in uniforms who are pretty useless, and then there are a lot of breathless armchair military pseudo-intellectuals who talk without knowing what they are doing. Then there are the politicians, who don't much care but are just trying to make points."[38] Officials in the Foreign Ministry and Ministry of National Defense, moreover, generally treated each other with barely concealed contempt, neither sharing information nor cooperating to develop policy recommendations.[39]

The Pentagon, urged on by Congress, set to work to revolutionize military affairs, undertaking missions to evaluate island defenses, including prevention of amphibious landing, submarine attack, or blockade and air war. From September 1999 to early 2000 the Office of the Secretary of Defense laid out as many as three hundred recommendations for solving operational problems.[40] The US could not transform the Taiwan military, but the Clinton administration sought to help begin the process.

The Rise of the Blue Team and the TSEA

In Washington conservative activists did not believe the Clinton administration could be trusted to overcome Taiwan's isolation and ensure a flow of hardware to the island. They decided to do so and to undermine Clinton's China policy at the same time. This so-called Blue Team, a name borrowed from the US side in military exercises, lacked a formal membership but, with financial backing from the right-wing political philanthropist Richard Mellon Scaife, gathered regularly. It may have drawn on the talents of as many as two dozen sympathizers, including Jim Doran, an aide to Senate Foreign Relations Committee (SFRC) Chairman Senator Jesse Helms (R-N.C.); Mark Lagon, an SFRC staffer; Richard Fisher, an aide to Representative Christopher Cox (R-Calif.); William Triplett, an aide to Senator Robert Bennett (R-Utah); Peter Brookes, a Republican staff member on the House International Relations Committee; Frank Gaffney of the conservative Center for Security Policy (a former Reagan-era DOD official); and the *Washington Times* reporter Bill Gertz as well as former intelligence officers and several scholars.[41] Among the two dozen, many possessed little actual interest in or knowledge of China or Taiwan, but they believed that Beijing posed a growing, and unacknowledged, threat to American security.

Between 1999 and 2001 this coalition, working sometimes with and sometimes parallel to Taiwan's lobbyists, orchestrated a series of measures requiring greater disclosure to Congress of classified data on Chinese missile deployments, the balance of forces across the Strait, and Taiwan's military readiness. The practices they targeted for reversal included barring Taiwan military personnel from access to equipment and locations not prohibited to Chinese PLA officers, selling Taiwan inferior versions of weaponry, and refusing to establish secure communications or institute joint exercises. "The executive branch . . . was slow to recognize the effect of what Congress was requiring" in raising Taiwan's profile, observed Kurt Campbell, deputy assistant defense secretary. A December 2000 DOD report to Congress, for instance, sought to emphasize Taiwan's importance, asserting that the need to maintain its defense capabilities derived not just from the TRA but also from US "national interest."[42]

Believing that the TRA was too weak and the PRC's military modernization too rapid, moreover, the Blue Team promoted a new piece of legislation: the Taiwan Security Enhancement Act (TSEA). The TSEA's origin is murky, but interviews pinpoint early conversations about remedies for Taiwan's vulnerability among mid-level US and Taiwan military officers, if not the Blue Team per se. Quickly convinced that the answer lay in legislation, however, the Taiwanese and their US counterparts turned to key congressional staff aides who could draft an effective bill and enlist the Blue Team to enact it. Thereafter, support from lobbyists at Cassidy & Associates and the Formosan Association for Public Affairs (FAPA) added resources to the campaign for the TSEA. In the Senate, Jesse Helms (R-N.C.) and Robert Torricelli (D-N.J.) cosponsored it (S. 693), and a companion measure was introduced by Benjamin A. Gilman (R-N.Y.) and Sam Gejdenson (D-Conn.) in the House (H. 1838).

The TSEA called for more vigorous congressional oversight of arms sales, including regular reports to Congress on Taiwan's defense requests. It provided for increased technical staffing of AIT, mandated senior (flag-rank) military travel to Taiwan, and authorized the sale of specific controversial weapons, including air-to-air missiles, diesel submarines, Aegis destroyers, and missile defense equipment that used satellite data. Finally, and perhaps most notably, the legislation supplied a direct communication link to the US Pacific Command in Hawaii, making possible US–Taiwan interoperability akin to a formal military alliance.

The Clinton administration condemned the TSEA as unnecessary and provocative; its provisions were already covered in the TRA. Many officials strongly objected, among them Admiral Dennis C. Blair, the commander in chief of the Pacific Command who insisted that the TSEA "doesn't give me the ability to do my job any better than I can do it today."[43] Sandy Berger, calling it the "Taiwan Insecurity Act," declared that he had recommended a presidential veto.[44] Critics denounced the TSEA as a mechanism for lobbyists to prove they were earning their retainers, and for members of Congress to generate votes in their districts.

Nevertheless, the TSEA remained popular in Congress, where protecting Taiwan "is a perfect blend of ideology and defense procurement," observed Kurt Campbell.[45] The TSEA passed in the House in a somewhat modified form on February 1, 2000, by a veto-proof vote of 341–70. Both Gilman, the Republican chairman of the International Relations Committee, and Majority Whip Thomas DeLay (R-Tex.) gave the measure vigorous support.[46]

Lobbying provided critical momentum. FAPA pushed enthusiastically on behalf of Taiwanese Americans, its leader, Coen Blaauw, convinced that a vague TRA needed to be supplemented with a practical to-do list. Thus, Blaauw asserted, the TSEA would make the TRA more effective, not undermine it.[47] A significant financial boost came directly from Taiwan through the Taiwan Studies Institute (TSI), a Taipei-based think tank led by Lin Chen-yi, who had been a major contributor to the DPP and a thirty-year friend to Chen Shui-bian. The TSI unexpectedly gave Sandwick International, and therefore its parent, Cassidy & Associates, $2 million to promote the bill without consulting the DPP, FAPA, TECRO, or the Foreign Ministry.[48]

Thereafter, lobbyists and interest groups struggled both to promote the bill and to claim credit. Carl Ford, a high-level Cassidy representative who served in both the Defense and State departments and on Capitol Hill, insisted that his lobbyists were crucial, arguing, "My experience has been that the US will do things for Taiwan only when the pain becomes so great that they have no other option. They don't do anything for Taiwan if they can avoid it because they have to pay a price with the PRC." Taiwan's own lobbying, observed Ford, was ineffectual and faulty, and "my sense is Taiwan is more timid than they need to be and that without somebody like Cassidy they would really be in deep, deep trouble."[49]

Taipei did labor under many constraints. First, US officials allegedly warned against vigorous lobbying for the TSEA lest it endanger US support for other measures desired by Taiwan. Since US–Taiwan relations remained fragile in the aftermath of the Strait crisis, such admonitions had deterrent value. Second, the Taiwan government was split. Lee Teng-hui did not campaign directly for the measure, but he sent money to lobbyists. On the other hand, Foreign Minister C. J. Chen argued that the TRA had served Taiwan well and would meet Taipei's requirements so long as Washington remained friendly. If it was not, the TSEA could not help. Accordingly, the Foreign Ministry opposed the bill and instructed TECRO not to promote it. (Only after the election of a DPP president did that change.) At TECRO, furthermore, people resented working with Cassidy, which made collaboration difficult. Finally, regardless of its own preferences, Taiwan feared alienating US proponents and opponents in more or less equal proportions. This dilemma also troubled Taiwan military officers, who wanted the weapons yet opposed too much American oversight and were beset by industry advocates.[50]

The Senate, as usual, proved to be a more difficult hurdle than the House. Cassidy had already told Taipei of likely defeat there and suggested enacting desirable provisions individually. Although Majority Leader Trent Lott (R-Miss.) continued to try to ram the TSEA through because of potential construction contracts for the Litton-Ingalls shipyards based in Pascagoula, Mississippi, he could not muster enough votes.[51] In the midst of the struggle, Chen Shui-bian's victory in the March 2000 presidential election further complicated the issue, raising the question whether he would wish to buy weapons requested by the KMT. Indeed, Senator Frank Murkowski (R-Alaska) suggested that Chen wanted the Senate to shelve the TSEA, and it did, even though Chen actually welcomed the act's aggressive approach.[52]

Failure of the TSEA, however, did not mean Congress had stopped worrying about Taiwan's defense. In the spring and summer of 2000 it brought stiff pressure to bear on Israel, including threats to cut aid drastically to prevent the sale to Beijing of advanced airborne radar warning technology. Washington argued that just one of the four planned Phalcon AWACS aircraft transfers, each slated to earn Israel $250 million, would allow China far better coordination for air strikes against Taiwan, which would threaten the island and jeopardize US forces should they intervene on Taipei's behalf. US action came late, after Chinese pilots had already begun to train on the aircraft, and deeply angered Beijing. Israel capitulated reluctantly to ensure US support at the Camp David 2000 summit between Prime Minister Ehud Barak and the Palestinian leader Yasser Arafat, although other arms sales to China continued.[53]

China's military expansion, in fact, accelerated in 1999. As a result of an extended and high-level debate on "peace and development" that emphasized the economy, Chinese leaders also concluded the US threat had increased and conditions in the Taiwan Strait had worsened. Therefore, they agreed to increase internal production and foreign procurement for Taiwan contingencies.[54]

During the Clinton administration, the military-to-military relationship between the United States and Taiwan expanded significantly. Taiwan purchased close to $21 billion in weapons, primarily from the US, making it the second-largest arms buyer in the world. Active-duty officers, who had not been able to visit until 1992, came at the rate of one hundred exchanges annually by the end of the decade. Pentagon assessments in 1999–2000 bolstered Taiwan's continuing requests for diesel-electric submarines, Aegis destroyers, and the P-3 Orion antisubmarine aircraft as part of a broad antisubmarine warfare (ASW) architecture.

Several factors nevertheless undermined the new intimacy. First, the US remained reluctant to introduce a new generation of technology and rekindle an arms race in the region. It limited sales of advanced missiles and stored one medium-range air-to-air variety in the US until conditions warranted repositioning.[55] Second, administration officials sought to avoid angering China. Initiatives meant to assist Taiwan did not occur before or after special events, holidays, or contacts with Beijing. Finally, Taiwan's officer corps viewed US scrutiny and assistance with mixed feelings. Reports to the US Congress detailing weaknesses in Taiwan's defense structure embarrassed them and possibly made them more vulnerable. Positive reports threatened to reduce sales. Officers also resented interference in setting priorities, especially when Americans urged passive defense measures rather than weapons.

Assent of the People

Following Lee's two-states declaration, the Institute of Taiwan Studies of the Chinese Academy of Social Sciences in Beijing drafted a white paper to expose his errors. Final approval did not come from the Taiwan Affairs Leading Small Group and Politburo Standing Committee until February 2000. As a result, release of "The One China Principle and the Taiwan Issue" coincided with Taiwan's presidential election campaign and the final push for China's and Taiwan's admission into the WTO. The paper conceded the need to negotiate on the "basis of equality," but also declared that "the government of the PRC is the sole legal government representing the whole of China."[56]

The Taiwan and US media, however, focused on a different passage, called Beijing's "third if." The white paper asserted that "if a grave turn of events occurs leading to the separation of Taiwan from China in any name, or if Taiwan is invaded and occupied by foreign countries, or if the Taiwan authorities refuse, sine die, the peaceful settlement of cross-Straits reunification," then Beijing would be "forced to adopt all drastic measures possible, including the use of force." In other words, *if* Taipei indefinitely delayed negotiating unification, China would coerce it. Zhu Rongji rightly protested that this contingency, far from being new, had been stated in the 1980s by Deng Xiaoping. But memories were short, the threat sounded serious, and Zhu's belligerence during Taiwan's election, coming from an otherwise "even-tempered pragmatist," seemed especially alarming.[57]

To the Clinton administration, which in the early months of 2000 sought to promote China's accession to the WTO, this posed an especially unwelcome development. On February 24, 2000, four days after the white paper's release, Clinton declared, "I believe to set . . . [China's membership] up as a choice between economic rights and human rights, or economic security and national security, is a false choice." Then he added, "The issues between Beijing and Taipei must be resolved peacefully and with the assent of the people of Taiwan."[58]

The key word, *assent,* which cautioned Beijing as it mollified Congress, built on ideas Clinton's AIT director, Richard Bush, had introduced in September 1998. Bush emphasized Washington's belief "that any result that enjoys broad public support will be more long lasting." Eager to refute suggestions by Chas Freeman, a former assistant secretary of defense, that the democratization of Taiwan had added unwelcome volatility to the cross-Strait situation, which required the "disciplining of Taiwan," Bush emphasized that "the people on Taiwan are wise and prudent," and democracy "contributes to peace and stability." As Bush would later write, Clinton effectively implemented dual deterrence.[59]

DURING the 1990s Taiwan developed a link to the United States that it had lacked before, its democracy. Washington had been aligned with Taipei for decades before this political change. It had signed the Mutual Defense Treaty at a moment when Taiwan's government was almost as repressive as China's. Democratization, however, broadened and deepened the relationship even as it introduced complications inherent in representative institutions. Democratization gratified Americans who had encouraged it, although cooperation became more difficult with an elected administration and autonomous legislature than it had been with an autocratic regime.

Democracy also played a role internally. For Clinton, Taiwan did not loom large as an issue compared to crises in Europe and the Middle East. It did motivate a small number of activists, however, who cared about Taiwan policy even if they didn't care about Taiwan and could extract a political penalty for inattention.

Lee exploited democracy, continuing and broadening the transformation he inherited from Chiang Ching-kuo, imbuing his people with a Taiwan consciousness and, ultimately, insisting that unification could occur only with a democratic China. Democracy's spread in Taiwan, moreover, allowed a previously quiescent public to enter the political arena, holding their own government to account for past failings and the US for support of authoritarianism. Mistrust of Washington had been largely silent, if widespread, but emerged as an important variable not just for bilateral relations but also in the way Taiwan people thought about the future.

WAR AGAINST TERRORISM

THE TERRORIST attacks on the US on September 11, 2001, defined the presidency of George W. Bush, although even before those events, Bush's advisers had a full agenda. They undertook initiatives to strengthen US military power, build a missile defense system, reinforce alliances in Asia, and end reliance on international treaties and coalitions (such as the Anti-Ballistic Missile Treaty, 1968). The administration reversed Clinton policies, rejecting humanitarian intervention, involvement in Arab-Israeli talks, the Agreed Framework with North Korea, and compromise with Russia. Rather than seek to make China a strategic partner, it initially perceived Beijing as a strategic competitor.

Terrorism in New York and Washington altered assumptions about America's place in the world. The US would have to work harder to stabilize and preserve its unipolar ascendancy. It could not allow any competitor to emerge to contest US power. No longer operating in a predictable cold war environment, moreover, US officials contemplated preemptive defense against threats from the "axis-of-evil"—Iran, Iraq, and North Korea—and rogue states such as Cuba, Syria, and Libya.

Responding to 9/11, the administration also launched a global war on terrorism, beginning with the Taliban in Afghanistan (2001). But it also invaded Saddam Hussein's Iraq (2003), an attack that was based on false intelligence about weapons of mass destruction and on concern about oil. This ensnared the US in a prolonged conflict, a version of nation building involving the messianic democratization of the Middle East.

In the midst of all this, the administration also completely reassessed China's importance, ending reflexive hostility and finding new fields for cooperation. After the EP-3 spy plane disaster (2001), in which American flyers became hostages amid bitterness, misunderstanding, and inadequate crisis management, Washington and Beijing moved toward repairing relations. Democracy and human rights did not play a role, but trade and the war on terrorism did. Beijing provided a measure of support for fighting terrorists through activities such as financial monitoring and border access. China significantly increased its bilateral trade surplus with the US. It simultaneously took advantage of the US absence from Southeast and East Asia, reaching out with diplomatic support and economic assistance to once-antagonistic nations. Of particular assistance to the US was China's hosting the Six-Party Talks about North Korea's nuclear ambitions. The US might have seen Chinese initiatives as threatening had they occurred at another historical moment, but in the wake of 9/11, to Taiwan's dismay, Beijing's needs and interests have become of increasing significance to the US and the world.

CHAPTER FOURTEEN

The Influence of Democracy

THE ELECTIONS of Chen Shui-bian and George W. Bush appeared exceptionally auspicious for the troubled US–Taiwan relationship. Chen's attainment of the presidency in 2000 affirmed the resilience and legitimacy of democracy in Taiwan as power devolved not just on a new leader, but also on a competing party. Less than a year later, Bush captured the White House and distanced himself from China while rebalancing America's posture in Asia. At the intersection of Taiwan's expanding democratization and shifting US security priorities, prospects for stabilizing and improving Washington-Taipei ties looked good. Only gradually did the realities of domestic politics, cultural and personal misunderstanding, and diverging defense needs intervene.

By the time George W. Bush entered the White House, Chen Shui-bian had been in office for eight months. In that time, his overtures to Beijing had been rebuffed repeatedly as China insisted he first concede that Taiwan is part of China. US efforts to shape Chen's message and encourage cross-Strait dialogue had not produced a breakthrough. Furthermore, Chen's programs had begun to fragment under intense KMT opposition, DPP factionalism, and government ineptitude.

Clinton administration officials had feared Chen's election, uneasy about DPP zeal and inexperience. Dreading an immediate cross-Strait crisis, they sought to soften the DPP's initial message and early decisions.[1] The new AIT chief in Taipei, Ray Burghardt, assisted Chen in composing a moderate inaugural address, emphasizing the language necessary to reassure hostile listeners in Beijing and nervous ones in Washington. His visits to the president-elect stirred controversy, particularly among newly ousted KMT politicians, who labeled US influence excessive. In fact, his advice and encouragement did weigh heavily, but so too did Chen's pragmatism. On the day of his inauguration, May 20, Chen declared his "4 Nos and 1 shall not," motivated at least as much by recognition that he must avoid war with China: "[As] long as the CCP regime has no intention to use military force against Taiwan, I pledge that during my term in office, I will not declare independence, I will not change the national title, I will not push forth the inclusion of the so-called 'state-to-state' description in the Constitution, and I will not promote a referendum to change the status quo in regards to the question of independence or unification. Furthermore, there is no question of abolishing the Guidelines for National Unification and the National Unification Council." Here Chen set aside positions long advocated by the DPP to take a safer, centrist stance. Moreover, as a goodwill gesture, he shared this text with Beijing before its delivery.[2]

Chen's conciliatory initiatives continued through the year and into 2001. Some imagined he would be a Taiwanese Richard Nixon—that is, the inveterate opponent of unification, neutralizing ideologically hard-core critics to reach an agreement with Beijing.[3] His December 31, 2000, New Year's message challenged China to "respect the existence and international dignity of the Republic of China"; he shocked DPP stalwarts by suggesting that "the integration of our economies, trade and culture can be a starting point for a new framework of permanent peace and political integration."[4]

The potential for improving cross-Strait relations, however, seemed limited. Chen told the *Los Angeles Times* that he would put relations with China ahead of fighting corruption and reviving Taiwan's troubled economy. He and his advisers appealed to Washington to take a greater role in restarting talks and, allegedly, sent an envoy to Wang Daohan, ARATS chairman, the day following his election. But Chen found that Beijing did not respond, despite earlier assurances that placatory inauguration remarks would pay off. Instead, Beijing asserted that it would be "listening to what he says and observing what he does."

In fact, China did not remain passive. American intelligence warned that the PLA appeared to be planning for a September blockade of Kaohsiung—a DPP stronghold, Taiwan's second-largest city, and the third-largest container port in the world—to compromise Chen. Although Kaohsiung remained untouched, general military intimidation continued.[5] PRC leaders welcomed the difficulties Chen had with the unruly KMT, a disunited DPP, and his own lack of experience. They sought to undermine him by mounting a united-front campaign to woo opposition politicians and co-opt businessmen. When the international technology market slowed Taiwan's economy, Beijing blamed Chen's refusal to remove barriers to investment in, and trade with, China.

Further, Beijing tried to counter Chen and appeal to Washington by recasting the one-China principle. The original Deng Xiaoping version "that there is but one China in the world, that the Government of the PRC is the sole legal government representing the whole of China, and that Taiwan is an inalienable part of Chinese territory," had no traction in Taiwan. During the summer of 2000 Deputy Prime Minister Qian Qichen repackaged it, declaring "there is only one China in the world and the mainland and Taiwan both belong to one China. China's sovereignty and territory are indivisible." Taipei rejected the reformulation as unequal and insincere, pointing out that Beijing continued to emphasize the earlier definition to the international community.[6]

Whether Chen would have engaged Beijing in a dialogue and what the parameters of such a conversation could have been strains the imagination. Circumscribed by the party faithful and personal conviction, Chen's maneuvering room would have been minimal. As it was, Beijing never tested Chen, never forced him to live up to his own most flexible initiatives.

Enter Bush

George W. Bush demonstrated little foreign policy interest or acumen in the protracted 2000 election campaign. He characterized China as a strategic competitor and occasionally empathized with Taipei. In July 1999 he told the *Washington Times* he planned to use US military forces against China if it attacked Taiwan. Bush supported the TSEA, which the Clinton White House had fought. Later, at a Boeing airplane plant in Seattle, he disparaged Clinton's administration for having "been inconsistent on Taiwan."[7] Nevertheless, as late as September, Chen Shui-bian remarked, "No matter which party wins . . . there will be no drastic changes in US policy toward Taiwan."[8] When Bush finally took office, his new administration appeared to have a modest foreign policy agenda and no popular mandate.

Bush's victory, however, provided Taiwan an advantageous constellation of people and policies. The Bush campaign had used Taiwan partly to censure Clinton, partly to emphasize Bush's commitment to democracy, and partly to satisfy special interests. Being good to Taiwan, however, reflected more than electioneering or Republican reflexes. Richard Armitage, the future deputy secretary of state, for instance, arranged a meeting between Taiwan officials and Bush before the election so that, should he win, each side would know what the other desired. These particular Republicans—the self-identified Vulcans and their friends—wanted to rectify US Asia policy and with it Taiwan's status.[9]

Shifting the central thrust of national security and foreign policy in the Asian arena had been a key priority of many Bush intimates since the Reagan years. They had concluded that no administration from Nixon on—Republican or Democrat—had paid enough attention to US friends and allies in Asia. Instead, the US had been mesmerized by China, whether because of the common enemy or because of the huge market, even when policy makers had not intended that Beijing should dominate Asian affairs. In 1999 an open letter sponsored by the Heritage Foundation and the Project for the New American Century laid out a contrary vision and allowed Armitage, Paul Wolfowitz, the future deputy secretary of defense, and I. Lewis "Scooter" Libby, the soon-to-be-national security adviser to Vice President Dick Cheney, to upbraid Clinton regarding Taiwan policy. "It has . . . become essential that the United States make every effort to deter any form of Chinese intimidation of [Taiwan]," they asserted, "and declare unambiguously that it will come to Taiwan's defense in the event of an attack or a blockade." In an extraordinary expansion of Washington's commitment, they offered what Eisenhower, the Mutual Defense Treaty, and the Taiwan Relations Act had all avoided: inclusion of Jinmen and Mazu islands in their proposed guarantee. What made this all the more bizarre was the DPP's indecision about holding the offshore islands given their symbolic link to the mainland.[10]

The newly minted Bush administration moved toward building a better US–Taiwan relationship in a more vigorous, well-informed, and purposeful way than Taipei could have expected. Officials dealing with Asia took George W. Bush as the pivot of their policies, but they followed a complex strategy that expanded on the president's preferences. Thus, the importance of Japan, alliances, and Taiwan rose as the significance of China fell. This did not mean that Bush or his team intended to abandon the China relationship or stop observing the one-China policy, but rather that constructive ties would be built with both governments.

Paul Wolfowitz articulated the concept most clearly. He had served as assistant secretary for East Asia in the State Department in the Reagan administration, working closely there with Armitage, and later as a top aide to Cheney at the Pentagon during the administration of George H. W. Bush when the F-16 sale to Taipei materialized. A cautious, deliberative thinker, Wolfowitz rejected the idea that a weak China could or should serve as a fundamental component of US policy. Conceding that Taiwan independence was not an option, he nevertheless called for preserving Taiwan from seizure by China. "We will not have peace in the Taiwan Strait if this promising democracy is made to disappear," he insisted in the spring of 2000, less than a year before Bush's inauguration.[11]

Wolfowitz strengthened Donald Rumsfeld, the new secretary of defense, in the notion that previous administrations had coddled the Chinese. Rumsfeld insisted that military exchanges with the Chinese gave them more than the US got and jeopardized American interests. Accordingly, he suspended visits and talks despite protests from around the US government and within the Defense Department. By contrast, he allowed arms sales to, and cooperation with, Taiwan to grow.[12]

Richard Armitage had focused on US–Japan relations, an interest reflected in the so-called Armitage report, issued in October 2000 by the National Defense University, which called for greater emphasis on the alliance. His coauthors included Wolfowitz, James Kelly, future assistant secretary of state for East Asia, and Torkel Patterson, soon to join the NSC as senior Asia director. Armitage had been involved in Asia for decades, fighting his own anticommunist war in various capacities in Vietnam. While serving on Robert Dole's senatorial staff in 1979, he had helped write the TRA. During the Reagan administration and on subsequent, frequent visits to Taiwan, he created a private network capable of financing underfunded security programs. In office as deputy secretary of state, he did what he could, within the constraints of the unofficial relationship, to communicate with Taipei. He observed that Taiwan's democracy had proven "inconvenient for some," but that "we look at Taiwan not as a problem but as an opportunity to show that democracy counts."[13]

Patterson, a Japan specialist like Armitage and Kelly, viewed China more harshly. The Chinese, he felt, demanded unwarranted deference from others. Rather than seek a solution, they cultivated the Taiwan confrontation in order to bolster the legitimacy of the communist regime and to justify expansion of military forces—an expansion exceeding that needed to deal with Taipei. Patterson opposed unification of Taiwan with China because that would undermine US security, which would endanger trade routes and influence in the region. He placed himself among administration alliance advocates like Rumsfeld, Armitage, and Secretary of State Colin Powell and against great power continentalists, who, he felt, did not understand that Asia was not Europe. Patterson also shared the president's ideological vision regarding the American mission abroad. "Taiwan for all its faults and stupidity, naiveté and immaturity, is on our side. They are the most democratic country in Asia. They are more democratic than Japan, more democratic than Singapore. . . . Some people say, 'Well, I really wouldn't care if Taiwan became part of China.' We should care about that. So anyway, what I am describing is the mindset that I had at the NSC, that we had there. When I left, it got lost."[14]

Dick Cheney's view of Taiwan was unsentimental and distrustful; he was alert to potential threats to Washington's prerogatives and interests. Cheney also could be harshly critical of China, which sometimes made him indirectly supportive of Taiwan. In 1992, while he was defense secretary, he had endorsed the sale of F-16 fighter aircraft to Taiwan, but it had been a rare moment of involvement with the island. His advisers had greater sympathy for Taipei and reservations about Beijing. Scooter Libby for one, as a protégé of Wolfowitz and legal counsel to the congressional Cox Committee on Chinese espionage in the 1990s, disparaged China and advocated better treatment of Taiwan.

Finally, Condoleezza Rice, Bush's foreign policy coach and his national security adviser, had had little exposure to Asia. In the earliest days of Bush's presidential run she wrote in *Foreign Affairs* that "The United States . . . has a deep interest in the security of Taiwan," which was threatened by China's efforts to "intimidate" it. Acknowledging "the longstanding U.S. commitment to a 'one China' policy," she noted the US also should be "containing Chinese power and security ambitions." She condemned Clinton for tilting toward Beijing, particularly in his recitation of the Three Nos. Five years later Bush would assert he had never read Rice's article, suggesting it had not influenced him. Rice, however, the foreign policy adviser with whom he had the most rapport, shaped his thinking. She understood Europe better than Asia and leaned toward condominium with great powers, but nevertheless nursed suspicions of China's intentions, particularly regarding Taiwan.[15]

Armitage and Wolfowitz, working in coordination with Patterson, choreographed policy decisions and implementation in ways reminiscent of the most effective period in the Reagan administration. Similarly, they controlled the message to Taiwan, shutting out competing voices. Their collaboration linked a wider community concerned about US–Taiwan relations, including Jim Kelly, the assistant secretary of state, who had worked on Taiwan at the Reagan NSC and Defense Department, as well as Randall Schriver, an Armitage protégé who moved from DOD to State to be a special assistant and later deputy assistant secretary for East Asia. As Patterson recalled, "On Taiwan there was nobody there who said this is the wrong policy. There was no objection. We were unanimous."[16]

Treatment of China elicited a greater variety of views. At one extreme, individuals in the administration, the military, Congress, and think tanks saw a looming China threat. The US should arm its friends against it, refuse to transfer technology to it, and stop signing agreements with it, lest Washington fortify a future enemy. China's prosperity solved nothing; it just meant more weapons. Clinton's designation of China as a "strategic partner" infuriated them.

A larger group, accepting China as a mounting danger, nevertheless favored limited engagement, not absolute containment. Influenced and supported by big business and moderate Republicans, they envisioned a strong and prepared US simultaneously trading with China and increasing support for Taiwan. Zalmay Khalilzad, writing at RAND, called their alternative view "congagement."[17]

Administration policy leaned toward the latter but sounded like the former. Washington had to demonstrate toughness with China. It had to be independent from past policies, to make clear to China that US interests would come first. Patterson insisted, "If you are not tough with China in the beginning, they will eat you alive later."[18] Accordingly, Bush would refuse to make deals with China and so would not need to compromise Taipei's rights and interests. US resolve would be demonstrated by its Taiwan policy.

In Defense of Taiwan

Indeed, the Bush administration began with bold gestures to redefine US policy toward Taiwan, granting greater dignity to Taipei, liberalizing rules for government-to-government interaction, and providing more visible assistance to the military establishment. It did this, disregarding China's anger and frustration. Rice confided in 2001 that the Bush team planned to take daring Taiwan-oriented steps quickly and rebuild China relations later. US priorities, not China's preferences, were to be foremost.[19]

The most telling example of this approach came with the April 23, 2001, announcement of arms sales, including Taiwan's first priority, submarines. Constituting the most costly weapons package since the F-16s of 1992, this deal grew out of intense preinaugural discussions in the Bush camp and with Taipei. The small inner circle that explored the requirements and implications included Armitage, Patterson, Wolfowitz, Kelly, Schriver, Libby, and Stephen Hadley (soon to join the NSC). Some met with delegations from Taiwan, while Patterson and Schriver quietly went to Taipei to ask Chen Shui-bian for a procurement list. They disregarded opposition from the Pacific commander in chief, Dennis Blair, believing their own accumulated military experience sufficient. Justification also rested on Taiwan's aged submarine fleet of four boats, two of which, World War II guppies, were the oldest in service worldwide.

The submarine sale satisfied right-wing administration critics as well as Taipei. Even the participants, however, cannot agree on whether the administration recognized how difficult it would be to build the submarines, or intended to provide the boats to Taiwan. The US had not built diesel-electric submarines in forty years. The US Navy didn't want them, emphasizing nuclear-powered craft instead. US companies, lacking experience, would require foreign designs that probably would be unobtainable. In China analysts thought Bush had cleverly avoided selling Aegis by promising a chimera. When US officials actually sought manufacturers and plans, they astonished the Chinese, but the search may well have been a sham.

For Taiwan the arms sales decisions allayed fears that Bush might prove unreliable. The $4 billion package included, in addition to the eight submarines, four Kidd-class destroyers, a dozen P-3 Orion antisubmarine aircraft, torpedoes, minesweeping helicopters, and amphibious assault vehicles, some of which previously had been barred as offensive. Although Bush did not provide Aegis, he said he would "be inclined" to sell them if Chinese missile deployments continued.[20]

Last-minute hesitation regarding the package, had there been any, would have vanished when, on April 1, 2001, a Chinese F-8 fighter plane collided with an American EP-3 surveillance aircraft. Dangerous encounters with Chinese fliers had been multiplying, which reflected China's objections to routine data collection along its coast that, along with satellite imaging, allowed the US to help Taiwan defend itself. On that April day the EP-3 observed PRC naval exercises mimicking invasion of a large offshore island. A Chinese pilot edged perilously close, hitting the larger plane's wing and crashing into the sea. The EP-3 made an emergency landing on China's Hainan Island, where authorities detained its crew for eleven days and seized high-tech equipment. Many Americans believed the episode portended greater conflict with China.[21]

Taiwan, watching nervously, imagined its interests could become a bargaining chip to extricate the crew and plane. Tsai Ing-wen, chair of the Mainland Affairs Council, continued to talk about being sold out even after the crew had been extricated.[22] But the US assured Taipei that arms sales and reconnaissance flights would continue, as would operations at its extensive National Security Agency signals intelligence (SIGINT) collection facility on Yangmingshan Mountain, outside Taipei. The huge complex, part of a covert collection partnership predating derecognition, processed massive volumes of intelligence on PLA capabilities and planning. It inherited Hong Kong–based interception facilities after 1997 and underwent thorough updating between 1995 and 2000. Taiwan might not share, or share in, all its surveillance, but it could not lose US support. Indeed, that April Taipei used the facility to monitor the EP-3 developments.[23]

If the airplane crisis did not disrupt arms sales, it also did not alter the administration's decision on the Aegis guided missile destroyers. The sale was anathema to China; US experts opposed it too, doubting Taiwan could afford them, man them, or integrate them into its defense infrastructure. Conservative Republicans, by contrast, saw Aegis as a test for the Bush team, ignoring divided opinion in Taiwan and the strong opposition of the US Navy. Aegis had not headed Taiwan's procurement list in 2001, and Tien Hung-mao, Taiwan's foreign minister, declared that Taiwan "could accept" a decision against Aegis to avoid "damaging . . . [the US] relationship over one weapon system." Tien's critics, Chen probably among them, thought he had made Bush's refusal of Aegis too easy.[24]

Washington, meanwhile, emphasized practical changes to strengthen Taiwan. The arms sales process itself appeared to be a barrier to effective weapons management, forcing Taiwan to submit a wish list annually in November and wait for the US to render its conclusions at an April meeting that was run, a onetime Pentagon official noted, "a bit like the Academy Awards."[25] Off-cycle approvals rarely occurred. The administration introduced a simplified procedure paralleling that used by other foreign purchasers, whereby requests were timed according to need and involved minimal publicity. Washington never consulted Taiwan's Ministry of National Defense, hastily informing officials of the change before Bush told the *Washington Post* on April 25, 2001. Taipei acknowledged this would make it harder for Beijing to protest, but distrust of Washington led officials to worry about holding the US accountable under the TRA.[26]

These events of April 2001 defined the US–Taiwan relationship at the beginning of the Bush presidency. They culminated with George W. Bush's declaration on national television that he saw the US having a clear obligation to defend Taiwan "and the Chinese must understand that." He told the audience of *Good Morning America* on April 25, 2001, that he would be willing "to do whatever it took to help Taiwan defend herself." The president insisted immediately that he had not changed policy, and his advisers asserted that he had just muffed his lines. Vice President Dick Cheney, however, said two days later, "Given what appears to be a somewhat more threatening posture of the mainland toward Taiwan over the last few months, ambiguity may be exactly the wrong thing to do. And to make it very clear that we're serious about seeing them proceed without resorting to force is, we thought, very important."[27]

For years thereafter policy makers argued about the actual meaning of Bush's words. That he intended to be tough, however, was certain. The president, once he was aware of Beijing's steady deployment of missiles across the Strait from Taiwan, insisted that China know they must not be used. During 2002 the US elaborated its weak and unfocused Taiwan-area war plan, OPLAN 5077-04, sharpening and broadening it, adding new elements, and emphasizing cooperation. A hotline linking Taipei's minister of national defense and the US secretary of defense was to follow. Proposed after the 1996 Strait crisis, the hotline didn't materialize when Taiwan sought to elevate it to the presidential level. Lee Teng-hui raised the idea again in 1999 because of military aircraft incursions across the Strait's centerline. He believed Washington's refusal was intended to punish him following his two-states declaration. Finally, in 2002, Wolfowitz authorized the controversial and clandestine technology.[28]

Administration backing for Taiwan, so intimately related to its democratic character, meant not just military support, but also resistance to negotiations between Taipei and an authoritarian China. The Bush administration considered Clinton-era promotion of a dialogue to have been inherently inequitable as well as fruitless. Wolfowitz wrote, "The more we seem to be pressing Taiwan to negotiate with China, the more fearful Taiwan becomes." Patterson insisted that the Chinese "use Taiwan as an excuse" for an "aggressive missile production program . . . [that would] continue whether Taiwan becomes part of China or not." Moreover, "making progress [in talks] is only important when you are going in the direction you want to go." That would not be true if Taiwan accepted the one-China principle before negotiating. "I don't think there needs to be any preconditions for dialogue," he asserted.[29]

Mutual Misunderstanding

Efforts by the Bush team to readjust US–Taiwan relations to heighten mutual confidence proved much more difficult than anyone had expected. American willingness to improve communications, provide greater support, and pledge stronger protections did not suffice. Misunderstanding overlay divergent priorities and quickly caused problems.

Chen spoke little English and lacked US experience, in striking contrast to the KMT ruling elite, which prided itself on its American friends and American degrees. The Clinton administration brought Chen to Washington to broaden his knowledge, but the country and its people remained largely opaque to him. Chen seemed ill at ease meeting Americans and, although he had constructive talks with officials, those encounters did not create a firm foundation for future interaction. His agenda and priorities reflected his local island experience. He had been born into a poor Taiwanese family. He served as a lawyer for jailed antigovernment militants and had been imprisoned himself for opposition to the KMT. His wife had been paralyzed in a possibly politically motivated attack when a truck struck her.[30] Finally, he had risen to the presidency from the platform of Taipei's mayoralty. These central events in his life had been partisan struggles against the KMT and, although the US had strongly backed democracy in Taiwan, it had also kept the KMT in power.

In the new DPP government, Americans gravitated to a group of English-speaking party luminaries. Oberlin-educated Hsiao Bi-khim, for instance, acted as a bridge, translating not just language but also systems, expectations, and mindsets in her posts in the DPP international division and the president's office. Chiou I-jen, first deputy secretary general of Chen's National Security Council and later secretary general of the president's office, became a crucial interlocutor and adviser. And, finally, Tsai Ing-wen, a lawyer and trade specialist who had been the principal agent behind Lee Teng-hui's two-states theory, concentrated on cross-Strait relations and tried to clarify Taipei's positions for Bush officials. Their ability to speak for Chen Shui-bian, however, was uneven and uncertain. Few at the top of the party could reach out to Washington, knew much about the US, or wanted to court Americans. How much Chen trusted those who could, particularly when their political ties were to another DPP faction or a previous president, proved difficult to determine.

Chen relied more heavily on advisers whose focus remained relentlessly domestic. This inner circle—including the "boy wonders" Ma Yung-cheng, Lin Chin-chang, and Luo Wen-chia—helped put him into office. Ma and Lin had been Chen allies since 1991, the former acting as a political strategist and the latter as a speechwriter; Luo handled publicity.[31] Wu Shu-chen, Chen's wife and the DPP's symbol of KMT ruthlessness, probably exercised even greater influence, sharing in deliberations and strengthening his convictions. The president minimized the participation of others, neglecting to convene his National Security Council or consult those whose official positions made them key foreign policy counselors.

Then there existed the DPP activists, often disenchanted with Washington and difficult for Chen to control, possessing their own visions of where the party should lead Taiwan. Vice President Annette Lu Hsiu-lien, a vibrant, outspoken former KMT political prisoner, gave no ground on her aggressively pro-independence positions. Just days after the inauguration, she insisted publicly that Beijing's one-China principle had no validity. Taiwan's status should not be seen as a remnant of China's civil war but should rather be considered undetermined. Beijing dismissed her as "scum of the nation." In comparison, Chen appeared to be a pragmatist.

The Kuomintang had reinforced the inward-looking nature of the DPP by excluding it from security discussions with the United States and China. Members of the party had not been schooled in military affairs and were all too aware that the armed forces had functioned as an adjunct of the KMT, not the nation. Even at senior levels of the DPP, little expertise existed regarding foreign policy and international organizations.

Lee Teng-hui provided the final, unpredictable variable. He evolved into so radical a presence—by, for example, establishing the pro-independence Taiwan Solidarity Union—that many wondered about his earlier ambitions regarding sovereignty and independence. Perhaps he had always advocated separatism or maybe, as Jim Kelly suggested, rather than "becoming more pro-independence, he has mostly become more pro–Lee Teng-hui" to retain political prominence.[32]

Understanding these different elements challenged the US. Taiwan as a one-party state with a limited future had seemed predictable, not requiring a robust contingent of AIT political observers. Americans assigned there sustained few connections with the opposition. When democracy abruptly changed the landscape, information about the new leadership had to come from human rights campaigners, congressional staff members, and businessmen. Fortunately, Richard Bush, president of AIT (1997–2002), having worked for Representative Stephen Solarz (D-N.Y.), a major force in convening hearings and proffering Taiwan-related resolutions in the 1980s, knew DPP stalwarts well.[33] More common was the reaction of Richard Armitage, who, although having met Chen at Lee Teng-hui's behest, reflected a broad perception of DPP radicalism: "We didn't speak the same language even though we may have been speaking in English."[34]

For TECRO and Taiwan lobbying, political upheaval had substantial consequences. Taiwan's representative offices in the US and its influence with Congress and the executive branch had been the preserve of the KMT. The new DPP authorities lacked appropriate personnel to staff diplomatic outposts and had to rely on former KMT figures like C. J. Chen. DPP factionalism, inexperience, and disorganization made dependence on nonparty people particularly uncomfortable and heightened suspicions about their behavior. TECRO's Chen, for instance, was caught in the middle, criticized in Taipei for being too close to Americans and suffering in Washington from doubts about his influence with his president. The problem became especially acute vis-à-vis the Taiwanese American community, which often worked at cross-purposes to the Foreign Ministry.

War and Politics

Before the end of the first year of the Bush-Chen era, several developments modified the trajectory of relations: the war on terrorism, China's inflexibility, and domestic politics. Washington's fundamental ideas on strategy, philosophy, politics, and economics endured, but tolerance for conflicting priorities notably diminished.

The attacks of September 11, 2001, on New York and Washington altered the Bush administration's worldview, minimizing the China threat. US–China relations had recovered from the EP-3 nadir by July, but Beijing recognized 9/11 as an opportunity for cooperation, offering help on gathering intelligence, tracing money flows, influencing Pakistan to assist in Afghanistan, and providing support at the UN.[35] Chinese officials squelched a brief outpouring of anti-American celebration and abandoned thoughts of trying to link US concessions on Taiwan to antiterrorist assistance. After meeting with Foreign Minister Tang Jiaxuan, Colin Powell declared, "There was no suggestion of a quid pro quo."[36]

Taiwan responded rapidly to US needs in Afghanistan and Iraq, but 9/11 did not constitute an opening for Taipei as it did for China. What Washington wanted from Taipei it could not give: stability and reliability. Chen's agenda required challenging Beijing and KMT rivals. US preoccupation with its war on terrorism and its increasing willingness to work with Beijing threatened Chen.[37]

The difference in perspective emerged as Chen rallied his core supporters and sought to startle Beijing onto a new course. Disappointment with China's refusal to engage his government plunged Chen into secret deliberations with his national security team and Lee Teng-hui during June and July 2002. Hinting at greater defiance to come, he twice declared publicly that Taiwan "should ponder 'walking down its own Road.'" Accordingly, on August 3, 2002, he departed from prepared remarks to observe to an overseas, pro-independence audience that one country existed on each side of the Taiwan Strait (yibian yiguo). Not having alerted members of his government or Washington, Chen experienced widespread censure as even the "blue team . . . expressed frustration." A member of President Chen's immediate staff acknowledged, "The statements have damaged the mutual trust between Taiwan and the US."[38]

Although Washington did grow apprehensive about Chen's intentions, it disappointed China by not visibly reining him in. Beneath the surface, diverging China-Taiwan priorities fractured administration cooperation and policy coordination. The split generally pitted the NSC and State against

DOD, the vice president's office, and sometimes the president. In this case US officials did not demand a retraction, nor did Bush label Chen a troublemaker, as Clinton had done with Lee in 1999, but worries grew that Taipei was misreading the extent and nature of US encouragement.

Beijing, meanwhile, attacked Chen by name for the first time since his inauguration, ending the policy of watching and listening. In October 2002 Jiang Zemin sought to aggravate tensions between Washington and Taipei when, during an informal summit at Bush's ranch in Crawford, Texas, he proposed that China move an unspecified number of mobile missiles from its coast—if the United States would reduce, and eventually end, arms sales to Taiwan. China's expanding short-range missile forces, with their increasing accuracy and potency, jeopardized not just Taiwan, but US bases in Japan and the US ability and willingness to assist Taipei. Washington had previously said it might curtail sales if the Chinese threat was reduced.[39]

The Bush administration responded cautiously. Publicly, it told China to take the offer directly to Taipei. Armitage emphasized, "China is operating under the mistaken assumption that the war against terrorism and Iraq will get them something in return on Taiwan, that the US will make concessions on Taiwan. This won't happen."[40] Taipei feared potential concessions, reacting with suspicion to what it called an insincere and dangerous proposal. Under the TRA and the Six Assurances, after all, Washington had pledged not to negotiate Taiwan arms sales with Beijing. A second objection was that mobile missiles could be as quickly redeployed as removed. Disruption of arms sales could not be abruptly reversed. Third, medium-range missiles could still target Taiwan from inland locations. Fourth, a missile deal would do nothing about other weapons being readied for an attack. Finally, Beijing could be waging psychological warfare, seeking to deter Aegis sales, to blame the US for Chinese missile placements, and to make the Taiwanese feel vulnerable. Nevertheless, the Defense Department did not dismiss the idea, secretly exploring how it could be utilized.[41]

The following spring, on May 20, 2003, Chen again surprised friends and foes, suddenly announcing plans for a referendum on membership in the World Health Organization. China had just blocked direct assistance to Taiwan during a deadly outbreak of Severe Acute Respiratory Syndrome (SARS), and a plebiscite promised to promote popular sovereignty and rally public support, despite the slowing economy and stalemate in the legislature. His statement came without warning, embarrassing the uninformed foreign minister, who was visiting the US.

Chen's referendum initiative demonstrated defiance of Beijing and resistance to "advice" from Washington. In no doubt about China's opposition, he also had just met secretly with the senior Asia director of Bush's NSC. In 2001 Torkel Patterson had been the first senior director to visit Taiwan and as an old Reagan-era friend had symbolically opened a direct White House dialogue. But in 2003 James Moriarty came. Chen considered him a hostile messenger carrying a disagreeable message. He paired Moriarty with the AIT Taipei head, Douglas Paal, whom he detested, as "panda-huggers," making it possible to question their credibility as representatives of a friendly president. Thus, when Moriarty said that despite congressional agitation there would be no trip to Washington and that a referendum was not welcome, Chen blamed these rebuffs on him rather than Bush.

Chen could not permit himself to be stymied on the popular referendum issue with an election impending. The DPP had long advocated referenda to provide the Taiwanese with a voice in public affairs that the KMT had denied them. Whether on WHO, nuclear power plant construction, constitutional reform, or security, a plebiscite magnified DPP core principles. Thus, Chen warned against coercion, declaring, "Taiwan is not a province of one country nor is it a state of another," and asserting that the one-China principle is "abnormal thinking." His posture alarmed China, which had plainly "forbidden" Taiwanese votes for independence or against unification. To Beijing Chen's proposal of a new constitution appeared just a device for realizing independence. Chen, however, appealed to Washington, proclaiming, "I don't think any democratic country can oppose our democratic ideals."[42]

In October 2003 Chen was in New York on what he subsequently deemed a breakthrough visit: meeting with Taiwanese Americans and members of Congress, accepting a human rights award, and addressing the press. Therese Shaheen, the AIT Washington director (2002–4), "made a giddy atmosphere even giddier" when she urged thanks be given to Chen's "secret guardian angel," George W. Bush. The pan-Blue political opposition in Taiwan complained that Washington had cast a powerful vote for Chen in the 2004 election with this boost to his status.[43] It even temporarily stopped opposing a referendum and the idea of a new constitution, proclaiming, for the first time, that independence might be a viable future option.[44] Predictably, Chen and his staff embraced Shaheen as an ally, someone personally influential with Bush and openly hostile to Paal. Her boisterous style challenged the low-profile nature of the AIT post, and Taipei welcomed her unconventionality and her pliability: "We didn't listen and she didn't make us listen."[45]

Shaheen's influence in the White House, however, was already fading. In the summer of 2003 her supporters injected her into an Oval Office meeting at which Paal was to engage the president. It quickly deteriorated into a brawl, during which Shaheen lectured Bush on the correct language to use regarding Taiwan independence. The president retorted, "I'm not a nuance guy—'Do not support.' 'Oppose.' It's the same to me."[46] Her protectors, Rumsfeld, Cheney, and the president's brother Jeb, temporarily preserved her job, either unaware or unconcerned about the mixed message to Taipei. Several years later Lawrence Wilkerson, the army colonel who served Powell as chief of staff, insisted that Paul Wolfowitz, Douglas Feith, the DOD undersecretary for policy, and Stephen Cambone, Rumsfeld's intelligence coordinator, supported by the US representative to the UN, John Bolton, joined Shaheen in encouraging Chen's independence aspirations. The others survived; Shaheen did not.[47]

Chen's priorities in the autumn of 2003 diverged substantially from those of George Bush. Bush and Rice sent Moriarty on two additional secret trips to Taipei to stop the rush toward referendum, but the New York welcome undermined White House pressure, and Chen rebuffed the US. The pan-Blue coalition in the Legislative Yuan also tried to restrain Chen by enacting barriers against presidents' calling referenda. Labeling China's missile deployment an imminent threat to Taiwan, however, Chen exploited a loophole to justify a "defensive referendum."

Bush personally concluded, given Chen's apparent betrayal, that only one option remained. Standing alongside Chinese Premier Wen Jiabao on December 9, 2003, Bush declared, "We oppose any unilateral decision by either China or Taiwan to change the status quo." Although referring to both, he aimed more narrowly, emphasizing, "The comments and actions made by the leader of Taiwan indicate that he may be willing to make decisions unilaterally to change the status quo, which we oppose."[48]

Thus, an angry president determined to break through Chen's practiced indifference departed dramatically from his public position on Taiwan. He had believed Chen would avoid embarrassing him. His decision, made with support from Rice, Powell, and others, therefore, did not reflect a feeling after 9/11 that "God, I need China, so I better get these Taiwans under control," recalled one official. "I talked to him for hours and hours on these issues," and

> I don't think that's right. . . . People who'll stick to their guns and take hits for him . . . those are his kind of leaders. . . . The president had taken hits from the Chinese on the arms package. If Chen had stuck to the Five Nos, the Four Nos and One Will Not, I think the president would have continued taking hits for Taiwan and not have been unhappy with him and pushed right back on the Chinese even after 9/11, even after we needed the Chinese on Korea

and so forth. The president was not afraid to beat the Chinese up on other is-sues like Tibet, not afraid at all. It had more to do with Chen proving himself to be unreliable.[49]

Instances when Chen kept his own counsel, acted outside institutions, and relied on instinct multiplied as he gained experience. Bush adminis-tration officials reluctantly concluded that no one consistently spoke for Chen. A brilliant tactical thinker, keenly attuned to the domestic and per-sonal implications of change, Chen seemingly grasped the strategic re-percussions for Taiwan only slowly. His resistance to the US seemed a combination of misunderstanding, opportunism, and mistrust, possibly worsened by inexperienced, uninformed aides. Less flamboyant than Lee, he nevertheless enjoyed political rows, and he allowed independence advocates—in Taiwan's streets and US interest groups—to radicalize his message.

Arms sales contributed to growing friction. Bush and his advisers, to their astonishment, found Taiwan reluctant to buy the April 2001 weap-ons package, capping a decade during which Taiwan's defense spending had fallen steadily. Taipei objected to the terms of the US offer, questioning the usefulness of some systems and rejecting inflated prices. Officials in-

sisted the US renegotiate charges on the basis of the legislature's willingness to spend, which evoked anger and derision. Buying old weapons—especially Kidd-class destroyers built twenty-five years earlier for the shah of
Iran—and having access only to defensive arms also rankled. Although
Chen Shui-bian pledged, "We will not develop . . . neither do we intend to
purchase any offensive weapons," others argued offense would be cheaper
and easier than defense.[50]

The conclusions reached at the Pentagon and among US defense analysts and weapons manufacturers were not complimentary to Taiwan. The
most devastating accused Taiwan of complacency and relying too heavily
on US forces. Rather than welcome Chen's disavowal of an arms race,
elements in the US defense community condemned him as irresponsible.
Some analysts scoffed at his assertion that "I think democracy . . . is the
greatest defense and the best arms that we have," complaining that Taiwan
refused to recognize its lack of preparedness and its inability to operate sophisticated weapons systems. Others lamented that Chen, like Lee Teng-
hui, sought only the symbolic support that pledges of weapons sales entailed.[51]

At the root of the arms sales dilemma lay conflicting estimates of China's
intentions. Americans believed China would attack if deprived of other
choices. Given DPP goals and China's increasing capabilities, a disastrous
clash seemed quite possible. In Taiwan, however, diminishing numbers believed China would strike. Some DPP politicians denied that Beijing could
invade or blockade, prevented by historic military weakness and a current
preoccupation with getting rich. Money spent for Taiwan's defense seemed
wasted. Taiwan had been the world's top arms buyer in the mid-1990s, but
Chen did not even request a special appropriation for the Bush package
until June 2004. The pan-Blue forces considered a robust defense super-
fluous as they contemplated recapturing the presidency and bettering relations with Beijing. But without growing defense expenditures, Taipei's ties
with US weapons manufacturers eroded, along with their willingness to
lobby on its behalf.

The Taiwan presidential campaign, then, escalated tensions already significantly worse than in 2002 or early 2003. Chen's maneuvering alienated
Bush even as Chen complained that Bush's emphasis on democracy seemed
reserved for Iraqis. "It is not right that while almost all people in the world
can enjoy the freedom from fear, only the people of Taiwan are denied this
basic right. According to the U.S.'s founding spirit," Chen protested, "the
resolution and efforts of the 23 million people in Taiwan to seek peace and
democracy should not be regarded as acts of provocation."[52]

Worried about how Chen would interpret and use his second election victory in 2004, the administration emphasized preserving the status quo, but the status quo "as we define it," not the DPP vision of Taiwan as a sovereign, independent state.[53] Bush also sent Moriarty's NSC successor, Michael Green, to Taipei to remind Chen of his inauguration promises in 2000. Green, a Japan specialist with deep roots in Japanese domestic politics, where conservatives vividly and fondly recalled their colonial experience in Taiwan, evinced sympathy for Taipei. His inherited attitudes and contacts protected him from the attacks Moriarty endured, and he moved quickly to assemble a Taiwan working group to promote better policy, eliminate interagency strife, and remove any suspicion of freelancing. His sober warnings to Taipei, therefore, were not easily disregarded.

Indeed, those most identified with efforts to raise Taiwan's profile, such as Richard Armitage, became harshly critical of Taiwan. Calling it the biggest landmine in US–China relations, late in 2004 he warned that in the event of war the TRA did not require the US to defend Taiwan. Further, he declared, "we all agree" that Taiwan is a part of China, jettisoning the distinction that Washington "acknowledged" but didn't "accept" the Chinese view of one China.[54]

THAT officials so supportive of Taipei should, in the space of just four years, turn into irritated and angry critics reflected the chronic contradictions of US–Taiwan relations. Taiwan could not be abandoned, but it could not be allowed to undermine relations with China or drag Washington into war. On the Taipei side, leaders followed a familiar path from illusion to disillusion. Hopeful that George W. Bush would be a champion, they found his growing attentiveness to Beijing dismaying and his insistence on caution and stability unacceptable.

The mutual trust that the Bush administration intended to foster with better treatment of Taipei foundered on the divergent priorities of the two governments. US political and strategic requirements dictated good relations with an increasingly powerful and influential PRC. Chen's domestic political problems and Taiwan's international aspirations could not be accommodated in a dangerous insurgent world—democracy or no democracy.

In fact, Taiwan's democracy magnified suspicion and strain as party heads found it increasingly difficult to balance internal demands for higher living standards with external challenges to the island's status. What seemed basic survival measures to Americans—acquisition of new weapons, training of troops, and sophisticated strategic planning—looked intolerable to pan-Green legislators worrying about a sluggish economy, and the pan-Blue opposition focused on the next election.

Furthermore, the Bush administration divided regarding the China-Taiwan situation and US–Taiwan relations. Unity splintered along institutional lines and ideological perspectives. DOD's emphasis on defense measures clashed with the NSC and State's focus on political solutions. Few advocated separation, but suspicion of Beijing's intentions animated realists and neoconservatives to worry about protecting strategic sea-lanes, high-tech industry, intelligence gathering, and voting rights. Yet at a time when Washington faced terrorists worldwide, almost all considered China's cooperation essential. Increasingly officials encouraged Taiwan to engage China.

The struggle to improve Taiwan's position in American diplomacy and world affairs did not end amid these frustrations, but these sources of mistrust diminished and diffused support. Chen and Bush, whose objectives and vision initially appeared complementary, became, in time, symbols of how far apart the needs and interests of Taiwan and the US remained. Terrorism and war made it unavoidable that attention shifted in Bush's second term to the Middle East and Europe. Chen's actions, however, facilitated US disengagement. Taiwan's domestic turmoil blunted its ability to reach out, accommodate to change, and utilize its advantages.

Conclusion:
The Uses of Adversity

IN MAY 1957 a mob wrecked the US Embassy in Taipei. Until then Americans believed that—with an alliance in place, the US Seventh Fleet patrolling the Taiwan Strait, and China at bay—they enjoyed stable, friendly, and cooperative relations with the ROC. The American ambassador was in Hong Kong at the time, addressing diplomatic colleagues and praising those ties. But as he uttered the words, a message arrived: crowds had assaulted his embassy, hurling a massive safe out the window onto his car; Americans had been injured, and classified papers littered the streets. The riot and the US's surprise demonstrated the depth of mistrust, and misunderstanding, between Taipei and Washington.

Superficially, the disorder erupted when a US court-martial acquitted an American serviceman for killing a Chinese in Taipei. It had been a lurid trial. Allegedly, the victim had been peering through a bathroom window at the killer's naked wife. Serious questions arose, however, about the plausibility of the evidence and the propriety of the defense. Nevertheless, Americans boisterously celebrated the verdict, evoking among the Chinese bitter memories of extraterritoriality, under which foreigners lived exempt from local law, and magnifying resentment against American racism.

Although recognizing that the public outrage was genuine, Washington concluded that Chiang Kai-shek had manipulated the anger to convey displeasure with US policies. Taiwan and the US disagreed about attacking

China and withdrawing from the offshore islands. To Chiang these differences comprised intolerable obstacles and threats. Taipei believed, as it did at other times, that it could not trust Washington to protect its interests, even as the US worried that it could not count on Taiwan to share its security priorities, that instead it would drag the US into war with China. Lack of trust between the United States and Taiwan, vividly illustrated by these 1957 events, had accumulated because of actions and policies undertaken by both sides intentionally, carelessly, and mistakenly. Even in 1957, distrust had been present for a long time, and it persisted. When, in 1969, Nixon abandoned cold war assumptions about the PRC and jettisoned the idea of a "Free China" as a bastion of American values, he radically altered and destabilized US–Taiwan ties. His decision to go to Beijing aggravated that distrust and institutionalized it. For Washington the initiative meant strategic advantage over the Soviets. But the new order had costs that the US did not pay. As is true of unequal relationships, the smaller and weaker participant absorbed most of the shocks.

Washington's new priorities stunned Taiwan's leaders, who had little room to maneuver and could not obstruct Sino-American reconciliation. Carter fulfilled the Nixon plan and opened diplomatic relations with Beijing, leaving Taiwan a nonstate in the eyes of its most critical ally. Slow to plan for an unwelcome future, Taiwan's leaders hurriedly prevailed on Congress, through lobbying, networking, espionage, and bribery, to secure the 1979 Taiwan Relations Act. It safeguarded Taiwan and facilitated future contacts. In time Taiwan sought international representation, fostered democratic reforms, and flirted with independence.

Allowing the public a voice spurred development of a Taiwan identity, and it magnified resentment against brutal KMT repression in which Americans had been complicit. US officials had practiced willful ignorance to accommodate cold war goals, supporting Chiang Kai-shek's government as it eliminated a generation of potential political leaders. Distrust of, and resentment against, the US, therefore, did not merely color the views of officials; it also endured among great swaths of ordinary people in Taiwan.

Even election of a purportedly sympathetic American president changed little. Ronald Reagan provided his Six Assurances about Taiwan's future, but, to the chagrin of many in Taiwan who trusted him, he did not upgrade relations or supply advanced aircraft. During his tenure, relations between Washington and Beijing actually improved. Bill Clinton also disappointed those who thought his campaign rhetoric disparaging China would yield advantages to Taiwan.

The Chen Shui-bian Dilemma

Like the 1957 riot, Chen Shui-bian's 2000 election to the presidency of Taiwan aggravated suspicions underlying US–Taiwan relations. The status quo constructed painfully by the US, Taiwan, and China, within which Taipei enjoyed autonomy but not independence, clashed with Chen's aspirations. Chen increasingly worried about his legacy, the partisan landscape, and the lack of US support for his goals, while the US worried about him.

Chen's position on independence also set him apart from the majority of Taiwan's people. Although in a truly free vote, the Taiwanese would choose separation, not unification, according to repeated opinion polls, Taiwan's pragmatic public dreams of independence, but accepts the status quo. Threats of war from China have been an effective brake on ideology and passion. Furthermore, for the youth of Taiwan, who might be expected to be more nationalistic, ethnic consciousness has not demanded renouncing China so long as political autonomy can be sustained and economic benefits flow.[1] Their seniors in the DPP emphasized difference and equated self-determination with democracy; the young do not.

Chen's transformational policies sparked anxiety abroad. To some degree they were meant to do so. Chen's calls for self-determination and membership in international organizations reminded the world of Taiwan's plight. The DPP confidently used Taiwan's new democracy to anchor Taiwan's ties to Americans. But constitutional reform, explicable, even justifiable, to remedy a dysfunctional political system, became a vehicle for asserting sovereignty. Surpassing Lee Teng-hui's assertions of ROC sovereignty, Chen moved vigorously to eliminate symbols of the KMT's mainland legacy, such as the National Unification Council.

Beijing's response combined promises with threats. Taiwan businessmen were welcomed on the mainland, and Beijing promoted trade, investment, and tourism. It made standing offers of political, economic, and even some military autonomy after Taiwan returns to China. Beijing began to talk about "preventing separation" rather than advancing unification. But China also continued modernizing its military, deploying missiles along its coast, and training troops that could invade Taiwan. It developed high-tech weaponry and satellite systems to deter US intervention. It passed an Anti-Secession Law in 2005 to legitimate its use of force, should that prove necessary. And it insisted that all Chinese on both sides of the Strait participate in a self-determination referendum, an approach that would swamp Taiwan's vote.

Washington does not want to linger in the Taiwan Strait now any more than it did in the 1950s. Challenges from terrorism and the Middle East have preoccupied officials since 9/11, much as the Soviets distracted Eisenhower and Dulles. Taiwan's dependence in the twenty-first century gave Americans leverage to constrain Chen Shui-bian and his colleagues, much as pressure was put on Chiang Kai-shek to disavow attacks on China. To Washington's relief, Taiwan's democracy afforded the opportunity through elections to see Chen go and the KMT take over from the DPP without waiting for dynastic succession, as had been true with the Chiangs. Thus, in the spring of 2008 Chen surrendered the government to the KMT after it threw the DPP out of power in a landslide.

The Politics of Hope

Ma Ying-jeou unsurprisingly entered office as president set to purge Taiwan of the tensions that fractured politics between 2000 and 2008 as well as the bitterness and distrust that came to characterize Taiwan's relations with the US and China. Although partisan, he did not embrace the strident agenda of some of his supporters and talked of broad reconciliation. On the issue most central to improving conditions with Beijing and Washington, he did not speak of independence but rather underlined ROC sovereignty, and he "pushed the possibility of unification with the mainland . . . far off into the indefinite future—a future that . . . includes both a democratic PRC and democratic approval from the people of Taiwan." It might be, as Jacques DeLisle, an influential scholar and observer of Taiwan, reasoned, that "most of the relevant actors seem to recognize how costly mutual mistrust had become, and so the new president has striking opportunities."[2] But Ma may have raised expectations to unattainable heights.

The dangers abound: escalating demands from China, complacency in Washington, and disappointment in Taiwan. Chinese leaders have to use their burgeoning power and international stature cautiously, not trying to bully Ma into a premature political agreement. They cannot risk treating Ma as an ordinary pan-Blue politician and insist on rapid and basic concessions. A series of economic accords have appreciably diminished tensions, but financial and commercial integration cannot insure peace as the advent of World War I demonstrated in Europe. Moreover, leaders cannot forget the ramifications of democracy in Taiwan, particularly the constraints voters place on Ma. Finally, they must not refuse to solve disputes because they fear the DPP could again take power, pocket concessions to Ma, and renew movement toward independence

Washington would be wrong to assume that problems ended with the departure of Chen and the DPP, even if early successes in cross-Strait relations appeared to support that conclusion. Ma had a honeymoon with Taiwan's citizens and with China, which sought to vindicate past policies by quickly agreeing to uncontroversial advances on economic issues. But although Chen had been personally responsible for much recent friction, many ideas that fueled his presidency remained popular afterwards, including assertive sovereignty, access to international organizations, and pride in a Taiwanese identity. The US has to remain alert and engaged.

Finally, Ma can hope to accomplish his objectives only if Taiwan is largely united behind him. Voters threw pan-Green out—tired of continual crises, incompetence and corruption—more vigorously than they put pan-Blue in. They remain split, challenging Ma to demonstrate strength regarding China and not accommodate too much. In the US they have to become accustomed to an era in which Taiwan will not have the same lobbying prowess or enthusiastic support from the Congress as in the past, which will render Taiwan more vulnerable vis-à-vis the US executive branch and China. Their support also is contingent on more than external relations. Taiwan voters will judge Ma primarily on domestic accomplishments, and dissatisfaction there can undermine support for his policies toward China and the US.

The US–Taiwan Relationship as an Obstacle to Settlement

US–Taiwan relations remain challenging; a long, discordant history is always just under the surface. The Taiwan Strait, after all, remains the most dangerous place on earth today. While much of the world focuses on threats from terrorists, only Taiwan can trigger war between nuclear-armed great powers. A rising China possesses unprecedented resources for solving its Taiwan problem, peacefully or not. Thus, for Washington, the hazards of its Taiwan ties accelerate at the same time as ardor for those ties declines. Since misjudgment, mistake, or mishap could, at any moment, plunge Taiwan, China, and the United States into a conflict all want to avoid, the abiding mistrust that prevents resolution must go.

Greater mutual confidence between the US and Taiwan would facilitate Washington's key contribution to resolving the Strait impasse: stabilization of the confrontation until answers are found. Ultimately, Beijing and Taipei will reach an acceptable agreement only through direct dialogue. For decades, however, secret talks between Taipei and Beijing have occurred and made few advances. Analysts blame ideology and politics, but they miss a crucial component of the persistently dysfunctional process: mistrust.

Mistrust colors relations among all the people involved, between the US and Taiwan as much as between Taiwan and China or China and the US. Mistrust is deep, broad, and justified. It flows from misperceptions, inflated expectations, unintended consequences, misinterpreted behavior, mistaken judgments, poor information, miscommunication, callousness, deceit, deception, and political manipulation.[3] It reveals conflicting worldviews and aspirations as well as tension derived from new, unpredictable democratic institutions. And it reflects the lack of personal contact between leaders barred from meeting.

Direct interaction among top officials of Taiwan and the United States is the only solution. It would promote transparency, enrich insight, and build trust. Its lack has contributed to destabilizing surprises and has aggravated cultural divergence, which remains despite strong American influence in Taiwan. George Bush never met Chen Shui-bian. There were no encounters like Reagan's with Gorbachev and Deng Xiaoping that might have moderated his dislike of Chen. The amplification of knowledge and intensified probing of diplomatic and policy positions inherent in meetings of leaders did not occur. Shortsightedly, Washington missed a relatively uncontroversial chance to grant a visa to Ma Ying-jeou and engage in high-level discussions before his inauguration.

Such a policy shift would not demand any significant alteration of existing relations. Representation would remain the same, as would other aspects of interaction, including military security. Washington would incur no new obligations to protect Taiwan, nor would its pressure on Taiwan to take self-defense more seriously abate.

Beijing has consistently rejected the possibility of high-level US–Taiwan interaction, believing it confers enhanced status on Taiwan's leaders and tighter cooperation across the Pacific. Occasions when Taiwan's presidents have transited through the US en route to other destinations have not, in fact, bestowed significant political benefits at home or abroad. Lee Teng-hui's Cornell trip enhanced his popularity, but he would have been reelected in any case, and Chen Shui-bian's brief appearances in California and New York were less significant than domestic factors in determining his political trajectory. Their effect would have been lessened if Beijing had not exaggerated the meaning of these events. China need not worry that the US will protect Taiwan more eagerly because of high-level contacts. Washington will rescue Taipei only if American national interests and Taiwan's plight coincide. Chinese leaders ought to encourage vigorous engagement to solve problems, even if it means forgoing the satisfaction of marginalizing Taiwan's leaders.

American officials and China specialists have also rebuffed efforts to elevate interaction. Some fear China, others believe the one-China policy constrains them, and some resist greater contact with, and responsibility for, Taipei. As one critic argued, "Washington cannot permit American ideological support for Taiwan's democracy . . . to undermine the politics of war and peace between the United States and China."[4] To some of these observers direct Washington talks with Beijing are a more effective way to settle the cross-Strait problem.

Direct talks have begun, but between Taipei and Beijing. After many years of rigidity on both sides, a new willingness to confront disputes took over in the spring of 2008. Ma Ying-jeou promised to proceed gradually through economic normalization to international space to a peace accord. He asserted in his inaugural address that he would deal with China "under the principle of 'no unification, no independence and no use of force,'" in accord with "Taiwan's mainstream public opinion."[5] China's Hu Jintao agreed to set aside status issues to find solutions in other areas.

This change makes US intervention, solicited at various times by Beijing and Taipei, unnecessary. That is a relief for American officials who shunned mediation and coercion, recalling previous failed efforts in China. Washington distrusted the motives of Beijing and Taipei, knowing impartiality had little appeal to either. The distrust was mutual: Taiwan and China suspected Washington's objectives. Far from being uninterested in results and dedicated only to a peaceful process, the US, they imagined, wanted to maintain Taiwan's de facto independence, whether for strategic reasons—protecting Japan's sea-lanes—or ideological objectives—using a model democracy to leverage change in China. Taipei worried about the economic and political ties Washington cultivated with Beijing, while Beijing feared America's obsession with democracy.[6]

Engagement means Washington need not and should not be central to Taiwan-China exchanges, but it does not dispense with its most basic responsibility. The US must stabilize the status quo, albeit a dynamic status quo, while talks proceed. It must commit to assist Taiwan if its relative weakness threatens equity. Ma requires support both to deal with China and to reassure his constituents, both to be cautious and to take risks.

Under these new conditions, even more than in the past, trust is vital for cooperation between Washington and Taipei. Only "strait" talk can make Taiwan less likely to be overwhelmed by China, accommodating too much or veering again toward independence and war. Transparent and forthcoming discussions between Washington and Taipei are critical to allay concerns about, or focus action on, differing objectives. The US can protect its interests only if it participates in the process of resolving cross-Strait tension.

Diplomacy at a higher, more authoritative level has the best chance of breaking down barriers between the US and Taiwan. Its absence has contributed to misunderstanding and mistrust. Strains across the Strait will be diverse and erratic in this time of flux, and Washington's ability to prevent unilateral change, to stabilize the situation, will be far more effective if leaders in Washington can work with those in Taipei in the search for answers. Taiwan may be inconvenient and politically messy. But American national interests, defined as much by values as by security or strategic goals, render sacrifice of Taiwan unacceptable. The US must do more than merely confront and be party to a Strait impasse. For itself and for Taiwan and China, the US has a political and moral obligation to contribute to a solution.

Abbreviations

ADB	Asian Development Bank
ADST	Association for Diplomatic Studies and Training, Foreign Service Oral History Project
AIDC	Aero Industry Development Center
AIT	American Institute in Taiwan
APEC	Asia-Pacific Economic Cooperation
ARATS	Association for Relations across the Taiwan Strait
ASW	antisubmarine warfare
BUSH	George H. W. Bush Library, College Station, Texas
CARTER	Jimmy Carter Library, Atlanta, Georgia
CCK	Chiang Ching-kuo
CCNAA	Coordination Council for North American Affairs
CCP	Chinese Communist Party
CFPF	Central Foreign Policy Files
CINCPAC	Commander in Chief, Pacific Command
CKS	Chiang Kai-shek
CNA	Central News Agency, Taipei
CWIHP	Cold War International History Project
DOD	Department of Defense
DPP	Democratic Progressive Party
DNSA	Digital National Security Archive
EA	Bureau of East Asian Affairs, State Department
FAPA	Formosan Association for Public Affairs
FBIS	Foreign Broadcast Information Service
FEER	*Far Eastern Economic Review*

FMS	foreign military sales
FOIA	Freedom of Information Act
FORD	Gerald Ford Presidential Library, Ann Arbor, Michigan
FRUS	*Foreign Relations of the United States*
HAKO	Henry A. Kissinger Office Files
IAEA	International Atomic Energy Commission
IDF	indigenous fighter aircraft
JCS	Joint Chiefs of Staff
JOHNSON	Lyndon Baines Johnson Library, Austin, Texas
KENNEDY	John F. Kennedy Library, Boston, Massachusetts
KMT	Kuomintang (Nationalist Party)
LAT	*Los Angeles Times*
LSK	Liu Shao K'ang
MAC	Mainland Affairs Council
MDT	Mutual Defense Treaty
MEMCON	Memorandum of Conversation
MFN	most-favored-nation status
MND	Ministry of National Defense
MOFA	Ministry of Foreign Affairs
MOFAA	Ministry of Foreign Affairs Archives, Taipei
MUDD	Seeley Mudd Manuscript Library, Princeton University
NARA	National Archives, College Park, Maryland
NPC	National People's Congress
NPMP	Nixon Presidential Materials Project
NSA	National Security Archive
NSB	National Security Bureau, Taiwan
NSC	National Security Council
NSAEBB	National Security Archive Electronic Briefing Book
NUC	National Unification Council
NYT	*New York Times*
PLA	People's Liberation Army
PRC	People's Republic of China
REAGAN	Ronald Reagan Library, Simi Valley, California
ROC	Republic of China
SCMP	*South China Morning Post* (Hong Kong)
SEF	Straits Exchange Foundation
SFRC	Senate Foreign Relations Committee
SIGINT	signals intelligence
TECRO	Taipei Economic and Cultural Representative Office
TMD	theater missile defense
TRA	Taiwan Relations Act
TRI	Taiwan Research Institute
TSEA	Taiwan Security Enhancement Act
TSI	Taiwan Studies Institute
USLO	US Liaison Office
USUN	US Mission to the United Nations

WHCF	White House Central Files
WP	*Washington Post*
WSJ	*Wall Street Journal*
WT	*Washington Times*
WTO	World Trade Organization

Notes

Introduction

1. The majority population on the island of Taiwan (upwards of 85 percent) is descended from eighteenth- and nineteenth-century immigrants from two southern China provinces, Fujian and Guangdong. They faced political repression after 1944, when the so-called mainlanders arrived.
2. Nancy Bernkopf Tucker, "Strategic Ambiguity or Strategic Clarity?" in *Dangerous Strait,* ed. Nancy Bernkopf Tucker (New York, 2005), 186–205.
3. Robert O. Keohane, "The Big Influence of Small Allies," *Foreign Policy* (Spring 1971): 161–82.
4. Erez Manela, "Imagining Woodrow Wilson in Asia: Dreams of East-West Harmony and the Revolt against Empire in 1919," *American Historical Review* 111 (December 2006): 1331–34, 1340, 1344–50.
5. Ernest R. May, *"Lessons" of the Past* (New York, 1973), ix–xiv and passim.

1. The Origins of Strategic Ambiguity

1. Odd Arne Westad, *Cold War & Revolution* (New York, 1993), 13–56, 140–54.
2. Chalmers Johnson, *Peasant Nationalism and Communist Power* (Stanford, 1962); Hans J. van de Ven, *War and Nationalism in China, 1925–1945* (London, 2003).
3. NSC 37, "The Strategic Importance of Formosa," December 1, 1948, U.S. Department of State, *FRUS, 1949,* vol. 9 (Washington D.C., 1975), 262; Joint Chiefs of Staff to Secretary Johnson, August 17, 1949, ibid., 376–78.

4. He Di, "'The Last Campaign to Unify China': The CCP's Unmaterialized Plan to Liberate Taiwan, 1949–1950," *Chinese Historians* 5 (Spring 1992): 1–16.

5. "Policy Information Paper—Formosa," Special Guidance No. 28, December 23, 1949, U.S. Senate, Committee on Armed Services and Committee on Foreign Relations, Hearings: *Military Situation in the Far East,* 82nd Cong., 1st sess., 1951, pt. 3, 1667–69.

6. Truman press conference, January 5, 1950; Dean Acheson, National Press Club speech, January 12, 1950, appeared as Dean Acheson, "Crisis in Asia—An Examination of US Policy," *Department of State Bulletin* 22 (January 23, 1950): 111–18

7. Gordon Chang and He Di, "The Absence of War in the U.S.–China Confrontation over Quemoy and Matsu in 1954–1955: Contingency, Luck, Deterrence?" *American Historical Review* 98 (December 1993): 1500–1524; He Di, "The Evolution of the People's Republic of China's Policy toward the Offshore Islands," in *The Great Powers in East Asia, 1953–1960,* ed. Warren I. Cohen and Akira Iriye (New York, 1990), 222–45; Niu Jun, "Chinese Decision Making in the Taiwan Strait," in *Managing Sino-American Crises,* ed. Michael Swaine and Zhang Tuosheng (Washington, D.C., 2006), 296–97, 301–4; Xia Yafeng, *Negotiating with the Enemy* (Bloomington, 2006), 261–62n20. Zhang Wenjin interview, September 1987, Beijing.

8. Nancy Bernkopf Tucker, "John Foster Dulles and the Taiwan Roots of the 'Two Chinas' Policy," in *John Foster Dulles and the Diplomacy of the Cold War,* ed. Richard Immerman (Princeton, 1990), 235–62.

9. Memcon Yeh, Koo, and Robertson, November 4, 1954, Box 192, V. K. Wellington Koo Papers, Columbia.

10. On the nuclear issue see Memorandum of Discussion, 240th NSC Meeting, March 10, 1955, *FRUS 1955–57,* vol. 2 (Washington, D.C., 1986), 347, 349; Rosemary Foot, *The Practice of Power* (Oxford, 1995), 167–76. On American policies see Robert Accinelli, *Crisis & Commitment* (Chapel Hill, 1996), 212–26; Gordon Chang, *Friends and Enemies* (Stanford, 1990), 116–42.

11. John Wilson Lewis and Xue Litai, *China Builds the Bomb* (Stanford, 1988), 34–39. On Soviet support see Vladislav Zubok and Constantine Pleshakov, *Inside the Kremlin's Cold War* (Cambridge, Mass., 1996), 217.

12. Dean Rusk never trusted Chiang's offer of troops. Dean Rusk, *As I Saw It* (New York, 1990), 175–76.

13. John Garver argues the opposite. Garver, *Sino-American Alliance* (Armonk, N.Y., 1997), 52–71.

14. NSC 146/2, "United States Objectives and Courses of Action with Respect to Formosa and the Chinese National Government," November 6, 1953, *FRUS 1952–54,* 14, pt. 1 (1985), 307–30; "Status of Aid Programs for the Republic of China," March 7, 1956, Box 31, folder: State Department, Karl Rankin Papers, MUDD.

15. Joint Strategic Plans Committee 958/257, July 18, 1955, RG 218, Combined Chiefs of Staff 381, Formosa (11-8-48), sec. 28, NARA; China Military Assistance Advisory Group Formosa to CINCPAC, September 18, 1955, ibid., 180530z, sec. 29; Morton Halperin, "The 1958 Taiwan Straits Crisis: A Doc-

umented History," RM 4900-ISA (prepared for the Rand Corp., Santa Monica, December 1966), 529; Dulles press and radio news conference, April 5, 1955, "China, People's Republic of," John Foster Dulles Papers, MUDD.

16. Jason Blatt, "Taiwan Documents Say US Thwarted Chiang Attack Plans in Mid-1950s," *SCMP*, April 15, 2002, FBIS, CPP20020415000033; on the riot see Nancy Bernkopf Tucker, ed., *China Confidential* (New York, 2001), 139–41. Plan K may be Operation Kuokwang (1965), revealed by the Ministry of National Defense in 2005 and also aborted by Washington. "Top-secret Plan to Retake Mainland in 1960s Unveiled," *China Post*, March 27, 2006, www.chinapost.com.tw, accessed March 28, 2006.

17. "Peking-Taipei Contacts: The Question of a Possible 'Chinese Solution,'" December 1971, CIA, *Caesar, Polo, and Esau Papers*, i–viii, 1–28, www.cia.gov; Garver, *Sino-American Alliance*, 140–41; Chen Jian, "Beijing's Changing Policies toward Taiwan," in *The United States and Cross-Straits Relations*, ed. Kenneth Klinkner (Urbana-Champaign, 2001), 32, 36–37; Li Ping and Ma Zhisun, eds., *Zhou Enlai nianpu, 1949–1976* [A Chronological Record of Zhou Enlai, 1949–1976] (Beijing, 1998), vol. 1: 623–24, vol. 2: 321, 524–25. Participants included the former Kuomintang generals Zhang Zhizhong and Fu Zuoyi.

18. Garver, *Sino-American Alliance*, 136; Chang, *Friends and Enemies*, 185; Ray S. Cline, *Chiang Ching-kuo Remembered* (Washington, D.C., 1989), 59–60.

19. Allen S. Whiting, "New Light on Mao; Quemoy 1958: Mao's Miscalculations," *China Quarterly* (June 1975): 265; Chen Jian, *Mao's China and the Cold War* (Chapel Hill, 2001), 202–4; Niu Jun, "Chinese Decision Making in the Taiwan Strait," 312–13.

20. Chen Jian, *Mao's China*, 174–75, 179–81, 199–202; Thomas Christensen, *Useful Adversaries* (Princeton, 1996), 205–25, 229–33.

21. John Lewis Gaddis, *We Now Know* (Oxford, 1997), 252.

22. John Foster Dulles, *War or Peace* (New York, 1950); Tucker, "John Foster Dulles and the Taiwan Roots," 235–36.

23. Halperin, "1958 Taiwan Straits Crisis," 102.

24. The traditional picture of Dulles as inflexible is in Townsend Hoopes, *The Devil and John Foster Dulles* (Boston, 1973). New records reveal a more sophisticated policy maker; see, for example, Immerman, *John Foster Dulles*.

25. Nancy Bernkopf Tucker, "John Foster Dulles and the Taiwan Roots," 251–59; Rusk, *As I Saw It*, 285; Warren I. Cohen, *Dean Rusk* (Totowa, N.J., 1980), 164. "Text of statement by Dulles on U.N.," NYT, July 9, 1954, A2.

26. William P. Snyder, "Dean Rusk to John Foster Dulles, May–June 1953: The Office, the First 100 Days, and Red China," *Diplomatic History* 7 (January 1983): 85–86; Wang Jisi, "The Origins of America's 'Two Chinas' Policy," in *Sino-American Relations, 1945–1955*, ed. Harry Harding and Yuan Ming (Wilmington, Del., 1989), 205; Tucker, "John Foster Dulles and the Taiwan Roots," 254–62; 711.56393/1-1259, Washington to Taipei, *FRUS 1958–60*, vol. 19 (Washington, D.C., 1996), 509–10.

27. 793.00/3-361, Memcon Kennedy with Prime Minister K. J. Holyoake, New Zealand, *FRUS 1961–63*, vol. 22 (Washington, D.C., 1996), 21; Kennedy,

speech given October 12, 1960, James C. Thomson Papers, Box 14: FE 1961–66, folder: Taiwan OSI 1960 Campaign Issue, KENNEDY; 611.93/3-2061, Drumright, Taipei, *FRUS 1961–63*, 37; Christopher Matthews, *Kennedy & Nixon* (New York, 1996), 158–63.

28. 793.00/7-1161, Admiral Harry D. Felt, CINCPAC, *FRUS 1961–63*, 92–93.
29. Snyder, "Dean Rusk to John Foster Dulles," 86; Rusk, *As I Saw It*, 285; Cohen, *Dean Rusk*, 164; 795.00/6-9953, #786, Lodge, *FRUS 1952–54*, vol. 3 (Washington, D.C., 1979), 661–62; 330/6-1053, Memcon, Henry Cabot Lodge, US representative to the UN, with staff, ibid., 663–65; 310.2/6-1153, Lodge to Dulles, ibid., 679–80.
30. The Kennedy administration considered diplomatic relations with Mongolia, but Taipei stopped it. 793.00/6-2161, Drumright, Taipei, *FRUS 1961–63*, 77; Memcon Kennedy with Rusk, July 28, 1961, ibid., 101.
31. Memcon President, Stevenson, Schlesinger, Cleveland, August 5, 1961, Schlesinger Papers, Box WH-22 Subject Files, folder: UN Speeches 8/3/61–8/11/61, KENNEDY; 303/4-51, Memcon Rusk with Yeh, *FRUS 1961–63*, 47.
32. Besides Cline, few knew beyond Bundy, JFK, Chiang Kai-shek, George Yeh (ambassador to the US), Chiang Ching-kuo, and Allen Dulles, the CIA director. *FRUS 1961–63*, 154–59; Bundy to U. Alexis Johnson, Deputy Undersecretary of State for Political Affairs, memo, August 22, 1961, ibid., 128.
33. Kai Bird, *The Color of Truth* (New York, 1998), 69–70, 157; Bundy to JFK, July 7, 1961, *FRUS 1961–63*, 89; Cline, *Chiang Ching-kuo Remembered*, 17–18, 24–26 (quote on 30); Jonathan Marshall, Peter Dale Scott, and Jane Hunter, *The Iran-Contra Connection* (Boston, 1987), 64–65.
34. Bundy told Kennedy the KMT believed the "wicked State Department" opposed the president's friendlier views. Bundy to Kennedy, August 22, 1961, *FRUS 1961–63*, 127.
35. 303/3-1761, Memcon Rusk with Dr. George K. C. Yeh, ROC Ambassador, *FRUS 1961–63*, 34–36.
36. Komer to Bundy and Rostow, June 15, 1961, NSF Countries, folder: China General 6/13/61 to 6/27/61, KENNEDY; Department of State Daily Opinion Summary, White House Central Files (WHCF), Box 387, folder: IT47/CO1-CO 50-2, KENNEDY. Komer consistently favored the two-Chinas approach to trap the PRC into refusing UN membership. Komer to Bundy and Rostow, March 1, 1961, NSF Countries, folder: China General, JFK, *FRUS 1961–63*, 19–20; Komer to Bundy and Rostow, May 2, 1961, ibid., 53–54.
37. Memcon Kennedy with Rusk, July 28, 1961, *FRUS 1961–63*, 100; Memcon President, Rusk, Stevenson, and Harlan Cleveland, May 24, 1961, *FRUS 1961–63*, 64; Cohen, *Dean Rusk*, 164–65.
38. Rusk, *As I Saw It*, 196–97.
39. Cohen, *Dean Rusk*, 61.
40. Telephone Conversation Transcript (Telcon) Rusk with McConaughy, September 28, 1961, *FRUS 1961–63*, 140n3.
41. McGhee to Rusk, memo, June 15, 1961, *FRUS 1961–63*, 72–73; 893.1901/5-3062, Harriman to McGhee, May 29, 1962, ibid., 237–38; Maxwell Taylor, "Impressions from Taiwan," September 20, 1962, ibid., 316.

42. 793.00/3-662 #615 Drumright, Taipei, *FRUS 1961–63*, 190; 793.00/3-3062 #658 Clough, Taipei, ibid., 202; Cline, *Chiang Ching-kuo Remembered*, 50–51; Jasper Becker, *Hungry Ghosts* (New York, 1996).

43. Cline to Bundy, April 14, 1962, *FRUS 1961–63*, 218n1; Jay Taylor, *The Generalissimo's Son* (Cambridge, Mass., 2000), 263.

44. 611.93/3-2762 Despatch 363 Taipei, *FRUS 1961–63*, 202n2, and 793.5/4-2662 #594 Ball, Washington, ibid., 219–21. The US withheld economic assistance to force reduced military expenditures. 811.0093/6-1562 #968 Clough, Taipei, ibid., 244–46.

45. Hilsman to Rusk, June 18, 1962, *FRUS 1961–63*, 248; Record of Meeting, June 20, 1961, ibid., 251–53; 793.54/6-2262 #1525 Green, Hong Kong, ibid., 272; Noam Kochavi, *A Conflict Perpetuated* (Westport, Conn., 2002), 116–19.

46. Hilsman to Harriman, June 21, 1962, *FRUS 1961–63*, 260–63.

47. Memcon Harriman with Dobrynin, June 22, 1962, *FRUS 1961–63*, 268–69, and 611.93/6-2362 #2136 Cabot, Warsaw, ibid., 273–75. On the talks see Robert S. Ross and Jiang Changbin, *Re-examining the Cold War* (Cambridge, Mass., 2001), 173–237.

48. "Peking-Taipei Contacts: The Question of a Possible 'Chinese Solution,'" December 1971, Polo Papers, CIA, 28; Memcon Kirk with Chiang Kai-shek, September 6, 1962, *FRUS 1961–63*, 309, 312.

49. Memcon Harriman with Dobrynin, June 22, 1962, FOIA, KENNEDY, NLK-92-10; Kochavi, *A Conflict Perpetuated*, 189–204.

50. On these plots see Nancy Bernkopf Tucker, *Patterns in the Dust* (New York, 1983), 181, 310n39; Kennedy notes, July 12, 1961, *FRUS 1961–63*, 98n1.

51. Roger Hilsman to Michael V. Forrestal, memo, July 9, 1963, Declassified Documents Reference System (1988), Fiche 191, no. 2841; Roger Hilsman to Secretary of State, memo, October 24, 1963, drafted by Jim Thomson, ibid., no. 2842; Editorial Note, *FRUS 1961–63*, 353–54.

52. Regarding JFK's preoccupation with a Chinese atomic bomb, see Chang, *Friends and Enemies*, 228–52.

53. Arthur M. Schlesinger Jr., *A Thousand Days* (Boston, 1965), 480.

54. LBJ heard it from Stevenson in November 1964, and Rostow in April 1966. Rostow urged that Ike be consulted before the administration took a two-Chinas position at the UN. Memorandum for the Record, November 18, 1964, *FRUS 1964–68*, vol. 30 (Washington, D.C., 1998), 127; Rostow to LBJ, memo, April 30, 1966, ibid., 294–95; Rostow to LBJ, memo, May 17, 1966, ibid., 303–4.

55. See reporting from Taipei #177, Clough, September 6, 1963, and Wright to Hilsman, December 19, 1963, *FRUS 1961–63*, 382–83, 413–16. On CCK's stay in Washington see Draft Minutes, Meeting, Bundy with Chiang Ching-kuo, September 10, 1963, and Memcon CCK with Kennedy, September 11, 1963, ibid., 383–92.

56. Memcon Kennedy with Chiang Ching-kuo, September 11, 1963, *FRUS 1961–63*,, 386–92. Either intelligence was bad or intelligence agencies were unwilling to give Chiang Kai-shek bad news. In April 1964 CKS told Rusk that

Beijing was three to five years from a bomb. Memcon Chiang with Rusk, April 16, 1964, *FRUS 1964–68*, 50.

57. #587 Johnson to Chiang Kai-shek, January 16, 1964, *FRUS 1964–68*, 4–5; #607 Rusk to Embassy Taipei, January 18, 1964, ibid., 8–9; Memcon Tsiang Ting-fu, ROC ambassador, with Rusk, January 24, 1964, ibid., 9–12; Ralph Clough, telephone interview, August 23, 2001.

58. Cline to McCone, March 2, 1964, *FRUS 1964–68*, 25–26. Chiang insisted there would be further coup attempts, but NIE 43-64, "Prospects for the Government of the Republic of China," dated March 11, was more reassuring. Komer to LBJ, March 16, 1964, *FRUS 1964–68*, 31.

59. *Meijun zai Hua gongzuo jishi (guwentuan zhi bu)* [Record of US Military Activities on Taiwan (Advisory Group)] (Taipei, October 1979), 24, 26, 121, as cited in Garver, *Sino-American Alliance*, 188; interview of anonymous intelligence source, winter 2005; CIA to Rusk, memo, November–December 1966, *FRUS 1964–68*, 477; "Reconnaissance Flights and Sino-American Relations," April 4 and 9, 2001, www.gwu.edu/~nsarchiv/NSAEBB/NSAEBB41.

60. 793.5622/9-962 #414 Circular from Washington, *FRUS 1961–63*, 318n2; Bundy to LBJ, January 10, 1965, *FRUS 1964–68*, 144.

61. Cline, *Chiang Ching-kuo Remembered*, 83–92. Cline's time line is different.

62. Rusk Policy Planning Meeting on "A Chinese Communist Nuclear Detonation and Nuclear Capability," October 15, 1963, *FRUS 1961–63*, 399–400; #328 Wright, Taipei, October 19, 1964, *FRUS 1964–68*, 112, and Report of Meetings, Cline with CKS, October 23–24, 1964, *FRUS 1964–68*, 116.

63. Komer to Bundy, November 25, 1964, *FRUS 1964–68*, 133; #869 Wright, Taipei, March 23, 1965, ibid., 155–57.

64. Rusk to Johnson, December 10, 1966, ibid., 490.

65. Memcon Chiang Ching-kuo with Robert McNamara, September 22, 1965, ibid., 209–14; Goldberg to LBJ, memo, March 9, 1967, ibid., 531. For LBJ's negative reply, see #156346, March 16, 1967, ibid., 539–40.

66. Memcon Wheeler with Chiang Kai-shek, December 29, 1965, ibid., 234–37.

67. Thomson to Bundy, April 15, 1965, ibid., 160–64 (quote on 163).

68. #489 Hummel, Taipei, October 28, 1965, ibid., 223; #1086 Hummel, Taipei, April 6, 1965, ibid., 279–80; Memo for the Files, April 25, 1966, ibid., 286–88. Transcript: U.S. Congress, Senate Foreign Relations Committee, U.S. Policy with Respect to Mainland China, 89th Cong., 2nd sess., 1966; Thomson to Bundy, July 9, 1965, Thomson Papers, folder: McGeorge Bundy Chronological File, 7/65–8/65, Box 11, KENNEDY.

69. Komer to Johnson, April 19, 1966, *FRUS 1964–68*, 285–86; Goldberg to Johnson, April 28, 1966, ibid., 293–94; Rusk to Johnson, May 14, 1966, ibid., 301–3; Rostow to Johnson, May 17, 1966, ibid., 303–4; Harriman to Moyers, June 3, 1966, ibid., 318–19.

70. See #315 Hummel, Taipei, September 14, 1965, NSF Country Files, Boxes 237–38, folder: China Cables, vol. 4, JOHNSON; Ray S. Cline interview, May 12, 1992, Washington, D.C.; George McT. Kahin, *Intervention* (Garden City, N.Y., 1986), 333; LBJ to Rostow, May 19, 1967, and Rostow to LBJ, May 8, 1967, *FRUS 1964–68*, 555, 555n1.

71. Rusk to McNamara, August 1, 1963, *FRUS 1961–63*, 375–78.
72. Ambassador Alan G. Kirk to JFK, March 29, 1963, President's Office Files, Countries, folder: China, Security, 1962–1963, Box 113a, KENNEDY.

2. Taiwan Expendable?

1. Henry Kissinger shaped the history of the China opening in *White House Years* (Boston, 1979), *The Years of Upheaval* (New York, 1982), and *Diplomacy* (New York, 1994). He upstaged Nixon, whose memoir, *RN* (New York, 1978), appeared first and was immediately overshadowed. Nixon grumbled in 1971 that Kissinger wanted to steal credit for the China opening. See H. R. Haldeman, *The Haldeman Diaries* (New York, 1994), 365, 367. Kissinger's dominance over the record meant that few questioned his assertions regarding Taiwan.
2. Two works proved especially helpful for this chapter: for its critique of Nixon and Kissinger, Jim Mann, *About Face* (New York, 1999); on China's role, Chen, *Mao's China*. US–Taiwan relations have begun getting attention; see Alan D. Romberg, *Rein in at the Brink of the Precipice* (Washington, D.C., 2003); Richard Bush, *At Cross Purposes* (Armonk, N.Y., 2004) and *Untying the Knot* (Washington, D.C., 2005); and Garver, *Sino-American Alliance*.
3. Marshall Green helped fund an oral history project at the Foreign Service Institute in Alexandria, Va., and coauthored (with John H. Holdridge and William N. Stokes) *War and Peace with China* (Bethesda, Md., 1994) to correct the record.
4. Telcons Henry Kissinger, NARA; Nixon White House Tapes, ibid.; and material on the NSA Web site, www.gwu.edu/~nsarchiv. Chinese records are in the Woodrow Wilson Center's *Cold War International History Project Bulletin*, cwihp.si.edu. Taiwan has no effective program for declassification of cold war–era documents.
5. The classic works are Ross Koen, *The China Lobby in American Politics* (New York, 1974), and Stanley Bachrack, *The Committee of One Million* (New York, 1976). The lobby delayed Koen's book for over a decade, reportedly threatening the publisher with legal action for defamation.
6. William Safire, *Before the Fall* (Garden City, N.Y., 1975), 366; Melvin Small, *The Presidency of Richard Nixon* (Lawrence, Kans., 1999), 118; and John K. Fairbank, *The United States and China*, 4th ed. (Cambridge, Mass., 1983), 457.
7. Wang Bingnan, *Nine Years of Sino-American Ambassadorial Talks* (Beijing, 1985), and Kenneth Young, *Negotiating with the Chinese Communists* (New York, 1968).
8. 193rd NSC Meeting, April 13, 1954, *FRUS, 1952–54*, vol. 14, pt. 1, 409–10.
9. Ronald W. Pruessen, "Over the Volcano: The United States and the Taiwan Strait Crisis, 1954–1955," in Ross and Jiang, *Re-examining the Cold War*, 81–82; David Mayers, *Cracking the Monolith* (Baton Rouge, 1986), 115–25.
10. U.S. Congress, Senate, Committee on Foreign Relations, Hearings: *U.S. Policy in Asia*, 86th Cong., 1st sess., November 1, 1959.

11. "FE—Office of Asian Communist Affairs," n.d., *FRUS 1961–63,* 397–99; James C. Thomson Jr., "On the Making of U.S. China Policy, 1961–69: A Study in Bureaucratic Politics," *China Quarterly* 50 (April–June 1972): 226, 229.

12. Thomson to Bundy, October 28, 1964, *FRUS 1964–68,* 118; Roger Hilsman, *To Move a Nation* (New York, 1967), 350–57; Thomson, "On the Making," 230–38.

13. #6436 Rice, Hong Kong, March 15, 1967, *FRUS 1964–68,* 535–36; Memcon, May 11, 1967, ibid., 564–66, and the cable that they discussed, #5546 Sullivan, Vientiane, March 10, 1967, ibid., 532–34; Jenkins to Rostow, memo, April 30, 1968, ibid., 672–74. Reference to the earlier Rice paper is made in Thomson, "On the Making," 223–24.

14. Leonard A. Kusnitz, *Public Opinion and Foreign Policy* (Westport, Conn., 1984), 115–16; Chang, *Friends and Enemies,* 272–73; U.S. Congress, Senate, Committee on Foreign Relations, Hearings, *US Policy with Respect to Mainland China,* 89th Cong., 2nd sess., March 1966. On the first containment without isolation, see Kochavi, *A Conflict Perpetuated,* 213–33.

15. Nancy Bernkopf Tucker, *Taiwan, Hong Kong, and the United States, 1945–1992: Uncertain Friendships* (New York, 1994), 53–62.

16. Garver, *Sino-American Alliance,* 84–88.

17. Tucker, "Dulles and the 'Two Chinas' Policy," 244–51; Kochavi, *A Conflict Perpetuated,* 64–67.

18. Robert S. Norris, William M. Arkin, and William Burr, "Where They Were," *Bulletin of the Atomic Scientists* (November–December 1999): 55–56.

19. Ibid.; Airgram 1037, Taipei to State, June 20, 1966, "Indications Government of the ROC Continues to Pursue Atomic Weaponry," NSAEBB, no. 20; "New Archival Evidence on Taiwanese 'Nuclear Intentions,' 1966–1976," www.gwu.edu/~nsarchiv/NSAEBB/NSAEBB20/.

20. Taylor, *Generalissimo's Son,* 286.

21. #993 Arthur Hummel, Taipei, March 17, 1966, folder: China cables, vol. 6, 3/66–9/66, Box 239, NSF Country Files, JOHNSON; Rusk to Johnson, memo, n.d., folder: China—Visit of C. K. Yen, 5/9–10/67, Briefing Book, Box 244–45, ibid.

22. Koen, *China Lobby in American Politics,* 41; Roger Morris, *Richard Milhous Nixon* (New York, 1990), 590–91; Kusnitz, *Public Opinion and Foreign Policy,* 95; Herbert S. Parmet, *Richard Nixon and His America* (Boston, 1990), 210.

23. Nixon, *RN,* 126, 256, 258, 282.

24. Arthur W. Hummel Jr. interview, May 1992, Washington, D.C.

25. Mann, *About Face,* 17–18.

26. Bachrack, *The Committee of One Million,* 261. And see Richard M. Nixon, "Asia after Viet Nam," *Foreign Affairs* 46 (October 1967): 111–25.

27. Kissinger, *White House Years,* 164; Walter Isaacson, *Kissinger* (New York, 1992), 334; Marvin Kalb and Bernard Kalb, *Kissinger* (New York, 1975), 248–53 (quote on 253); Ray Garthoff, *Détente and Confrontation* (Washington, D.C., 1965), 214–15. John Gaddis ascribes more interest to Kissinger in *Strategies of Containment* (New York, 1982), 282.

28. James Lilley, *China Hands* (New York, 2004), 156; John Holdridge, *Crossing the Divide* (Lanham, Md., 1997), 35.

29. Robert S. Litwak says Nixon worried about Democrats in the bureaucracy. Litwak, *Détente and the Nixon Doctrine* (New York, 1984), 64–65; Garry Wills, *Nixon Agonistes* (Boston, 1970), 87–90.

30. Marvin Liebman, *Coming Out Conservative* (San Francisco, 1992), 180, 189; Bachrack, *The Committee of One Million,* 261; "'China Lobby,' Once Powerful Factor in U.S. Politics, Appears Victim of Lack of Interest," *NYT,* April 26, 1970, A14; #9917 Walter McConaughy, Taipei, n.d. (ca. April 1970), vol. I: Visit of Vice Premier CCK of China, April 21–23, 1970, Box 913, VIP Visits, NSC Files, NPMP, NARA.

31. Mann, *About Face,* 22; Foot, *Practice of Power,* 107.

32. Conversation 532-17: Nixon, Haig, McConaughy, June 30, 1971, Nixon White House Tapes, NARA.

33. #27529 State to Taipei, February 24, 1970, Paul Kreisberg, FOIA.

34. Clough quoted in Tucker, *China Confidential,* 97.

35. James Shen, *The U.S. and Free China* (Washington, D.C., 1983), 66; #1314 McConaughy, Taipei, March 24, 1970, vol. I, Box 913, NSC Files, NPMP, NARA.

36. A-206 Dean, Hong Kong, to SecState, July 21, 1970, Subject-Numeric Files 1970–73, POL Chicom—US, RG 59, NSA.

37. Nguyen Tien Hung and Jerrold L. Schecter, eds., *The Palace File* (New York, 1989), 34–35.

38. Ch'ien Fu Report, spring 1970, file 412.21, Vice Premier Chiang's Visit to the US, 00313-00346, MOFAA; #157 MOFA to Chow Shu-kai, April 14, 1970, folder: specific telegrams to ROC ambassador, file 412.21, ibid.; #3022 (#694) Chow to MOFA, April 15, 1970, folder: specific telegrams to MOFA, ibid.

39. Shen, *U.S. and Free China,* 51; Taylor, *Generalissimo's Son,* 296–98 (quote on 297); Memcon Kissinger, Holdridge, CCK, James Shen, and Chow, April 22, 1970, vol. I, Box 913, NSC Files, NPMP, NARA.

40. Taylor, *Generalissimo's Son,* 300.

41. Kissinger to Agnew, memo, August 22, 1970, folder: Vice President's Briefing Book, August 1970, ROC, Box 406, NSC Subject Files, NPMP, NARA; Objectives Paper, n.d. [ca. August 1970], ibid.

42. Wei Tao-ming, Foreign Minister, to President's Office, December 10, 1969, files 551 and 565, Agnew Visits, MOFAA; Memcon Agnew with Vice President Yen Chia-kan, January 1970, ibid.; Tai Rei-ming, Ministry of Foreign Affairs, to CKS, memo, August 18, 1970, ibid.

43. Kissinger, *Years of Upheaval,* 92; Kissinger, *White House Years,* 713, 729; Haig to Kissinger, memo, March 25, 1971, folder: Items to discuss with the President 1/1/71–7/31/71, Box 336, Planning Coordination Staff Director's Files (Winston Lord), RG 59, NARA; Andrew Kydd, "Which Side Are You On? Bias, Credibility, and Mediation," *American Journal of Political Science* 47(October 2003): 597–611.

44. Taiwan's status as "undetermined" appears in National Security Study Memorandum 106, "US China Policy," February 16, 1971. Romberg, *Rein In,* 22–25.

45. Kissinger to Nixon, May 3, 1971, Box 1031: Exchanges Leading Up to the HAK Trip to China—December 1969–July 1971 (1), NSC Files, NPMP, NSA.

46. A-25 Warsaw to SecState, January 24, 1970; Stoessel-Lei Talks, Report of the 135th Meeting, January 20, 1970, Subject-Numeric Files 1970–73, POL Chicom—US, RG 59, NSA.

47. Nixon, *RN,* 547.

48. Kissinger, *White House Years,* 749; Memcon Kissinger with Zhou, July 9, 1971, 4:35–11:20 PM, Box 1033, China HAK Memcons, July 1971, NSC Files, NPMP, NSA.

49. A May 1971 Zhou Enlai report included eight principles for opening relations, but they fell short of what Kissinger offered. Chen, *Mao's China,* 263–64; Memcon Kissinger with Zhou, July 9, 1971, 4:35–11:20 PM, Box 1033, China HAK Memcons, July 1971, NSC Files, NPMP, NSA; Kissinger, *White House Years,* 749.

50. Memcon Kissinger and Zhou, July 10, 1971, 12:10–6:00 PM and 11:20–11:50 PM, Box 1033: China HAK Memcons, July 1971, NSC Files, NPMP, NSA.

51. C-56410, MacArthur, Commander in Chief, Far East, to Dept. Army, Washington, May 29, 1950, folder 4, "Formosa File, March 1948–October 1950," Box 8, RG 6: Far East Command Records, MacArthur Memorial Bureau of Archives, Norfolk, Va.

52. Conversation 534-3: Nixon and Kissinger, July 1, 1971, Nixon Tapes, NPMP, NARA.

53. *Zhonghua renmin gongheguo shilu* [A Factual Record of the People's Republic of China], vol. 3 (Changchun, 1994), 713–14.

54. Service quoted in Tucker, *China Confidential,* 254; Kissinger, *White House Years,* 705.

55. William Burr, ed., *The Kissinger Transcripts* (New York, 1998), 42.

56. Memcon Kissinger with Zhou, July 9, 1971, 4:35–11:20 PM, NPMP, NSA.

57. Anatoly Dobrynin, *In Confidence* (New York, 1995), 226–28; Jussi Hanhimaki, "'Dr. Kissinger' or 'Mr. Henry'? Kissingerology, Thirty Years and Counting," *Diplomatic History* 27 (November 2003): 650–51; Taylor, *Generalissimo's Son,* 304.

58. #3632 McConaughy, Taipei, July 26, 1971, folder: UN6 Chicom, July 23, 1971, Box 3211, UN (Chicom-Chinat), CFPF, 1970–73, RG 59, NARA.

59. Conversation 532-17: Nixon, Haig, McConaughy, June 30, 1971, Nixon Tapes, NPMP, NARA.

60. TelCon 1-91: Nixon and Kissinger, April 14, 1971, ibid., transcript created by Sharon Chamberlain, George Washington University.

61. Taylor, *Generalissimo's Son,* 304; Mann, *About Face,* 37.

62. Shen, *U.S. and Free China,* 110.

63. Haig to Kissinger, memo, with Helms report attached, August 26, 1971, folder: August 1971, Box 340, Winston Lord Chronology File, May 1971 through February 1972, SPC/SP Lord, NARA.

64. Memcon Kissinger and Zhou, July 10, 1971, 11:20–11:50 PM, NSA.

65. Haig to Kissinger, memo, February 23, 1971, folder: Items to discuss with the President 1/1/71–7/31/71, Box 336, RG 59, NARA; Richard Allen interview, February 1, 2001, Washington, D.C.

66. Jonathan Salant, "New Recordings Show Nixon No Fan of Reagan," Associated Press, December 11, 2003; interview, Roger Sullivan, February 2, 2001, Medford, Mass.

67. Kissinger disparaged Reagan's trip to Taiwan as purely political. Memcon Kissinger with Zhou, October 21, 1971, 4:42–7:17 PM, Box 1034, Polo II—HAK China Trip October 1971, NSC Files, NPMP, NSA; Michael Deaver, *Behind the Scenes* (New York, 1987), 66.

68. Kissinger to Nixon, memo, "My August 16 Meeting with the Chinese Ambassador in Paris," August 16, 1971, Box 330: China Exchanges July–October 20, 1971, SPC/SP Lord, NSA; Conversation 581-1: Nixon and Kissinger, September 30, 1971, Nixon Tapes, NSAEBB, no. 70, "Negotiating U.S.–Chinese Rapprochement," document #6, Chamberlain transcript, www.gwu.edu/~nsarchiv/NSAEBB/NSAEBB70/doc6.pdf.

69. Conversation 582-3: Nixon and Kissinger, September 30, 1971, Nixon Tapes, document #8, www.gwu.edu/~nsarchiv/NSAEBB/NSAEBB70/doc8.pdf.

70. Winston Lord to Kissinger, November 20, 1970, with draft memo from Kissinger to Nixon, and Lord to Kissinger, memo (includes Nixon quote), November 25, 1970, folder: Winston Lord, November 1970, Box 334: Winston Lord Chronological File, September 1970–November 1970, SPC/SP Lord, NARA.

71. NSSM 107, "The Entire UN Membership Question: U.S.–China Policy," folder: UN6 Chicom, March 15, 1971, Box 3210, UN (Chicom-Chinat), CFPF, 1970–73, RG 59, NARA.

72. Kissinger, *White House Years,* 773.

73. Conversation 532-17: Nixon, Haig, McConaughy, June 30, 1971, Nixon Tapes, NPMP, NARA.

74. Yost to Rogers, February 8, 1971, folder: UN6 Chicom, February 1, 1971, Box 3209, UN (Chicom-Chinat), CFPF, 1970–73, RG 59, NARA.

75. #3387 McConaughy, Taipei, July 11, 1971, folder: UN6 Chinat, July 1, 1971, Box 3211, UN (Chicom-Chinat), ibid.

76. Memcon Chow Shu-kai with Marshall Green, etc., January 25, 1971, folder: UN6 Chicom, January 20, 1971, Box 3209, UN (Chicom-Chinat), ibid.; Samuel DePalma, Assistant Secretary International Organization Affairs, to Kissinger, memo, February 6, 1971, transmitting study pursuant to NSSM 107, "The Entire UN Membership Question: U.S.–China Policy," folder: UN6 Chicom, March 15, 1971, Box 3210, UN (Chicom-Chinat), ibid.

77. Presentation of Credentials, May 18, 1971, folder: [EX] CO34-1, Republic of China (Formosa-Taiwan) 1/1/71– [1 of 2], Box 18, Subject Files, WHCF, NPMP, NARA.

78. #134611 State to Taipei, July 24, 1971, folder: UN6 Chinat, July 23, 1971, Box 3211, UN (Chicom-Chinat), CFPF, 1970–73, RG 59, NARA; #3680 McConaughy, Taipei, July 28, 1971, NARA.

79. Holdridge to Kissinger, August 19, 1971, folder: [EX] CO34-1, Republic of China (Formosa-Taiwan) 1/1/71– [1 of 2], Box 18, Subject Files, WHCF, NPMP, NARA.

80. Hummel quoted in Tucker, *China Confidential,* 209

81. 303/4-561 Rusk to Embassy, *FRUS 1961–63,* 46 (quote); #087 Yost, USUN,

January 13, 1971, folder: UN6 Chicom, January 1, 1971, Box 3209, UN (Chicom-Chinat), CFPF, 1970–73, RG 59, NARA.

82. Kissinger to Nixon, May 3, 1971, Box 1031: Exchanges Leading Up to HAK Trip to China, December 1969–July 1971 (1), NSC Files, NPMP, NSA.

83. #1255 McConaughy, Taipei, March 20, 1971, folder: UN6 Chicom, March 15, 1971, Box 3210, UN (Chicom-Chinat), CFPF, 1970–73, RG 59, NARA.

84. #2063 Bennett, USUN, July 30, 1971, folder: UN6 Chicom, July 23, 1971, Box 3211, ibid.; #2280 Bush, USUN, August 18, 1971, folder: UN6 Chicom, August 16, 1971, Box 3212, ibid.; #4206 McConaughy, Taipei, August 24, 1971, folder: UN6 Chicom, August 20, 1971, ibid.; Shen, *U.S. and Free China*, 62.

85. #4553 McConaughy to Rogers, September 10, 1971, folder: UN6 Chicom, September 10, 1971, Box 3213, UN (Chicom-Chinat), CFPF, 1970–73, RG 59, NARA; Rogers to Nixon, memo, September 11, 1971, folder: UN6 Chicom, September 10, 1971, NARA.

86. Conversation 581-6: Nixon, Rogers, and Kissinger, September 30, 1971, Nixon Tapes, NPMP, NARA, Chamberlain transcript.

87. Garver, *Sino-American Alliance*, 261.

88. According to H. R. Haldeman, Kissinger believed Rogers manipulated the UN vote to cast blame on him. *Haldeman Diaries*, entries for October 18, 1971, 365, and October 27, 1971, 369. Conversation 581-6: Nixon, Rogers, and Kissinger, September 30, 1971, Nixon Tapes, NPMP, NARA, Chamberlain transcript; Kissinger, *White House Years*, 770, 772, 776. "Defeated man" comment by Treasury Secretary John Connally, which Kissinger said was "what the President thinks." Telcon October 1, 1971, folder: 1971, 1–4 October (8), Box 11, NPMP, NARA; Nixon quote, October 2, 1971, 1:22 PM, ibid.; Frederick Ch'ien Fu, *Qian Fu Hui Yi Lu: Hua Fu Lu Qi Qu, 1977–1988* [Ch'ien Fu's Memory Lane: The Bumpy U.S. Goverment Road] (Taipei, 2005), 154–56.

89. Thayer quoted in Tucker, *China Confidential*, 264–65.

90. Walter Pincus and Bob Woodward, "Presidential Posts and Dashed Hopes: Appointive Jobs Were Turning Point," *WP*, August 9, 1988; Parmet, *George Bush* (New York, 1997), 152.

91. Telcon Nixon and Kissinger, April 27, 1971, Box 1031 (1), NPMP, NSA; #3738 Bush, USUN, October 21, 1971, folder: UN6 Chicom, October 21, 1971, Box 3215, UN (Chicom-Chinat), CFPF, 1970–73, RG 59, NARA.

92. Telcon Henry Kissinger with William Rogers, October 4, 1971, 8:50 AM, Box 11, folder: 1971, 1–4 October (8), NPMP, NARA.

93. George Bush, *Looking Forward* (Garden City, N.Y., 1987), 114–16.

94. Conversation 532-17: Nixon, Haig, McConaughy, June 30, 1971, Nixon Tapes, NPMP, NARA.

95. Telcons Nixon with Kissinger, March 30, 1971, 9:35 AM, Box 9, folder: 1971, 25–31 March (6), NPMP, NARA.

96. Memcon Kissinger with Zhou, October 21, 1971, 10:30 AM–1:45 PM, Box 1034, Polo II—HAK China Trip October 1971, NSC Files, NPMP, NSA; Kissinger, *White House Years*, 782.

97. Memcon Nixon and Kissinger with Zhou, February 22, 1972, 2:10–6:00 PM, Box 87, "Beginning February 20, 1972," President's Office Files, NPMP, NSA.

98. Garver, *Sino-American Alliance,* 256–62.

3. Survival

1. Robert Goldberg, *Barry Goldwater* (New Haven, 1995), 265; Nixon to Wayne, January 13, 1972, WHCF, Subject Files, CO 34 China [1969–70], Box 18, folder: [EX] CO 34-1 Republic of China (Formosa-Taiwan) 1/1/71– [2 of 2], NPMP, NARA.

2. Parmet, *Richard Nixon and His America,* 623; Haldeman, *Haldeman Diaries,* entries for October 26, 1971, 368, and October 27, 1971, 369; Telcon Henry Kissinger with Ronald Reagan, October 29, 1971, 5:15 PM, folder: 1971 15–30 October (11), Box 11, NPMP, NARA; Telcon Kissinger with Walter Judd, November 23, 1971, 4:42 PM, folder: 1971 15–23 November (2), ibid.

3. #067545 State, December 15, 1971, WHCF, Subject Files, CO 34 China [1969–70], Box 17, NPMP, RG 59, NARA.

4. C. J. Chen interview, November 7, 2003, Washington, D.C.

5. #5589 McConaughy, November 1, 1971, CFPF, 1970–73, Box 3216, UN (Chicom-Chinat), folder: UN6 Chicom, November 1, 1971, RG 59, NARA.

6. #5459 Clarke, Taipei, October 27, 1971, and #5362 McConaughy, October 27, 1971 CFPF, 1970–73, Box 3216 UN (Chicom-Chinat), folder: UN6 Chicom, October 27, 1971, RG 59, NARA.

7. Talking Points, Department of State, n.d., Box 184: Haldeman Binder Dealing with Trip to China, folder: Visit of Richard Nixon to PRC February 1972 Briefing Papers, Mr. Haldeman 3 of 3, WHSF, Staff Memoranda and Office Files of H. R. Haldeman, NPMP, NARA.

8. Taylor, *Generalissimo's Son,* 308.

9. Memcon Kissinger with Zhou, October 25, 1971, 9:50–11:40 PM, NSC, Box 1034, Polo II—HAK China Trip October 1971, Transcript of Meetings, NPMP, NARA and NSA.

10. Memcon Kissinger with Zhou, October 26, 1971, 5:30–8:10 PM, NSC, Box 1034, Polo II—HAK China Trip October 1971, Transcript of Meetings, NPMP, NARA and NSA; Bush, *At Cross Purposes,* 126.

11. Memcon Haig with Zhou, January 3, 1972, midnight, NSC, Box 1037, China—AM Haig January Visit Jan. 1972, NPMP, NARA and NSA.

12. Memcon Nixon and Kissinger with Zhou, February 22, 1972, 2:10–6:00 PM, Box 87, "Beginning February 20, 1972," President's Office Files, NPMP, NSA.

13. Memcon Nixon and Kissinger with Zhou, February 24, 1972, 5:15–8:05 PM, President's Office Files, Memoranda for the President, Box 87, "Beginning February 20, 1972," NPMP, NARA and NSA.

14. Memcon Nixon and Kissinger with Zhou, February 28, 1972, 8:30–9:30 AM, President's Office Files, Memoranda for the President, Box 87, "Beginning February 20, 1972," NPMP, NARA and NSA.

15. Kissinger, *White House Years,* 1082–83; Kissinger, *Diplomacy,* 744. Green's version is in Green, Holdridge, and Stokes, *War and Peace with China,* 162–65.

16. Lord, Holdridge, and Green quoted in Tucker, *China Confidential,* 274–75; Bush, *At Cross Purposes,* 124–78.

17. Secto 212 For Eagleburger from Bremer, November 27, 1974, folder: PRC–State Department Telegrams to Secretary of State—NODIS (3), Box 15, NSA—President Country Files, FORD; Memcon Kissinger with Vice Foreign Minister Qiao Guanhua, February 26–27, 1972, 10:20 PM–1:40 AM, HAKO, Box 92, Dr Kissinger's Meetings in the PRC during the Presidential Visit, February 1972, NPMP, NARA and NSA; Kissinger, *White House Years,* 1082–84; Bush, *At Cross Purposes,* 129–30.

18. The Chinese and English texts of the communiqué are not the same. The Chinese language is stronger. See Dong, *Zhong Mei guanxi ciliao xuanbian,* 3–8; Joint Communiqué between the PRC and the USA, Shanghai, February 27, 1972, *Public Papers of the Presidents of the United States: Richard Nixon, 1972* (Washington, D.C., 1974), 376–79.

19. Quoted by John Garver in *Sino-American Alliance,* 274.

20. On demands for a UN seat, see Peng, *A Taste of Freedom,* 260.

21. Garver, *Sino-American Alliance,* 275; memo to Kissinger, March 2, 1972, Box 343, folder: Kissinger's Noon/Evening Notes, February 1, 1972–March 31, 1972, NSC, Subject Files, NPMP, NARA; Bush, *At Cross Purposes,* 134; Holdridge, *Crossing the Divide,* 99; Taylor, *Generalissimo's Son,* 308.

22. William Gleysteen, ADST, 90.

23. #6724 McConaughy, Taipei, November 7, 1973, Box 371: Bilateral PRC Officials April 22, 1974 thru China-Sec Kissinger, folder: China-Sec Kissinger, SPC/SP Lord, NARA; Shen, *U.S. and Free China,* 107–10; Memcon Kissinger with Shen, March 1, 1972, *FRUS 1969–72,* vol. 17, 825–30; Memcon Nixon and Kissinger with Shen, March 6, 1972, ibid., 835–40.

24. See John S. Service, *The Amerasia Papers* (Berkeley, 1971); Gary May, *China Scapegoat* (Prospect Heights, Ill., 1979); O. Edmund Clubb, *The Witness and I* (New York, 1974); E. J. Kahn, *The China Hands* (New York, 1975).

25. Kissinger to Nixon, memo, January 4, 1972, National Security Adviser/Memoranda of Conversations, 1973–77, Box 1: Memcons—Nixon Admin, undated, folder: January 5, 1973—Nixon, Republic of China Officials, FORD; Memcon Nixon with Yen, January 5, 1973, ibid.; Yen to Nixon, February 15, 1973, WHCF, Subject Files, Box 18, folder: [EX] CO 34-1 Republic of China (Formosa-Taiwan) 1/1/73– , NPMP, NARA.

26. "Residual Relations with Taiwan," n.d., Box 380: China Notes thru Exclusively Eyes Only—Lord China Notes, folder: Exclusively Eyes Only—Lord China File, SPC/SP Lord, NARA.

27. Ibid.; meeting between Henry Kissinger and Zhou Enlai, Guest House Villa #3, Peking, November 12, 1973, 3:00–5:30 PM, China and the United States Collection #00279, DNSA.

28. Gleysteen, ADST, 91.

29. Sullivan interview; Chas Freeman quoted in Tucker, *China Confidential,* 288.

30. Burr, *Kissinger Transcripts,* 85, 117; Freeman and James Lilley quoted in Tucker, *China Confidential,* 289.

31. Norris, Arkin, and Burr, "Where They Were."

32. Kissinger to Nixon, memo, February 27, 1973, "My Asian Trip," NPMP, NARA.

33. Shen to Kissinger, July 11, 1973, WHCF, Subject Files, CO 34 China [1969–70], Box 20, folder: [EX] CO 34-2 Republic of China (Formosa-Taiwan) 6/1/73–12/31/73, NPMP, NARA.

34. Shen, *U.S. and Free China,* 146–47.

35. Taylor, *Generalissimo's Son,* 313; Bruce Dickson, *Democratization in China and Taiwan* (New York, 1997), 206.

36. "Major Problems in East Asia," 1973, Box 382: Cambodia—Sensitive Chron March 1975 thru Issue Papers from the Bureaus, folder: Issue Papers from the Bureau [1 of 2], SPC/SP Lord, NARA; #1152 McConaughy, Taipei, March 12, 1971, CFPF, 1970–73, Box 3210, UN (Chicom-Chinat), folder: UN6 Chicom, March 15, 1971, RG 59, NARA.

37. William Gleysteen interview, February 28, 2001, Washington, D.C.; Solomon to Kissinger, January 19, 1974, Box 371: Bilateral PRC Officials April 22, 1974, thru China—Sec Kissinger, folder: China—Sec Kissinger, SPC/SP Lord, NARA.

38. Shen, *U.S. and Free China,* 131.

39. Meeting, Henry Kissinger with Zhou Enlai, November 12, 1973, #00279, DNSA; Kissinger to Nixon, memo, November 19, 1973, Box 374: Sec. Kissinger's Trip to China Oct 1975 thru China Sensitive July 1973–Feb 1974, folder: China—Sensitive, Special WL File, Misc & Reports, SPC/SP Lord, NARA; meeting, Henry Kissinger with Zhou Enlai, Great Hall of the People, November 11, 1973, 3:15–7:00 PM, #00278, DNSA.

40. Kissinger to Nixon, memo, November 19, 1973, Box 374: Sec. Kissinger's Trip to China Oct. 1975 thru China Sensitive July 1973–Feb. 1974, folder: China—Sensitive, Special WL File, Misc & Reports, SPC/SP Lord, NARA; Kissinger, *Years of Upheaval,* 691–92 (quote on 692).

41. Solomon to Kissinger, January 19, 1974, Box 371: Bilateral PRC Officials April 22, 1974 thru China—Sec Kissinger, folder: China—Sec Kissinger, SPC/SP Lord, NARA.

42. Hummel and Lord to Kissinger, memo, January 29, 1974, Box 371: Bilateral PRC Officials April 22, 1974 thru China—Sec Kissinger, folder: China—Sec Kissinger, SPC/SP Lord, NARA.

43. #1171 USLO, Peking, n.d., Box 370: Sec. Visit to Peking: NSC Reference Book—Taiwan, Nov. 1974, S/P Mr. Lord thru Sec's Meeting with the Chinese October 2, 1974, folder: Sec. Kissinger's Visit to Peking, October 1973, S/PC Mr. Lord, vol. I [folder 1 of 2], SPC/SP Lord, NARA. The State Department's Intelligence and Research Bureau expressed greater urgency in "Peking Changes Taiwan Line," Intelligence Note, April 2, 1974, Box 331: China Exchanges April 1–August 8, 1974, thru October–December 1975, folder: China Exchanges April 1–August 8, 1974, SPC/SP Lord, NARA.

44. Margaret MacMillan, *Nixon in China* (Toronto, 2006), 76.

45. Robert Ross, *Negotiating Cooperation* (Stanford, 1995), 65.

46. Memcon Kissinger and Shen, November 15, 1971, *FRUS 1969–72*, vol. 17 (2006), 593; #231267 Kissinger to Taipei, November 24, 1973, Box 374: Sec. Kissinger's trip to China Oct. 1975 thru China Sensitive July 1973–Feb. 1974, folder: China Sensitive July 1973–Feb. 1974, SPC/SP Lord, NARA.

47. Sullivan interview.

48. Hummel and Lord to Kissinger, memo, January 29, 1974, Box 371: Bilateral PRC Officials April 22, 1974 thru China—Sec Kissinger, folder: China—Sec Kissinger, SPC/SP Lord, NARA.

49. Ralph Clough, *Island China* (Cambridge, Mass., 1978), 168–70; John Garver, "Taiwan's Russian Option: Image and Reality," *Asian Survey* 18 (July 1978): 751–66; Solomon to Kissinger, January 19, 1974, Box 371: Bilateral PRC Officials April 22, 1974 thru China—Sec Kissinger, folder: China—Sec Kissinger, SPC/SP Lord, NARA; Lord and Hummel to Kissinger, memo, April 12, 1974, Box 376: China Sensitive Chron August 17–October 15, 1974 thru China Sensitive Chron February–April 1974, folder: China-Sensitive Feb.–April 1974, SPC/SP Lord, NARA.

50. Leonard to Sullivan, memo, n.d., Box 16, folder: DEF 19-8 FMS FY'75 and out year 1974, Subject Files of the Office of Chinese Affairs, RG 59, NARA.

51. Telcon Ford with Kissinger, February 8, 1972, 5:35 PM, folder: 1972 5–10 February (3), NARA; Shen, *U.S. and Free China*, 13.

52. Leonard Unger interview, August 1993, Potomac, Md.; Lord and Hummel to Kissinger, memo, April 12, 1974, Box 376: China Sensitive Chron August 17–October 15, 1974 thru China Sensitive Chron February–April 1974, folder: China—Sensitive Feb.–April 1974, SPC/SP Lord, NARA.

53. Roger Sullivan (EA/ROC) to Arthur Hummel (EA), memo, May 15, 1974, Box 375: China Sensitive Chron March–June 1975 thru China Sensitive Chron Spec. Winston Lord File: Nov. 1974 re HAK Trip to Peking, folder: China Sensitive May 1–June 30, 1974, SPC/SP Lord, NARA; Jeanne W. Davis (NSC) to John Marsh, memo, June 28, 1974, Box 65: Vice Presidential Meetings with Foreign and Diplomatic Officials, May 1974–June 1974, folder: May–June 1974, Ford Vice Presidential Papers, FORD.

54. Roger Sullivan (EA/ROC) to the files, memo, April 29, 1974, Box 16, folder: DEF-1 Policy, Plans, Readiness (General), 1974, Subject Files of the Office of ROC Affairs, 1951–75, RG 59, NARA; Roger Sullivan (EA/ROC) to Arthur Hummel (EA), memo, May 15, 1974, Box 375: China Sensitive Chron March–June 1975 thru China Sensitive Chron Spec. Winston Lord File: Nov 1974 re HAK Trip to Peking, folder: China Sensitive May 1–June 30, 1974, SPC/SP Lord, NARA; Gleysteen, ADST, 102–3.

55. Norris, Arkin, and Burr, "Where They Were."

56. Memcon Unger with Schlesinger, April 12, 1974, Box 1: Taipei [Taiwan] Top Secret Embassy Files E3257B [E3373], 1959–77, RG 84, NARA; Catherine Sung and William Ide, "Nuclear Redeployment Preceded US Pullout," *Taipei Times*, October 20, 1999; Gleysteen interview.

57. #1682 Gleysteen, Taipei, May 11, 1974, Box 376: China Sensitive Chron August 17–October 15, 1974 thru China Sensitive Chron February–April 1974,

folder: China Sensitive May 1–June 30, 1974, SPC/SP Lord, NARA; #3105 Unger, Taipei, May 18, 1974, ibid.; #106570 Rush, State, May 21, 1974, ibid.; #1871 Unger, Taipei, May 24, 1974, ibid.; #128587 Sisco, State Department, June 17, 1974, Box 1: Embassy Taipei 1959–1977, folder: DEF 15-9 Reductions—ROC 1974, RG 84, NARA.

58. Decision on May 24, 1974, Box 376: China Sensitive Chron August 17–October 15, 1974 thru China Sensitive Chron February–April 1974, folder: China-Sensitive Feb.–April 1974, SPC/SP Lord, NARA (quote); Roger Sullivan (EA/ROC) to Arthur Hummel (EA), memo, May 15, 1974, Box 375: China Sensitive Chron March–June 1975 thru China Sensitive Chron Spec. Winston Lord File: Nov. 1974 re HAK Trip to Peking, folder: China Sensitive May 1–June 30, 1974, ibid.; Burton Levin (EA/ROC) to Harvey, Taipei, October 23, 1974, Box 16, folder: DEF 7 Defense Visits (to and from ROC) 1974, Subject Files of the Office of Chinese Affairs, RG 59, NARA. State could not stop Defense officials, particularly those overseas, from traveling to Taiwan.

4. Collapse and Reprieve

1. Gerald Ford, *A Time to Heal* (New York, 1979), 97, 121, 128–29; Patrick Tyler, *A Great Wall* (New York, 1999), 185.

2. Joint Report to the US House of Representatives on Mission to China, June 23–July 7, 1972, Robert T. Hartmann Papers, Box 43: House of Representatives Subject File: China—Ford/Boggs Trip, folder: China—Ford/Boggs Trip—Report to the House of Representatives, FORD; Ford, *A Time to Heal, 96.*

3. Central Intelligence Agency Chronology of the Kissinger-Nixon China Initiative, Rand Corporation (hereafter CIA Chron), 43; Memcon Kissinger with Qiao Guanhua, PRC Foreign Minister, October 2, 1974, Box 374: Sec. Kissinger's Trip to China Oct. 1975 thru China Sensitive July 1973–Feb. 1974, folder: Meeting with PRC Foreign Minister September 28, 1975, SPC/SP Lord, NARA.

4. Memcon Ford, Bush, and Scowcroft, October 15, 1974, National Security Assistant Memcons, 1973–77, Box 6: Memcons Ford Administration—September 21, 1974, Ford . . . Vignes, folder: October 15, 1974—Ford, George Bush, FORD.

5. George H. W. Bush, Peking Diary, November 3, 1974, vol. 1, 77–78, BUSH; #100 Bush to Kissinger, January 15, 1975, Box 331: China Exchanges April 1–August 8, 1974 thru October–December 1975, folder: China Exchanges January 1–May 31, 1975, SPC/SP Lord, NARA.

6. Ch'ien, *Hui Yi Lu,* 267; Tyler, *Great Wall,* 202; Smyser and Solomon to Kissinger, memo, April 11, 1975, NSA/PCF/EAP, Box 4, folder: China, Republic of, FORD.

7. John Donnell, "South Vietnam in 1975: The Year of the Communist Victory," *Asian Survey* 16 (January 1976): 4; Taylor, *Generalissimo's Son,* 269; Thomas Marks, *Counterrevolution in China* (London, 1996), 198–215. Taiwan also assisted Lon Nol in Cambodia.

8. Smyser to Scowcroft, May 19, 1975, NSA/PCF/EAP, Box 4: Cambodia—

Seizing of the Mayaguez, May 1975 (1), folder: China, Republic of, FORD; Smyser and Solomon to Kissinger, May 29, 1975, NSA/PCF/EAP, Box 4: Cambodia—Seizing of the Mayaguez, May 1975 (1), folder: China, Republic of (4), FORD; draft response to CCK message to Ford, SecState to Taipei, n.d., ibid.; Solomon and Froebe to Kissinger, July 16, 1975, with cover note from McFarlane to Solomon, NSA/PCF/EAP, Box 5, folder: China, Republic of (5), ibid.

9. #91 Bush to Ford, voyager channel, May 23, 1975, Office of the Assistant to the President for National Security Affairs Henry Kissinger and Brent Scowcroft Files (1972) 1974–77, Box A1: Temporary Parallel File, folder: Kissinger-Scowcroft West Wing Office File, China Exchanges—unnumbered (13), FORD.

10. Habib, Gleysteen, Lord, and Solomon to Kissinger, memo, May 9, 1975, Box 375: China Sensitive Chron March–June 1975 thru China Sensitive Chron Spec. Winston Lord File: Nov. 1974 re HAK Trip to Peking, folder: China Sensitive March–June 1975, SPC/SP Lord, NARA.

11. Mann, *About Face,* 69; Habib, Lord, Gleysteen, and Solomon to Kissinger, memo July 3, 1975, Office of the Assistant to the President for National Security Affairs Henry Kissinger and Brent Scowcroft Files, (1972) 1974–77, Box A1: Temporary Parallel File, folder: Kissinger-Scowcroft West Wing Office File, China Exchanges—unnumbered (15), FORD; Memcon Kissinger, Habib, Lord, Gleysteen, Solomon, July 6, 1975, Box 332: China Exchanges January–September 1975 thru August 1976–January 1977, folder: China Exchanges, label missing, SPC/SP Lord, NARA.

12. Hartmann to Ford, October 1975, Hartmann Papers, Box 131, folder: Hartmann Memos—President (2), FORD.

13. Congressional correspondence, November 1975, WHCF Subject Files, Box 13: CO 34-1 ROC (Formosa-Taiwan) 11/1/75 (Executive) to CO 34-2 PRC (Gen), folder: CO 34-1 ROC (Formosa-Taiwan) 11/1/75–12/3/75, FORD; Burton Levin (EA/ROC) to Habib, memo, December 4, 1975, Box 381: President's China Trip thru Cambodia April 1975, folder: President's China Trip, SPC/SP Lord, NARA.

14. Barry Goldwater, *With No Apologies* (New York, 1979), 234–35, 242; Goldwater with Casserly, *Goldwater* (New York, 1988), 259; Goldberg, *Barry Goldwater,* 248, 265.

15. Memcon Ford with Kissinger and Scowcroft, August 30, 1976, National Security Adviser Memcons, 1973–77, Box 20, folder: August 30, 1976—Ford, Kissinger, FORD.

16. Kissinger to Ford, memo, August 1974, Box 371: Bilateral PRC Officials April 22, 1974 thru China-Sec Kissinger, folder: Secretary's Visit to Peking Bilateral Issues—S/P, SPC/SP Lord, NARA; "Briefing Paper for the President," August 14, 1974, Box 376: China Sensitive Chron August 17–October 15, 1974 thru China Sensitive Chron February–April 1974, folder: China-Sensitive July 1–August 16, 1974, SPC/SP Lord, NARA, emphasis in original.

17. #5091 Unger, Taipei, August 14, 1974, NSA/PCF/EAP, Box 5, folder: China, Republic of—State Department Telegrams to SecState—EXDIS (1), FORD.

18. Memcon CCK with Unger, November 7, 1974, Box 375: China Sensitive Chron March–June 1975 thru China Sensitive Chron Spec. Winston Lord File: Nov. 1974 re HAK Trip to Peking, folder: China Sensitive October 16–December 31 1974, SPC/SP Lord, NARA; Paul M. Popple, DCM, Taipei, to William H. Gleysteen, DAS, November 14, 1974, ibid.

19. #6814 Unger, Taipei, NSA/PCF/EAP, Box 5, folder: China, Republic of—State Department Telegrams to SecState—NODIS (3), FORD.

20. #7012 Unger, Taipei November 22, 1974, Box 375: China Sensitive Chron March–June 1975 thru China Sensitive Chron Spec. Winston Lord File: Nov. 1974 re HAK Trip to Peking, folder: China Sensitive Chron October 16–December 31, 1974, SPC/SP Lord, NARA.

21. #5933 Unger, Taipei, September 24, 1974, NSA/PCF/EAP, Box 5, folder: China, Republic of—State Department Telegrams to SecState—NODIS (1), FORD.

22. Michael J. Glennon, "Liaison and the Law: Foreign Intelligence Agencies' Activities in the United States," *Harvard International Law Journal* 25 (Winter 1984): 2, 2n2, 3n5; U.S. Congress, House, Hearings, *Taiwan Agents in America and the Death of Prof. Wen-chen Chen,* 97th Cong., 1st sess., July 30 and October 6, 1981; David Kaplan, *Fires of the Dragon* (New York, 1992), 141–52, 506–7.

23. Chas Freeman noted his weekly reports to Assistant Secretary Richard Holbrooke were being read in Taipei, but the FBI failed to establish the source. Hummel and Freeman quoted in Tucker, *China Confidential,* 298 and 337; Kaplan, *Fires,* 177.

24. Jay Taylor in *Generalissimo's Son,* 317, states categorically that Chiang "approved" the plan. I am inclined to agree, since this operation was too dangerous to do without authorization. But when Unger confronted Chiang, he "looked increasingly baffled," claiming to find the story "unbelievable" and disparaging the "utter folly and stupidity" of the effort. #0668 Unger, Taipei, February 6, 1975, NSA/PCF/EAP, Box 5, folder: China, Republic of—State Department Telegrams to SecState—NODIS (2), FORD.

25. #019383 Kissinger, January 28, 1974, NSA/PCF/EAP, Box 5, folder: China, Republic of—State Department Telegrams from SecState—NODIS (1), FORD; #0513 Unger, Taipei, January 29, 1974, ibid.; Solomon, Froebe, and Jennings to Kissinger, memo, January 31, 1974, ibid., Box 4, folder: China, Republic of (2); unmarked paper left with CCK, February 6, 1975, Box 5, folder: China, Republic of—State Department Telegrams from SecState—NODIS (1); #041760 Kissinger, February 24, 1975, ibid., NODIS (2); Patrick Tyler, "Taiwanese Spies Said to Penetrate Top U.S. Agencies," *WP,* June 1, 1982, A1; Kaplan, *Fires,* 184–91.

26. Kaplan, *Fires,* 237–40.

27. #1037 Taipei, June 20, 1966, Subject Numeric Files, 1964–66, folder: DEF 12-1 Chinat, NSAEBB20 "New Archival Evidence on Taiwanese 'Nuclear Intentions,' 1966–1976," www.gwu.edu/~nsarchiv/NSAEBB/NSAEBB20/; David Albright and Corey Gay, "Taiwan: Nuclear Nightmare Averted," *Bulletin of the Atomic Scientists* (January–February 1998): 56.

28. SNIE 43-1-72 "Taipei's Capabilities and Intentions Regarding Nuclear Weapons Development," November [16?], 1972, NSAEBB 221; Morton Abramowitz to Ray Cline, November 15, 1972, ibid.; Memcon Dr. E. Abel, West German Embassy, with H. Daniel Brewster (SCI/AE), State Department, November 22, 1972, Subject-Numeric Files, 1970–73, AE 11-2 Chinat, RG 59, NSAEBB 20; Moser to Green, December 14, 1972, ibid., FSE 13 Chinat; #2051 State to Embassies, Bonn, Brussels, and Taipei, January 4, 1973, ibid.; #0338 McConaughy, Taipei, January 16, 1973, ibid.; #12137 State to McConaughy, January 20, 1973, ibid.; #685 McConaughy, Taipei, January 31, 1973, ibid.; #828 McConaughy, Taipei, February 8, 1973, ibid; Leonard Spector, *Nuclear Proliferation Today* (New York, 1984), 342–43n2.

29. Sullivan to Hummel, memo, October 29, 1973, NSAEBB 221.

30. #51747 State to Taipei, March 21, 1973, NSAEBB 20; #7051 Taipei to State, November 23, 1973, NSAEBB 221.

31. "Prospects for Arms Production and Development in the Republic of China," Interagency Intelligence Memorandum, NIO IIM 76-020, May 1976, NSA/PCF/EAP, Box 5, folder: China, Republic of (10), FORD; #6272 Unger, Taipei, September 15, 1976, NSA/PCF/EAP, Box 5, folder: China, Republic of—State Department Telegrams to SecState—EXDIS (2), FORD; Memcon Unger with Ambassador James C. H. Shen, November 18, 1976, Box 1: Embassy Taipei 1959–1977, folder: DEF 12 Nuclear Weapons 1976, RG 84, NARA; #91733 Robinson to Taipei, September 4, 1976, NSAEBB 221.

32. #5091 Unger, Taipei, August 14, 1974, NSA/PCF/EAP, Box 5, folder: China, Republic of—State Department Telegrams to SecState—EXDIS (1), FORD.

33. #7108 Unger, Taipei, November 30, 1974, Box 375: China Sensitive Chron March–June 1975 thru China Sensitive Chron Spec. Winston Lord File: Nov. 1974 re HAK Trip to Peking, folder: China–Sensitive Chron Oct. 16–Dec. 31, 1974, SPC/SP, Lord, NARA.

34. Gleysteen, ADST, 111.

35. Habib to Kissinger, memo, January 4, 1975, Box 375: China Sensitive Chron March–June 1975 thru China Sensitive Chron Spec. Winston Lord File: Nov. 1974 re HAK Trip to Peking, folder: China—Sensitive Chron January–February 1975, SPC/SP Lord, NARA; Habib to Deputy Secretary, memo, January 7, 1975, ibid.; #0079 Unger, Taipei, January 7, 1975, ibid.; #0113 Unger, Taipei, January 8, 1975, ibid.; #003603 Kissinger to Unger, January 8, 1975, ibid. On Shen's access see Barnes to Scowcroft, December 30, 1975, NSA/PCF/EAP, Box 5, folder: China, Republic of (9), FORD.

36. Robert H. Miller (EA-Acting) to Kissinger, July 3, 1976, Box 377: Control List of China Material to Mr. Eagleburger 1976 thru China Sensitive Chron July 1–September 30, 1976, folder: WL China Sensitive Chron July 1–September 30, 1976, SPC/SP Lord, NARA.

37. Burton Levin (EA/ROC) to Leonard Unger, November 13, 1974, with NSSM 212 attached, Box 1: Embassy Taipei, 1959–1977, folder: DEF-9 Military Asst–ROC 1974, RG 84, NARA. The embassy welcomed the report, except for its assessments of Taiwan's military inferiority. Unger to Levin, December

3, 1974, ibid.; Levin to Unger, February 6, 1975, folder: DEF-19 Military Asst-ROC 1975, ibid.

38. "The Operational Issues Associated with a Normalization Agreement," Box 370: Sec. Visit to Peking: NSC Reference Book—Taiwan, Nov. 1974, S/P Mr. Lord thru Sec's Meeting with the Chinese October 2, 1974, folder: Sec's Meeting with the Chinese, October 2, 1974, SPC/SP Lord, NARA.

39. Kissinger to Ford, January 6, 1975, Box 331: China Exchanges April 1–August 8, 1974 thru October–December 1975, folder: China Exchanges January 1–May 31, 1974, SPC/SP Lord, NARA; Smyser and Solomon to Kissinger, December 12, 1974, ibid.; "The Operational Issues Associated with a Normalization Agreement"; Box 370: Sec. Visit to Peking: NSC Reference Book—Taiwan, Nov. 1974, S/P Mr. Lord thru Sec's Meeting with the Chinese October 2, 1974, folder: Sec's Meeting with the Chinese, October 2, 1974, SPC/SP Lord, NARA; Kissinger to Ford, memo, "Our Future Relationship with the PRC," n.d., Box 381: President's China Trip thru Cambodia April 1975, folder: President's China Trip, SPC/SP Lord, NARA.

40. Unger to Lord, December 21, 1974, Box 375: China Sensitive Chron March–June 1975 thru China Sensitive Chron Spec. Winston Lord File: Nov. 1974 re HAK Trip to Peking, folder: China—Sensitive Chron January–February 1975, SPC/SP Lord, NARA.

41. Hummel to Kissinger, memo, November 1, 1976, Box 377: Control List of China Material to Mr. Eagleburger 1976 thru China Sensitive Chron July 1–September 30, 1976, folder: WL China Sensitive Chron October 1–December 31, 1976, SPC/SP Lord, NARA; Habib to Clements, draft, n.d., ibid.

42. George H. Aldrich (L) to Lord and Hummel, memo, November 14, 1974, Box 371: Bilateral PRC Officials April 22, 1974 thru China–Sec Kissinger, folder: China–Sec Kissinger, SPC/SP Lord, NARA.

43. Scowcroft to Aldrich, memo, n.d., Box 375: China Sensitive Chron March–June 1975 thru China Sensitive Chron Spec. Winston Lord File: Nov. 1974 re HAK Trip to Peking, folder: China Sensitive Special Winston Lord File: November 1974 re Kissinger Trip to Peking, SPC/SP Lord, NARA.

44. Aldrich to Hummel, memo, November 14, 1974, Box 371: Bilateral PRC Officials April 22, 1974 thru China–Sec Kissinger, folder: Sec Visit to Peking Bilateral Issues—S/P Mr. Lord November 1974 #1 [folder 2 of 2], SPC/SP Lord, NARA.

45. Memcon Kissinger, Habib, Lord, Gleysteen, Solomon, July 6, 1975, Box 332: China Exchanges January–September 1975 thru August 1976–January 1977, folder: China Exchanges, label missing, SPC/SP Lord, NARA.

46. "The Taiwan Side of Normalization," Box 373: President Ford's Visit to Peking International Issues December 1–5, 1975 (2 of 2) thru Visit of Sec. Kissinger to Peking, October 19–23, 1975, folder: Visit of Sec. Kissinger to Peking, October 19–23, 1975, SPC/SP Lord, NARA.

47. Freeman quoted in Tucker, *China Confidential,* 315–16.

48. Unger to Lord, January 7, 1975, Box 375: China Sensitive Chron March–June 1975 thru China Sensitive Chron Spec. Winston Lord File: Nov. 1974 re HAK

Trip to Peking, folder: China—Sensitive Chron January–February 1975, SPC/SP Lord, NARA.

49. CIA Chron, 44; #1530 Bruce, Peking, NSA/PCF/EAP, Box 15: Country File—PRC—State Department Telegrams, folder: PRC—State Department Telegrams to SecState—EXDIS (1), FORD; Hummel to Kissinger, memo, September 14, 1974, Box 376: China Sensitive Chron August 17–October 15, 1974 thru China Sensitive Chron February–April 1974, folder: China-Sensitive Chron August 17–October 15, 1974, SPC/SP Lord, NARA; Tyler, *Great Wall*, 186–87.

50. Hummel, Lord, and Solomon to Kissinger, memo, September 27, 1974, Box 370: Sec. Visit to Peking: NSC Reference Book—Taiwan, Nov. 1974, S/P Mr. Lord thru Sec's Meeting with the Chinese October 2, 1974, folder: Sec's Meeting with the Chinese, October 2, 1974, SPC/SP Lord, NARA; Background Report, "Normalization of Relations, and the Taiwan Issue," ibid.

51. Tyler, *Great Wall*, 197; Ross, *Negotiating Cooperation*, 78; Xue Mohong et al., eds., *Dangdai zhongguo waijiao* [Contemporary Chinese Diplomacy] (Beijing, 1988), 226.

52. Habib, Lord, Gleysteen, Solomon, "Peking's Current Posture towards Normalization," cover memo, July 3, 1975, Office of the Assistant to the President for National Security Affairs Henry Kissinger and Brent Scowcroft Files (1972) 1974–77, Box A1: Temporary Parallel File, folder: Kissinger-Scowcroft West Wing Office File, China Exchanges—unnumbered (15), FORD; CIA Chron, 47.

53. Habib, Lord, Gleysteen, and Solomon, memo, July 3, 1975, Office of the Assistant to the President for National Security Affairs Henry Kissinger and Brent Scowcroft Files (1972) 1974–77, Box A1: Temporary Parallel File, folder: Kissinger-Scowcroft West Wing Office File, China Exchanges—unnumbered (15), FORD.

54. Tyler, *Great Wall*, 215, 219.

55. Romberg, *Rein In*, 47; Ross, *Negotiating Cooperation*, 86; Herbert E. Horowitz (INR/REA) to Gleysteen (EA), memo, November 26, 1975, Box 381: President's China Trip thru Cambodia April 1975, folder: President's China Trip, SPC/SP Lord, NARA. The State Department's Intelligence and Research staff contradicted the CIA, dismissing the CIA's evidence as contingency planning.

56. Ross, *Negotiating Cooperation*, 60–67.

57. "Talking Points on the Taiwan Issue," July 1976, National Security Adviser Presidential Name File, Box 3, folder: Scott, Hugh, FORD; Memcon Scott, Gates, and Zhang, July 13, 1976, ibid.; Scott to Ford, July 27, 1976, WHCF Subject Files, folder: CO 34-2 PRC 5/1/75–1/20/77, box 13, FORD.

58. #1288 Gates, Peking, July 14, 1976, Box 332: China Exchanges January–September 1975 thru August 1976–January 1977, folder: China Exchanges March 1976–July 1976, SPC/SP Lord, NARA; Memcon Kissinger, Habib, Lord, Hummel, Gleysteen, and Rodman, July 14, 1976, ibid.

59. #180639 Kissinger, July 21, 1976, Box 377: Control List of China Material to Mr. Eagleburger 1976 thru China Sensitive Chron July 1–September 30, 1976,

folder: WL China Sensitive Chron July 1–September 30, 1976, SPC/SP Lord, NARA; "Peking's Hard Line on Taiwan," Intelligence and Research Harold H. Saunders to Kissinger, October 4, 1976, folder: China Sensitive Chron October 1–December 31, 1976, ibid.; Scowcroft to Ford, memo, n.d. (summer 1976), ibid.

60. Memcon Kissinger, Unger, and Habib, January 15, 1976, Box 378: China Sensitive Chron April 1–June 30, 1976 thru China Sensitive Chron July 1–September 30, 1976, folder: China-Sensitive January 1, 1976–March 31, 1976, SPC/SP Lord, NARA; Tyler, *Great Wall*, 225.

5. Derecognition

1. Chas Freeman quoted in Tucker, *China Confidential,* 316.
2. Gaddis Smith, *Morality, Reason & Power* (New York, 1986), 86–87; Jimmy Carter, *Keeping Faith* (New York, 1982), 188.
3. Armacost and Oksenberg to Brzezinski and Aaron, February 18, 1977, National Security Adviser, Staff Material, Far East, Box 2, folder: Armacost Chron File, February 18–28, 1977, CARTER; "East Asia: Where Do We Stand? Where Are We Going?" folder: April 1–12, 1977, ibid.
4. Oksenberg to Brzezinski, January 31, 1977, National Security Adviser, Staff Material, Far East, Box 1, folder: Armacost Chron File, January 1977, CARTER.
5. Freeman quoted in Tucker, *China Confidential,* 322.
6. Tyler, *Great Wall*, 234–35; Harry Thayer quoted in Tucker, *China Confidential*, 323; Zbigniew Brzezinski, *Power and Principle* (New York, 1983), 41.
7. Michel Oksenberg to the author, November 1, 2000; Gleysteen, ADST, 143–45. Patrick Tyler's version of the Oksenberg-Holbrooke airplane confrontation (in his book *A Great Wall,* 256) angered Oksenberg.
8. Zbigniew Brzezinski interview, September 18, 2002, Washington, D.C.
9. Brzezinski, *Power and Principle,* 198.
10. Ibid., 196; Brzezinski interview.
11. Tyler, *Great Wall,* 236–39.
12. Richard Holbrooke interview, March 13, 2001, New York City.
13. Brzezinski interview.
14. Cyrus Vance, *Hard Choices* (New York, 1983), 77.
15. Ibid., 79; "Taiwan's Fate Seen as Lesson in Israel," *LAT,* December 17, 1978.
16. Brzezinski, *Power and Principle,* 200.
17. Brzezinski to Carter, ca. July 1977, "China Policy Review: Recent Developments," National Security Adviser, Staff Material, Far East, Box 4, folder: Armacost Chron File, July 1–14, 1977, CARTER; Brzezinski, *Power and Principle,* 200; Oksenberg to Brzezinski, January 31, 1977, National Security Adviser, Staff Material, Far East, Box 1, folder: Armacost Chron File, January 1977, CARTER; Presidential Review Memorandum, "People's Republic of China," National Security Adviser, Staff Material, Far East, Box 2, folder: Armacost Chron File, March 1–9, 1977, CARTER. PRM 24 was leaked to the *New York Times,* June 24, 1977, A1, A3.

18. Gleysteen, ADST, 137.
19. Carter, *Keeping Faith,* 187; Brzezinski to Carter, May 17, 1977, National Security Adviser, Brzezinski Material Country File, Box 11, folder: China (Republic of China), January 1977–May 1978, CARTER; Bill Curry, "Winning Taiwan Friends," *WP,* June 9, 1977, 1.
20. Linda Matthews, "Taiwan Facing Fact It May Be Defending Itself Alone," *LAT,* November 6, 1977, 8.
21. #292 Abramowitz, Seoul, March 13, 1978, National Security Adviser, Staff Material, Far East, Box 6, folder: Armacost Chron File, March 10–21, 1978, CARTER.
22. "Arms Sales to the Republic of China," n.d., National Security Adviser, Staff Material, Far East, Box 7, folder: Armacost Chron File, April 11–18, 1978, CARTER (quote); Far East to Brzezinski, September 16, 1977, ibid., Box 4, folder: Armacost Chron File, September 1–14, 1977, CARTER.
23. Richard L. Lawson, Lt. General, Director for Plans and Policy, JCS/DOD, to DOD/AS/ISA, July 12, 1978, National Security Adviser, Brzezinski Material Country File, Box 11, folder: China (Republic of China), June–October 1978, CARTER.
24. Armacost and Oksenberg/Denend to Brzezinski, April 18, 1978, National Security Adviser, Staff Material, Far East, Box 7, folder: Armacost Chron File, April 11–18, 1978, CARTER; Holbrooke interview.
25. Robert S. Strauss to Henry Owen, Assistant to the President for Economic Affairs, June 1, 1978, National Security Adviser, Brzezinski Material Country File, Box 11, folder: China (Republic of China), June–October 1978, CARTER; Sheldon S. Cohen to Strauss, May 17, 1978, ibid.; Oksenberg to Brzezinski, July 5, 1978, ibid.
26. "Arms Sales to the Republic of China (ROC)," DOD Annex, July 1978, National Security Adviser, Staff Material, Far East, Box 65, folder: Platt Chron File, July 1978, CARTER; Harlan W. Jencks, "Taiwan in the International Arms Market," in *Taiwan in World Affairs,* ed. Robert Sutter and William Johnson (Boulder, Colo., 1994), 79 (quote).
27. Oksenberg to Brzezinski, November 7, 1978, National Security Adviser, Staff Material, Far East, Box 1, folder: Armacost East and West Reports File, November–December 1978, CARTER.
28. Jerold Schecter to Brzezinski, memo, January 29, 1977, WHCF, Subject Files Countries, CO-15, folder: CO 34-1 January 20, 1977–June 30, 1977, NA; Taylor, *Generalissimo's Son,* 328.
29. Taylor, *Generalissimo's Son,* 326.
30. Ibid., 324; "East Asia: Where Do We Stand? Where Are We Going?" folder: April 1–12, 1977, CARTER; Report #11, April 29, 1977, Brzezinski Collection, Box 41, folder: Weekly Reports [to the President], 1–15: [February 1977–June 1977], CARTER.
31. #332 Taipei to State, January 19, 1977, NSAEBB 221.
32. "Nuclear Proliferation in Taiwan and Korea," ca. February 1978, National Security Adviser, Staff Material, Far East, Box 1, folder: Armacost Evening and Weekly Reports File, January–February 1978, CARTER; Weekly Report,

Far East to Brzezinski, February 9, 1978, ibid; Joseph Yager, ed., *Nonproliferation and U.S. Foreign Policy* (Washington, D.C., 1980), 69n12, 70; #67316
State to Taipei, March 26, 1977, NSAEBB 221; Brzezinski to Carter, April 29,
1977, ibid.; #2646 Taipei, May 6, 1977, ibid.

33. #6065 Taipei, September 8, 1978, NSAEBB 221.

34. Tyler, "Taiwanese Spies Said to Penetrate Top U.S. Agencies"; Kaplan, *Fires,*
240–41.

35. Telcon Oksenberg with Shen, April 26, 1978, National Security Adviser,
Brzezinski Material Country File, Box 11, folder: China (Republic of China),
January 1977–May 1978, CARTER; Oksenberg to Brzezinski, May 30, 1978,
ibid.; Oksenberg to Brzezinski, July 28, 1978, August 1, 1978, and August 3,
1978, WHCF, Subject Files Countries, CO-15, folder: CO 34-1 January 20,
1977–January 20, 1981, NARA; Brzezinski interview.

36. Jiang Liangren, "Zhengtan shang di wannianqing—Shen Chang-huan"
[Shen Chang-huan Is an Evergreen Tree on the Political Stage], *Bashi niandi*
[Eighties Monthly], October 19–25, 1985, 24, quoted in Linda Chao and
Ramon H. Myers, *The First Chinese Democracy* (Baltimore, 1998), 80.

37. John Chang Hsiao-yen interview, November 10, 2000, Taipei; Mark Pratt interview, September 30, 2000, Washington, D.C.

38. Sullivan interview; Shaw Yu-ming interview, June 1993, Washington, D.C.

39. Holbrooke interview; C. J. Chen interview, November 7, 2003.

40. Taylor, *Generalissimo's Son,* 332; Sullivan interview; Chang Hsiao-yen interview.

41. Taylor, *Generalissimo's Son,* 332; Mark Pratt, ADST, tape 7; CIA report in
Oksenberg, weekly report to Brzezinski, July 20, 1978, National Security Ad-
viser, Staff Material, Far East, Box 1, folder: Armacost Evening and Weekly
Reports File, July–August, 1978, CARTER.

42. Lilley, *China Hands,* 210; Jim Lilley interview, March 26, 2001, Washington,
D.C.

43. J. Stapleton Roy interview, February 2, 2002, Washington, D.C.; Shen, *U.S.
and Free China,* 228–29; Brzezinski interview.

44. Evening Report, East Asia to Brzezinski, October 25, 1978, National Security
Adviser, Staff Material, Far East, Box 1, folder: Armacost Evening and Weekly
Reports File, September–October 1978, CARTER.

45. Intelligence Items, East Asia to Brzezinski, November 22, 1978, National Security Adviser, Staff Material, Far East, Box 1, folder: Armacost Evening and
Weekly Reports File, November–December 1978, CARTER.

6. Final Act

1. Vance, *Hard Choices,* 79.

2. "Statements re Arms Sales," Vertical File/ China MR-NLC-98-215 [2], folder:
MR-NLC-98-215 [1], CARTER; Mann, *About Face,* 83; Romberg, *Rein In,*
78.

3. Michel Oksenberg, "Reconsiderations: A Decade of Sino-American Relations," *Foreign Affairs* 61 (Fall 1982): 183.

4. Memcon Vance with Huang, August 24, 1977, Vertical File/China MR-NLC-98-215 [2], folder: MR-NLC-98-215 [2], CARTER.
5. Memcon Vance with Deng, August 24, 1977, ibid.
6. Tyler, A *Great Wall*, 245; Vance, *Hard Choices*, 82. The second Strategic Arms Limitation Treaty, like canal reversion, faced widespread domestic opposition. Vance also feared alienating Moscow after two years of difficult negotiations.
7. Tyler, *Great Wall*, 245–46.
8. Oksenberg to Brzezinski and Aaron, September 6, 1977, National Security Adviser, Brzezinski Material Country File, Box 8, folder: China (People's Republic of), July–September 1977, CARTER; Oksenberg to Brzezinski, September 6, 1977, ibid.; Oksenberg to Brzezinski, October 25, 1977, ibid., folder: China (Peoples Republic of), October 1977–January 1978. Huang Hua later insisted to Leonard Woodcock that he had told Vance that the US was trying to create two Chinas. #2654 Woodcock, Beijing, Vertical File/China, MR-NLC-98-215 [2], folder: MR-NLC-98-214 [1], CARTER; Gleysteen, ADST, 138.
9. Armacost and Oksenberg to Brzezinski, March 24, 1977, National Security Adviser, Staff Material, Far East, Box 6, folder: Armacost Chron File, March 22–31, 1977, CARTER.
10. Tyler, *Great Wall*, 167. These points were: (1) one China; (2) no independence for Taiwan; (3) no third party in Taiwan; (4) peaceful resolution; and (5) no attack on China.
11. Vance, *Hard Choices*, 115–16; Brzezinski, *Power and Principle*, 214; Carter to Brzezinski, n.d., Douglas Paal Papers, Box 1 (92355), folder: [China/U.S. Meetings/Trips, May 1978–September 1982] (Binder) (1 of 1), REAGAN.
12. Brzezinski, *Power and Principle*, 218–19; Memcon Brzezinski with Hua, May 22, 1978, Vertical File/China MR-NLC-98-215 [2], folder: MR-NLC-98-215 [2], CARTER.
13. Brzezinski, *Power and Principle*, 224; Carter, *Keeping Faith*, 197.
14. Brzezinski interview; Vance, *Hard Choices*, 116.
15. Brzezinski, *Power and Principle*, 227.
16. Holbrooke and Oksenberg to Woodcock, Voyager Channel, September 8, 1978, Vertical File/China MR-NLC-98-215 [2], folder: MR-NLC-98-215 [3], CARTER; Memcon Holbrooke with Han, September 12, 1978, ibid., folder: MR-NLC-98-214 [1]; Oksenberg to Brzezinski, September 13, 1978, Vertical File/China MR-NLC-98-215 [2], folder: MR-NLC-98-215 [3], CARTER.
17. Brzezinski to Carter, September 11, 1978, Vertical File/China MR-NLC-98-215 [2], folder: MR-NLC-98-215 [3], CARTER.
18. Memcon Carter with Chai, September 19, 1978, Vertical File/China MR-NLC-98-215 [2], folder: MR-NLC-98-215 [3], CARTER.
19. Oksenberg, "A Decade of Sino-American Relations," 188.
20. #224 Woodcock, Beijing, December 13, 1978, Vertical File/ China MR-NLC-98-215 [2], F: MR-NLC-98-214 [2], CARTER.
21. Romberg, *Rein In*, 94.
22. #236 Woodcock, Beijing, Vertical File/China MR-NLC-98-215 [2], folder:

MR-NLC-98-214 [2], CARTER; Brzezinski, *Power and Principle*, 229, 231; Tyler, *Great Wall*, 262–69.

23. Romberg, *Rein In*, 93, 99–101; Shirley Kan, *China/Taiwan: Evolution of the "One China" Policy: Key Statements from Washington, Beijing, and Taipei* (Washington, D.C., 2000), 4.

24. Carter, *Keeping Faith*, 209–10; *Time* interview conducted January 24 (printed February 5), 1979, CIA Chron, 75. Deng told Senator Sam Nunn (D-Ga.), "We can't tie our own hands. . . . Taiwan authorities led by Chiang Ching-kuo would become reckless and . . . Taiwan would enter into no talks at all . . . and this will lead to a settlement by armed force." #0162 CINCPAC for POLAD (Political Adviser), Peking, January 11, 1979, Vertical File/China MR-NLC-98-215 [2], folder: MR-NLC-98-214 [2], CARTER.

25. Carter, *Keeping Faith*, 200.

26. Yeh, "Carter Refuses to Apologize to Taiwan for Diplomatic Switch," Agence France-Presse, March 30, 1999, www.lexis-nexis.com (accessed July 26, 2003).

27. Oksenberg to Brzezinski, July 28, 1977, National Security Adviser, Brzezinski Material Country File, Box 11, folder: China (Republic of China), January 1977–May 1978, CARTER. Sent to Carter in Weekly Report #23, July 29, 1977, Box 41, folder: 16-30 [June 1977–September 1977], CARTER.

28. Vance, *Hard Choices*, 118; Evening Report, July 17, 1978, National Security Adviser, Staff Material, Far East, Box 1, folder: Armacost Evening and Weekly Reports File, July–August 1978, CARTER; ibid., July 25, 1978; #11164 telegram, ROC Embassy, Washington, D.C., to MOFA, July 18, 1978, and #11324 telegram, ROC Embassy, Washington, D.C., to MOFA, July 20, 1978, folder: Dole, Stone and Goldwater, MOFAA.

29. Martin Schram, "China Policy: A Born-Again Brzezinski," *WP*, February 8, 1979, A1.

30. Roy interview, February 2, 2001.

31. Taylor, *Generalissimo's Son*, 336–37; G. Eugene Martin interview, April 2002, Washington, D.C.; James Soong Chu-yu interview, November 18, 2000, Taipei.

32. Taylor, *Generalissimo's Son*, 338; Soong interview.

33. David Dean interview, June 1991, Washington, D.C.

34. Warren Christopher, *Chances of a Lifetime* (New York, 2001), 92; Mann, *About Face*, 95; Frederick Ch'ien Fu interview, November 8, 2000, Taipei.

35. Christopher, *Chances*, 93; Mann, *About Face*, 95; Carter, *Keeping Faith*, 201; #0409 Unger, Taipei, December 27, 1978, Box 10, folder: China (PRC): Reaction to Normalization, December 22–28, 1978, CARTER; #0423 Unger, Taipei, December 28, 1978, ibid.; Sullivan interview; Soong interview; Stephen Chen interview, May 1992, Washington, D.C. Chen acknowledged that police protection was intentionally lax, and relations with Americans remained difficult for months.

36. "President Chiang Ching-kuo's Five Principles on U.S.–ROC Relations in the Postnormalization Period," December 29, 1978, in *America and Island China*,

ed. Stephen Gibert and William Carpenter (Lanham, Md., 1989), 208–9; Soong interview.

37. Christopher, *Chances,* 94.

38. David Dean, ADST, 88. Fifteen years later, when William Brown saw Christopher, "the question immediately popped out of his mouth: 'Do you think that Fred Chen [*sic*] was responsible for this incident or was part of it?'" William A. Brown, ADST, 302.

39. David Lee Tawei, *The Making of the Taiwan Relations Act* (New York, 2000), 18.

40. Taylor, *Generalissimo's Son,* 340–41; Tucker, *Patterns in the Dust,* 69.

41. Vance to Carter, January 11, 1979, Plains Files, Subject Files, State Department Evening Reports, Box 39, folder: State Department Evening Reports, December 1978, CARTER; Loh I-cheng, "Taiwan: 'We'll Fight, We'll Die for Freedom,'" *New York Daily News,* December 26, 1978, 34; "Ugly Americanism," *WSJ,* February 6, 1979, 18; Loh I-cheng interview, November 8, 2000, Taipei.

42. Robert Lipshutz to Herbert Hansell, memo, January 2, 1979, Staff Offices, Counsel Lipshutz, Box 7, folder: China—Taiwan Presidential Memorandum and Legislation, December 1978–June 1979 [CF, O/A 710], CARTER; note by Lee Marks, n.d., folder: China—Twin Oaks (and other real property in the United States), December 1978–June 1979 [CF, O/A 710], ibid.

43. Meeting between Kissinger and Deng, November 28, 1974, CH #00329, DNSA, 9.

44. Lee Ta-wei, *Making of the Taiwan Relations Act,* 16.

45. Marks, *Counterrevolution in China,* 261–63; Taylor, *Generalissimo's Son,* 344.

46. Lee Ta-wei, *Making of the Taiwan Relations Act,* 35–38.

47. Hodding Carter III to Deputy Secretary, January 9, 1979, Brzezinski Collection, Geographic Files, Box 9, folder: China [People's Republic of] January–March 1979, CARTER.

48. Lee Ta-wei, *Making of the Taiwan Relations Act,* 39, 69, 177; Tucker, *Taiwan, Hong Kong, and the United States,* 135–36.

49. Nixon to Carter, December 20, 1978, Brzezinski Collection, Geographic Files, Box 9, folder: China [People's Republic of]—Alpha Channel: [December 1978–January 1980], CARTER.

7. The Taiwan Relations Acts

1. Brzezinski, *Power and Principle,* 415.

2. Holbrooke interview; Herbert Hansell interview, March 6, 2001, Washington, D.C.

3. Memcon Brzezinski, Vance, Brown, Holbrooke, Aaron, Abramowitz, Armacost, and Oksenberg, April 11, 1978, National Security Adviser, Staff Material, Far East, Box 7, folder: Armacost Chron File, April 11–18, 1978, CARTER; Goldwater to Carter, May 15, 1978, WHCF, Subject Files Countries, CO-16, folder: CO 34-1, January 1, 1978–May 31, 1978, NARA.

4. Memcon Brzezinski, Vance, Brown, Holbrooke, Aaron, Abramowitz, Armacost, and Oksenberg, April 11, 1978, National Security Adviser, Staff Material, Far East, Box 7, folder: Armacost Chron File, April 11–18, 1978, CARTER.

5. "Study of US Foreign Relations Legislation," Tab 7, Staff Offices, Counsel, Lipshutz, Box 7, folder: China Briefing Book, CARTER.

6. Hansell called on an eminent legal scholar, Stephan Risenfeld of the Hastings Law School, to carry it out. Hansell interview.

7. C. J. Chen interview, November 7, 2003.

8. Michel Oksenberg, "Congress, Executive-Legislative Relations, and American China Policy," in *The President, the Congress, and Foreign Policy,* ed. Edmund S. Muskie, Kenneth Rush, and Kenneth W. Thompson (Lanham, Md., 1986), 216; C. J. Chen interview, November 7, 2003; Stanley Roth interview, May 7, 2004, Rosslyn, Va.

9. Allen interview.

10. "Diplomatic Relations with the People's Republic of China and Future Relations with Taiwan," December 1978, National Security Adviser, Staff Material, Far East, Box 65, folder: Platt Chron File, December 1978, CARTER.

11. Hansell interview.

12. David E. McGiffert to Chairman, SCC Ad Hoc Group on China, January 23, 1979, National Security Adviser, Staff Material, Far East, Box 8-64, folder: Meetings February 19–28, 1979, CARTER.

13. Hansell interview.

14. Michel Oksenberg interview, April 1999, Washington, D.C., and Oksenberg, "Congress," 218.

15. Lee Ta-wei, *Making of the Taiwan Relations Act,* 56; Ch'ien interview.

16. Vance to Carter, January 23, 1979, Plains Files, Subject Files, State Department Evening Reports, Box 39, folder: State Department Evening Reports, January 1979, CARTER.

17. Carter, *Keeping Faith,* 211.

18. Text of the Taiwan Relations Act in Gibert and Carpenter, *America and Island China,* 222–29, quotes on 223.

19. Richard Bush analyzes Congress's decisions in *At Cross Purposes,* 150–60.

20. #5750 Vance to Beijing, March 28, 1979, National Security Adviser, Staff Material, Far East, Box 9, folder: China (PRC), January–March 1979, CARTER; #4868 Beijing to Washington, March 31, 1979, ibid.

21. Carl Ford interview, February 16, 2001, Washington, D.C.

22. Tyler, "Taiwanese Spies Said to Penetrate Top U.S. Agencies"; Kaplan, *Fires,* 275.

23. Chas Freeman quoted in Tucker, *China Confidential,* 336–37; Sullivan interview.

24. Vance to Carter, January 9, 1979, Plains Files, Subject Files, State Department Evening Reports, Box 39, folder: State Department Evening Reports, December 1978, CARTER; Vance to Carter, January 11, 1979, ibid.; Christopher to Carter, January 18, 1979, ibid.; Loh interview.

25. Brzezinski to Carter, February 8, 1979, National Security Adviser, Staff Mate-

rial, Far East, Box 66, folder: Platt Chron File, February 1–13, 1979, CARTER.

26. Charles Cross, *Born a Foreigner* (Boulder, Colo., 1999), 257.
27. Ibid., 257–60 (quotes on 259–60).
28. David Dean, ADST, 88.
29. Cross, *Born a Foreigner,* 257; Charles Cross Diary, May 27, 1981.
30. Taylor, *Generalissimo's Son,* 344–45; Pratt interview; Bush, *At Cross Purposes,* 78–80.
31. Marc J. Cohen, *Taiwan at the Crossroads* (Washington, D.C., 1988)), 261–62; Bush, *At Cross Purposes,* 80–84.

8. The Reagan Difference

1. Lauren Barrett, *Gambling with History* (New York, 1984), 56–57.
2. Even the staunch Republican and Reagan supporter Richard Cheney, who became vice president in 2000, believed that Reagan was not "intellectually curious." Haynes Johnson, *Sleepwalking through History* (New York, 1991), 323.
3. Kiron K. Skinner, Annelise Anderson, and Martin Anderson, eds., *Reagan, in His Own Hand* (New York, 2001), 36, 45–46 (quotes), 57, 58–59, 61–62.
4. Ibid., 43–44 (quote); Mann, *About Face,* 115; Allen interview. On turmoil in Taiwan see Shelley Rigger, *Politics in Taiwan* (New York, 1999), 110–24.
5. Tyler, *Great Wall,* 290, 453n5; Mann, *About Face,* 116. Fifty thousand in 1977 dollars would equal $171,000 in 2008.
6. Catherine Forslund, *Anna Chennault* (Wilmington, Del., 2002), 133; Don Oberdorfer, "Two Top Reagan Advisers Are on Taiwan's Payroll," *WP,* June 6, 1980, www.lexis-nexis.org, accessed October 19, 1999.
7. Marshall and Hunter, *The Iran-Contra Connection,* 61; Reagan to Sam Yorty, former mayor of Los Angeles, August 18, 1980, in Kiron K. Skinner, Annelise Anderson, and Martin Anderson, eds., *Reagan: A Life in Letters* (New York, 2003), 528; Peter Hannaford, ed., *Recollections of Reagan* (New York, 1997), x.
8. Allen interview. This version of the meeting with Deng is based on Tyler, *Great Wall,* 291–93; James Sterba, "Reagan Reawakens Issue of Taiwan Ties," *NYT,* August 24, 1980, A1; Jay Matthews, "China Calls Bush Visit a Failure," *WP,* August 24, 1980, A1–2.
9. George Bush and Brent Scowcroft, *A World Transformed* (New York, 1998), 93; Sterba, "Reagan Reawakens Issue of Taiwan Ties," A1.
10. "The Chinese Assail Reagan Aide's Plan," *NYT,* December 4, 1980, A7.
11. Tyler, *Great Wall,* 295; Lilley, *China Hands,* 220.
12. Cross Diary, January 16–18, 1981; John Holdridge quoted in Tucker, *China Confidential,* 356.
13. U.S. Senate, Committee on Foreign Relations, "Implementation of the Taiwan Relations Act: The First Year," in Gibert and Carpenter, *America and Island China,* 268.
14. Ch'ien interview.

15. C. J. Chen joined him in making this case. Cross Diary, February 19, 1981; Cross mentions Ch'ien passim, but especially on April 17, 1981.

16. Taylor, *Generalissimo's Son,* 363; David Dean interview, February 13, 2003, McLean, Va. Shen became secretary general in the president's office in 1984.

17. Lou Cannon, *President Reagan: The Role of a Lifetime* (New York, 1991), 187–89.

18. Alexander Haig, *Caveat* (New York, 1984), 200.

19. Tyler, *Great Wall,* 295; Ronald Reagan, *An American Life* (New York, 1990), 361.

20. Maxine Cheshire, "Behind the Scenes at Reagan's Night Out," *WP,* May 21, 1981, D1; Tyler, *Great Wall,* 308.

21. "Taiwan Relations Act," April 10, 1979, in Gibert and Carpenter, *America and Island China,* 223.

22. Lilly, *China Hands,* 230.

23. Mann, *About Face,* 113. The NSC proposed a CIA study of repercussions of such a downgrade. Gregg to McFarlane, July 6, 1982, David Laux Files, Box 90385, folder: Taiwan Arms Sales, vol. II 1982 (3 of 7), REAGAN.

24. Tyler, *Great Wall,* 299–300.

25. Arthur Hummel quoted in Tucker, *China Confidential,* 360; Mann, *About Face,* 122; Steven Weisman, "Haig Remark on China Puzzles White House Aides," *NYT,* June 27, 1981, A5.

26. Cross Diary, June 22, 1981.

27. Cross, *Born a Foreigner,* 267.

28. Carter to Reagan, September 9, 1981, FOIA request NLC 98-262; Zbigniew Brzezinski, "What's Wrong with Reagan's Foreign Policy?" *NYT Magazine,* December 6, 1981.

29. Leslie Gelb, "Arms for China and Taiwan: Twists in Diplomacy," *NYT,* October 16, 1981, A2.

30. Ross, *Negotiating Cooperation,* 314n68.

31. Anne Shutt, "As FX Decision Nears, Taiwan Sees Fighter as Symbol of US Attitudes," *Christian Science Monitor,* September 3, 1981, 6.

32. Lilley, *China Hands,* 234; Arthur Hummel quoted in Tucker, *China Confidential,* 363.

33. Gelb, "Arms for China and Taiwan," A2; Jim Lilley quoted in Tucker, *China Confidential,* 363.

34. Lilley, *China Hands,* 233. John Holdridge, by contrast, says Haig acted without Reagan's approval. Holdridge, *Crossing the Divide,* 212–13.

35. Tad Szulc, "The Reagan Administration's Push toward China Came from Warsaw," *LAT,* January 17, 1982, sec. 4, 1. The Chinese credited Reagan's reversal to their own belligerency and problems in Poland. Ross, *Negotiating Cooperation,* 191.

36. Mark Mohr interview, April 14, 2003, Washington, D.C.; Donald Gregg to William Clark, memo, January 12, 1982, William P. Clark Files, Box 6: Taiwan [Arms Sales], January 10–14, 1982, REAGAN; Janice Hinton, "The Sale of the FX Aircraft to Taiwan," Rand Graduate Institute, Santa Monica, Calif., January 1982, discusses the FX options.

37. Ch'ien, *Hui Yi Lu*, 2: 213; Mohr interview. Mohr, although deputy director of the Taiwan desk, could not read critical (NODIS) cable traffic because he disagreed with Haig's policy. Mohr says Bremer threatened to transfer him if he continued to talk to Taiwan representatives.

38. Tsai Wei-ping to William P. Clark, June 22, 1982, Laux Files, Box 90385, folder: Taiwan Arms Sales, vol. II 1982 (2 of 7), REAGAN; Arthur Hummel quoted in Tucker, *China Confidential,* 363–64; Harvey Feldman, "Taiwan, Arms Sales, and the Reagan Assurances," *American Asian Review* 19 (Fall 2001): 81.

39. Lilley to Allen, October 5, 1981, Laux Files, Box 90385, folder: Taiwan–U.S. (includes TRA) (7 of 7), REAGAN.

40. Marks, *Counterrevolution in China,* 267–69; Steven Hood, *The Kuomintang and the Democratization of Taiwan* (Boulder, Colo., 1997), 76; Tien Hung-mao, *The Great Transition* (Stanford, 1989), 81–83 (quote on 81); Kaplan, *Fires,* 328–29.

41. Lilley interview, March 26, 2001; Lilley, *China Hands,* 242; Donald Gregg to William P. Clark, May 24, 1982, Laux Files, Box 90385, folder: Taiwan Arms Sales, vol. II 1982 (2 of 7), REAGAN.

42. Douglas Brinkley, ed., *The Reagan Diaries* (New York, 2007), 76; Reagan to Deng Xiaoping, April 5, 1982, Reagan to Zhao Ziyang, April 5, 1982, and Reagan to Hu, May 3, 1982, in Gibert and Carpenter, *America and Island China,* 296–98; Lilley, *China Hands,* 242–43.

43. Lilley interview, March 26, 2001.

44. Mann, *About Face,* 125.

45. Arthur Hummel quoted in Tucker, *China Confidential,* 359.

46. #02720 Lilley, Taipei, May 19, 1982, Laux Files, Box 90385, folder: Taiwan Arms Sales, vol. II 1982 (2 of 7), REAGAN; Donald Gregg to William Clark, memo, June 1, 1982, ibid.; Haig to Reagan, memo, June 29, 1982, ibid., (5 of 7), REAGAN.

47. Arthur Hummel in Tucker, *China Confidential,* 367.

48. #2419 Stoessel to Taipei, June 9, 1982, Laux Papers, Box 90385, folder: Taiwan Arms Sales, vol. II 1982 (1 of 7), REAGAN.

49. Tsai to Clark, June 22, 1982, Laux Papers, Box 90385, folder: Taiwan Arms Sales, vol. II 1982 (2 of 7), REAGAN.

50. Shen, *U.S. and Free China,* 289; Colin Powell, *My American Journey* (New York, 1995), 289; Barrett, *Gambling,* 333.

51. Don Oberdorfer, "Reagan Renews Assurance on Taiwan Arms," *WP,* July 3, 1982, A13; #02951 Taipei, May 29, 1982, transcript of Goldwater's press conference at Chiang Kai-shek Airport, Laux Files, Box 90385, folder: Taiwan Arms Sales, vol. II 1982 (2 of 7), REAGAN.

52. Taylor, *Generalissimo's Son,* 371; Oberdorfer, "Reagan Renews Assurance"; Reagan to Nackey Scripps Gallowhur, June 28, 1982, in Ralph E. Weber and Ralph A. Weber, eds., *Dear Americans* (New York, 2003), 66; Bill Peterson, "Conservatives Push for Taiwan Arms," *WP,* July 9, 1982, A5; Percy to Clark, July 2, 1982, Laux Files, Box 90385, folder: Taiwan Arms Sales, vol. II 1982 (6 of 7), REAGAN.

53. Entry for June 8, 1983, in Hau Pei-tsun, *Ba nian can mou zong zhang ze ji* [Diary of Eight Years as Chief of the General Staff] (Taipei, 2000), 117–18.

54. Gaston Sigur quoted in Tucker, *China Confidential*, 368–69; Dean interview, February 13, 2003.

9. American Assurances

1. Don Oberdorfer, "China Sees Diplomatic Victory in Pact," *WP*, August 18, 1982, www.lexis-nexis.com (accessed March 17, 2005).

2. Dean interview, February 13, 2003.

3. Mohr, Dean (February 13, 2003), Ch'ien, and John Chang interviews; Feldman, "Taiwan, Arms Sales, and the Reagan Assurances," 79, 81; Lilley, *China Hands,* 247.

4. Feldman, "Taiwan, Arms Sales, and the Reagan Assurances," 86.

5. Ibid., 77–78; Ch'ien, *Hui Yi Lu,* 214–20.

6. Feldman, "Taiwan, Arms Sales, and the Reagan Assurances," 87–88. Elsewhere, Feldman concluded that the nonpaper had been Gaston Sigur's work; Lilley interview, March 26, 2001.

7. Feldman, "Taiwan, Arms Sales, and the Reagan Assurances," 89–90.

8. Ch'ien, *Hui Yi Lu,* 220.

9. William Rusher, contribution to Hannaford, ed., *Recollections of Reagan,* 150; Oberdorfer, "China Sees Diplomatic Victory in Pact."

10. "China Says U.S. Is Trying to Distort Taiwan Pact," *NYT,* August 22, 1982, A5.

11. This discussion is based on a George Shultz interview, June 8, 2004, Palo Alto, Calif.; William Brown, ADST, 54; Dean interview, February 13, 2003; "Reagan Responds to Conservative Criticism," *Human Events,* February 26, 1983, 19. Ch'ien said he first learned of it six years later; see *Hui Yi Lu,* 224; Lilley, *China Hands,* 249. General Hau Pei-tsun first refers to it in his diary (*Ba nian can mou zong zhang ze ji*) on July 22, 1988.

12. "Reagan Responds to Conservative Criticism."

13. Ronald Steel, "Shultz's Revenge," *New York Review of Books,* September 23, 1993, 34.

14. George Shultz, *Turmoil and Triumph* (New York, 1993), 382.

15. Shultz interview.

16. Edward Neilan, "Reagan's Odyssey Confirms Importance of Ties to Japan," *WT,* November 11, 1983; C. J. Chen interview, March 16, 2001, Washington, D.C.; Soong interview.

17. Mann, *About Face,* 128.

18. Ibid., 128–29; Jim Mann, *Rise of the Vulcans* (New York, 2004), 115.

19. Gaston Sigur quoted in Tucker, *China Confidential,* 358; William Clark Jr. interview, March 29, 2001, Washington, D.C.

20. Gary Weis interview, January 22, 2001, Mt. Vernon, Va.; Mann, *Rise of the Vulcans,* 127.

21. Dean interview, February 13, 2003; Mann, *Rise of the Vulcans,* 127.

22. Harry Harding, *A Fragile Relationship* (Washington, D.C., 1992), 135–36.

23. Arthur Hummel quoted in Tucker, *China Confidential,* 358.

24. John Poindexter to Bud McFarlane, November 1983, Laux Papers, Box 90385, Box 1 of 2, folder: Taiwan–US (including TRA) (7 of 7), REAGAN.

25. Ross, *Negotiating Cooperation,* 234.

26. Nayan Chanda, "A Technical Point," *FEER* 131 (August 26, 1986): 26.

27. Lilley interview, March 26, 2001; Hau, *Ba nian,* entry for October 3, 1983, 409–10.

28. Ch'ien, *Hui Yi Lu,* 226; Weis interview; Mohr interview.

29. Interview with Department of State official, not for attribution, 2003.

30. Selig Harrison, "Interview with Hu Yaobang," *FEER* 133 (July 24, 1986): 26–27; Ross, *Negotiating Cooperation,* 217; Weis interview; Shultz, *Turmoil and Triumph,* 386.

31. Bernard Gwertzman, "U.S. Backs Bank Seat for China," *NYT,* March 22, 1983, D14; "Reagan Reaffirms Line on Recognition of China," *Financial Times,* November 30, 1983, 6.

32. William Rusher, contribution to Hannaford, *Recollections of Reagan,* 150–51; Hau, *Ba nian,* entries for July 10 and 20, 1983, 358–59, 365. A US military source who wished to remain unnamed also complained about the "junk" that was sold to Taiwan in the 1980s.

33. Hau, *Ba nian,* entries for January 10 and February 16, 1984, 459–60, 478.

34. Carl Goldstein, "The New China Lobby," *FEER* 132 (November 6, 1986): 44–45.

35. Hau, *Ba nian,* entry for August 16, 1987, 1186.

36. Ibid., entry for September 2, 1987, 1196.

37. Jencks, "Taiwan in the International Arms Market," 87.

38. "U.S. Industry Aiding Taiwan in Developing National Fighter to Meet Threat from PRC," *Aviation Week & Space Technology* (March 31, 1986), 31; Hau, *Ba nian,* entries for May 4 and September 8, 1984, 530–31, 605; Douglas Paal interview, March 9, 2001, Washington, D.C.; David Laux interview, August 17, 2000, Arlington, Va.; David Keegan interview, January 12, 2001, Washington, D.C.; Tang Fei interview, May 30, 2001, Washington, D.C.

39. Taylor, *Generalissimo's Son,* 391; Lilley, *China Hands,* 252–53; Hau, *Ba nian,* entries for May 3, 22, and 23, 1985, 726, 734; July 2, 1985, 759–60.

40. Taylor, *Generalissimo's Son,* 393.

41. Hau, *Ba nian,* entries for November 1 and 11, 1984, 632, 637.

42. Nayan Chanda, "Defence: Hi-Tech Diplomacy: US Technology Sales to India and China to Reap Political Gains," *FEER* 131 (February 20, 1986): 36; Hau, *Ba nian,* entry for November 20, 1987, 1238; Jim Mann, "Taiwan to Lobby against US Naval Aid to China," *LAT,* January 23, 1985, www.lexisnexis.com accessed October 10, 1999.

43. Lou Cannon, "Finding Capitalism in China Provides an Out on Old Stance," *WP,* May 7, 1984, A2.

44. Shultz interview; Brinkley, *Reagan Diaries,* 211.

45. "Reagan Said to Assure Taiwan on His China Visit," *NYT,* April 26, 1984, A4; Reagan, *An American Life,* 368–69; Glen Emery, "Conservatives See Taipei as 'Litmus Test' for Reagan," *WT,* January 12, 1984, A5.

46. Ch'ien to Clark, memo, November 10, 1983, Laux Papers, Box 90385, Box 1 of 2, folder: Taiwan–US (including TRA) (7 of 7), REAGAN; Christopher Wren, "Reagan and Zhao Reportedly Clash on Foreign Policy," *NYT*, April 28, 1984, A1.

47. Edward Neilan, "Nationalists Fear Arms Sales to Peking," *WT*, April 26, 1984, A6; "Across the Strait," *Newsweek*, May 7, 1984, 32.

48. Roger Fontaine, "Peking Arms, Atom Deals Worry Taipei Government," *WT*, May 2, 1984, A12 (quote); Mark Baker, "China and U.S. Agree Nuclear Power Deal," *Financial Times*, April 27, 1984, A20; Harding, *Fragile Relationship*, 185–86.

49. Richard Fairbanks, Assistant Secretary for Congressional Relations, to Solarz, draft, November 12, 1981, Laux Papers, Box 90385, Box 1 of 2, folder: Taiwan–US (including TRA) (7 of 7), REAGAN.

50. Taylor, *Generalissimo's Son*, 386.

51. Ibid., 385–91; Hood, *Kuomintang and the Democratization of Taiwan*, 79. Robert Sutter, then of the US Congressional Research Service, discovered that Wang and his associates received promotions while incarcerated and were paroled early. Tucker, *Taiwan, Hong Kong, and the United States*, 183.

52. Jeane Kirkpatrick, "Dictatorships and Double Standards," *Commentary*, November 1979; Cannon, *President Reagan*, 85, 434. Kirkpatrick had minimal influence on policy and less on Asia issues, but her views reflected a general predisposition of the Reagan administration about human rights and US policy. Judith Ewell, "Barely in the Inner Circle: Jeane Kirkpatrick," in *Women and American Foreign Policy*, ed. Edward P. Crapol (Westport, 1987), 158–65.

53. Taylor, *Generalissimo's Son*, 391.

54. Hau, *Ba nian*, entries for January 26 and 28, 1984, 469, 470–71.

55. Albright and Gay, "Taiwan: Nuclear Nightmare Averted," 59–60; Hau, *Ba nian*, entry for October 18, 1983, 418–19, November 9, 1983, 429–30; January 20, 1988, 1270; Tim Weiner, "How a Spy Left Taiwan in the Cold," *NYT*, December 20, 1997, A7. Jim Lilley observed to Weiner, "You pick a comer, put the right case officer on him and recruit him carefully . . . and keep in touch."

56. Jeffrey Smith and Don Oberdorfer, "Taiwan to Close Nuclear Reactor," *WP*, March 24, 1988, A32; Stephen Engelberg with Michael Gordon, "Taipei Halts Work on Secret Plant to make Nuclear Bomb Ingredient," *NYT*, March 23, 1988, A1, 15; Hau, *Ba nian*, entry for January 20, 1988, 1270; Hau Pei-tsun interview, November 9, 2000, Taipei.

57. John K. Singlaub, *Hazardous Duty* (New York, 1991), 453–56, 464–66, 492; Johnson, *Sleepwalking*, 280–86; Robert Gates, *From the Shadows* (New York, 1997), 311–13; Benjamin Weiser, "Singlaub Suggested an Earlier Fund Diversion," *WP*, March 20, 1987, A1, 14.

58. Oliver L. North to Robert C. McFarlane, "Assistance for the Nicaraguan Resistance," December 4, 1984, Iran-Contra Affair, 2983–99, IC00644, DNSA.

59. Christopher Andrew, *For the President's Eyes Only* (New York, 1995), 480; Theodore Draper, *A Very Thin Line* (New York, 1991), 84.

60. "Iran-Contra Affair," Report of the Congressional Committees, 100th Congress, 1st sess., Washington, D.C., 1987, 44–45, 63, 69–70, 124; Richard H. Melton to Elliott Abrams, secret memorandum, May 12, 1986, Iran-Contra Affair, 1983–88, EC02801, DNSA.

61. Weiser, "Singlaub Suggested an Earlier Fund Diversion," A14.

62. Frederick Kempe, *Divorcing the Dictator* (New York, 1990), 287, 315, 325. In 1989 Taiwan's deep pockets funded debt relief in Costa Rica with a $1.5 billion contribution. Susumu Awanohara, "Political Purse Strings," *FEER* (October 19, 1989): 10.

63. Joel Millman, "Taiwan's Central American Links," *Jane's Defence Weekly,* November 26, 1988, 1330; Kempe, *Divorcing the Dictator,* 58, 287–88. Taiwan also sold arms to the left in El Salvador, according to Larry Rohter, "Noriega's Lawyer Presses Ex-Pilot," *NYT,* October 2, 1991, A20.

64. Lilley interview, March 26, 2001; Dean interview, February 13, 2001.

65. Martin Lasater, *The Taiwan Issue in Sino-American Strategic Relations* (Boulder, Colo., 1984), 137–39. Many Americans thought it was conciliatory, and Jim Lilley credited US policy. Lilley, *China Hands,* 231.

66. Martin Lasater, "The PRC's Force Modernization: Shadow over Taiwan and U.S. Policy," *Strategic Review* (Winter 1984): 62. Though the concept had been discussed earlier, "One country, two systems" is usually dated from a conversation between Deng and Professor Winston Yang Liyu of Seton Hall University on June 26, 1983. Chen Jian sets it in the context of a discussion on February 22, 1984, with a delegation from the Center for Strategic and International Studies led by Zbigniew Brzezinski. Chen, "Beijing's Changing Policies toward Taiwan," 25–52.

67. Mann, *About Face,* 154.

68. Dickson, *Democratization in China and Taiwan,* 211–12.

69. Hau, *Ba nian,* entry for November 7, 1986, 833–34.

70. Shultz interview; Harding, *Fragile Relationship,* 161.

71. Martin Lasater, "Reading Tea Leaves on America's Taiwan Policy," *WSJ,* April 27, 1987, 25; Hau, *Ba nian,* entry for October 1, 1987, 1208. Shultz does not mention his 1987 trip in his memoir.

72. Ray Cline interview; Carl Goldstein, "Security Links Remain Despite Lost Diplomatic Ties," FEER 131 (May 8, 1986): 30; Victor Marchetti and John D. Marks, *The CIA and the Cult of Intelligence* (New York, 1980), 256.

10. Shifting Ground

1. Parmet, *George Bush,* 148, 157.

2. Ibid., 172–73.

3. High-level official commenting at the Miller Center for Public Affairs Conference, University of Virginia, December 1999.

4. Parmet, *George Bush,* 182; Memcon Mao with Kissinger, Bush, et al., October 21, 1975, in Burr, *Kissinger Transcripts,* 397; Michael Duffy and Dan Goodgame, *Marching in Place* (New York, 1992), 180.

5. George Bush, "Our Deal with Peking: All Cost, No Benefit," *WP*, December 24, 1978, D1.

6. David Greenberg, "Fathers & Sons: George W. Bush and His Forebears," *New Yorker*, July 12 and 19, 2004, 96; Lilley, *China Hands*, 216–17.

7. David Dean, "U.S. Relations with Taiwan," in Chiu Hungdah, Hsing-wei Lee, and Chih-yu Wu, eds., *Implementation of the Taiwan Relations Act: An Examination after Twenty Years* (Baltimore, 2001); Parmet, *George Bush*, 176.

8. Bush, "Our Deal with Peking."

9. "Bush Said to Continue US Cooperation with ROC on Basis of TRA," CNA, December 23, 1988, www.lexis-nexis.com (accessed Jun 3, 2004).

10. Andrew Rice, "Brent Scowcroft Calls Iraq War 'Overreaction,' ," *New York Observer*, September 6, 2004; Duffy and Goodgame, *Marching in Place*, 137–38.

11. Mann, *About Face*, 79–80.

12. James Baker, *The Politics of Diplomacy* (New York, 1995), 29–32.

13. Parmet, *George Bush*, 349.

14. Martin Anderson, a close Reagan adviser, told this to Bush's biographer Parmet. Parmet, *George Bush*, 361.

15. "Taiwan Comments on 'Distressing' Rumors of US Mediation with China," BBC Summary of World Broadcasts, Part 3: The Far East, Africa and Latin America, February 27, 1989, FE/0395/A1/1; "Bush Should Not Be Pressed to Nudge ROC toward Reunification," CNA, February 25, 1989, www.lexis-nexis.com (accessed June 3, 2004), discusses a *WSJ* editorial; Laux interview, August 17, 2000.

16. Robert Sutter, *U.S. Policy toward China* (Lanham, Md., 1998), 26, 29.

17. Chao and Myers, *First Chinese Democracy*, 192–96; interview with an anonymous American official, September 2004, Washington, D.C. Shaw Yu-ming, then director-general of the Government Information Office, recalled a similar experience at the University of Chicago in 1968. Shaw Yu-ming interview, November 17, 2000, Taipei.

18. Clayton Jones, "China Killings Spark Muted Outcry," *Christian Science Monitor*, June 19, 1989, 4.

19. Lin Wen-cheng and Lin Chen-yi, "National Defense and the Changing Security Environment," in *Assessing the Lee Teng-hui Legacy in Taiwan's Politics*, ed. Bruce Dickson and Chao Chien-min, (Armonk, N.Y., 2002), 242; Winston Lord, "China and America: Beyond the Big Chill," *Foreign Affairs* 68 (Fall 1989): 1–26.

20. David Dean quoted in Tucker, *China Confidential*, 449.

21. Daniel A. Mica and J. Terry Emerson, eds., *Fredrick F. Chien* (Tempe, Ariz., 1995), 20; Mann, *About Face*, 269; Ding Mou-shih interview, November 9, 2000, Taipei.

22. Harding, *Fragile Relationship*, 282–83; Mann, "Western Nations Open Way for Taiwan to Join GATT," *LAT*, September 19, 1992, A6. The US coached Taipei, and in September 1992, with US support and Beijing's acquiescence, GATT established a working group to facilitate Taipei's admission.

23. Harry Harding notes that this term was used most frequently by Robert Scalapino, *The Last Leninists* (Washington, D.C., 1992), 20. See Harry Harding, "Taiwan and Greater China," in *Taiwan in the World,* ed. Robert G. Sutter and William R. Johnson (Boulder, Colo., 1994), 246.

24. Leslie Gelb, "Breaking China Apart," *NYT,* November 13, 1991, A25.

25. Steven Goldstein, "The Impact of Domestic Politics on Taiwan's Mainland Policy," *Harvard Studies on China* 2 (1998): 62–90. Goldstein notes that the MAC was created to curb, not advance, activity by Taiwan enterprises on the mainland. Lilley, *China Hands,* 367.

26. Richard Bush, "Lee Teng-hui and 'Separatism,'" in *Dangerous Strait,* ed. Nancy Bernkopf Tucker (New York, 2005), 77–78.

27. Sheryl WuDunn, "Taiwan Opposition Pushes for Independence," *NYT,* September 19, 1991, A6.

28. Dennis Engbarth, "Taiwan's Defense Ministry Denies Coup Rumors," *SCMP,* August 17, 1993.

29. Alan Wachman, *Taiwan: National Identity and Democratization* (Armonk, N.Y., 1994), 147–51 and passim; Chao Chien-min, "DPP's Factional Politics and the Issue of Taiwan Independence," in *Assessing Chen Shui-bian's First Year,* Sigur Center Paper no. 14 (Washington, D.C., 2001), 59.

30. James Lilley, "A Formula for China-Taiwan Relations," *Asian WSJ,* September 6, 1991, 10.

31. Lisa Beyer, "The Center Holds—for Now," *Time,* September 3, 1990, 35; Jim Mann, "Next Step: Taiwan to US—We're Back," *LAT,* July 28, 1992, H1; Gelb, "Breaking China Apart"; Nicholas Kristof, "China Attacks Ex–U.S. Envoy for Stand on Taiwan," *NYT,* August 18, 1991, A6.

32. Ed Ross interview, August 20, 2004, Arlington, Va.; Ford interview.

33. Smith, *Morality, Reason & Power,* 61–64; Sheryl WuDunn, "For Taiwan, New Access to Western Arms," *NYT,* September 24, 1991, A7 (quote); Peter Stone, "Exporting Weapons," *Atlanta Constitution,* January 3, 1993, B1; Lyn Bixby, "Peace Pays Dividends for Makers of Weapons," *Hartford Courant,* October 25, 1992, A1.

34. "Relationship between ROC and US Congress to Remain Stable," CNA, November 10, 1988, www.lexis-nexis.com (accessed June 3, 2004).

35. WuDunn, "For Taiwan, New Access to Western Arms"; Peter Wickenden, "Taiwan 2: Two Confident Steps Forward," *Financial Times,* October 10, 1991, 34.

36. #01972 Stanley Brooks, Taipei, to AIT Washington, March 21, 1991, FOIA case. The first IDF squadron went into service in February 1994.

37. #05160 Brooks, Taipei, to AIT Washington for Donald Anderson (DOS/EAP/DAS), Douglas Paal (NSC), and James Lilley (DOD/EAP/AS), FOIA.

38. Don Oberdorfer, "1982 Arms Policy with China Victim of Bush Campaign, Texas Lobbying," *WP,* September 4, 1992, A31.

39. Robert Suettinger, *Beyond Tiananmen* (Washington, D.C., 2003), 141.

40. Robert Koenig, "Politics Made Bush Speed Up F-15 Sale, House Members Say," *St. Louis Post-Dispatch* (September 24, 1992), A22; John Goshko, "U.S. Agrees to Provide Israel with Helicopters, Place Other Equipment There,"

WP (September 27, 1992), www.lexis-nexis.com (accessed January 26, 2005); R. W. Apple Jr., "The 1992 Campaign: Political Pulse—Missouri: Missouri's Words of Advice to Bush: Jobs, Jobs, Jobs," *NYT,* September 29, 1992, www .lexis-nexis.com (accessed January 26, 2005).

41. Mann, *About Face,* 266; Lilley, *China Hands,* 377.

42. #04677 Hallford, Taipei, to AIT Washington, July 2, 1991, FOIA. Hallford believed Ministry of National Defense officials were willing to provide information because they saw the fighter gap as real. Lee Teng-hui interview, October 17, 2003, Tamsui, Taiwan.

43. Mattel was a leading toy company. "This Sale Is a Mirage," *Time,* July 13, 1992, 9; Mann, "Next Step." In 1999 the Defense Department, in "The Security Situation in the Taiwan Strait," contended that "its technical sophistication . . . is believed to be superior to any aircraft produced and deployed by China to date." "The Security Situation in the Taiwan Strait," Report to Congress Pursuant to the FY99 Appropriations Bill, February 26, 1999, 8, www.fas.org/news/taiwan/1999/twstrait_02261999.htm (accessed June 10, 2008.

44. Comments to the author by a participant in the interagency discussion groups, not for attribution, 1993; Mann, *About Face,* 264.

45. #04677 Hallford, Taipei, to AIT Washington, July 2, 1991, FOIA. Negotiations with Israel in the 1980s for the Kfir aircraft might similarly have been meant to create leverage. Yitzhak Shichor, "Israel's Military Transfers to China and Taiwan," *Survival* (Spring 1998): 72–73.

46. Lee Teng-hui, *The Road to Democracy* (Tokyo, 1999), 134.

47. Natale Bellocchi interview, July 15, 2003, Potomac, Md.; Mann, *About Face,* 265.

48. Joseph Borich (EAP/RA/TC) to Lynn Pascoe (EAP), memo, October 16, 1992, FOIA.

49. Weis interview; Ch'ien interview; Lien Chan interview, November 17, 2000, Taipei; Tang Fei interview; Andrew Yang Nien-tzu, defense analyst, as cited in Mann, "Next Step"; Jim Mann, "Targeting Taiwan for Arms Deals," *LAT,* March 14, 1994, A1.

50. Mann, "Next Step."

51. #04160 Hallford, Taipei, to AIT Washington, June 13, 1991, FOIA.

52. Brian Hsu, "Hau Defends Himself over Warship Deal," *Taipei Times,* October 23, 2000, 1.

53. James Mann, "Taiwan Arms Deals Open Doors to Civilian Contracts," *LAT,* March 15, 1994, A1; Qian Qichen, *Ten Episodes in China's Diplomacy* (New York, 2005), 231–43. Investigation of the scandal continued some fifteen years after the original deal was closed. Both *Le Monde* and the *Taipei Times* covered the investigation of the scandal fifteen years after the original deal was closed.

54. Geoffrey Crothall and Michael Chugani, "Furious Beijing in Arms Talks Threat," *SCMP,* September 4, 1992, 1.

55. Susumu Awanohara, "Arms Sales B: Pork Barrel Roll," *FEER* 155 (September 17, 1992): 12.

56. Barbara Starr, "F-16 Sale Justified by 'Discrepancy,'" *Jane's Defence Weekly,* September 12, 1992, 5.

57. Suettinger, *Beyond Tiananmen,* 141.

58. It is not known whether this story is true. NSC Project Oral History Roundtables: The China Policy and the NSC (November 4, 1999), 22.

59. Lena Sun and Stuart Auerbach, "F-16, Grain Decisions Draw Flack," *WP,* September 4, 1992, A27.

60. John Garver, *Face Off* (Seattle, 1997), 52–60.

61. Suettinger, *Beyond Tiananmen,* 143.

62. For a discussion of the secret talks, see chapter 12.

63. On the relationship between Wang and Jiang Zemin, see David M. Lampton, *Same Bed, Different Dreams* (Berkeley, 2001), 342–46. Koo published his memoir shortly before his death.

64. "Beijing and Taipei Agree to Disagree on 'One China,'" *Renmin Ribao,* November 16, 1992. According to Su Chi and Cheng An-kuo, "The main difference was that Taipei meant 'one China' to say, 'Taiwan and the mainland are both parts of China,' while Beijing only meant: 'Taiwan is a part of China.' In other words, we held out for parity, while Beijing demanded hegemony." Su and Cheng, *"One China, Different Interpretations"—A Historical Account of the Consensus of 1992* (Taipei, 2002), I–VIII, www.taiwansecurity.org (accessed August 2003); Su Chi, "Domestic Determinants of Taiwan's Mainland Policy," paper presented at the Peace across the Taiwan Strait Conference, Oxford University, May 2002; Xu Shiquan, "Possible Key to Deadlock of Cross-Strait Relations," typescript, July 27, 2000. Chen Shui-bian claimed that SEF Vice President Hsi Hwei-yow denied there was a 1992 consensus. Koo Chen-foo wrote that Taiwan delegates suggested saying there were different interpretations but China would not agree. Lillian Wu, "Chen Shui-bian Says '1992 Consensus' Cannot Be Accepted Since It Doesn't Exist," CNA; text in English, FBIS, CPP20050503000100.

65. Goldstein, "The Impact of Domestic Politics on Taiwan's Mainland Policy," 73. DPP whip Chen Shui-bian, however, protested his party's exclusion, circumscribing the negotiators' flexibility. Bush, *Untying the Knot,* 161.

66. #247625 Washington to AIT Taipei, August 1, 1992, FOIA.

67. #06049 AIT Taipei to AIT Washington, August 25, 1992, for Lynn Pascoe (DOS/EAP/DAS), Douglas Paal (NSC), and James Lilley (DOD/EAP/AS), FOIA.

68. Dean interview, February 13, 2003; Raymond Whitaker, "Peking Anger at US Fighter Sale," *Independent* (London), September 4, 1992, 10; Ford interview.

69. Rand Beers (PM) and Lynn Pascoe (EAP) to Frank Wisner (T), Action Memorandum, September 11, 1992, FOIA; Crothall and Chugani, "Furious Beijing in Arms Talks Threat"; Julian Baum, "Arms Sales A: A Foot in the Door: US Decision Opens New Options to Taiwan Military," *FEER,* 155 (September 17, 1992): 12; Ford interview; Lien interview.

70. Jencks, "Taiwan in the International Arms Market," 96.

71. U.S. Congress, House, International Relations Committee, Asia and Pacific

Subcommittee, Hearings, *Taiwan, China and the Taiwan Security Enhancement Act,* September 15, 1999; Ford interview; Michael R. Gordon, "Secret U.S. Study Concludes Taiwan Needs New Arms," *NYT,* April 1, 2001, www.lexis-nexis.com (accessed August 11, 2004).

72. William Clark Jr., "Policy toward Taiwan Needs a Clinton Redo," *International Herald Tribune,* August 30, 1994.

11. Change and Continuity

1. Jason DeParle, "The Man inside Bill Clinton's Foreign Policy," *NYT Magazine,* August 20, 1995, www.nytimes.com (accessed October 19, 1999).
2. Anthony Lewis, "The Clinton Doctrine," *NYT,* January 22, 1993, A17; Anthony Lake, "From Containment to Enlargement," address presented to the Nitze School of Advanced International Studies, Washington, D.C., September 21, 1993; DeParle, "The Man inside Bill Clinton's Foreign Policy."
3. Warren Christopher, *In the Stream of History* (Stanford, 1998), 31. The phrase "peaceful evolution" troubled the Chinese, who saw it as a strategy to overthrow the government, not unlike Dean Acheson's comment in the China White Paper of 1949.
4. Ibid., 61–64 (quotes on 64).
5. Christopher, *Chances,* 238–39.
6. Ibid., 92, 94.
7. Winston Lord quoted in Tucker, *China Confidential,* 476–77.
8. Benedict Anderson, *Imagined Communities* (New York, 1991); Dickson and Chao, *Assessing the Lee Teng-hui Legacy,* 5.
9. Simon Long, "Republic of China: Friends Are Easy to Make, Influence Is Hard to Come By," *Daily Telegraph,* October 18, 1993, 7.
10. Garver, *Face Off,* 24, 31.
11. "Aristide Urges Total Embargo against Haiti," *St. Louis Post-Dispatch,* October 29, 1993, www.lexis-nexis.com (accessed August 6, 2004).
12. Geoffrey Crothall, "US Accused of Blocking Attempts to Reunify," *SCMP,* September 1, 1993, 11.
13. Suettinger, *Beyond Tiananmen,* 204.
14. Mann, *About Face,* 317.
15. Bellocchi interview; Suettinger, *Beyond Tiananmen,* 204–5.
16. Lee Teng-hui interview.
17. Winston Lord quoted in Tucker, *China Confidential,* 478; Peter Tomsen interview, January 4, 2002, Va.
18. Mann, *About Face,* 319.
19. Suettinger, *Beyond Tiananmen,* 206; Romberg, *Rein In,* 158–60. Until 2002 the chief of the General Staff outranked the defense minister and reported directly to the president. But he could come to Washington, and the minister could not.
20. Chang Jaw-ling, "The Making of Clinton's New Taiwan Policy," paper presented at Conference on US Taiwan Policy Consultation, New York, Decem-

ber 1994; Dirk Kirschten, "The Other China," *National Journal* 26 (October 8, 1994), www.nationaljournal.com (accessed October 28, 1999); Julian Baum, "Regrets Only," *FEER* 157 (September 22, 1994): 15.

21. Robb's opening statement, U.S. Congress, Senate, Committee on Foreign Relations, Hearing of the East Asian and Pacific Affairs Subcommittee, *Review of U.S. Policy toward Taiwan,* September 27, 1994; Hank Brown quoted in Kirschten, "The Other China."

22. Ambassador James R. Lilley, testimony, U.S. Congress, Senate, Committee on Foreign Relations, Hearing of the East Asian and Pacific Affairs Subcommittee, *Review of US Policy toward Taiwan,* September 27, 1994. Such names as Republic of China or Taiwan would reintroduce too much "officiality" into the relationship.

23. Transcript of Background Briefing on Taiwan Policy Review by Senior Administration Official, September 7, 1994.

24. Romberg, *Rein In,* 161n20. On national security grounds Clinton planned to ignore Congress's actions regarding visas.

25. Ch'ien, disregarding Lee's political motives, argued against co-opting the UN campaign from the DPP in 1993 because it couldn't succeed. Lee denied there was friction or knew Ch'ien opposed the trip. Zou Jing-wen, *Li Denghui Zhizheng Gaobai Shilu* [Record of Revelations on Lee Teng-hui's Administration] (Taipei, 2001), 265; Dean interview, February 13, 2003; Tomsen interview; Nadia Tsao, "Lobbying Firm Draws Fire," *Taipei Times,* July 10, 2000, www.taipeitimes.com/News/local/archives/2000/07/10/43189 (accessed March 24, 2002).

26. Richard Bush interview, December 16, 2004, Washington, D.C.; Mann, *About Face,* 320; Elaine Sciolino, "Taiwan's Lobbying in US: Mixing Friendship and Hardball," *NYT,* April 9, 1996, A12. On the slush fund, see Ting Yu-chou with Wang Shichun, *Ting Yu-chou Hui-I-lu* [Memoirs of Ting Yu-chou] (Taipei, 2004), ch. 19, 28–29, in FBIS Translated Excerpts, CPP20050707000248 and CPP20050708000239; and Lawrence Chung, "Leakage of Classified Documents," *Straits Times,* March 27, 2002. Liu, an economist who served as the head of the KMT's Business Management Committee, supervised the use of the party's $3 billion in assets, out of which the TRI was financed beginning in early 1994. According to Elaine Sciolino, Cassidy was already on retainer in 1994 (at $125,000 per month) and received an additional $2.5 million for the visa campaign.

27. James Mann, "Congress and Taiwan: Understanding the Bond," in Ramon Myers, Michel Oksenberg, and David Shambaugh, eds., *Making China Policy* (Lanham, Md., , 2001), 209.

28. Lampton, *Same Bed, Different Dreams,* 48; Simon Beck, "Taiwan Out from Under Its Shell," *SCMP,* February 16, 1995, www.lexis-nexis.com (accessed April 13, 2005).

29. Sutter, *U.S. Policy toward China,* 71.

30. Jiang Zemin's original speech, "Continuing to Strive toward the Reunification of China," is excerpted in "Jiang on Taiwan Straits," where the eight points are highlighted, http://2006.chinataiwan.org/web/webportal/

W5097695/Uadmin/A5111811.html (accessed May 5, 2008). See Michael Swaine, "Chinese Decision-Making Regarding Taiwan, 1979–2000," in David M. Lampton, *The Making of Chinese Foreign and Security Policy* (Stanford, 2001), 314.

31. Lee, *The Road to Democracy*, 122–23; Romberg, *Rein In*, 163–64; Garver, *Face Off*, 41–46; Chang Jung-feng interview, November 15, 2000, Taipei.

32. Robert Suettinger interviews, March 16, 2001, Arlington, Va., and January 1, 2006, Bethesda, Md. According to a Xinhua commentary: "Anyone with some political common sense knows that it is the U.S. Government and not the Congress that formulates and implements the country's foreign policies." Romberg, *Rein In*, 167; Robert Ross, "The 1995–1996 Taiwan Strait Confrontation: Coercion, Credibility, and Use of Force," *International Security* 25 (Fall 2000): 91.

33. Mann, *About Face*, 323–24.

34. William J. Clinton, *My Life* (New York, 2004), 270, 326.

35. Nicholas Kristof, "Taiwan, Winning New Friends, Hopes for Another One in Clinton," *NYT*, January 18, 1993, A10.

36. Stone, "Exporting Weapons."

37. Barton Gellman, "U.S. and China Nearly Came to Blows in 1996," *WP*, June 21, 1998, A21; Romberg, *Rein In*, 175n62. The idea that a Jiang visit could be linked to, and help excuse, a Lee visit was apparently not discussed.

38. William J. Perry and Ashton B. Carter, *Preventive Defense* (Washington, D.C., 1999), 93.

39. Suettinger, *Beyond Tiananmen*, 215; Tyler, *Great Wall*, 25.

40. Zou, *Li Denghui Zhizheng Gaobai Shilu*, 286.

12 Taiwan Strait Crisis

1. Winston Lord quoted in Tucker, *China Confidential*, 480.

2. Bush, *Untying the Knot*, 52–53; Tucker, *China Confidential*, 481; Qian, *Ten Episodes in China's Diplomacy*, 247.

3. Ross, "The 1995–1996 Taiwan Strait Confrontation," 91–95.

4. Winston Lord quoted in Tucker, *China Confidential*, 481; Andrew Hsia interview, November 17, 2000, Taipei.

5. Qian Qichen, *Ten Episodes in China's Diplomacy*, 244.

6. Mann, *About Face*, 328; Testimony of Winston Lord, Hearing of the East Asian and Pacific Affairs Subcommittee of the SFRC, "U.S. Policy toward China," September 27, 1994.

7. This meant substituting "defensive-defense" (*shoushi fangyu*) for "offensive-defense as one" (*gong shou yi ti*). Alexander Chieh-cheng Huang, "Taiwan's View of Military Balance and the Challenge It Presents," in *Crisis in the Taiwan Strait*, ed. James Lilley and Chuck Downs (Washington, D.C., 1997), 282–83.

8. Tai Ming Cheung, "Chinese Military Preparations against Taiwan over the Next 10 Years," in Lilley and Downs, *Crisis*, 47–48, 53–54.

9. Jean-Pierre Cabestan, "Taiwan's Mainland Policy: Normalization, Yes; Reuni-

fication, Later," in *Contemporary Taiwan,* ed. David Shambaugh, (Oxford, 1998), 235.

10. Suettinger, *Beyond Tiananmen,* 232; Qian, *Ten Episodes in China's Diplomacy,* 248.

11. The reader will recall that an oral promise to that effect had been made years earlier by both Nixon and Kissinger, but they had been unwilling to put those politically risky words on paper. In May 1978 Carter did commit to paper his request that Brzezinski reiterate Nixon's so-called five points.

12. Garver pointed to Clinton's omission of a reference to peaceful settlement as a critical oversight; see *Face Off,* 74–75, 80. The Chinese took note of US complaints that summer and of its silence in the fall. Ross, "The 1995–96 Taiwan Strait Confrontation," 101, 103; Suettinger, *Beyond Tiananmen,* 247.

13. Garver, *Face Off,* 101; Christie Su, "President Says No to Nuclear Arms," *Free China Journal,* August 4, 1995.

14. Garver, *Face Off,* 82; Ross, "The 1995–1996 Taiwan Strait Confrontation," 96–98; Department of State daily press briefings, September 18, 1995, and September 21, 1995.

15. William Perry, telephone interview, July 21, 2004; Patrick Tyler, "As China Threatens Taiwan, It Makes Sure U.S. Listens," *NYT,* January 24, 1996, A3; Gellman, "U.S. and China Nearly Came to Blows," A20.

16. Perry, telephone interview. Ross would appear to be wrong on this; see his "1995–1996 Taiwan Strait Confrontation," 104.

17. Tang Shubei, deputy director of Beijing's Taiwan Affairs Office, interview, March 6, 1996, in Patrick Tyler, "Beijing Steps Up Military Pressure on Taiwan Leader," *NYT,* March 7, 1996.

18. Tyler, *Great Wall,* 7.

19. Suettinger, "U.S. 'Management' of Three Taiwan Strait 'Crises,'" in Swaine and Zhang, *Managing Sino-American Crises,* 282–83; Suettinger, *Beyond Tiananmen,* 251; Tyler, *Great Wall,* 27. Tyler dates the Shalikashvili meeting with Clinton incorrectly.

20. Perry and Carter, *Preventive Defense,* 96.

21. Mann, *About Face,* 336–37; Suettinger, *Beyond Tiananmen,* 255; Tyler, *Great Wall,* 22, 33–34. Navy officers believed the Strait was too narrow for a serious show of force.

22. Charles Hutzler, "Hired Guns," *WSJ,* July 16, 2004.

23. Joseph Prueher interview, October 27, 2000, Beijing; Maggie Farley, "U.S. Carrier Off Taiwan Trails Analysts' Worries in Its Wake," *LAT,* March 19, 1996, 8; Tyler, *Great Wall,* 33.

24. Americans saw Beijing's limitation to a single additional missile as a sign of success. Luo Yuan of China's Academy of Military Sciences contended that firing even one missile after the US intervened showed that China would not be deterred. Luo Yuan interview, October 25, 2000, Beijing.

25. "Ma Seeks Scripts for Possible Mainland Attack," *China Post,* May 4, 2004, www.chinapost.com.tw/taiwan/2004/05/04/48440/Ma-seeks.htm (accessed April 21, 2008).

26. Mark Stokes, interview by e-mail, November 21, 2004.

27. John Pomfret, "Taiwanese Mistake Led to 3 Spies' Executions," *WP,* February 20, 2000, A1, 29; interviews with civilian and military US government intelligence consumers and a general from Taiwan's military intelligence bureau, autumn 2004.

28. The participants included Su Chih-cheng, a protégé of Lee Teng-hui, and Cheng Shu-min, chair of China Television in Taiwan. They met on nine occasions between 1988 and 1992 with mainland counterparts, who were probably Yang Side, a PLA career officer, the secretary general of the Taiwan Affairs Leading Small Group, the director of the Central Committee's Taiwan Work Office, and a representative of Yang Shangkun, and Wang Zhaoguo, 1991–96 Director of the Taiwan Affairs Office of the CCP Central Committee and 1990–96 Director of the Taiwan Affairs Office of the State Council, as well as Wang Daohan. Others said to have been involved on the Taiwan side were Chen Charng-ven, an attorney, a member of the board of the SEF, and the head of Taiwan's Red Cross, and Shi Hwei-yow, deputy secretary general of SEF 1993–96 and vice chairman of MAC 1996–97. On the Beijing side there were Tang Shubei, deputy director of the PRC State Council's Taiwan Affairs Office and vice chairman of ARATS, and Zhou Ning. "Secret Contacts Said to Have Been Conducive to Cross-Strait Peace," CNA, July 19, 2000; "Historic 1993 China, Taiwan Talks Took Five Years of Groundwork," Agence France-Presse, July 19, 2000, www.lexis-nexis.com (accessed July 20, 2004); Su and Cheng, *"One China, Different Interpretations,"* I–VIII; "Taiwan's New Government Won't Hold Secret Talks with China," Agence France-Presse, July 20, 2000, www.lexis-nexis.com (accessed July 20, 2004); Jay Chen and Flor Wang, "US Should Have Been Informed of Secret Emissaries between Taiwan, China," CNA, July 20, 2000 ; Bush, *Untying the Knot,* 289.

29. Lee Teng-hui noted twenty-seven trips by Su Chih-cheng. Zou, *Li Denghui Zhizheng Gaobai Shilu,* 182; Cabestan, "Taiwan's Mainland Policy," 227; Mann, *About Face,* 337; Gary Klintworth, "Lessons Learned," in Greg Austin, ed., *Missile Diplomacy and Taiwan's Future* (Canberra, 1997), 253; Katsuhiko Shimizu, "Who Are the new Emissaries between Taiwan and China?—A Secret Connection between Chinese President Jiang Zemin and Taiwan's Former President Lee Teng-hui," *Aera,* September 11, 2000, FBIS, East Asia, JPP20000905000062.

30. Tyler, *Great Wall,* 33.

31. Huang, "Taiwan's View of Military Balance," 284–85; Michael Swaine and James Mulvenon, *Taiwan's Foreign and Defense Policies* (Santa Monica, Calif., 2001), 29.

32. Interview of Pentagon official, April 2002, Washington, D.C.; Perry, telephone interview.

33. Lin and Lin, "National Defense and the Changing Security Environment," 243.

34. Prueher interview; Bruce J. Dickson, "Taiwan's Challenge to U.S. Foreign Policy," in Dickson and Chao, *Assessing the Lee Teng-hui Legacy,* 275, 285n12.

35. According to the contents of classified documents revealed during the 2002 slush-fund scandal (see *Next Magazine,* March 21, 2002, 10–23), Japanese

Prime Minister Hashimoto Ryutaro and Vice Defense Minister Akiyama Masahiro were paid by Taiwan to include the island under the purview of a US–Japan TMD agreement. Chung, "Leakage of Classified Documents."

36. Lake repeated the observation twice and made certain I had written it down. Anthony Lake interview, October 27, 1999, Washington, D.C.; Swaine, "Chinese Decision-Making Regarding Taiwan," 329.

37. Jeff Bader interview, November 1, 2004, Washington, D.C.

38. Suettinger, *Beyond Tiananmen,* 250, 257; Ray Burghardt interview, November 6, 2000, Taipei; Tien Hung-mao interview, spring 2000, Washington, D.C.

39. James Kelly interview, March 17, 2006, Washington, D.C.; Michael J. Green interview, April 11, 2006, Washington, D.C.

40. Sara Fritz, "Probe of Donors Said to Include Taiwan Envoy," *LAT,* October 29, 1996; Keith Richburg and Dan Morgan, "Taiwanese: Ex-Clinton Aide Said He Was Raising Money: No Direct Request Made, Political Scientist Says," *WP,* October 30, 1996, A16; Laurence Zuckerman, "Taiwan Keeps a Step Ahead of China in U.S. Lobbying," *NYT,* March 14, 1997, www.lexis-nexis.com (accessed January 26, 2005).

41. Jason Hu Chih-chiang, telephone interview, February 2, 2005.

42. Hu, telephone interview; Mann, "Congress and Taiwan," 212.

43. Department of Defense, "Executive Summary of Report to Congress on Supplementation of the Taiwan Relations Act," Report by the Office of Net Assessment in the Office of the Secretary of Defense, pursuant to Public Law 106-113, in Lester L. Wolff, Jon D. Holstine, and John J. Brady, eds., *A Legislative History of the Taiwan Relations Act,* vol. 4 (Arlington, Va., 2004), 547.

44. John Pomfret, "In Fact and Tone, U.S. Expresses New Fondness for Taiwan," *WP,* April 30, 2002, A12.

45. James Mann, "U.S. Has Secretly Expanded Military Ties with Taiwan," *LAT,* July 24, 1999, www.lexis-nexis.com (accessed December 2000); Micheal D. Slack, in a telephone interview, February 4, 2005, revealed a contemporary study from the State Department's political-military affairs office that also emphasized skills over equipment.

46. John Corbett and Mark Stokes interviews, February 21, 2001, Washington, D.C.; Bush, *Untying the Knot,* 113;

47. Off-the-record observation by a senior Taiwan military official, May 2001.

48. Interviews with US and Taiwan military officers, 2001. On defense contractors see Michael D. Swaine, *Taiwan's National Security, Defense Policy, and Weapons Procurement Processes* (Santa Monica, Calif., 1999), 69–70. Also critical on the US side was Karl Eikenberry, and on the Taiwan side Lt. General Herman Schwai, Generals Fu Taixing and Liu Xiangbin, and a staff officer, Yu Hsiao-pin. Michael Pillsbury, "The US Role in Taiwan's Defense Reforms," paper presented at ITDSS Conference, February 29, 2004, Taipei; Randall Schriver interview, January 29, 2001, Rossyln, Va.

49. Kurt Campbell interview, January 25, 2001, Washington, D.C.

50. Pillsbury, "The US Role in Taiwan's Defense Reforms"; Darryl Johnson interview, November 25, 2001, Washington, D.C.

13. Setting the Record Straight

1. Tucker, "Strategic Ambiguity or Strategic Clarity?" in Tucker, *Dangerous Strait,* 188–98.

2. Mann, *About Face,* 355; Romberg, *Rein In,* 182; Keith Richburg, "Taiwan Says President's Remarks Misinterpreted," *WP,* November 10, 1997, www .lexis-nexis.com (accessed February 2, 2005); Lee San Chouy, "Taiwan Fears the Long-Term Impact," *Straits Times,* October 27, 1997, A32.

3. R. W. Apple Jr., "A Domestic Sort with Global Worries," *NYT,* August 25, 1999, A10.

4. Suettinger, *Beyond Tiananmen,* 343, 436; Bader interview; James Steinberg interview, March 13, 2001, New York, N.Y.

5. Zou, *Li Denghui Zhizheng Gaobai Shilu,* 299; Lu Shumin interview, October 27, 2000, Beijing; James Mann, "U.S.–China Summit Has Taiwan Jittery," *LAT,* May 27, 1998, A7; Lee Siew Hua, "US Allays Taiwan Fears over Beijing Summit," *Straits Times,* May 14, 1998, www.lexis-nexis.com (accessed August 5, 2005).

6. Quote from *Time* magazine of June 22, 1998, in Lin and Lin, "National Defense and the Changing Security Environment," 246.

7. Hu, telephone interview; Nicholas Kristof, "Taipei Is on Alert for Sign of Betrayal," *NYT,* June 27, 1998, A9; Peter Landers, Susan Lawrence, and Julian Baum, "Hard Target," *FEER* 180 (September 24, 1998); Lampton, *Same Bed, Different Dreams,* 107; Robert Sutter, "Taiwan–Mainland China Talks: Competing Approaches and Implications for U.S. Policy," Congressional Research Service Report, 98-887F, October 28, 1998, 3; John Pomfret, "Clinton Declaration on Independence Irks Taiwan," *WP,* July 1, 1998, A26.

8. John Pomfret, "China Tells Taiwan to 'Face Reality,'" *WP,* July 10, 1998, A28.

9. Bader interview; Susan Shirk interview, June 7, 2004, San Diego, Calif.

10. Andrew Nathan, "What's Wrong with American Taiwan Policy," *Washington Quarterly* (Spring 2000): 97–98.

11. Lampton, *Same Bed, Different Dreams,* 102–3.

12. Bush interview, December 16, 2004; Flor Wang, "AIT Chairman Reassures Taiwan on US Policy," CNA, July 8, 1998, www.lexis-nexis.com (accessed January 17, 2005).

13. Philip Shenon, "No Policy Turn, U.S. Assures Taiwan Again," *NYT,* July 7, 1998, A9; "President Lee Reiterates ROC Sovereignty to US Envoy," CNA, July 6, 1999, www.lexis-nexis.com (accessed July 1999).

14. Swaine and Mulvenon, *Taiwan's Foreign and Defense Policies,* 139; Susan Shirk interview.

15. Lee Teng-hui, "U.S. Can't Ignore China," *WSJ,* August 3, 1998, in Kan, *China/Taiwan: Evolution of the "One China" Policy,* 37; Nicholas Kristof, "Taiwan Chief Sees Separate Identity," *NYT,* September 2, 1998, A4.

16. Swaine and Mulvenon, *Taiwan's Foreign and Defense Policies,* 148.

17. Stephen Fidler and Tony Walker, "Big Powers Flex Muscles over Taiwan," *Fi-*

nancial Times, February 10, 1999, www.lexis-nexis.com (accessed February 1999); "Report to Congress on Theater Missile Defense Architecture Options for the Asia-Pacific Region," May 4, 1999, www.dod.mil/pubs/tmd050499 .pdf (accessed July 25, 2005).

18. Landers, Lawrence, and Baum, "Hard Target"; Erik Eckholm and Steven Lee Myers, "Taiwan Asks U.S. to Let It Obtain Top-Flight Arms," *NYT,* March 1, 2000, A12.

19. Swaine and Mulvenon, *Taiwan's Foreign and Defense Policies,* 35; Eckholm and Myers, "Taiwan Asks U.S. to Let It Obtain Top-Flight Arms."

20. Bonnie Glaser, "Chinese Missiles and Taiwan TMD: Can a New Round of the Cross-Strait Arms Race Be Averted?" Paper presented at Fifth Roundtable on US–China Policy and Cross-Strait Relations, National Committee on American Foreign Policy, August 29–31, 1999, 6. Richard Bush notes specifically that members of Congress avoided this most logical option. Bush, *At Cross Purposes,* 157.

21. This two-states discussion is a result of many interviews with high-level officials and former officials in Taiwan (2000) and the US as well as; Bush, "Lee Teng-hui and 'Separatism,'" 87–89.

22. Lee Teng-hui interview; Lee, *The Road to Democracy,* 130; Zou, *Li Denghui Zhizheng Gaobai Shilu,* passim.

23. Lin Bih-jaw interview, November 16, 2000, Tamsui, Taiwan.

24. Chang Jung-feng interview; Su Chi interview, November 10, 2000, Taipei; Zou, *Li Denghui Zhizheng Gaobai Shilu,* 229 (quote).

25. Shirk interview; Bush, *Untying the Knot,* 220; Zou, *Li Denghui Zhizheng Gaobai Shilu,* 228.

26. Seth Faison, "Taiwan President Implies His Island Is Sovereign State," *NYT,* July 13, 1999, www.lexis-nexis.com (accessed January 20, 2005); coverage of Su Chi press conference in *United Daily News,* July 13, 1999; Su Chi, *Weixian bianlu: Cong lianguolun dao yibian yiguo* [Brinkmanship: From the Two States Theory to One Country on Each Side] (Taipei, 2003), 77–114.

27. Zou, *Li Denghui Zhizheng Gaobai Shilu,* 245.

28. Yang Jiemian, "Clinton Administration's Taiwan Policy Readjustment," *Beijing Meiguo Yanjiu,* December 5, 1999, FBIS; "China's Show of Force to Taiwan," *Advertiser* (South Australia), July 19, 1999, www.lexis-nexis.com (accessed September 1, 2006).

29. Lee Teng-hui, *Jianzheng Taiwan: Chiang Ching-kuo yu wo* [Witness Taiwan: President Chiang Ching-kuo and Me] (Taipei, 2004), 82.

30. Peter S. Goodman, "Foreign Funding Can Be Problematic for U.S. Academics," *WP,* November 29, 1996, www.lexis-nexis.com (accessed February 7, 2005); Zou, *Li Denghui Zhizheng Gaobai Shilu,* 293–95; Kenneth Lieberthal interview, July 25, 2001, Washington, D.C.

31. Lee, *The Road to Democracy,* 130.

32. Ching Cheong, "Don't Take Sides, Taiwan Urges US," *Straits Times,* July 30, 1999, www.lexis-nexis.com (accessed February 2, 2005); Zou, *Li Deng-hui Zhizheng Gaobai Shilu,* 256.

33. Interview with anonymous high-level Clinton administration official, August

2003; David E. Sanger, "Clinton and Jiang Heal Rift and Set New Trade Course," *NYT,* September 12, 1999, 1.

34. Interviews with anonymous high-level officials in Washington and Taipei.

35. Lee Teng-hui, *Ya Zhou de Zhi Lue* [Asia's Wisdom and Strategy] as excerpted in the *Taipei Liberty Times,* July 22, 2000, FBIS, CPP20000724000144.

36. Coverage of Clinton's news conference, *NYT,* July 22, 1999, www.lexis-nexis .com (accessed March 7, 2004); Ray Burghardt interview, April 18, 2005, New York, N.Y.

37. John Pomfret, "Chinese Threat Tests Taiwan's Preparedness," *WP,* July 27, 1999, A13; David A. Shlapak, David T. Orletsky, and Barry A. Wilson, *Dire Strait?* (Santa Monica, Calif., 2000), 19n22.

38. Interview with anonymous senior American official, August 2004.

39. Swaine, *Taiwan's National Security, Defense Policy, and Weapons Procurement Processes,* 9, 11, 13–16, 24.

40. Pillsbury, "The US Role in Taiwan's Defense Reforms," 2.

41. Robert G. Kaiser and Steven Mufson, "'Blue Team' Draws a Hard Line on Beijing," *WP,* February 22, 2000; Michael T. Klare, "'Congagement' with China? GOP Hawks Want Containment; Others Favor More Trade and More Toughness," *Nation,* April 30, 2001.

42. Jim P. Doran, Senior Professional Staff Member for Asia and Pacific Affairs, "U.S. Defense Policy toward Taiwan: Indefensible," Staff Trip Report to the Senate Foreign Relations Committee, March 8, 2001; James Mann, "Push for Taiwan Arms Sale Shows the Hand of Politics," *LAT,* April 23, 2001; Report to Congress on Implementation of the Taiwan Relations Act, Pursuant to PL 106-113, December 19, 2000, www.napsnet@nautilus.org (accessed December 22, 2000).

43. Thomas Ricks, "Admiral Takes Stand against Pro-Taiwan Legislation," *WP,* March 8, 2000, A32.

44. David Sanger, "Decision in Taiwan: The White House," *NYT,* March 20, 2000, A8.

45. Mann, "Push for Taiwan Arms Sale Shows the Hand of Politics."

46. For the text of each bill see Congressional, H.R. 1838, either 1999, 106th Cong., 1st sess., or 2000, 106th Cong., 2nd sess., www.lexis-nexis.com, congressional.

47. Coen Blaauw, telephone interviews, July 30, 2004, and August 2, 2004, Washington, D.C; Tsao, "Lobbying Firm Draws Fire."

48. Judy Sarasohn, "Special Interest, One Taiwan Account Lost, Another Gained," *WP,* July 6, 2000, A19; Jim Mann, "Taiwan's New Era Looks a Lot Like Old One," *LAT,* July 12, 2000, A1, A5. Cassidy had earlier been retained by the Taiwan Research Institute, an arm of the KMT, which paid it $10 million over six years. The TSI worked with the DPP and had been established in 1995 as the Makoto Foundation.

49. Peter Brookes interview, December 27, 2000, Washington, D.C.; Ford interview.

50. Interviews with high-level officials from the US and Taiwan governments, 1999; C. J. Chen interview, November 7, 2003; Hu, telephone interview.

51. Mann, "Push for Taiwan Arms Sale Shows the Hand of Politics"; Ford interview.

52. Steven Mufson and Helen Dewar, "Senate GOP Tables Taiwan Bill; Island's Leaders Urge Delay of Military Plan during Transition," *WP,* April 27, 2000, A24; Joseph Kahn and Erik Eckholm, "Senate Republicans Try to Delay Vote on Taiwan Security Bill," *NYT,* April 28, 2000, A11; Ted Galen Carpenter, "Prospects for the TSEA under Bush," *Taipei Times,* February 7, 2001, www .taiwansecurity.org (accessed February 2001); Eckholm and Myers, "Taiwan Asks to Let It Obtain Top-Flight Arms."; Chen Shui-bian to Jesse Helms, May 1, 2000, provided by Coen Blaauw of FAPA.

53. Janine Zacharia, "The Phalcon: Squandering Years of Cooperation?" *Jerusalem Post,* June 30, 2000, www.lexis-nexis.com (accessed July 15, 2004); Herb Keinon, "Peres Offers China Farms, Not Phalcons," *Jerusalem Post,* August 18, 2000; Richard McGregor, "China Furious at US Role in Foiling Israel Defence Deal," *Financial Times,* July 14, 2000; Ann Scales and Charles M. Sennott, "Barak Offers a Concession to Clinton: Israelis, at Camp David Talks, Say They Won't Sell Plane to China," *Boston Globe,* July 13, 2000.

54. David Finkelstein, *Washington's Taiwan Dilemma, 1949–1950* (Fairfax, Va., 1993), 21–30.

55. "US Arms Sales Would Boost Taiwan's Defense Capacity: Analysts," Agence France-Presse, September 29, 2000, www.taiwansecurity.org (accessed October 13, 2000).

56. Xu Shiquan interview, October 25, 2000, Beijing; Cindy Sui, "U.S. Urges Chinese 'Restraint' on Taiwan," *WP,* February 19, 2000, A22; Shelley Rigger, *From Opposition to Power* (Boulder, Colo., 2001), 213; "The One China Principle and the Taiwan Issue," February 21, 2000, http://english.peopledaily .com.cn/features/taiwanpapar/taiwan.html (accessed February 15, 2005).

57. Clay Chandler, "China Threatens Voters in Taiwan," *WP,* March 16, 2000, 1, 22. The *Post* communicated its view in its editorial titled "Premier Zhu Don Corleone," *WP,* March 16, 2000, A26.

58. Bill Clinton, speech to the US Business Council, February 24, 2000, Washington, D.C., www.fas.org/news/china/2000/000224-prc2.htm (accessed June 8, 2005).

59. Jay Chen and Sophia Wu, "Taiwan's Democratization Contributes to Peace: AIT Chief," CNA, September 17, 1998, www.lexis-nexis.com (accessed December 5, 2004); Richard Bush, "The United States Role in the Taiwan Straits Issue," speech presented at the University of Illinois at Carbondale, December 7, 1998; Bush, *Untying the Knot,* 262.

14. The Influence of Democracy

1. Dickson, "Taiwan's Challenge to U.S. Foreign Policy," 279.

2. President Chen Shui-bian's inauguration speech, "Taiwan Stands Up," May 20, 2000, Office of the President, www.gio.gov.tw (accessed April 21, 2008).

3. Steven Mufson, "U.S. Sees Election as 'Fresh Opportunity' to Resolve Tensions," *WP,* March 19, 2000, A29.

4. Chen Shui-bian, "Bridging the New Century," December 31, 2000, www.gio .gov.tw/taiwan-website/4-oa/chen/press891231.htm.

5. "Wang Daohan Meeting with Chen Shui-bian's Envoy Cited," *Hong Kong Tung Fang Jih Pao,* April 7, 2000, FBIS, CPP20000407000030; Joseph Fewsmith and Stanley Rosen, "The Domestic Context of Chinese Foreign Policy: Does 'Public Opinion' Matter?" in *The Making of Chinese Foreign and Security Policy,* ed. Lampton, 173; Bush, *Untying the Knot,* 116; Justin Brown, "America sends envoys to calm China-Taiwan rhetoric," *Christian Science Monitor,* March 22, 2000, www.lexis-nexis.com (accessed June 14, 2005); "Chinese Reassure U.S. on Dispute with Taiwan," *Atlanta Journal and Constitution,* April 2, 2000, www.lexis-nexis.com (accessed June 14, 2005); Andrew Perrin, "Taiwanese Don't Fear Blockade," *Courier Mail* (Queensland, Australia), May 18, 2000, 18.

6. Vice Premier Qian Qichen, interview by Wu Hsiao-li, Phoenix TV, Hong Kong, September 11, 2000, FBIS, CPP2000911000019; John Pomfret, "Beijing Signals New Flexibility on Taiwan," *WP,* January 5, 2001, www.lexis-nexis.com (accessed March 16, 2005); Zhao Shuisheng, "Coping with Chen Shui-bian's Administration: Beijing's Wait-and-See Policy and Two-Pronged Strategy," in *Assessing Chen Shui-bian's First Year* (Washington, D.C., 2001), 67–83.

7. David Postman and Catherine Tarpley, "Bush at Boeing, Backs China Trade," *Seattle Times,* May 18, 2000, A1; Charles Babington and Dana Milbank, "Bush Advisers Try to Limit Damage," *WP,* April 27, 2001, A19; "Liu Case Controversy: Hong Kong Newspaper Prints Secret NSB Details," *Taipei Times,* March 25, 2002.

8. Dennis Van Vranken Hickey, "Continuity and Change: The Administration of George W. Bush and US Policy toward Taiwan," *Journal of Contemporary China* 13 (August 2004): 464.

9. Richard Armitage interview, March 1, 2006, Arlington, Va.

10. "US Foreign-Policy Experts Call for Defense of Taiwan," August 24, 1999, www.globalsecurity.org/wmd/library/news/taiwan/1999/e-08-25-99-17.htm (accessed June 14, 2005); Jonathan S. Landay, "How Far Would US Go to Protect Taiwan?" *Christian Science Monitor,* September 3, 1999, 3. Armitage nevertheless spoke positively about strategic ambiguity. Jane Perlez, "Bush Carries Some Baggage in Developing China Stance," *NYT,* August 29, 1999, A15.

11. Robert G. Kaiser and Steven Mufson, "Taiwan: Crisis in the Making?" *WP,* March 16, 2000, A22; Mann, *Rise of the Vulcans,* 114–15, 234–35; Paul Wolfowitz, "Remembering the Future," *National Interest* (Spring 2000): 42–45 (quote on 45).

12. Andrew Tully, "Why Rumsfeld Wants to Engage China," *Asia Times Online,* February 12, 2005, www.atimes.com/atimes/China/GB12Ad01.html (accessed February 14, 2005).

13. Steven Mufson, "U.S.–China Ties in the Balance: Rights Resolution Could Signal Harder Line toward Beijing," *WP,* February 17, 2001, www.lexis-nexis .com (accessed August 25, 2004); Armitage interview; for a critical view see

Chalmers Johnson, "No Longer the 'Lone' Superpower: Coming to Terms with China," Japan Policy Research Institute, Working Paper no. 105 (March 2005).

14. Torkel Patterson interview, April 13, 2006, Rosslyn, Va.

15. Condoleezza Rice, "Promoting the National Interest," *Foreign Affairs* 79 (January–February 2000): 56–57.

16. Patterson interview.

17. Klare, "'Congagement' with China?"; Zalmay M. Khalilzad et al., *The United States and a Rising China: Strategic and Military Implications* (Santa Monica, Calif., 1999).

18. Patterson interview.

19. Mann, *Rise of the Vulcans,* 281.

20. David Sanger, "Bush Is Offering the Taiwanese Some Arms but Not the Best," *NYT,* April 24, 2001, http://query.nytimes.com/gst/fullpage.html?res= 9B04E3DC1639F937A15757C0A9679C8B63&scp=1&sq=bush+is+ offering+the+taiwanese+some+arms&st=nyt (accessed May 13, 2008).

21. John Keefe, *Anatomy of the EP-3 Incident, April 2001* (Alexandria, Va., 2002). Keefe was serving as special assistant to the US ambassador in Beijing at the time.

22. William Foreman, "Taiwan Worried about US-China Deal," Associated Press, April 12, 2001, www.lexis-nexis.com (accessed August 25, 2004).

23. "US 'Keeps Tabs on China via Signals Base in Taipei,'" Agence France-Presse, January 18, 2002; Wendell Minnick, "Taiwan–USA Link Up on SIGINT," *Jane's Defence Weekly,* January 24, 2001; Wendell Minnick, "Spook Mountain," *Asia Times,* March 6, 2003, www.atimes.com/atimes/activities/ ChinaEC06 Ad03.html (accessed June 29, 2007). For a discussion about satellite photography and the National Security Bureau, see www.fas.org (accessed June 23, 2000).

24. John Pomfret, "Taiwan Faces Divide over Possible U.S. Radar Deal," *WP,* April 20, 2001, A14; Sanger, "Bush Is Offering the Taiwanese Some Arms"; Neil Lu and Fang Wen-hung, "ROC Foreign Minister Seeks Correction from US Newspaper," CNA, April 20, 2001.

25. Greg Torode, "And the Award Goes to—Taiwan," *SCMP,* April 19, 2001.

26. Maubo Chang, "Taiwan: Government Not Informed of USA Dropping Annual Arms Sales Review," CNA, April 25, 2001.

27. Brian Knowlton, "Analysts See Comments as a Toughening of American Position," *International Herald Tribune,* April 25, 2001; transcript of CNN's *Larry King Live,* "Dick Cheney Discusses the Beginning of the Bush Administration," April 27, 2001.

28. Zou, *Li Denghui Zhizheng Gaobai Shilu,* 234–35; Wendell Minnick, "Washington Establishes Military Hotline with Taipei," *Jane's Defence Weekly,* October 29, 2003; Mark Stokes, e-mail interview.

29. Monique Chu, "US Likely to Walk Similar Taiwan Strait Line," *Taipei Times,* December 18, 2000, 3; "U.S. Official Supports Cross-Strait Dialogue with No Preconditions," CNA, June 22, 2001; Wolfowitz, "Remembering the Future."

30. It remains unclear whether the driver, Chang Jung-tsai, committed a crime. He was not prosecuted even after Chen became president.

31. Rigger, *From Opposition to Power,* 221–26.

32. Kelly interview.

33. Bush, *At Cross Purposes,* 179–218; Bush, *Untying the Knot,* 345–46.

34. Armitage interview.

35. Shirley Kan, "US–China Counter-Terrorism Cooperation: Issues for US Policy," Congressional Research Service brief no. RS21995, May 12, 2005, 4.

36. John Pomfret, "China Also Wants U.S. Help against 'Separatists,'" *WP,* September 19, 2001, A11; Charles Snyder, "Powell Assures Taipei There's No Deal with China," *Taipei Times,* September 23, 2001.

37. Ting, *Ting Yu-chou Hui-I-lu,* CPP20050708000239, ch. 25.

38. Lin Mei-chun, "Media Took Remarks Out of Context: Chen," *Taipei Times,* August 7, 2002, www.taipeitimes.com/News/front/archives/2002/08/07/159289 (accessed May 8, 2005); "Chen Repeats Call for Taiwan to Take 'Own Road,'" *China Post,* July 30, 2002.

39. Bonnie Glaser, "China's Taiwan Policy in the Wake of 'One Country on Each Side," paper presented at the Conference on US–Taiwan–China Relations of the National Committee on American Foreign Policy and the Chinese-Eurasia Foundation, October 7–8, 2002, New York, N.Y.; John Pomfret, "China Suggests Missile Buildup Linked to Arms Sales to Taiwan," *WP,* December 10, 2002, A1 (accessed April 20, 2005).

40. Dennis Van Vranken Hickey, "Continuity and Change: The Administration of George W. Bush and US Policy toward Taiwan," *Journal of Contemporary China* 13 (August 2004): 474.

41. Interview with a senior US official, 2004, Washington, D.C.

42. John Pomfret, "Taiwanese Leader Condemns Beijing, 'One China' Policy," *WP,* October 7, 2003, A18.

43. Taiwan political parties identify themselves by color. The pan -Blue coalition included the KMT, James Soong's People's First Party, and the Chinese New Party. The pan-Green group incorporated the DPP, Lee Ten-hui's Taiwan Solidarity Union, and the Taiwan Independence Party.

44. Liu Yung-hsiang, "Shaheen's Manipulation Leads to Inconsistency in U.S. Policy toward Taiwan," *China Times,* November 17, 2003, A13; Frank Ching, "Fallen Angel or the Devil in Disguise?," *SCMP,* April 13, 2004, 12.

45. Susan Lawrence, "Diplomatic but Triumphal Progress," *FEER* 167 (November 13, 2003): 34; interview with Taiwan official, September 2004; Therese Shaheen interview, December 13, 2004, Potomac, Md.

46. Susan Lawrence, "The Guardian Angel Finally Had Enough," *FEER* (April 22, 2004): 24–28 (quote on 25).

47. Jeff Stein, "Defense Officials Tried to Reverse China Policy, Says Powell Aide," *CQ Homeland Security,* June 1, 2007, http://public.cq.com/docs/hs/hsnews110-000002523531.html (accessed June 29, 2007).

48. "Bush, Wen Meet at the White House: Text of the Chinese and American Leaders' Comments," *WP,* December 9, 2003, www.washingtonpost.com/

ac2/wp-dyn?pagename=article&node=&contentId=A49483-2003Dec9
&notFound=true (accessed February 20, 2004).

49. Green interview.

50. Chen Shui-bian, interview, *WT,* July 17, 2001.

51. Philip P. Pan and David Hoffman, "Taiwan's President Maintains Hard Line;
Chen Shui-bian Rebukes China in Interview,", *WP,* March 30, 2004, www
.lexis-nexis.com, accessed April 5, 2004.

52. Bush, *Untying the Knot,* 252.

53. U.S. Congress, House International Relations Committee, Asia and Pacific
Subcommittee, April 21, 2004, Hearing: Taiwan Relations Act, Testimony
of James Kelly, www.lexis-nexis.com, congressional (accessed February 22,
2005).

54. Secretary Colin L. Powell, interview by Anthony Yuen of Phoenix TV, October 25, 2004, China World Hotel, Beijing, www.state.gov/secretary/former/
powell/remarks/37361.htm. The earlier session, also on October 25, was with
Mike Chinoy of CNN International TV, ibid.; Joseph Kahn, "Warnings by
Powell to Taiwan Provoke a Diplomatic Dispute," *NYT,* October 28, 2004,
www.lexis-nexis.com, accessed February 22, 2005; Jacky Hsu, "KMT calls
for urgent review of ties with US," *SCMP,* December 23, 2004, ibid.; David G.
Brown, "Campaign Fallout," *Comparative Connections,* Pacific Forum CSIS
(Center for Strategic and International Studies), October–December 2004,
www.csis.org/pacfor (accessed April 21, 2005). Alan Romberg points out that
almost all senior US officials since 1971 have been sloppy and uttered this
"sweeping misstatement of policy." Romberg, *Rein In,* 226.

Conclusion

1. Shelley Rigger, *Taiwan's Rising Rationalism* (Washington, D.C., 2006), 4–23,
56–59.

2. In fairness, it must be noted that DeLisle also wrote of and analyzed "daunt-
ing challenges" for Ma. Jacques DeLisle, "Taiwan under President Ma Ying-
jeou," Foreign Policy Researach Institute E-Note, June 2008, www.fpri.org.

3. Robert Jervis, *Perception and Misperception in International Politics* (Princeton, N.J., 1976).

4. Ross, "The 1995–1996 Taiwan Strait Confrontation," 123

5. Ma Ying-jeou, "Taiwan's Renaissance," *China Post,* May 21, 2008, www
.chinapost.com.tw/taiwan/national/national%20news/2008/05/21/157332/
p1/Full%2Dtext.htm.

6. Nancy Bernkopf Tucker, "If Taiwan Chooses Unification, Should the United
States Care?" *Washington Quarterly* 25 (Summer 2002) 15–28.

Interviews

Chang King-yuh   November 16, 2000, Taipei

Chen Chien-jen (C. J. Chen)   March 16, 2001, November 7, 2003, and February 20, 2004, Washington, D.C.

Stephen Chen Hsi-fan   May 1992, Washington, D.C.

Chen Mingming   November 2000, Beijing

Frederick Ch'ien Fu   November 8, 2000, Taipei

Chiou I-jen   July 2, 1999, Washington, D.C., and November 6, 2000, Taipei

Chu Shulong   October 30, 2000, Beijing

Chu Yunhan   November 6, 2000, Taipei

William Clark Jr.   March 29, 2001, Washington, D.C.

William P. Clark   August 4, 2004, by telephone

Ray S. Cline   May 12, 1992, Washington, D.C.

Ralph Clough   August 23, 2001, by telephone

John Corbett   February 21, 2001, Washington, D.C.

Charles Cross   March 3, 2001, Washington, D.C.

David Dean   June 1991, Washington, D.C.; February 13, 2003, McLean, Va.

Arthur Ding Shu-fan   April 2000, Washington, D.C.

Ding Mou-shih   November 9, 2000, Taipei

Harvey Feldman   May 21, 2001, Washington, D.C.

Michael Finegan   October 27, 2000, Washington, D.C.

David Finkelstein   February 6, 2001, Alexandria, Va.

Carl Ford   February 16, 2001, Washington, D.C.

Charles (Chas) W. Freeman Jr.   December 20, 1994, Washington, D.C.

Norman Fu Chien-chung . March 6, 2004, Bethesda, Md.

Kent Fung   November 17, 2000, Taipei

Robert Gallucci   March 19, 2001, Washington, D.C.

Bonnie Glaser   2000–2008, repeated discussions

William Gleysteen   February 28, 2001, Washington, D.C.

Michael J. Green   April 11, 2006, Washington, D.C.

David Gries   February 23, 2001, Washington, D.C.

Rupert Hammond-Chambers   June 15, 2004, Rosslyn, Va.

Herbert Hansell   March 6, 2001, Washington, D.C.

Hau Pei-tsun   November 9, 2000, Taipei

Richard Holbrooke   March 13, 2001, New York City

Andrew Hsia   November 17, 2000, Taipei

Alexander Huang   November 16, 2000, Taipei

Huang Renwei   November 2, 2000, Shanghai

Jason Hu Chih-chiang   November 17, 2000, Taipei; February 2, 2005,
   by telephone

Arthur W. Hummel Jr.   May 1992, Washington, D.C.

Kenneth Jarrett   January 30, 2001, Washington, D.C.

Darryl Johnson   November 20 and 26, 2001, Washington, D.C.

Arnold Kanter   March 20, 2001, Washington, D.C.

Michael Kau Ying-mao   November 9, 2000, Taipei

David Keegan   January 12, 2001, Washington, D.C.

James A. Kelly   March 17, 2006, Washington, D.C.

Robert M. Kimmitt   June 21, 2006, Rosslyn, Va.

Frank Kramer   September 14, 2004, Washington, D.C.

Anthony Lake   October 27, 1999, Washington, D.C.

David Laux   August 11, 2000, by telephone; August 17, 2000, Arlington, Va.

David Lee Ta-wei   November 16, 2000, Taipei

Lee Teng-hui   October 17, 2003, Tamsui, Taiwan

Kenneth Lieberthal   July 25, 2001, Washington, D.C.

Lien Chan   November 17, 2000, Taipei

James Lilley   March 26, 2001, and March 13, 2003, Washington, D.C.

Lin Bi-jaw   November 16, 2000, Tamsui, Taiwan

C. K. Liu   November 13, 2000, Taipei

Eugene Loh I-cheng   November 8, 2000, Taipei

Winston Lord   October 17, 2000, Washington, D.C.

Luo Yuan   October 25, 2000, Beijing

Lu Shumin   October 27, 2000, Beijing

G. Eugene Martin   April 17, 2002, Rosslyn, Va.

Michael McDevitt   August 18, 2004, Alexandria, Va.

Mark Mohr   April 14, 2003, Washington, D.C.

Michel Oksenberg   April 1999, Washington, D.C.

Douglas Paal   March 9, 2001, Washington, D.C.

Torkel Patterson   April 13, 2006, Rosslyn, Va.

William Perry   July 21, 2004, by telephone

Mark Pratt   September 30, 2000, Washington, D.C.

Joseph Prueher   October 27, 2000, Beijing

David Ruether   March 23, 2001, Rosslyn, Va.

Alan Romberg   August 7, 2000, Bethesda, Md.

Ed Ross   August 20, 2004, Arlington, Va.

Stanley Roth   May 7, 2004, Rosslyn, Va.

J. Stapleton Roy   March 29, 2001, and February 2, 2002, Washington, D.C.

Barbara Schrage   June 28, 2004, Rosslyn, Va.

Randall Schriver   January 29, 2001, Rosslyn, Va.; December 28, 2004, Washington, D.C.

Therese Shaheen   December 13, 2004, Potomac, Md.

Shaw Yu-ming   June 1993, Washington, D.C.; November 17, 2000, Taipei

Shen Lyushun   October 1999, Washington, D.C.

Susan Shirk   June 7, 2004, San Diego, Calif.

George Shultz   June 8, 2004, Palo Alto, Calif.

Vincent Siew   November 8, 2000, Taipei

Michael D. Slack   February 4, 2005, by telephone

Richard Solomon   October 13, 2000, Washington, D.C.

James Soong Chu-yu   May 23, 2000, Washington, D.C.; November 18, 2000, Taipei

James Steinberg   March 13, 2001, New York City

Mark Stokes   February 21, 2001, Washington, D.C.; November 21, 2004, by e-mail

Su Chi   November 10, 2000, Taipei

Robert Suettinger   March 16, 2001, Arlington, Va.; January 1, 2006, Bethesda, Md.

Roger Sullivan   February 2, 2001, Medford, Mass.

Christopher Szymanski   March 5, 2001, Washington, D.C.

Tang Fei   May 30, 2001, Washington, D.C.

Tang Shubei   October 31, 2000, Beijing

Jim Thomson   October 27, 2001, by telephone

Tien Hung-mao   March 31, 2000, Washington, D.C.; November 13, 2000, Taipei

John Tkacik   September 2, 1997, Washington, D.C.

Peter Tomsen   January 4, 2002, Virginia

Tsai Ing-wen   November 2000, Taipei

Harry Tseng   September 2, 2004, Washington, D.C.

Leonard Unger   August 1993, Potomac, Md.

Ezra Vogel   April 13, 2000, Cambridge, Mass.

Gary Weis   January 22, 2001, Mt. Vernon, Va.

Xu Shiquan   March 30 and October 25, 2000, Beijing

Andrew Yang Nien-dzu   April 6, 2000, Washington, D.C.

Steve Yates October 3, 2002, Washington, DC

Steve Young November 15, 2000, Taipei

Yu Hsiao-pin November 7, 2001, Washington, D.C.

Zhang Nianchi November 1, 2000, Shanghai

Zhang Wenjin September 1987, Beijing

Zhou Mingwei October 31, 2000, Beijing

Bibliography

Primary Sources

Unpublished Documents

George H. W. Bush Library, College Station, Texas
  George H. W. Bush Peking Diary, Bush Library, www.bushlibrary.tamu.edu.
Jimmy Carter Library, Atlanta, Georgia
  Collections: Vertical File, Brzezinski Collection, White House Central Files, Counsel-Lipshutz, National Security Adviser Brzezinski Material and Staff Materials, Plains Files, Staff Offices, Name File.
Cold War International History Project
  Woodrow Wilson International Center for Scholars, Washington, D.C.
Digital National Security Archive
  China and the United States: From Hostility to Engagement, 1960–1998; Iran-Contra Affair, 1983–1988.
Gerald Ford Presidential Library, Ann Arbor, Michigan
  Collections: National Security Adviser, National Security Council, Presidential Handwriting File, Legislative Interdepartmental Group Files, Ford Vice Presidential Files, White House Central Files, Ron Nessen Papers, Robert T. Hartman Papers, Gerald Ford Papers, James E. Connor Papers, White House Operations.
Lyndon Baines Johnson Library, Austin, Texas
  Collections: Lyndon Baines Johnson, National Security, White House Central Files, Tom Johnson Notes of Meetings.
John F. Kennedy Library, Boston, Massachusetts
  Collections: National Security, China General, James C. Thomson, President's Office, Roger Hilsman, Arthur Schlesinger, John F. Kennedy.

V. K. Wellington Koo Papers, Butler Library Manuscript Division, Columbia University, New York, New York

Ministry of Foreign Affairs Archives, Taipei, Taiwan

Seeley G. Mudd Manuscript Library, Princeton University, Princeton, New Jersey
John Foster Dulles, Karl Rankin.

National Archives, College Park, Maryland
RG 59: General Records of the Department of State; RG 84: Post Files; RG 218: Joint Chiefs of Staff Record Group; RG 381: Combined Chiefs of Staff.

National Security Archive, www.gwu.edu/~nsarchiv
NSAEBB, no. 20, "New Archival Evidence on Taiwanese 'Nuclear Intentions,' 1966–1976."
NSAEBB, no. 41, "Reconnaissance Flights and Sino-American Relations, 1969–1970."
NSAEBB, no. 70, "Negotiating U.S.–Chinese Rapprochement."

Nixon Presidential Materials Project
Henry Kissinger Telephone Conversation Transcripts (Telcons), White House Tapes, National Security Council Files, White House Central Files, White House Special Files.

Ronald Reagan Library, Simi Valley, California
Collections: Douglas Paal, David Laux, Gaston Sigur, Executive Secretariat.

Oral History

Association for Diplomatic Studies and Training Foreign Service Oral History Project
Donald Anderson, William A. Brown, Ralph Clough, David Dean, Charles (Chas) W. Freeman Jr., William Gleysteen, Marshall Green, John Holdridge, Herbert Horowitz, Arthur W. Hummel Jr., Paul Kreisberg, Herbert Levin, James R. Lilley, Winston Lord, David Osborn, Mark Pratt, David Reuther, John S. Service, Thomas P. Shoesmith, Gaston Sigur, Richard Solomon, Harry E. T. Thayer.

Carter Presidency Project, Jimmy Carter Library
David Aaron, Madeleine Albright, Zbigniew Brzezinski, Leslie Denend, William Odom.

National Security Council Project Oral History Roundtables. www.cissm.umd.edu /projects/nsc.php.

Unpublished Papers, Speeches, Testimony

Bush, Richard. "The United States' Role in the Taiwan Straits Issue." Speech presented at the University of Illinois at Carbondale, December 7, 1998.

Central Intelligence Agency. Chronology of the Kissinger-Nixon China Initiative, Rand Corporation, obtained through FOIA request.

Chang Jaw-ling. "The Making of Clinton's New Taiwan Policy." Paper presented at the Conference on US Taiwan Policy Consultation, New York, December 1994.

Chen Shui-bian. "Taiwan Stands Up." Inauguration speech, May 20, 2000. Office of the President. www.gio.gov.tw.

Chiou I-jen. "The Policy Dilemma and New Expectations." Speech presented at the American Assembly Luncheon, Taipei, June 21, 1999.

Clinton, William J. Speech presented to the Business Council, February 24, 2000. www.lexis-nexis.com, accessed June 8, 2005.

Charles T. Cross Diary. In possession of Cross.

Democratic Progressive Party. "White Paper on Foreign Policy for the 21st Century," November 28, 1999. www.taiwandocuments.org/dppo2.htm.

"Dick Cheney Discusses the Beginning of the Bush Administration." *Larry King Live,* April 27, 2001. http://transcripts.cnn.com/TRANSCRIPT/0104/lkl.00.html.

Doran, Jim P. "U.S. Defense Policy toward Taiwan: Indefensible." Staff Trip Report to the Senate Foreign Relations Committee, March 8, 2001.

Glaser, Bonnie. "China's Taiwan Policy in the Wake of 'One Country on Each Side.'" Paper presented at the Conference on US–Taiwan–China Relations of the National Committee on American Foreign Policy and the Chinese-Eurasia Foundation, New York, October 7–8, 2002.

———. "Chinese Missiles and Taiwan TMD: Can a New Round of the Cross-Strait Arms Race Be Averted?" Paper presented at the Fifth Roundtable on US–China Policy and Cross-Strait Relations, National Committee on American Foreign Policy, New York, August 29–31, 1999.

Hinton, Janice. "The Sale of the FX Aircraft to Taiwan." Rand Graduate Institute, January 1982.

"Implementation of the Taiwan Relations Act." Report to Congress Pursuant to PL 106-113, December 19, 2000. napsnet@nautilus.org, accessed December 22, 2000.

Lake, Anthony. "From Containment to Enlargement." Address given at the Nitze School of Advanced International Studies, Washington, D.C., September 21, 1993.

The National Security Strategy of the United States of America, September 2002. www.whitehouse.gov/nsc/nss/2002/index.html, accessed July 2003.

Nuclear Posture Review, 16, December 31, 2001. www.globalsecurity.org, accessed July 2003.

"The One China Principle and the Taiwan Issue." February 21, 2000. http://english.peopledaily.com.cn/features/taiwanpaper/taiwan.html, accessed February 15, 2005.

Pillsbury, Michael. "The US Role in Taiwan's Defense Reforms." Paper presented at the Institute for Taiwan Defense and Strategic Studies Conference, Taipei, February 29, 2004.

Qian Qichen. "Adhere to the Basic Policy of 'One Country, Two Systems' and Strive to Promote the Development of Cross Strait Relations." Speech presented to Beijing Xinhua Domestic Service (in Chinese), January 24, 2002, FBIS.

"The Security Situation in the Taiwan Strait." Report to Congress Pursuant to the FY99 Appropriations Bill, February 26, 1999. www.fas.org/news/taiwan/1999/twstrait_02261999.htm, accessed June 10, 2008.

Su Chi. "Domestic Determinants of Taiwan's Mainland Policy." Paper presented at the Peace across the Taiwan Strait Conference, Oxford University, May 2002.

"Theater Missile Defense Architecture Options for the Asia-Pacific Region." Report to Congress, May 4, 1999. www.dod.mil/pubs/tmd050499.pdf, accessed July 25, 2005.

Xu Shiquan. "The One China Principle: Positions of CCP, KMT and DPP." Typescript, July 22, 2000.

———. "Possible Key to Deadlock of Cross-Strait Relations." Typescript, July 27, 2000.

Yang, Philip Y. M. "From Strategic Ambiguity to Three Noes: The Changing Nature of the U.S. Policy toward Taiwan." Paper presented at a conference, "U.S. and Its Allies," Tel Aviv, November 9–11, 1998. www.taiwansecurity.org/TS/TS-Yang-2.htm, accessed April 23, 2002.

Zhu Rongji. Press conference, National People's Congress, March 15, 2000, CCTV transcript.

Published Government Documents

Central Intelligence Agency. *The Caesar, Polo, and Esau Papers.* www.cia.gov.

Public Papers of the Presidents of the United States: Richard Nixon, 1972. Washington, D.C.: Government Printing Office, 1974.

Joint Communiqué, PRC and the USA, Shanghai, February 27, 1972, 376–79.

United States Department of State. *Foreign Relations of the United States.*

FRUS 1949, vol. 9: *The Far East: China* (Washington, D.C.: Government Printing Office, 1975).

FRUS 1952–54, vol. 3: *United Nations Affairs* (1979).

FRUS 1952–54, vol. 14, pt. 1: *China and Japan* (1985).

FRUS 1955–57, vol. 2: *China* (1986).

FRUS 1958–60, vol. 19: *China* (1996).

FRUS 1961–63 vol. 22: *Northeast Asia* (1996).

FRUS 1964–68, vol. 30: *China* (1998).

FRUS 1969–72, vol. 17: China (2006)

Congressional Hearings and Testimony: www.lexis-nexis.com.

U.S. Congress. Hearing: *The U.S. China and Taiwan: American Policy in a Zone of Crisis.* Testimony of Winston Lord, Assistant Secretary of State for East Asian and Pacific Affairs, March 25, 1996.

U.S. Congress, House. Hearings: *Taiwan Agents in America and the Death of Prof. Wen-chen Chen.* 97th Cong., 1st sess., July 30 and October 6, 1981. Washington D.C.: Government Printing Office, 1982.

U.S. Congress, House Foreign Affairs Committee, Subcommittee on International Security, International Organizations and Human Rights and the Subcommittee on Asia and the Pacific. John R. Bolton, president, National Policy Forum. Testimony on Taiwan and the UN, July 14, 1994.

U.S. Congress, House International Relations Committee, Asia and Pacific Subcommittee. Hearings: *Taiwan, China and the Taiwan Security Enhancement Act,* September 15, 1999.

————.Hearings: *Taiwan Relations Act,* Testimony of James Kelly, April 21, 2004.

U.S. Congress, Senate Committee on Armed Services and Committee on Foreign Relations. Hearings: *Military Situation in the Far East.* 82nd Cong., 1st sess., 1951, pt. 3, 1667–69.

U.S. Congress, Senate Committee on Foreign Relations. Hearings: *Review of US Policy Toward Taiwan.* Testimony of Ambassador James R. Lilley, Senator Charles S. Robb, September 27, 1994.

————. Hearings: *U.S. Policy in Asia.* 86th Cong., 1st sess., November 1, 1959.

————. Hearings: *U.S. Policy with Respect to Mainland China.* 89th Cong., 2nd sess., March 1966.

————. Hearings of the East Asian and Pacific Affairs Subcommittee: *U.S. Policy toward China.* Testimony of Winston Lord, September 27, 1994.

Books and Articles

Newspapers and Journals: broad runs of newspapers and journals were consulted; it is impossible to list every article that proved useful.

Accinelli, Robert. *Crisis & Commitment.* Chapel Hill: University of North Carolina Press, 1996.

Acheson, Dean. "Crisis in Asia—An Examination of US Policy." *Department of State Bulletin* 22 (January 23, 1950): 111–18.

"Across the Strait." *Newsweek,* May 7, 1984, 32.

Albright, David, and Corey Gay. "Taiwan: Nuclear Nightmare Averted." *Bulletin of the Atomic Scientists* 54(January–February 1998): 54–60.

Ambrose, Stephen E. *Eisenhower.* Vol. 2. New York: Simon and Schuster, 1984.

————. *Nixon.* Vol. 2. New York: Simon and Schuster, 1989.

Anderson, Benedict. *Imagined Communities.* New York: Verso, 1991.

Anderson, Scott, and Jon Lee Anderson. *Inside the League.* New York: Dodd, Mead, 1986.

Andrew, Christopher. *For the President's Eyes Only.* New York: HarperCollins, 1995.

Apple, R. W., Jr. "A Domestic Sort with Global Worries." *NYT,* August 25, 1999, A10.

————. "The 1992 Campaign: Political Pulse—Missouri; Missouri's Words of Advice to Bush: Jobs, Jobs, Jobs." *NYT,* September 29, 1992.

"Aristide Urges Total Embargo against Haiti." *St. Louis Post-Dispatch,* October 29, 1993. www.lexis-nexis.com, accessed August 6, 2004.

Austin, Greg, ed. *Missile Diplomacy and Taiwan's Future.* Canberra: Australian National University, 1997.

Awanohara, Susumu. "Arms Sales B: Pork Barrel Roll." *FEER* 155 (September 17, 1992): 12.

————. "Political Purse Strings." *FEER* 146 (October 19, 1989): 10.

Babington, Charles. "All Quiet on the Right Wing Front." *WP,* April 19, 2001.

————. "Clinton Urges Trade, Shrinking U.S. Debt." *WP,* February 25, 2000, A4.

Babington, Charles, and Dana Milbank. "Bush Advisers Try to Limit Damage." *WP,* April 27, 2001, A19

Bachrack, Stanley D. *The Committee of One Million*. New York: Columbia University Press, 1976.

Baker, James A., III. *The Politics of Diplomacy*. New York: Putnam, 1995.

Baker, Mark. "China and U.S. Agree on Nuclear Power Deal." *Financial Times,* April 27, 1984, A20.

Barnett, A. Doak. *The FX Decision*. Washington, D.C.: Brookings Institution Press, 1981.

Barrett, Lauren I. *Gambling with History*. New York: Penguin, 1984.

Baum, Julian. "Arms Sales A: A Foot in the Door: US Decision Opens New Options to Taiwan Military." *FEER* 155 (September 17, 1992)12–13.

———. "Regrets Only." *FEER* 157 (September 22, 1994): 15.

Beck, Simon. "Taiwan Out from Under Its Shell." *SCMP,* February 16, 1995. www.lexis-nexis.com, accessed April 13, 2005.

Becker, Jasper. *Hungry Ghosts*. New York: Henry Holt, 1996.

"Beijing and Taipei Agree to Disagree on 'One China.'" *Renmin Ribao,* November 16, 1992.

Beyer, Lisa. "The Center Holds—for Now." *Time,* September 3, 1990, 35.

Bird, Kai. *The Color of Truth*. New York: Simon and Schuster, 1998.

Bixby, Lyn. "Peace Pays Dividends for Makers of Weapons." *Hartford Courant,* October 25, 1992, A1.

Blatt, Jason. "Taiwan Documents Say US Thwarted Chiang Attack Plans in Mid-1950s." *SCMP,* April 15, 2002. FBIS, China, CPP20020415000033.

Borg, Dorothy, and Waldo Heinrichs, eds. *Uncertain Years*. New York: Columbia University Press, 1980.

Brands, H. W., Jr. "Testing Massive Retaliation, Credibility and Crisis Management in the Taiwan Strait." *International Security* 12 (Spring 1988): 124–51.

Brinkley, Douglas, ed. *The Reagan Diaries*. New York: HarperCollins, 2007.

Brown, David G. "Campaign Fallout." *Comparative Connections,* Pacific Forum CSIS, October–December 2004. www.csis.org/pacfor, accessed April 21, 2005.

———. "Deadlocked but Stable." *Comparative Connections,* Pacific Forum CSIS, April–June 2004. www.csis.org/pacfor, accessed April 21, 2005.

———. "Unproductive Military Posturing." *Comparative Connections,* Pacific Forum CSIS, July–September 2004. www.csis.org/pacfor, accessed April 21, 2005.

Brown, Justin. "America Sends Envoys to Calm China-Taiwan Rhetoric." *Christian Science Monitor,* March 22, 2000. www.lexis-nexis.com, accessed June 14, 2005.

Brzezinski, Zbigniew. *Power and Principle*. New York: Farrar, Straus and Giroux, 1983.

———. "What's Wrong with Reagan's Foreign Policy?" *NYT Magazine,* December 6, 1981.

Bundy, William. *A Tangled Web*. New York: Hill and Wang, 1998.

Burr, William, ed. *The Kissinger Transcripts*. New York: New Press, 1998.

Bush, George H. W. *Looking Forward*. Garden City, N.Y.: Doubleday, 1987.

———. "Our Deal with Peking: All Cost, No Benefit." *WP*, December 24, 1978, D1.

Bush, George H. W., and Brent Scowcroft. *A World Transformed*. New York: Alfred A. Knopf, 1998.

Bush, Richard C. *At Cross Purposes*. Armonk, N.Y.: M. E. Sharpe, 2004.

———. "Lee Teng-hui and 'Separatism.'" In *Dangerous Strait,* ed. Nancy Bernkopf Tucker, 70–92. New York: Columbia University Press, 2005.

———. *Untying the Knot*. Washington, D.C.: Brookings Institution Press, 2005.

"Bush Said to Continue US Cooperation with ROC on Basis of TRA." CNA, December 23, 1988. www. lexis-nexis.com, accessed June 3, 2004.

"Bush Should Not Be Pressed to Nudge ROC toward Reunification." CNA, February 25, 1989. www.lexis-nexis.com, accessed June 3, 2004.

Cabestan, Jean-Pierre. "Taiwan's Mainland Policy: Normalization, Yes; Reunification, Later." In *Contemporary Taiwan,* ed. David Shambaugh, 216–39. Oxford: Clarendon Press, 1998.

Campbell, Kurt M., and Derek J. Mitchell. "Crisis in the Taiwan Strait?" *Foreign Affairs* 80 (July–August 2001): 14–25.

Cannon, Lou. "Finding Capitalism in China Provides an Out on Old Stance." *WP*, May 7, 1984, A2.

———. *President Reagan: The Role of a Lifetime*. New York: Simon and Schuster, 1991.

Carpenter, Ted Galen. "President Bush's Muddled Policy on Taiwan." Cato Institute Foreign Policy Briefing, no. 82, March 15, 2004.

———. "Prospects for the TSEA under Bush." *Taipei Times,* February 7, 2001. www.taiwansecurity.org, accessed February 2001.

Carter, Ashton B., and William J. Perry. "China on the March." *National Interest* (March–April 2007): 16–22.

Carter, Jimmy. *Keeping Faith*. New York: Bantam Books, 1982.

"Carter Comments Berated." FT Asia Intelligence Wire, April 1, 1999, Agence France-Presse. www.lexis-nexis.com, accessed July 26, 2003.

Chanda, Nayan. "Defence: Hi-Tech Diplomacy: US Technology Sales to India and China to Reap Political Gains." *FEER* 131 (February 20, 1986): 36.

———. "A Technical Point." *FEER* 131 (August 26, 1986): 26.

Chandler, Clay. "China Threatens Voters in Taiwan." *WP*, March 16, 2000, 1, 22.

Chang, Gordon H. *Friends and Enemies*. Stanford: Stanford University Press, 1990.

Chang, Gordon H., and He Di. "The Absence of War in the U.S.–China Confrontation over Quemoy and Matsu in 1954–1955: Contingency, Luck, Deterrence?" *American Historical Review* 98 (December 1993): 1500–1524.

Chang, Maubo. "Taiwan: Government Not Informed of USA Dropping Annual Arms Sales Review." CNA, April 25, 2001.www.lexis-nexis.com, accessed August 25, 2004.

Chang, Parris H. "Lessons from the Taiwan Strait Crisis of 1996." *Topics* (American Chamber of Commerce in Taiwan) (August 1996): 46–48.

Chao Chien-min. "DPP's Factional Politics and the Issue of Taiwan Independence." In *Assessing Chen Shui-bian's First Year.* Sigur Center Paper no. 14. Washington, D.C., May 2001, 55–66.

Chao, Linda, and Ramon H. Myers. *The First Chinese Democracy.* Baltimore: Johns Hopkins University Press, 1998.

Chen, Edwin. "Talks Yield a U.S. Warning to Taiwan and Pledge by China to Ease Trade Gap." *LAT,* December 10, 2003. www.lexis-nexis.com, accessed April 11, 2004.

Chen, Jay. "U.S. Policy on 'One China' Remains Unchanged." CNA, October 1, 2002. www.lexis-nexis.com, accessed December 5, 2004.

Chen, Jay, and Flor Wang. "US Should Have Been Informed of Secret Emissaries between Taiwan, China." CNA, July 20, 2000. www.lexis-nexis.com, accessed December 5, 2004.

Chen, Jay, and Sofia Wu. "Taiwan's Democratization Contributes to Peace: AIT Chief." CNA, September 17, 1998, www.lexis-nexis.com, accessed December 5, 2004.

———. "U.S. Committed to Helping Taiwan Defend Itself." CNA, April 9, 2002, www.lexis-nexis.com, accessed June 2003.

Chen Jian. "Beijing's Changing Policies toward Taiwan." In *The United States and Cross-Straits Relations,* ed. Kenneth Klinkner. Urbana-Champaign: University of Illinois Press, 2001.

———. *China's Road to the Korean War.* New York: Columbia University Press, 1994.

———. *Mao's China and the Cold War.* Chapel Hill: University of North Carolina Press, 2001.

"Chen Repeats Call for Taiwan to Take 'Own Road.'" *China Post,* July 30, 2002.

Chen Shui-bian. "Meeting Challenges, Moving Forward: New Year Message." *Taipei Journal,* January 4, 2002, 7.

Cheshire, Maxine. "Behind the Scenes at Reagan's Night Out." *WP,* May 21, 1981, D1.

Cheung, Ray, "Two Sides Tied in 'Nots' over the US Stance on Taiwan." *SCMP,* November 19, 2003, A7.

Cheung Tai Ming. "Chinese Military Preparations against Taiwan over the Next 10 Years." In *Crisis in the Taiwan Strait,* ed. James Lilley and Chuck Downs, 45–71. Washington, D.C.: National Defense University Press, 1997.

Ch'ien Fu, Frederick. *Qian Fu Hui Yi Lu: Hua Fu Lu Qi Qu, 1979–1988* [Ch'ien Fu's Memory Lane: The Bumpy U.S. Government Road]. 2 vols. Taibei Shi: Tian xia yuan jian chu ban gu fen you xian gong si, 2005.

"'China Lobby,' Once Powerful Factor in U.S. Politics, Appears Victim of Lack of Interest." *NYT,* April 26, 1970, A14.

"China Says U.S. Is Trying to Distort Taiwan Pact." *NYT,* August 22, 1982, A5.

"China's Show of Force to Taiwan." *Advertiser* (South Australia), July 19, 1999. www.lexis-nexis.com, accessed September 1, 2006.

"Chinese Assail Reagan Aide's Plan." *NYT,* December 4, 1980, A7.

"Chinese Reassure U.S. on Dispute with Taiwan." *Atlanta Journal and Constitution,* April 2, 2000. www.lexis-nexis.com, accessed June 14, 2005.

Ching Cheong. "Don't Take Sides, Taiwan Urges US." *Straits Times,* July 30, 1999. www.lexis-nexis.com, accessed February 2, 2005.

Ching, Frank. "Fallen Angel or the Devil in Disguise?" *SCMP*, April 13, 2004, 12.

Chiu Hungdah, ed. *China and the Taiwan Issue*. New York: Praeger, 1979.

Chiu Hungdah, Hsing-wei Lee, and Chih-yu Wu, eds. *Implementation of the Taiwan Relations Act: An Examination after Twenty Years*. Baltimore: Maryland Series in Contemporary Asian Studies, 2001.

Christensen, Thomas J. "Posing Problems without Catching Up." *International Security* 25 (Spring 2001): 5–40 ..

―――. *Useful Adversaries*. Princeton: Princeton University Press, 1996.

Christopher, Warren. *Chances of a Lifetime*. New York: Scribner, 2001.

―――. *In the Stream of History*. Stanford: Stanford University Press, 1998.

Chu, Monique. "US Likely to Walk Similar Taiwan Strait Line." *Taipei Times*, December 18, 2000, 3.

Chung, Lawrence. "Leakage of Classified Documents." *Straits Times*, March 27, 2002.

Chu Yun-han. "Democratic Consolidation in the Post-KMT Era: The Challenge of Governance." In *Taiwan's Presidential Politics*, ed. Muthiah Alagappa, 88–114. Armonk, N.Y.: M. E. Sharpe, 2001.

―――. "Making Sense of Beijing's Policy toward Taiwan." In *China under Jiang Zemin*, ed. Tien Hung-mao and Chu Yun-han, 193–212. Boulder, Colo.: Lynne Rienner, 2000.

Clark, William, Jr. "Policy toward Taiwan Needs a Clinton Redo." *International Herald Tribune*, August 30, 1994.

Cline, Ray S. *Chiang Ching-kuo Remembered*. Washington, D.C.: United States Global Strategy Council, 1989.

Clinton, William J. *My Life*. New York: Alfred A. Knopf, 2004.

Clough, Ralph N. *Island China*. Cambridge: Harvard University Press, 1978.

Clubb, O. Edmund. *The Witness and I*. New York: Columbia University Press, 1974.

Cohen, Marc J. *Taiwan at the Crossroads*. Washington, D.C.: Asia Resource Center, 1988.

Cohen, Warren I. *Dean Rusk*. Totowa, N.J.: Cooper Square, 1980.

Cohen, Warren I., and Akira Iriye, eds. *The Great Powers in East Asia, 1953–1960*. New York: Columbia University Press, 1990.

Cole, Bernard D. *Taiwan's Security*. New York: Taylor and Francis, 2007.

Cook, Blanche Wiesen. *The Declassified Eisenhower*. Garden City, N.Y.: Doubleday, 1981.

Crampton, Thomas. "Taipei Says Paris Betrayed Secrets on Frigate Deal to China." *International Herald Tribune*, March 22, 2002.

Cross, Charles T. *Born a Foreigner*. Boulder, Colo.: Rowman and Littlefield, 1999.

Crothall, Geoffrey. "US Accused of Blocking Attempts to Reunify." *SCMP*, September 1, 1993, 11.

Crothall, Geoffrey, and Michael Chugani. "Furious Beijing in Arms Talks Threat." *SCMP*, September 4, 1992, 1.

Curry, Bill. "Winning Taiwan Friends." *WP*, June 9, 1977, 1.

Dean, David. "U.S. Relations with Taiwan." In *Implementation of the Taiwan Relations Act: An Examination after Twenty Years*, ed. Chiu Hungdah, Hsing-wei Lee, and Chih-yu Wu. Baltimore: Maryland Series in Contemporary Asian Studies, 2001.

Dean, Jason. "U.S. Official Backs Taiwan Status and Its Negotiations with China." *WSJ*, January 29, 2002. www.lexis-nexis.com.

Deaver, Michael K. *Behind the Scenes*. New York: William Morrow, 1987.

DeLisle, Jacques. "Law's Spectral Answers to the Cross-Strait Sovereignty Question." *Orbis* 46 (Fall 2002): 733–52.

DeParle, Jason. "The Man inside Bill Clinton's Foreign Policy." *NYT Magazine*, August 20, 1995. www.lexis-nexis.com, accessed October 19, 1999.

Dickson, Bruce J. *Democratization in China and Taiwan*. New York: Oxford University Press, 1997.

———. "Taiwan's Challenge to U.S. Foreign Policy." In *Assessing the Lee Teng-hui Legacy in Taiwan's Politics*, ed. Bruce J. Dickson and Chao Chien-min, 264–85. Armonk, N.Y.: M. E. Sharpe, 2002.

Dickson, Bruce J., and Chao Chien-min, eds. *Assessing the Lee Teng-hui Legacy in Taiwan's Politics*. Armonk, N.Y.: M. E. Sharpe, 2002.

Dillin, John. "Pentagon Braces for a Makeover." *Christian Science Monitor*, February 12, 2001. www.lexis-nexis.com, accessed August 25, 2004.

Dobrynin, Anatoly. *In Confidence*. New York: Times Books, 1995.

Dong Mei. *Zhong Mei guanxi ciliao xuanbian* [Selected Compilation of Materials on US–China Relations]. Beijing: Shishi chubanshe, 1982.

Donnell, John C. "South Vietnam in 1975: The Year of the Communist Victory." *Asian Survey* 16 (January 1976): 1–13.

Draper, Theodore. *A Very Thin Line*. New York: Hill and Wang, 1991.

Duffy, Michael, and Dan Goodgame. *Marching in Place*. New York: Simon and Schuster, 1992.

Dulles, John Foster. *War or Peace*. New York: Macmillan, 1950.

Eckholm, Erik, and Steven Lee Myers. "Taiwan Asks U.S. to Let It Obtain Top-Flight Arms." *NYT*, March 1, 2000, A12.

Emery, Glen. "Conservatives See Taipei as 'Litmus Test' for Reagan." *WT*, January 12, 1984, A5.

Engbarth, Dennis. "Taiwan's Defense Ministry Denies Coup Rumors." *SCMP*, August 17, 1993. lexis-nexis.com, accessed August 25, 2004.

Engelberg, Stephen, with Michael R. Gordon, "Taipei Halts Work on Secret Plant to Make Nuclear Bomb Ingredient." *NYT*, March 23, 1988, A1, 15.

Erlanger, Steven. "'Ambiguity' on Taiwan." *NYT*, March 12, 1996, A1.

Ewell, Judith. "Barely in the Inner Circle: Jeane Kirkpatrick." In *Women and American Foreign Policy*, ed. Edward P. Crapol, 158–65. Westport, Conn.: Greenwood, 1987.

Fairbank, John K. *The United States and China*. 4th ed. Cambridge: Harvard University Press, 1983.

Faison, Seth. "Taiwan President Implies His Island Is Sovereign State." *NYT*, July 13, 1999. www.lexis-nexis.com, accessed January 20, 2005.

Farley, Maggie. "U.S. Carrier Off Taiwan Trails Analysts' Worries in Its Wake." *LAT*, March 19, 1996, 8.

Feigenbaum, Evan A. *Change in Taiwan and Potential Adversity in the Strait.* Santa Monica, Calif.: Rand, 1995.

Feldman, Harvey. "Taiwan, Arms Sales, and the Reagan Assurances." *American Asian Review* 19 (Fall 2001): 81.

Feldman, Harvey, Michael Y. M. Kau, and Ilpyong J. Kim, eds. *Taiwan in a Time of Transition.* New York: Paragon House, 1988.

Fewsmith, Joseph, and Stanley Rosen. "The Domestic Context of Chinese Foreign Policy: Does 'Public Opinion' Matter?" In *The Making of Chinese Foreign and Security Policy in the Era of Reform,* ed. David Lampton, 151–87. Stanford: Stanford University Press, 2001.

Fidler, Stephen, and Tony Walker. "Big Powers Flex Muscles over Taiwan." *Financial Times,* February 10, 1999. www.lexis-nexis.com, accessed February 1999.

Finkelstein, David M. *Washington's Taiwan Dilemma, 1949–1950.* Fairfax, Va.: George Mason University Press, 1993.

Fitchett, Joseph. "Europeans Reject Role in Taiwan Arms Deal." *International Herald Tribune,* April 27, 2001. www.lexis-nexis.com, accessed August 24, 2004.

Fontaine, Roger. "Peking Arms, Atom Deals Worry Taipei Government." *WT,* May 2, 1984, A12.

Foot, Rosemary. *The Practice of Power.* Oxford: Clarendon Press, 1995.

Ford, Gerald. *A Time to Heal.* New York: Harper and Row, 1979.

Forman, William. "Taiwan Worried about US–China Deal." Associated Press, April 12, 2001. www.lexis-nexis.com, accessed August 25, 2004.

Forney, Matt, and Nigel Holloway. "Sunny Side Up." *FEER* 159 (July 25, 1996): 14–15.

Forslund, Catherine. *Anna Chennault.* Wilmington, Del.: Scholarly Resources, 2002.

Freeman, Chas W., Jr. "Preventing War in the Taiwan Strait: Restraining Taiwan— and Beijing." *Foreign Affairs* (Fall 1998): 6–11.

Fritz, Sara. "Probe of Donors Said to Include Taiwan Envoy." *LAT,* October 29, 1996. www.lexis-nexis.com, accessed October 19, 1999.

Gaddis, John Lewis. *Strategies of Containment.* New York: Oxford University Press, 1982.

———. *We Now Know.* Oxford: Clarendon Press, 1997.

Gargan, Edward A. "China Breaks the Ice to Offer Political Talks with Taiwan." *NYT,* February 25, 1998, A6.

Garrison, Jean A. *Making China Policy.* Boulder, Colo.: Lynne Rienner, 2005

Garthoff, Raymond L. *Détente and Confrontation.* Washington, D.C.: Brookings Institution Press, 1965.

Garver, John W. *Face Off.* Seattle: University of Washington Press, 1997.

———. *The Sino-American Alliance.* Armonk, N.Y.: M. E. Sharpe, 1997.

———. "Sino-American Relations in 2001." *International Journal* (Spring 2002): 283–310.

———. "Taiwan's Russian Option: Image and Reality." *Asian Survey* 18 (July 1978): 751–66.

Gates, Robert M. *From the Shadows*. New York: Simon and Schuster, 1997.

Gelb, Leslie H. "Arms for China and Taiwan: Twists in Diplomacy." *NYT,* October 16, 1981, A2.

———. "Breaking China Apart." *NYT,* November 13, 1991, A25.

Gellman, Barton. "Reappraisal Led to New China Policy." *WP,* June 22, 1998.

———. "U.S. and China Nearly Came to Blows in 1996." *WP,* June 21, 1998, A20–21.

Gertz, Bill. Interview of Chen Shui-bian. *WT,* July 17, 2001.

———. "Pentagon Confirms defense Talks between Taiwan, U.S." *WT,* July 20, 2001.

Gibert, Stephen P., and William M. Carpenter, eds. *America and Island China*. Lanham, Md.: University Press of America, 1989.

Glaser, Bonnie. "Washington's Hands-On Approach to Managing Cross-Strait Tension." PacNet no. 21, May 13, 2004, CSIS Pacific Forum. www.csis.org/pacfor.

Glennon, Michael J. "Liaison and the Law: Foreign Intelligence Agencies' Activities in the United States." *Harvard International Law Journal* 25 (Winter 1984): 1–42.

Goh, Evelyn. *Constructing the US Rapprochement with China, 1961–1974*. New York: Cambridge University Press, 2005.

Goldberg, Robert Alan. *Barry Goldwater*. New Haven: Yale University Press, 1995.

Goldstein, Carl. "The New China Lobby." *FEER* 132 (November 6, 1986): 44–45.

———. "Security Links Remain Despite Lost Diplomatic Ties." *FEER* 131 (May 8, 1986): 30

Goldstein, Steven. "The Impact of Domestic Politics on Taiwan's Mainland Policy." *Harvard Studies on China* 2 (1998): 62–90.

Goldwater, Barry M. *With No Apologies*. New York: William Morrow, 1979.

Goldwater, Barry M., with Jack Casserly. *Goldwater*. New York: Doubleday, 1988.

Goodman, Peter S. "Foreign Funding Can Be Problematic for U.S. Academics." *WP,* November 29, 1996. www.lexis-nexis.com, accessed February 7, 2005.

Gordon, Michael R. "Secret U.S. Study Concludes Taiwan Needs New Arms." *NYT,* April 1, 2001. www.lexis-nexis.com, accessed August 11, 2004.

Goshko, John M. "U.S. Agrees to Provide Israel with Helicopters, Place Other Equipment There." *WP,* September 27, 1992. www.lexis-nexis.com, accessed January 26, 2005.

Green, Marshall, John H. Holdridge, and William N. Stokes. *War and Peace with China*. Bethesda, Md.: Dacor Press, 1994.

Green, Michael J., and Benjamin L. Self. "Japan's Changing China Policy: From Commercial Liberalism to Reluctant Realism." *Survival* 38 (Summer 1996): 34–58.

Greenberg, David. "Fathers & Sons: George W. Bush and His Forebears." *New Yorker,* July 12 and 19, 2004, 92–98.

Greenstein, Fred I. *The Hidden-Hand Presidency*. New York: Basic Books, 1982.

Gwertzman, Bernard. "U.S. Backs Bank Seat for China." *NYT,* March 22, 1983, D14.

Haig, Alexander M., Jr. *Caveat.* New York: Macmillan, 1984.

Haldeman, H. R. *The Haldeman Diaries.* New York: Putnam, 1994.

Halperin, Morton. "The 1958 Taiwan Straits Crisis: A Documented History," RM 4900-ISA. Santa Monica, Calif.: Rand, December 1966.

Hanhimaki, Jussi M. "'Dr. Kissinger' or 'Mr. Henry'? Kissingerology, Thirty Years and Counting." *Diplomatic History* 27 (November 2003): 637–77.

Hannaford, Peter, ed. *Recollections of Reagan.* New York: William Morrow, 1997.

Harding, Harry. *The Fragile Relationship.* Washington, D.C.: Brookings Institution Press, 1992.

———. "'One China' or 'One Option': The Contending Formulas for Relations across the Taiwan Strait." *Notes from The National Committee on United States–China Relations* 29 (Fall–Winter 2000): 8–11.

Harding, Harry, and Yuan Ming, eds. *Sino-American Relations, 1945–1955.* Wilmington, Del.: Scholarly Resources, 1989.

Harrison, Selig. "Interview with Hu Yaobang." *FEER* 132 (July 24, 1986): 26–27.

Hau Pei-tsun. *Ba Nian Can Mou Zong Zhang Ze Ji* [Diary of Eight Years as Chief of the General Staff]. Taibei Shi: Tian xia yuan jian chu ban gu fen you xian gong si, 2000.

He Di. "The Evolution of the People's Republic of China's Policy toward the Offshore Islands." In *The Great Powers in East Asia, 1953–1960,* ed. Warren I. Cohen and Akira Iriye, 222–45. New York: Columbia University Press, 1990.

———. "'The Last Campaign to Unify China': The CCP's Unmaterialized Plan to Liberate Taiwan, 1949–1950." *Chinese Historians* 5 (Spring 1992): 1–16.

Helm, Leslie. "Fighter Plane Sale to Taiwan Also Worries Japanese." *LAT,* September 5, 1992, 12A.

Hersh, Seymour M. *The Price of Power.* New York: Summit Books, 1983.

Hille, Kathrin, and Victor Mallet. "The Widening Strait." *Financial Times,* March 18, 2004. www.lexis-nexis.com, accessed May 5, 2007.

Hilsman, Roger. *To Move a Nation.* Garden City, N.Y.: Doubleday, 1967.

"Historic 1993 China, Taiwan Talks Took Five Years of Groundwork." Agence France-Presse, July 19, 2000. www.taiwansecurity.org, accessed July 20, 2000.

Holdridge, John H. *Crossing the Divide.* Lanham, Md.: Rowman and Littlefield, 1997.

Hood, Steven J. *The Kuomintang and the Democratization of Taiwan.* Boulder, Colo.: Westview, 1997.

Hoopes, Townsend. *The Devil and John Foster Dulles.* Boston: Little, Brown, 1973.

Hsiung, James C., and Steven I. Levine, eds. *China's Bitter Victory.* Armonk, N.Y.: M. E. Sharpe, 1992.

Hsu, Brian. "Hau Defends Himself over Warship Deal." *Taipei Times,* October 23, 2000, 1.

Hsu, Jacky. "KMT Calls for Urgent Review of Ties with US." *SCMP,* December 23, 2004. www.lexis-nexis.com, accessed February 22, 2005.

Huang, Mab. *Intellectual Ferment for Political Reforms in Taiwan, 1971–1973.* Ann Arbor: University of Michigan Center for Chinese Studies, 1976.

Hung, Nguyen Tien, and Jerrold L. Schecter, eds. *The Palace File*. New York: Harper and Row, 1989.

Hutzler, Charles. "Hired Guns." *WSJ*, July 16, 2004.

"IAEA Found Undisclosed Activity on Taiwan in 1995." *Nucleonics Week* 42 (February 15, 2001). http://proquest.umi.com, accessed June 26, 2004

Immerman, Richard H., ed. *John Foster Dulles and the Diplomacy of the Cold War*. Princeton: Princeton University Press, 1990.

Isaacson, Walter. *Kissinger*. New York: Simon and Schuster, 1992.

Jencks, Harlan W. "Taiwan in the International Arms Market." In *Taiwan in World Affairs*, ed. Robert G. Sutter and William R. Johnson, 73–111. Boulder, Colo.: Westview, 1994.

Jervis, Robert. *Perception and Misperception in International Politics*. Princeton: Princeton University Press, 1976.

Johnson, Chalmers. "No Longer the 'Lone' Superpower: Coming to Terms with China." Japan Policy Research Institute, Working Paper no. 105 (March 2005).

———. *Peasant Nationalism and Communist Power*. Stanford: Stanford University Press, 1962.

Johnson, Haynes. *Sleepwalking through History*. New York: W. W. Norton, 1991.

Jones, Clayton. "China Killings Spark Muted Outcry." *Christian Science Monitor*, June 19, 1989, 4.

Judis, John. "The Decline of Principled Conservative Hostility to China: Sullied Heritage." *New Republic*, April 23, 2001, 19–25.

Kagan, Robert. "At Last, Straight Talk on China." *WP*, April 29, 2001.

Kagan, Robert, and William Kristol. "Stand by Taiwan." *Weekly Standard*, December 22, 2003, 8.

Kahin, George McT. *Intervention: How America Became Involved in Vietnam*. Garden City, N.Y.: Doubleday, 1986.

Kahn, E. J., Jr. *The China Hands*. New York: Viking Press, 1975.

Kahn, Joseph. "Warnings by Powell to Taiwan Provoke a Diplomatic Dispute." *NYT*, October 28, 2004. www.lexis-nexis.com, accessed February 22, 2005.

Kahn, Joseph, and Erik Eckholm. "Senate Republicans Try to Delay Vote on Taiwan Security Bill." *NYT*, April 28, 2000, A11.

Kaiser, Robert G., and Steven Mufson. "'Blue Team' Draws a Hard Line on Beijing." *WP*, February 22, 2000. www.lexis-nexis.com, accessed February 22, 2000.

———. "Taiwan: Crisis in the Making?" *WP*, March 16, 2000, A22.

Kalb, Marvin, and Bernard Kalb. *Kissinger*. New York: Dell, 1975.

Kan, Shirley. *China/Taiwan: Evolution of the "One China" Policy: Key Statements from Washington, Beijing, and Taipei*. Washington, D.C.: Congressional Research Service RL30341, 2000.

———. *Taiwan: Major US Arms Sales since 1990*. Washington D.C.: Congressional Research Service RL30957, 2005.

———. "US–China Counter-Terrorism Cooperation: Issues for US Policy." Congressional Research Service brief no. RS21995, May 12, 2005, 4.

Kaplan, David E. *Fires of the Dragon.* New York: Atheneum, 1992.

Kaplan, John. *The Court-Martial of the Kaohsiung Defendants.* Berkeley: University of California Press, 1981.

Keefe, John. *Anatomy of the EP-3 Incident, April 2001.* Alexandria, Va.: Project Asia, CNA Corporation, 2002.

Keinon, Herb. "Peres Offers China Farms, Not Phalcons." *Jerusalem Post,* August 18, 2000. www.lexis-nexis.com, accessed January 26, 2005.

Keller, Bill. "Reagan's Son." *NYT Magazine,* January 26, 2003, 26–31, 34–36, 44, 62.

Kempe, Frederick. *Divorcing the Dictator.* New York: Putnam, 1990.

Keohane, Robert O. "The Big Influence of Small Allies." *Foreign Policy* (Spring 1971): 161–82.

Kerr, George H. *Formosa Betrayed.* Boston: Houghton Mifflin, 1965.

Khalilzad, Zalmay M., et al. *The United States and a Rising China: Strategic and Military Implications.* Santa Monica, Calif.: Rand, 1999.

Kirkpatrick, Jeane J. "Dictatorships and Double Standards." *Commentary,* November 1979. www.commentarymagazine.com/viewarticle.cfm/dictatorships-double-standards-6189.

Kirschten, Dirk. "The Other China." *National Journal* 26 (October 8, 1994). www.nationaljournal.com, accessed October 28, 1999.

Kissinger, Henry. *Diplomacy.* New York: Simon and Schuster, 1994.

———. *The White House Years.* Boston: Little, Brown, 1979.

———. *The Years of Renewal.* New York: Simon and Schuster, 1999.

———. *The Years of Upheaval.* Boston: Little, Brown, 1982

Klare, Michael T. "'Congagement' with China? GOP Hawks Want Containment; Others Favor More Trade and More Toughness." *Nation,* April 30, 2001. www.thenation.com/doc/20010430/klare, accessed June 11, 2008).

Klinkner, Kenneth, ed. *The United States and Cross-Straits Relations.* Urbana-Champaign: University of Illinois Press, 2001.

Klintworth, Gary. "Lessons Learned." In *Missile Diplomacy and Taiwan's Future,* ed. Greg Austin, 241–61. Canberra: Australian National University, 1997.

Knowlton, Brian. "Analysts See Comments as a Toughening of American Position." *International Herald Tribune,* April 25, 2001.

Kochavi, Noam. *A Conflict Perpetuated.* Westport, Conn.: Praeger, 2002.

Koen, Ross. *The China Lobby in American Politics.* New York: Harper and Row, 1974.

Koenig, Robert L. "Politics Made Bush Speed Up F-15 Sale, House Members Say." *St. Louis Post-Dispatch,* September 24, 1992, A22.

Kristof, Nicholas D. "China Attacks Ex–U.S. Envoy for Stand on Taiwan." *NYT,* August 18, 1991, A6.

———. "Taipei Is on Alert for Sign of Betrayal." *NYT,* June 27, 1998, A9.

———. "Taiwan, Winning New Friends, Hopes for Another One in Clinton." *NYT,* January 18, 1993, A10.

———. "Taiwan Chief Sees Separate Identity." *NYT,* September 2, 1998, A4.

Kristol, William, and Gary Schmitt. "A Dangerous New Policy toward Taiwan?"

Weekly Standard, December 2, 2003. www.taiwandc.org/wstand-2003-01 .htm, accessed March 24, 2005.

Kusnitz, Leonard A. *Public Opinion and Foreign Policy.* Westport, Conn.: Greenwood, 1984.

Kydd, Andrew. "Which Side Are You On? Bias, Credibility, and Mediation." *American Journal of Political Science* 47 (October 2003): 597–611.

Lague, David. "Coming About." *FEER* 164 (December 13, 2001): 19

———. "U.S. Holds Tighter to Taiwan's Hand." *FEER* 164 (August 30, 2001): 12–16.

Lai Tse-han, Ramon H. Myers, and Wei Wou. *A Tragic Beginning.* Stanford: Stanford University Press, 1991.

Lampton, David M., ed. *The Making of Chinese Foreign and Security Policy in the Era of Reform.* Stanford: Stanford University Press, 2001.

———. *Same Bed, Different Dreams.* Berkeley: University of California Press, 2001.

Landay, Jonathan S. "How Far Would US Go to Protect Taiwan?" *Christian Science Monitor,* September 3, 1999, 3.

Landers, Peter, Susan Lawrence, and Julian Baum. "Hard Target." *FEER* 161 (September 24, 1998): 20–21.

Lasater, Martin L. "The PRC's Force Modernization: Shadow over Taiwan and U.S. Policy." *Strategic Review* (Winter 1984): 62.

———. "Reading Tea Leaves on America's Taiwan Policy." *WSJ,* April 27, 1987, 25.

———. *The Taiwan Issue in Sino-American Strategic Relations.* Boulder, Colo.: Westview, 1984.

Lawrence, Susan V. "Diplomatic but Triumphal Progress." *FEER* 166 (November 13, 2003): 34.

———. "The Guardian Angel Finally Had Enough." *FEER* 167 (April 22, 2004): 24–28.

Lee, David Tawei. *The Making of the Taiwan Relations Act.* New York: Oxford University Press, 2000.

Lee San Chouy. "Taiwan Fears the Long-Term Impact." *Straits Times,* October 27, 1997. www.lexis-nexis.com, accessed February 2, 2005.

"Lee Says Coup Was Imminent in Frigate Scandal." *China Post,* August 14, 2002. www.chinapost.com.tw/news/2002/08/14/29681/Lee%2Dsays.htm.

Lee Siew Hua. "US Allays Taiwan Fears over Beijing Summit." *Straits Times,* May 14, 1998. www. lexis-nexis.com, accessed August 5, 2005.

Lee Teng-hui. *Jianzheng Taiwan: Chiang Ching-kuo yu wo* [Witness Taiwan: President Chiang Ching-kuo and Me]. Taipei: Lee Teng-hui Oral History Project, 2004.

———. *The Road to Democracy.* Tokyo: PHP Institute, 1999.

———. "U.S. Can't Ignore China." *WSJ,* August 3, 1998. Reprinted in *China/Taiwan: Evolution of the "One China" Policy: Key Statements from Washington, Beijing, and Taipei,* ed. Shirley Kan, CRS-36. Washington, D.C.: Congressional Research Service RL30341, 2000.

————. *Ya Zhou de Zhi Lue* [Asia's Wisdom and Strategy]. As excerpted in the *Taipei Liberty Times,* July 22, 2000. FBIS, CPP2000007 24000144.

"Lee Teng-hui Illegally Used 3.5 Billion Taiwan Dollars." *Next Magazine* (Taiwan), March 21, 2002, 10–23.

Lee, Thompson. "Restoring the Balance." *Free China Review* (November 1992): 42–43.

Lehman, Nicholas. "Without a Doubt." *New Yorker,* October 14 and 21, 2002, 164–79.

Lewis, Anthony. "The Clinton Doctrine." *NYT,* January 22, 1993, A17.

Lewis, John Wilson, and Xue Litai. *China Builds the Bomb.* Stanford: Stanford University Press, 1988.

Liebman, Marvin. *Coming Out Conservative.* San Francisco: Chronicle Books, 1992.

"Lien-ho Pao on US Official Patterson's 'Taboo' Remarks on Cross-Strait Dialogue." FBIS, June 24, 2001, CPP20010624000076.

Lilley, James. *China Hands.* New York: Public Affairs, 2004.

————. "A Formula for China-Taiwan Relations." *Asian WSJ,* September 6, 1991, 10.

Lilley, James, and Chuck Downs, eds. *Crisis in the Taiwan Strait.* Washington, D.C.: National Defense University Press, 1997.

Lin Mei-chun. "Media Took Remarks Out of Context: Chen." *Taipei Times,* August 7, 2002. www.taipeitimes.com/News/front/archives/2002/08/07/159289, accessed May 8, 2005.

Lin Wen-cheng and Lin Chen-yi. "National Defense and the Changing Security Environment." In *Assessing the Lee Teng-hui Legacy in Taiwan's Politics,* ed. Bruce J. Dickson and Chao Chien-min, 241–63. Armonk, N.Y.: M. E. Sharpe, 2002.

Li Ping and Ma Zhisun, eds. *Zhou Enlai nianpu, 1949–1976* [A Chronological Record of Zhou Enlai, 1949–1976]. 2 vols. Beijing: Zhongyang wenxian, 1998.

Litwak, Robert S. *Détente and the Nixon Doctrine.* New York: Cambridge University Press, 1984.

"Liu Case Controversy: Hong Kong Newspaper Prints Secret NSB Details." *Taipei Times,* March 25, 2002. www.taipeitimes.com /News/taiwan/archives/2002/ 03/25/129108, accessed March 25, 2002.

Liu Yung-hsiang. "Shaheen's Manipulation Leads to Inconsistency in U.S. Policy toward Taiwan." *China Times,* November 17, 2003, A13.

Loh I-cheng. "Taiwan: 'We'll Fight, We'll Die for Freedom.'" *New York Daily News,* December 26, 1978, 34.

————. *Wei chen wu li ke hui tian: Lu Yizheng de waijiao sheng ya* [Valiant but Fruitless Endeavors: Memoirs of I-cheng Loh] (Taibei Shi: Tian xia yuan jian chu ban gu fen you xian gong si, 2002).

Long, Simon. "Republic of China: Friends Are Easy to Make, Influence Is Hard to Come By." *London Daily Telegraph,* October 18, 1993, 7.

Lord, Winston. "China and America: Beyond the Big Chill." *Foreign Affairs* 68 (Fall 1989): 1–26.

Lu, Neil, and Fang Wen-hung. "ROC Foreign Minister Seeks Correction from US Newspaper." CNA, April 20, 2001. www.lexis-nexis.com, accessed May 3, 2001.

MacMillan, Margaret. *Nixon in China.* Toronto: Viking Canada, 2006.

Manela, Erez. "Imagining Woodrow Wilson in Asia: Dreams of East-West Harmony and the Revolt against Empire in 1919." *American Historical Review* 111 (December 2006): 1327–51.

Mann, Jim. *About Face.* New York: Alfred A. Knopf, 1999.

———. *Beijing Jeep.* New York: Simon and Schuster, 1989.

———. "Congress and Taiwan: Understanding the Bond. In *Making China Policy,* ed. Ramon H. Myers, Michel C. Oksenberg, and David Shambaugh, 201–19. Lanham, Md.: Rowman and Littlefield, 2001.

———. "Next Step: Taiwan to US—We're Back." *LAT,* July 28, 1992, H1.

———. "The Personal Connection between China, Bush Clan." *Seattle Times,* December 27, 2000. http://community.seattletimes.nwsource.com/archive/?date=20001227&slug=TT5B2NKOK, accessed April 21, 2008.

———. "Push for Taiwan Arms Sale Shows the Hand of Politics." *LAT,* April 23, 2001.

———. *Rise of the Vulcans.* New York: Viking, 2004.

———. "Taiwan Arms Deals Open Doors to Civilian Contracts." *LAT,* March 15, 1994, A1.

———. "Taiwan's New Era Looks a Lot Like Old One." *LAT,* July 12, 2000, A1, 5.

———. "Taiwan to Lobby against US Naval Aid to China." *LAT,* January 23, 1985.

———. "Targeting Taiwan for Arms Deals." *LAT,* March 14, 1994, A1.

———. "U.S.–China Summit Has Taiwan Jittery." *LAT,* May 27, 1998, A7.

———. "U.S. Has Secretly Expanded Military Ties with Taiwan." *Los Angeles Times,* July 24, 1999. www.lexis-nexis.com, accessed December 2000.

———. "Western Nations Open Way for Taiwan to Join GATT." *LAT,* September 19, 1992, A6.

Marchetti, Victor, and John D. Marks. *The CIA and the Cult of Intelligence.* New York: Dell, 1980.

Marks, Thomas A. *Counterrevolution in China.* London: Frank Cass, 1996.

Marshall, Jonathan, Peter Dale Scott, and Jane Hunter. *The Iran-Contra Connection.* Boston: South End Press, 1987.

"Ma Seeks Scripts for Possible Mainland Attack." *China Post,* May 4, 2004. www.chinapost.com.tw/taiwan/2004/05/04/48440/Ma-seeks.htm, accessed April 21, 2008.

Matthews, Christopher. *Kennedy & Nixon.* New York: Simon and Schuster, 1996.

Matthews, Jay. "China Calls Bush Visit a Failure." *WP,* August 24, 1980, A1–2.

Matthews, Linda. "Taiwan Facing Fact It May Be Defending Itself Alone." *LAT,* November 6, 1977, 8.

May, Ernest R. *"Lessons" of the Past.* New York: Oxford University Press, 1973.

May, Gary. *China Scapegoat.* Prospect Heights, Ill.: Waveland Press, 1979.

Mayers, David Allan. *Cracking the Monolith.* Baton Rouge: Louisiana State University Press, 1986.

McDevitt, Michael. "The Quadrennial Defense Review and East Asia." PacNet Newsletter no. 43, October 26, 2001. www.csis.org/pacfor.

McGregor, Richard. "China Furious at US Role in Foiling Israel Defence Deal." *Financial Times,* July 14, 2000.

"Medal for Ex–US Rep to Taipei 'an Abuse of Power.'" *Straits Times,* June 24, 2004. www.lexis-nexis.com, accessed September 22, 2004.

Melanson, Richard A., and David Mayers, eds. *Reevaluating Eisenhower.* Urbana: University of Illinois Press, 1987.

Mica, Daniel A., and J. Terry Emerson, eds. *Fredrick F. Chien.* Tempe: Arizona State University Press, 1995.

Millman, Joel. "Taiwan's Central American Links." *Jane's Defence Weekly,* November 26, 1988.

Minnick, Wendell. "Spook Mountain." *Asia Times,* March 6, 2003. www.atimes .com/atimes/China/EC06Ad03.html.

———. "Taiwan Prepares for US Military Attaché." *Jane's Defence Weekly,* August 3, 2005.

———. "Taiwan–USA Link Up on SIGINT." *Jane's Defence Weekly,* January 24, 2001. www.fas.org/irp/news/2001/01/jdw-taiwan-sigint.html.

Mirsky, Jonathan. "Taiwan on the Edge." *New York Review of Books,* May 27, 2004, 44–46.

Mitton, Roger. "Beijing Not Amused by 'Shaheen Speak.'" *Straits Times,* November 29, 2003. www.lexis-nexis.com, accessed September 22, 2004.

Moens, Alexander. *Foreign Policy under Carter.* Boulder, Colo.: Westview, 1990.

Morrin, Richard, and Claudia Deane. "Lobbyists Seen Lurking behind Tank Funding." *WP,* November 19, 2002, A23.

Morris, Roger. *Richard Milhous Nixon.* New York: Henry Holt, 1990.

———. *Uncertain Greatness.* New York: Harper and Row, 1977.

Mufson, Steven. "U.S.–China Ties in the Balance; Rights Resolution Could Signal Harder Line toward Beijing." *WP,* February 17, 2001. www.lexis-nexis.com, accessed August 25, 2004.

———. "U.S. Sees Election as 'Fresh Opportunity' to Resolve Tensions." *WP,* March 19, 2000, A29.

Mufson, Steven, and Helen Dewar. "Senate GOP Tables Taiwan Bill; Island's Leaders Urge Delay of Military Plan during Transition." *WP,* April 27, 2000, A24.

Myers, Ramon H., Michel C. Oksenberg, and David Shambaugh, eds. *Making China Policy.* Lanham, Md.: Rowman and Littlefield, 2001.

Nathan, Andrew. "What's Wrong with American Taiwan Policy." *Washington Quarterly* (Spring 2000): 93–106.

Neilan, Edward. "Nationalists Fear Arms Sales to Peking." *WT,* April 26, 1984, A6.

———. "Reagan's Odyssey Confirms Importance of Ties to Japan." *WT,* November 11, 1983.

Nelson, Chris. "China 'Pushing' Missile/Taiwan Arms Sale 'Swap' . . . U.S. Not Buying." *Nelson Report,* December 10, 2002. www.samuelsinternational .com/NelRpt.html.

Niu Jun. "Chinese Decision Making in the Taiwan Strait." In *Managing Sino-American Crises,* ed. Michael D. Swaine and Zhang Tuosheng, 293–326. Washington, D.C.: Carnegie Endowment for International Peace, 2006.

Nixon, Richard M. "Asia after Viet Nam." *Foreign Affairs* 46 (October 1967): 111–25.

———. *RN.* New York: Grosset and Dunlap, 1978.

Norris, Robert S., William M. Arkin, and William Burr. "Where They Were." *Bulletin of the Atomic Scientists* (November–December 1999): 26–35.

Nye, Joseph S., Jr. "A Taiwan Deal." *WP,* March 8, 1998, C7.

Oberdorfer, Don. "China Sees Diplomatic Victory in Pact." *WP,* August 18, 1982. www.lexis-nexis.com, accessed March 17, 2005.

———. "1982 Arms Policy with China Victim of Bush Campaign, Texas Lobbying." *WP,* September 4, 1992, A31.

———. "Reagan Renews Assurance on Taiwan Arms" *WP,* July 3, 1982, A13.

———. "Two Top Reagan Advisers Are on Taiwan's Payroll." *WP,* June 6, 1980. www.lexis-nexis.com, accessed October 19, 1999.

O'Hanlon, Michael. "Why China Cannot Conquer Taiwan." *International Security* 25 (Fall 2000): 51–86.

Oksenberg, Michel. "Congress, Executive-Legislative Relations, and American China Policy." In *The President, the Congress, and Foreign Policy,* ed. Edmund S. Muskie, Kenneth Rush, and Kenneth W. Thompson, 207–30. Lanham, Md.: University Press of America, 1986.

———. "Reconsiderations: A Decade of Sino-American Relations." *Foreign Affairs* 61 (Fall 1982).

Pan, Philip P. "Rice Rebuffs China on Taiwan Arms Sales." *WP,* July 9, 2004. www.lexis-nexis.com, accessed February 25, 2005.

———. "Vote Favors Independent Taiwan." *WP,* December 2, 2001, A30, 33.

Pan, Philip P., and David Hoffman. "Taiwan's President Maintains Hard Line; Chen Rebukes China in Interview." *WP,* March 30, 2004, A1.

Pan Zhongqi, "US Taiwan Policy of Strategic Ambiguity: A Dilemma of Deterrence." *Journal of Contemporary China* 12 (May 2003): 402–7.

Pao, Maureen. "What George W. Bush Doesn't Know." *FEER* 164 (April 12, 2001): 20.

Parmet, Herbert S. *George Bush.* New York: Scribner, 1997.

———. *Richard Nixon and His America.* Boston: Little, Brown, 1990.

Peng Ming-min. *A Taste of Freedom.* New York: Holt, Rinehart and Winston, 1972.

Perlez, Jane. "Bush Carries Some Baggage in Developing China Stance." *NYT,* August 29, 1999, A15.

Perrin, Andrew. "Taiwanese Don't Fear Blockade." *Courier Mail* (Queensland, Australia), May 18, 2000, 18.

Perry, William J., and Ashton B. Carter. *Preventive Defense.* Washington, D.C.: Brookings Institution Press, 1999.

Peterson, Bill. "Conservatives Push for Taiwan Arms." *WP,* July 9, 1982, A5.

Phillips, Steven E. *Between Assimilation and Independence.* Stanford: Stanford University Press, 2003.

Pincus, Walter, and Bob Woodward. "Presidential Posts and Dashed Hopes: Appointive Jobs Were Turning Point." *WP,* August 9, 1988.

Pomfret, John. "Beijing Signals New Flexibility on Taiwan." *WP,* January 5, 2001. www.lexis-nexis.com, accessed March 16, 2005.

———. "China Also Wants U.S. Help against 'Separatists.'" *WP,* September 19, 2001, A11.

———. "China Suggests Missile Buildup Linked to Arms Sales to Taiwan." *WP,* December 10, 2002, A1.

———. "China Tells Taiwan to 'Face Reality.'" *WP,* July 10, 1998, A28.

———. "Chinese Threat Tests Taiwan's Preparedness." *WP,* July 27, 1999, A13.

———. "Clinton Declaration on Independence Irks Taiwan." *WP,* July 1, 1998, A26.

———. "In Fact and Tone, U.S. Expresses New Fondness for Taiwan." *WP,* April 30, 2002, A12.

———. "Taiwanese Leader Condemns Beijing, 'One China' Policy." *WP,* October 7, 2003, A18

———. "Taiwanese Mistake Led to 3 Spies' Executions." *WP,* February 20, 2000, A1, 29.

———. "Taiwan Faces Divide over Possible U.S. Radar Deal." *WP,* April 20, 2001, A14.

———. "U.S. Seeks China-Taiwan Dialogue." *WP,* February 21, 1998, A16.

Postman, David, and Catherine Tarpley. "Bush at Boeing, Backs China Trade." *Seattle Times,* May 18, 2000, A1.

Powell, Colin. *My American Journey.* New York: Random House, 1995.

"Premier Zhu Don Corleone." *WP,* March 16, 2000, A26.

"President Chiang Ching-kuo's Five Principles on U.S.–ROC Relations in the Post-normalization Period." In *America and Island China,* ed. Stephen P. Gibert and William M. Carpenter, 208–9. Lanham, Md.: University Press of America, 1989.

"President Lee Reiterates ROC Sovereignty to US Envoy." CNA, July 6, 1999. www.lexis-nexis.com, accessed July 1999.

Pruessen, Ronald W. "Over the Volcano: The United States and the Taiwan Strait Crisis, 1954–1955." In *Re-examining the Cold War,* ed. Robert S. Ross and Jiang Changbin, 77–105. Cambridge: Harvard University Asia Center, 2001.

Qian Qichen. *Ten Episodes in China's Diplomacy.* New York: HarperCollins, 2005.

Reagan, Ronald. *An American Life.* New York: Simon and Schuster, 1990.

———. Reagan: A Life in Letters. Ed. Kiron K. Skinner, Annalise Anderson, and Martin Anderson. New York: Free Press, 2003.

———. *Reagan, in His Own Hand.* Ed. Kiron K. Skinner, Annelise Anderson, and Martin Anderson. New York: Free Press, 2001.

"Reagan Reaffirms Line on Recognition of China." *Financial Times,* November 30, 1983, 6.

"Reagan Responds to Conservative Criticism." *Human Events,* February 26, 1983, 19.

"Reagan Said to Assure Taiwan on His China Visit." *NYT,* April 26, 1984, A4.

Reeves, Richard. *President Nixon.* New York: Simon and Schuster, 2001.

"Relationship between ROC and US Congress to Remain Stable." CNA, November 10, 1988. www.lexis-nexis.com.

Ren Yi. "The 'Taiwan Lobby' in the United States." *Shijie Zhishi,* February 1, 1981, 4–5. FBIS, March 10, 1981, B1–4.

Ren Yujun. "The Taiwan Authorities Once Thought of Using US Nuclear Weapons to Retaliate against the Mainland." *Beijing Renmin Wang,* September 4, 2001. FBIS, September 6, 2001, CPP20010906000011.

Rice, Andrew, "Brent Scowcroft Calls Iraq War 'Overreaction.'" *New York Observer,* September 6, 2004.

Rice, Condoleezza. "Promoting the National Interest." *Foreign Affairs* 79 (January–February 2000). www.globalpolicy.org/empire/analysis/2001/01CRice.htm.

Richburg, Keith. "Taiwan Says President's Remarks Misinterpreted." *WP,* November 10, 1997, A32.

Richburg, Keith, and Dan Morgan. "Taiwanese: Ex-Clinton Aide Said He Was Raising Money; No Direct Request Made, Political Scientist Says." *WP,* October 30, 1996, A16.

Ricks, Thomas. "Admiral Takes Stand against Pro-Taiwan Legislation." *WP,* March 8, 2000, A32.

Rigger, Shelley. "Competing Conceptions of Taiwan's Identity: The Irresolvable Conflict in Cross-Strait Relations." *Journal of Contemporary China* 6 (July 1997): 307–17.

———. *From Opposition to Power.* Boulder, Colo.: Lynne Rienner, 2001.

———. "New Crisis in the Taiwan Strait?" Foreign Policy Research Institute E-Notes, September 5, 2003, www.fpri.org/enotes/20030905.rigger.newcrisis taiwan.html, accessed April 22, 2008.

———. *Politics in Taiwan.* New York: Routledge, 1999.

———. *Taiwan's Rising Rationalism.* Washington, D.C.: East-West Center, 2006.

Rohter, Larry. "Noriega's Lawyer Presses Ex-Pilot." *NYT,* October 2, 1991, A20.

Romberg, Alan D. "Addressing the China Question: The U.S. Role." Occasional Paper no. 47, July 2002. www.stimson.org/china/pdf/romberg-oxford.pdf, accessed June 2003.

———. "'China's Sacred Territory, Taiwan Island': Some Thoughts on American Policy." Occasional Paper no. 44, Henry L. Stimson Center, January 2002. www.stimson.org/pub.cfm?id=54, accessed June 2003.

———. *Rein in at the Brink of the Precipice.* Washington, D.C.: Stimson Center, 2003.

Ross, Robert S. *Negotiating Cooperation.* Stanford: Stanford University Press, 1995.

———. "The 1995–1996 Taiwan Strait Confrontation: Coercion, Credibility, and Use of Force." *International Security* 25 (Fall 2000): 87–123.

Ross, Robert S., and Jiang Changbin, eds. *Re-examining the Cold War.* Cambridge: Harvard University Asia Center, 2001.

Rusk, Dean. *As I Saw It.* New York: W. W. Norton, 1990.

Russell, Richard L. "What if . . . 'China Attacks Taiwan!'" *Parameters* (Autumn 2001): 76–91.

Safire, William. *Before the Fall*. Garden City, N.Y.: Doubleday, 1975.

Salant, Jonathan D. "New Recordings Show Nixon No Fan of Reagan." Associated Press, December 11, 2003. www.lexis-nexis.com, accessed December 14, 2003.

Sanger, David E. "Bush Is Offering the Taiwanese Some Arms but Not the Best." *NYT*, April 24, 2001. 34.

———. "Clinton and Jiang Heal Rift and Set New Trade Course." *NYT*, September 12, 1999, 1.

———. "Decision in Taiwan: The White House." *NYT*, March 20, 2000, A8.

Sarasohn, Judy. "Special Interest, One Taiwan Account Lost, Another Gained." *WP*, July 6, 2000, A19.

Scalapino, Robert A. *The Last Leninists*. Washington, D.C.: Center for Strategic and International Studies, 1992.

Scales, Ann, and Charles M. Sennott. "Barak Offers a Concession to Clinton; Israelis, at Camp David Talks, Say They Won't Sell Plane to China." *Boston Globe,* July 13, 2000.

Schlesinger, Arthur M., Jr. *The Imperial Presidency*. Boston: Houghton Mifflin, 1973.

———. *A Thousand Days*. Boston: Houghton Mifflin, 1965.

Schram, Martin. "China Policy: A Born-Again Brzezinski." *WP*, February 8, 1979, A1.

Schulzinger, Robert D. *Henry Kissinger*. New York: Columbia University Press, 1989.

Sciolino, Elaine. "Taiwan's Lobbying in US: Mixing Friendship and Hardball." *NYT*, April 9, 1996, A12.

"Secret Contacts Said to Have Been Conducive to Cross-Strait Peace." CNA, July 19, 2000.

Self, Benjamin L. "An Alliance for Engagement: Rationale and Modality." In *An Alliance for Engagement,* ed. Benjamin L. Self and Jeffrey W. Thompson, 145–65. Washington, D.C.: Henry L. Stimson Center, 2002.

Service, John S. *The Amerasia Papers*. Berkeley: Center for Chinese Studies, University of California, 1971.

Shambaugh, David, ed. *Contemporary Taiwan*. Oxford: Clarendon Press, 1998.

Shane, Scott. "Since 2001, Sharp Increase in the Number of Documents Classified by the Government." *NYT*, July 3, 2005, A14.

Shaw Yu-ming. "Taiwan: A View from Taipei." *Foreign Affairs* 63 (Summer 1985): 1050–63.

Shen, James C. *The U.S. and Free China*. Washington, D.C.: Acropolis Books, 1983.

Shenon, Philip. "No Policy Turn, U.S. Assures Taiwan Again." *NYT*, July 7, 1998, A9.

Shichor, Yitzak. "Israel's Military Transfers to China and Taiwan." *Survival* 40 (Spring 1998): 68–92.

Shimizu, Katsuhiko. "Who Are the New Emissaries between Taiwan and China?—A Secret Connection between Chinese President Jiang Zemin and Taiwan's Former President Lee Teng-hui." *Aera* (Tokyo), September 11, 2000. FBIS, East Asia, JPP20000905000062.

Shlapak, David A., David T. Orletsky, and Barry A. Wilson. *Dire Strait?* Santa Monica, Calif.: Rand, 2000.

Shultz, George P. *Turmoil and Triumph.* New York: Scribner's, 1993.

Shutt, Anne. "As FX Decision Nears, Taiwan Sees Fighter as Symbol of US Attitudes." *Christian Science Monitor,* September 3, 1981, 6.

Singlaub, John K. *Hazardous Duty.* New York: Summit Books, 1991.

Small, Melvin. *The Presidency of Richard Nixon.* Lawrence: University of Kansas Press, 1999.

Smith, Gaddis. *Morality, Reason & Power.* New York: Hill and Wang, 1986.

Smith, R. Jeffrey, and Don Oberdorfer. "Taiwan to Close Nuclear Reactor." *WP,* March 24, 1988, A32.

Snyder, Charles. "Powell Assures Taipei There's No Deal with China." *Taipei Times,* September 23, 2001. www.taipeitimes.com/news/front/archives/2001/09/23/104133.

Snyder, Glenn H. "The Security Dilemma in Alliance Politics." *World Politics* 36 (July 1984): 461–95.

Snyder, William P. "Dean Rusk to John Foster Dulles, May–June 1953: The Office, the First 100 Days, and Red China." *Diplomatic History* 7 (January 1983): 79–86.

Southerland, Daniel. "Chiang Envisions Change for Taiwan." *WP,* October 13, 1986, A18.

Spector, Leonard. *Nuclear Proliferation Today.* New York: Random House, 1984.

Starr, Barbara. "F-16 Sale Justified by 'Discrepancy,'" *Jane's Defence Weekly,* September 12, 1992, 5.

Steel, Ronald, "Shultz's Revenge." *New York Review of Books,* September 23, 1993, 34–40.

Stein, Jeff. "Defense Officials Tried to Reverse China Policy, says Powell Aide." *CQ Homeland Security,* June 1, 2007. http://public.cq.com/docs/hs/hsnews110-00000z523531.html, accessed June 29, 2007.

Sterba, James P. "Reagan Reawakens Issue of Taiwan Ties." *NYT,* August 24, 1980, A1

Stolper, Thomas E. *China, Taiwan, and the Offshore Islands.* Armonk, N.Y.: M. E. Sharpe, 1985.

Stone, Peter. "Exporting Weapons." *Atlanta Constitution,* January 3, 1993, B1.

Su Chi. *Weixian bianlu: Cong lianguolun dao yibian yiguo* [Brinksmanship: From the Two States Theory to One Country on Each Side]. Taipei: Tianxia yuanjian, 2003.

Su Chi and Cheng An-kuo. *"One China, Different Interpretations"—A Historical Account of the Consensus of 1992.* Taipei: National Policy Foundation, 2002. www.taiwansecurity.org, accessed August 2003.

Su, Christie. "President Says No to Nuclear Arms." *Free China Journal,* August

4, 1995. http://taiwanjournal.nat.gov.tw/ct.asp?XItem=13429&CTNode=122.

Suettinger, Robert. *Beyond Tiananmen*. Washington, D.C.: Brookings Institution Press, 2003.

———. "Of Successors, Memories, and Guidance: Qian Qichen Defines His Legacy." *China Leadership Monitor*, no. 10 (Spring 2004). www.hoover.org/publication/clm/issues/2904246.html.

Sui, Cindy. "U.S. Urges Chinese 'Restraint' on Taiwan." *WP*, February 19, 2000, A22.

Sun, Lena, and Stuart Auerbach. "F-16, Grain Decisions Draw Flack." *WP*, September 4, 1992, A27.

Sung, Catherine, and William Ide. "Nuclear Redeployment Preceded US Pullout." *Taipei Times*, October 20, 1999.

Sutter, Robert G. "Taiwan–Mainland China Talks: Competing Approaches and Implications for U.S. Policy." Congressional Research Service Report 98-887F, October 28, 1998.

———. *U.S. Policy toward China*. Lanham, Md.: Rowman and Littlefield, 1998.

Sutter, Robert G., and William R. Johnson, eds. *Taiwan in World Affairs*. Boulder, Colo.: Westview, 1994.

Swaine, Michael D. "Chinese Decision-Making Regarding Taiwan, 1979–2000." In *The Making of Chinese Foreign and Security Policy in the Era of Reform*, ed. David M. Lampton, 289–336. Stanford: Stanford University Press, 2001.

———. *Taiwan's National Security, Defense Policy, and Weapons Procurement Processes*. Santa Monica, Calif.: Rand, 1999.

Swaine, Michael D., and James C. Mulvenon. *Taiwan's Foreign and Defense Policies*. Santa Monica, Calif.: Rand, 2001.

Swaine, Michael D., and Zhang Tuosheng, eds. *Managing Sino-American Crises*. Washington, D.C.: Carnegie Endowment for International Peace, 2006.

Szulc, Tad. "The Reagan Administration's Push toward China Came from Warsaw." *LAT*, January 17, 1982, IV, 1.

"Taiwan Comments on 'Distressing' Rumors of US Mediation with China." BBC Summary of World Broadcasts, Part 3, February 27, 1989, FE/0395/A1/1.

"Taiwan Open to Signing of Cross-Strait Interim Agreements." CNA, March 26, 1999. www.lexis-nexis.com, accessed May 1999.

"Taiwan's Fate Seen as Lesson in Israel." *LAT*, December 17, 1978.

"Taiwan's New Government Won't Hold Secret Talks with China." Agence France-Press, July 20, 2000. www.taiwansecurity.org, accessed July 25, 2000.

Takashi Oka. "China Casts Doubt on Reagan Visit." *Christian Science Monitor*, December 1, 1983, 1.

Taylor, Jay. *The Generalissimo's Son*. Cambridge: Harvard University Press, 2000.

"This Sale Is a Mirage." *Time*, July 13, 1992, 9.

Thomson, James C., Jr. "On the Making of U.S. China Policy, 1961–69: A Study in Bureaucratic Politics." *China Quarterly* 50 (April–June 1972): 220–43.

Tien Hung-mao. *The Great Transition*. Stanford: Hoover Institution Press, 1989.

Ting Yu-chou with Wang Shichun. *Ting Yu-chou Hui-I-lu* [Memoirs of Ting Yu-chou]. Taipei: T'ien-hsia Publishing, 2004, in FBIS Translated Excerpts, CPP20050706000218–CPP20050708000239.

"Top-secret Plan to Retake Mainland in 1960s Unveiled." *China Post*, March 27, 2006. www.chinapost.com.tw, accessed March 28, 2006.

Torode, Greg. "And the Award Goes to—Taiwan." *SCMP*, April 19, 2001. www.lexis-nexis.com, accessed August 31, 2004.

———. "Fig-Leaf Diplomacy." *SCMP*, March 24, 2002. www.lexis-nexis.com, accessed August 31, 2004.

Traub, James. "The Bush Years: W's World." *NYT Magazine*, April 26, 2001. http://query.nytimes.com/gst/fullpage.html?res=9B0CEED6153AF937 A25752C0A9679C8B63&scp=18sq=Bush+years%3A+W%27+world&st =nyt, accessed June 12, 2008.

Tsao, Nadia. "Lobbying Firm Draws Fire." *Taipei Times*, July 10, 2000. www .taipeitimes.com/News/local/archives/2000/07/10/43189, accessed March 24, 2002.

———. "What Does Taiwan Want from Sub Deal?" *Taipei Times*, November 19, 2003. www.taipeitimes.com/News/editorials/archives/2003/11/19/ 2003076443, accessed January 6, 2004.

Tucker, Nancy Bernkopf. "China and America 1941–1991." *Foreign Affairs* 70 (Winter 1991–92): 75–92.

———, ed. and comp. *China Confidential*. New York: Columbia University Press, 2001.

———, ed. *Dangerous Strait*. New York: Columbia University Press, 2005.

———. "If Taiwan Chooses Unification, Should the United States Care?" *Washington Quarterly* 25 (Summer 2002): 15–28.

———. "John Foster Dulles and the Taiwan Roots of the 'Two Chinas' Policy." In *John Foster Dulles and the Diplomacy of the Cold War*, ed. Richard H. Immerman, 235–62. Princeton: Princeton University Press, 1990.

———. *Patterns in the Dust*. New York: Columbia University Press, 1983.

———. *Security Challenges for the United States, China and Taiwan at the Dawn of the New Millennium*. Alexandria, Va.: Project Asia, CNA Corporation, 2000.

———. "Strategic Ambiguity or Strategic Clarity?" In *Dangerous Strait*, ed. Nancy Bernkopf Tucker, 186–211. New York: Columbia University Press, 2005.

———. *Taiwan, Hong Kong, and the United States, 1945–1992: Uncertain Friendships*. New York: Macmillan/Twayne, 1994.

———. "The Taiwan Factor in the Vote on PNTR for China and Its WTO Accession." *National Bureau for Asian Research Analysis* (July 2000). www.nbr .org/publications/issue.aspx?ID=244.

———. "War or Peace in the Taiwan Strait." *Washington Quarterly* 19 (Winter 1996): 171–87.

Tully, Andrew. "Why Rumsfeld Wants to Engage China." *Asia Times Online*, February 12, 2005. www.atimes.com/atimes/China/GB12Ad01.html, accessed February 14, 2005.

Tyler, Patrick. "The (Ab)normalization of U.S.–Chinese Relations." *Foreign Affairs* 78 (September–October 1999): 93–122.

———. "As China Threatens Taiwan, It Makes Sure U.S. Listens." *NYT,* January 24, 1996, A3.

———. "Beijing Steps Up Military Pressure on Taiwan Leader." *NYT,* March 7, 1996. www.lexis-nexis.com, accessed March 24, 2002.

———. *A Great Wall.* New York: Public Affairs, 1999.

———. "Taiwanese Spies Said to Penetrate Top U.S. Agencies." *WP,* June 1, 1982, A1.

"Ugly Americanism." *WSJ,* February 6, 1979, 18.

"US Arms Sales Would Boost Taiwan's Defense Capacity: Analysts." Agence France-Presse, September 29, 2000. www.taiwansecurity.org, accessed October 13, 2000.

"US Foreign-Policy Experts Call for Defense of Taiwan." August 24, 1999. www.globalsecurity.org/wmd/library/news/taiwan/1999/e-08-25-99-17.htm, accessed June 14, 2005.

"U.S. Industry Aiding Taiwan in Developing National Fighter to Meet Threat from PRC." *Aviation Week and Space Technology* 124 (March 31, 1986): 31.

"US 'Keeps Tabs on China via Signals Base in Taipei,'" Agence France-Presse, January 18, 2002. www.lexis.nexis.com, accessed March 25, 2004.

"U.S. Official Supports Cross-Strait Dialogue with No Preconditions." CNA, June 22, 2001. www.lexis-nexis.com, accessed March 30, 2003.

Vance, Cyrus. *Hard Choices.* New York: Simon and Schuster, 1983.

Van den Ven, Hans J. *War and Nationalism in China, 1925–1945.* London: Routledge, 2003.

Van Vranken Hickey, Dennis. "Continuity and Change: The Administration of George W. Bush and US Policy toward Taiwan." *Journal of Contemporary China* 13 (August 2004): 461–78.

Van Vranken Hickey, Dennis, and Li Yitan. "Cross-Strait Relations in the Aftermath of the Election of Chen Shui-bian." *Asian Affairs* 28 (Winter 2002): 201–18.

Wachman, Alan. *Taiwan: National Identity and Democratization.* Armonk, N.Y.: M. E. Sharpe, 1994.

———. *Why Taiwan?* Stanford: Stanford University Press, 2007.

Wang Bingnan. *Nine Years of Sino-American Ambassadorial Talks.* Beijing: World Knowledge Press, 1985.

"Wang Daohan Meeting with Chen Shui-bian's Envoy Cited." *Hong Kong Tung Fang Jih Pao,* April 7, 2000. FBIS, CPP20000407000030.

Wang, Flor. "AIT Chairman Reassures Taiwan on US Policy." CNA, July 8, 1998. www.lexis-nexis.com, accessed January 17, 2005.

Wang Jisi. "The Origins of America's 'Two Chinas' Policy." In *Sino-American Relations, 1945–1955,* ed. Harry Harding and Yuan Ming, 198–212. Wilmington, Del.: Scholarly Resources, 1989.

Weber, Ralph E., and Ralph A. Weber, eds. *Dear Americans.* New York: Doubleday, 2003.

Weiner, Tim. "How a Spy Left Taiwan in the Cold." *NYT,* December 20, 1987, A7.

Weiser, Benjamin. "Singlaub Suggested an Earlier Fund Diversion." *WP,* March 20, 1987, A1, 14.

Weisman, Steven R. "Haig Remark on China Puzzles White House Aides." *NYT,* June 27, 1981, A5.

Weisskopf, Michael. "Taiwan's Role in a United China Would Be Equal, Deng Pledges." *WP,* July 19, 1983, A11.

Westad, Odd Arne. *Cold War and Revolution.* New York: Columbia University Press, 1993.

Whitaker, Raymond. "Peking Anger at US Fighter Sale." *Independent* (London), September 4, 1992, 10.

Whiting, Allen S. "New Light on Mao; Quemoy 1958: Mao's Miscalculations." *China Quarterly* (June 1975): 263–70.

Wickenden, Peter. "Taiwan 2: Two Confident Steps Forward." *Financial Times,* October 10, 1991, 34.

Wills, Garry. *Nixon Agonistes.* Boston: Houghton Mifflin, 1970.

Winckler, Edwin. "Institutionalization and Participation on Taiwan: From Hard to Soft Authoritarianism." *China Quarterly* 99 (September 1984): 491–99.

Wolff, Lester L., Jon D. Holstine, and John J. Brady, eds. *A Legislative History of the Taiwan Relations Act.* Vol. 4. Arlington, Va.: Pacific Community Institute, 2004.

Wolfowitz, Paul. "Remembering the Future." *National Interest* (Spring 2000): 35–46.

Wren, Christopher. "Reagan and Zhao Reportedly Clash on Foreign Policy." *NYT,* April 28, 1984, A1.

Wu, Lillian. "Chen Shui-bian Says '1992 Consensus' Cannot Be Accepted Since It Doesn't Exist," CNA, May 3, 2005. FBIS, CPP20050503000100.

WuDunn, Sheryl. "For Taiwan, New Access to Western Arms." *NYT,* September 24, 1991, A7.

———. "Taiwan Opposition Pushes for Independence." *NYT,* September 19, 1991, A6.

Xia Yafeng. *Negotiating with the Enemy.* Bloomington: Indiana University Press, 2006.

Xue Mohong et al, eds. *Dangdai zhongguo waijiao* [Contemporary Chinese Diplomacy]. Beijing: Zhongguo shehui kexue, 1988.

Yager, Joseph A., ed. *Nonproliferation and U.S. Foreign Policy.* Washington, D.C.: Brookings Institution Press, 1980.

Yang, Andrew Nien-dzu. "Crisis, What Crisis? Lessons of the 1996 Tension and the ROC View of Security in the Taiwan Strait." Council of Advanced Policy Studies (CAPS) Paper no. 20, Taipei, December 1997.

———. "The 1996 Missile Exercises: China's Political Manipulation and Taiwan's Crisis Management." CAPS Paper no. 27, Taipei, March 2000.

Yang Jiemian. "Clinton Administration's Taiwan Policy Readjustment." *Beijing Meiguo Yanjiu,* December 5, 1999, FBIS.

Yeh, Benjamin. "Carter Refuses to Apologize to Taiwan for Diplomatic Switch." Agence France-Presse, March 30, 1999. www.lexis-nexis.com, accessed July 26, 2003.

Young, Kenneth T. *Negotiating with the Chinese Communists.* New York: McGraw-Hill, 1968.

Zacharia, Janine. "The Phalcon: Squandering Years of Cooperation?" *Jerusalem Post,* June 30, 2000. www.lexis-nexis.com, accessed July 15, 2004.

Zhang Shu Guang. *Deterrence and Strategic Culture.* Ithaca: Cornell University Press, 1992.

Zhao Shuisheng, ed. *Across the Taiwan Strait.* New York: Routledge, 1999.

———. "Coping with Chen Shui-bian's Administration: Beijing's Wait-and-See Policy and Two-Pronged Strategy." In *Assessing Chen Shui-bian's First Year,* 67–83. Sigur Center Paper no. 14. Washington, D.C., May 2001.

Zhonghua renmin gongheguo shilu [A Factual Record of the People's Republic of China]. Vol. 3. Changchun: Jilin renmin chubanshe, 1994.

Zi Zhongyun and He Di, eds. *Meitai Guanxi Sishinian* [Forty Years of US–Taiwan Relations]. Beijing: People's Press, 1991.

Zou Jing-wen. *Li Denghui Zhizheng Gaobai Shilu* [Record of Revelations on Lee Teng-hui's Administration]. Taipei: INK, 2001.

Zubok, Vladislav, and Constantine Pleshakov. *Inside the Kremlin's Cold War.* Cambridge: Harvard University Press, 1996.

Zuckerman, Laurence. "Taiwan Keeps a Step Ahead of China in U.S. Lobbying." *NYT,* March 14, 1997. www.lexis-nexis.com, accessed January 26, 2005.

Index